KU-187-946

Colaiste Oideachais Mhuire Gan Smal
Luimneach

CRISIS IN EUROPE

1560–1660

Essays from *Past and Present*

CONTRIBUTORS

John Bossy
Alan Cole
Mark H. Curtis
J. H. Elliott
Pierre Goubert
E. J. Hobsbawm
V. G. Kiernan
Brian Manning
Roland Mousnier
Terence Ranger
Michael Roberts
Keith Thomas
H. R. Trevor-Roper

CRISIS IN EUROPE
1560–1660

Essays from *Past and Present*

Edited by
TREVOR ASTON

with an Introduction by
CHRISTOPHER HILL

WITHDRAWN FROM STOCK

ROUTLEDGE & KEGAN PAUL
London

27296

First published 1965
by Routledge & Kegan Paul Ltd
Broadway House, 68-74 Carter Lane
London, EC4V 5EL

Second impression 1966
Third impression 1969
Fourth impression 1970
First published as a paperback 1974

Reprinted by photolithography in Great Britain
by Bookprint Limited, Crawley, Sussex

© *Routledge & Kegan Paul Ltd 1965*

No part of this book may be reproduced
in any form without permission from
the publisher, except for the quotation
of brief passages in criticism

ISBN 0 7100 6889 1

Coláiste Oideachais
Mhuire Gan Smál
Luimneach
Class No. 940·23
Acc. No. 19768

CONTENTS

CONTENTS

PREFACE

MR. CHRISTOPHER HILL, in his Introduction, explains the general background to these articles and the journal from which they are drawn. The actual selection of the articles was done by the Editorial Board of the journal. In making our selection, we omitted all articles which had already been reprinted or incorporated in books by their authors, with the sole exception of the article by Professor Pierre Goubert which may be more accessible to readers than his two volumes on *Beauvais et le Beauvaisis de 1600 à 1730* (Paris, 1960). The collection thus presents a good deal less than the sum of work which appeared on its subject in *Past and Present* 1952–62; and (in addition to articles mentioned by Mr. Hill on page 2), it may be worth drawing attention to the following (issue number, and date being given in brackets): Christopher Hill, 'Puritans and the Poor' (No. 2, Nov. 1952); S. F. Mason, 'Science and Religion in Seventeenth-Century England' (No. 3, Feb. 1953); W. G. Hoskins, 'The Rebuilding of Rural England' (No. 4, Nov. 1953); Eric Mercer, 'The Houses of the Gentry' (No. 5, May 1954); Lawrence Stone, 'The Inflation of Honours' (No. 14, Nov. 1958); Francis Haskell, 'The Market for Italian Art in the Seventeenth Century' (No. 15, Apr. 1959); and C. B. Macpherson, 'Harrington's Opportunity State' (No. 17, Apr. 1960).

Since the volume was planned, further important contributions have appeared in *Past and Present*, closely bearing on themes in the anthology. In particular may be mentioned: W. T. MacCaffrey, 'Elizabethan Politics: the First Decade, 1558–1568' (No. 24, Apr. 1963); the debate on Harrington between John F. H. New and C. B. Macpherson (in Nos. 24 and 25, Apr. and July 1963); Joan Simon, 'The Social Origins of Cambridge Students 1603–1640' (No. 26, Nov. 1963); Christopher Hill, 'William Harvey and the Idea of Monarchy' (No. 27, Apr. 1964); Lawrence Stone, 'The

Educational Revolution in England, 1560–1640' (No. 28, July 1964); and H. F. Kearney, 'Puritanism, Capitalism and the Scientific Revolution' (*ibid.*).

The articles here appear for the most part in their original form. All authors were invited to make necessary corrections and minor alterations in the text and notes; and a few additions have been made to references in the footnotes, but no attempt was made to bring these generally up to date. Some preliminary matter in Dr. Manning's article has been omitted in this reprinting. Otherwise the substantial alterations are twofold. First, it was impossible to reprint all the contributions to the symposium on Professor Trevor-Roper's article on the General Crisis; this necessarily involved the author adjusting his reply to the contributions. Second, Dr. Hobsbawm has added a short postscript to his two original articles.

We hope that this volume may be the first of several anthologies, in which the articles are by no means necessarily limited to pieces which first appeared in *Past and Present*.

I am grateful to the publishers for undertaking the labours of compiling the index.

Corpus Christi College,
Oxford

TREVOR ASTON

I

INTRODUCTION

Christopher Hill

THE first number of *Past and Present* appeared in February 1952, so that the periodical is now thirteen years old. During these years it has expressed an attitude towards history which is peculiarly its own, and which has, we hope, contributed something of value to historical scholarship. The title of the present volume, with its emphasis on change and movement, and the articles themselves, drawn from those which appeared in *Past and Present* between 1952 and 1962, exemplify this attitude. In the first number of the periodical the Editors stated their aims in an Introduction. We took issue both with the then fashionable tendency to reject all historical generalization and with the danger of oversimplified application to history of techniques drawn from other disciplines, whether economics, psychology, sociology or anthropology. 'Our main task', we said, 'is to record and explain these "transformations that society undergoes by its very nature".' (The words are those of Ibn Khaldun, the fourteenth-century Arab scholar.) Polybius was cited for the view that 'the facts themselves may be interesting, but hardly useful. It is the study of causes that makes history fruitful.' Yet the Editors stated a preference for 'example and fact' rather than 'methodological articles and theoretical dissertations'.[1]

The articles reprinted in this volume illustrate the preoccupation with historical change which has always characterized *Past and Present*, and the willingness to range over large areas in the

[1] *Past and Present*, no. 1 (Feb. 1952), pp. i–iii. The words in the last quotation are those of Marc Bloch and Lucien Febvre.

attempt to find causal explanations. The contributors would, I imagine, agree on few points except that it is the duty of the historian to explain, not merely to record. It is this belief which gives unity to the present book. Its guiding conception is that in the seventeenth century there was a 'general crisis'. This idea was first put forward by Dr. Hobsbawm in nos. 5 and 6 of *Past and Present* (1954); it was developed by Professor Trevor-Roper in no. 16 (1959), and his stimulating article was followed by a discussion in no. 18 (1960), from which contributions by Professor Mousnier and Dr. Elliott, together with Professor Trevor-Roper's reply, are here reprinted. The related articles of Dr. Elliott on Spain and Professor Roberts on Sweden followed in nos. 20 and 22 (1961 and 1962). Mr. Kiernan's article on foreign mercenaries and absolute monarchy (no. 11, 1957) covers similar ground, though not specifically related to the question of a general crisis in the seventeenth century. Dr. Manning's article on the nobles, the people and the constitution (no. 9, 1956) deals with a crisis in England, as Dr. Ranger's article on Strafford (no. 19, 1961) with a crisis in Ireland; and Professor Goubert discusses the victims of crisis in France (no. 10, 1956), though none of these refer specifically to the theme put forward by Dr. Hobsbawm and Professor Trevor-Roper. Attention should also be drawn to articles not included in the present volume: Professor J. V. Polišenský, 'The Thirty Years' War' (no. 6, 1954), Professor B. F. Porshnev, 'The Legend of the Seventeenth Century in French History' (no. 8, 1955), R. Ludloff, 'Industrial Development in Sixteenth- to Seventeenth-century Germany' (no. 12, 1957), and to the Report of a *Past and Present* Conference on 'Seventeenth-century Revolutions' in no. 13 (1958).[2]

In most countries reactions to the seventeenth-century crisis were expressed in religious forms. Another group of articles here reprinted deals with the relation between religion and society in England. Sociological analyses of Puritanism are familiar enough; but Dr. Bossy's sociological approach to 'The Character of English Catholicism' (no. 21, 1962) is as novel as it is intriguing. Professor Curtis relates Puritan lecturers to the society which produced them (no. 23, 1962), and Messrs. Cole and Thomas (nos.

[2] Dr. Hobsbawm has continued the discussion in an article in *Science and Society*, xxiv (1960): 'The Seventeenth Century in the Development of Capitalism'.

10 and 13, 1956 and 1958) deal with the radical sects which appeared during the revolution which was England's reaction to the crisis.

Now that they are collected together in book form, these articles, I believe, suggest that a basis of agreement may have been reached on some features of seventeenth-century history:

1. There was an economic and political crisis all over western and central Europe in the seventeenth century.

2. Though reactions to this crisis took very different forms in different countries, the existence of the underlying crisis itself makes it worth while comparing these reactions in the light of differing national circumstances.

3. These national circumstances must be analysed in relation to social and political structures and to religious institutions and beliefs.

4. The outcome of the crisis in the Netherlands and England, where political revolutions led to significant economic and social changes, was decidedly different from the outcome in other European countries; though France and Sweden in some respects may represent a half-way house.

5. The history of the British Isles (and no doubt of the Netherlands too, though this is not dealt with in the present volume) may be illuminated by considering continental parallels for the path which England did not take; just as the history of France, Spain, Italy may be illuminated by considering their abortive revolts in the light of the successful revolutions in the Netherlands and England.

6. This suggests that, applied with discretion, the comparative method is a useful tool for the historian, the nearest he can get to a laboratory test. It is yet another argument against the narrow parochialism which still afflicts the teaching of history in too many schools and universities, and which still leads us to think of English history as something unique and God-given.

One of the declared aims of *Past and Present* was 'to widen the somewhat narrow horizon of traditional historical studies among the English-speaking public', to attempt to break down barriers of nationality and social system. We have not yet been as successful as we would have wished in 'bringing to non-specialist readers knowledge of Indian, Chinese, Arab, African or Latin-American history',[3] but the present volume suggests that in one field at least we have helped to widen horizons.

[3] *Past and Present*, no. 1 (Feb. 1952), p. iv.

II

THE CRISIS OF THE SEVENTEENTH CENTURY*

E. J. Hobsbawm

I

IN the first part of this essay I wish to suggest that the European economy passed through a 'general crisis' during the seventeenth century, the last phase of the general transition from a feudal to a capitalist economy. Since 1300 or so, when something clearly began to go seriously wrong with European feudal society,[1] there have been several occasions when parts of Europe trembled on the brink of capitalism. There is a taste of 'bourgeois' and 'industrial' revolution about fourteenth-century Tuscany and Flanders or early sixteenth-century Germany. Yet it is only from the middle of the seventeenth century that this taste becomes more than a seasoning to an essentially medieval or feudal dish. The earlier urban societies never quite succeeded in the revolutions they foreshadowed. From the early eighteenth century, however, 'bourgeois' society advanced without substantial checks. The seventeenth century crisis thus differs from its predecessors in that it led to as fundamental a solution of the difficulties which had

[1] E. Perroy, R. Boutruche, R. H. Hilton have discussed this in recent years in *Annales E.S.C.*, and elsewhere. See also the discussion among M. Dobb, P. M. Sweezy, H. K. Takahashi, R. H. Hilton and C. Hill in *Science and Society*, xiv–xvii (1950–3), and the general survey by M. Malowist in *Kwartalnik Historiczny*, i (1953). (I am indebted to the Polish Institute, London, for a translation of this.)

* From nos. 5 and 6 (1954).

previously stood in the way of the triumph of capitalism, as that system will permit. In the first part of this essay I propose to marshal some of the evidence for the existence of a general crisis, which is still disputed by some, and to suggest an explanation of it. In the second part I propose to discuss some of the changes it produced, and how it was overcome. It is very probable that a great deal of historical work will be done on this subject and period in the next few years. Indeed, lately historians in various countries have tentatively suggested something like that 'general check to economic development' or general crisis with which this paper deals.[2] It may therefore be convenient to take a bird's eye view of the field, and to speculate about some sort of working hypothesis, if only to stimulate better ones, or further work.

THE 'GENERAL CRISIS'

A good deal of evidence for the 'general crisis' is available. We must, however, be careful to avoid the argument that a general crisis equals economic retrogression, which has bedevilled much of the discussion about the 'feudal crisis' of the fourteenth and fifteenth centuries. It is perfectly clear that there *was* a good deal of retrogression in the seventeenth century. For the first time in history the Mediterranean ceased to be a major centre of economic and political, and eventually of cultural influence and became an impoverished backwater. The Iberian powers, Italy, Turkey were plainly on the downgrade: Venice was on the way to becoming a tourist centre. With the exception of a few places dependent on the north-western States (generally free ports) and the pirate metropolis of Algiers, which also operated in the Atlantic,[3] there was little advance. Farther north, the decline of Germany is patent,

[2] F. Braudel, *La Méditerranée . . . au temps de Philippe II* (Paris, 1949), p. 1097. R. Romano, 'Industries textiles et conjoncture à Florence au XVIIe siècle', *Annales E.S.C.*, viie année (1952), p. 510. French historians regard the 'phase de contraction du XVIIe siècle' as 'un fait maintenant établi' (P. Chaunu in *Rev. Hist.*, ccx [1953], p. 379). In what follows I owe a great deal to discussion with J. Meuvret who confirmed many of my non-specialist guesses. However I doubt whether he would agree with much of this paper.

[3] C. A. Julien, *Histoire de l'Afrique du Nord* (Paris, 1931), pp. 538 ff; the 'industrial revolution' in piracy, due to the introduction of northern sails by English and Dutch after 1604 may be noted.

though not wholly unrelieved. In the Baltic Poland, Denmark and the Hanse were on the way down. Though the power and influence of Habsburg Austria increased (perhaps largely because others declined so dramatically), her resources remained poor, her military and political structure rickety even at the period of her greatest glory in the early eighteenth century. On the other hand in the Maritime Powers and their dependencies—England, the United Provinces, Sweden, and in Russia and some minor areas like Switzerland—the impression is one of advance rather than stagnation; in England, of decisive advance. France occupied an intermediate position, though even here political triumph was not balanced by great economic advance until the end of the century, and then only intermittently. Indeed an atmosphere of gloom and crisis fills the discussions there after 1680, though conditions in the previous half-century can hardly have been superior. (Possibly the huge catastrophe of 1693–4 accounts for this.[4]) It was in the sixteenth not the seventeenth century that invading mercenaries marvelled at how much there was to loot in France, and men in Richelieu's and Colbert's era looked back on Henry IV's as a sort of golden age. It is indeed possible that, for some decades in the middle of the century, the gains made in the Atlantic did not replace the losses in the Mediterranean, central Europe and the Baltic, the total proceeds from both stagnating or perhaps declining. Nevertheless what is important is the decisive advance in the progress of capitalism which resulted.

The scattered figures for European *population* suggest, at worst an actual decline, at best a level or slightly rising plateau between the mounting slopes of the population curve in the later sixteenth and eighteenth centuries. Except for the Netherlands, Norway and perhaps Sweden and Switzerland and some local areas, no major increases in population appear to be recorded. Spain was a byword for depopulation, southern Italy may have suffered, and the ravages of the mid-century in Germany and eastern France are well known. Though Pirenne has argued that Belgian population increased, figures for Brabant do not seem to bear him out. Hungarian population fell; that of Poland even more. English population growth probably slowed down rapidly and may actually have

[4] J. Meuvret in *Mélanges d'Histoire Sociale*, v (1944), pp. 27–44; in *Population*, i (1946), pp. 643–50 and an unpublished paper on the effects of the 1693–4 and 1709–10 famines on French diplomacy.

ceased after 1630.[5] In fact it is not easy to see why Clark concludes that 'the seventeenth century in most of Europe saw, like the sixteenth, a moderate increase in population'.[6] Mortality was certainly higher than in either the sixteenth or eighteenth. No century since the fourteenth has a worse record for epidemic disease and recent work has demonstrated that its ravages cannot be dissociated from those of famine.[7] While a handful of court and

[5] There are, of course, no reliable statistics and not always good indirect indices. This paragraph is based, in particular, on: K. Larsen, *History of Norway* (Princeton, 1948) (figures only for 1665 and after); K. Mayer, *The Population of Switzerland* (New York, 1952), and Patavino's estimate for 1608 which is as great as Mayer's for 1700, in H. Nabholz, Muralt, Feller, Bonjour, Dürr, *Gesch. d. Schweiz* (Zurich, 1932–8), ii, p. 5; H. Wopfner, *Gueterteilung u. Uebervoelkerung* (Berlin 1938), pp. 202 ff; H. v. z. Muehlen, 'Entstehung d. Gutsherrschaft in Oberschlesien', in *Vierteljahrschrift f. Soz.- und Wirtschaftgesch.*, xxxviii, pp. 334–60; K. L. Beloch, *Bevoelkerungsgeschichte Italiens* (Leipzig, 1937), i, pp. 153, 225 ff; E. Keyser, *Bevoelkerungsgesch. Deutschlands* (Leipzig, 1941), pp. 304 ff, 361 ff; G. Roupnel, *La Ville et la campagne dijonnaises au xvii*[e] *siècle* (Paris, 1922); P. Goubert, 'Problèmes démographiques du Beauvaisis au 17e s.' (*Annales, E.S.C.*, viie année [1952], pp. 452–68), for an area which seems to have suffered rather less; G. Debien, *En Haut-Poitou; Défricheurs au Travail (XV–XVIII siècles)*, and for absence of forest-clearing and recovery of forests, *Bull. Soc. Hist. Mod.*, lvii (1953), pp. 6–9; H. Pirenne, *Hist. de Belgique* (Bruxelles, 1900), iv, pp. 439–40; A. Cosemans, *Bevolkering v. Brabant en de 17*[e] *eeuw* (Brussels, 1939), pp. 224–4; G. N. Clark, *The Seventeenth Century* (Oxford, 1929); J. Rutkowski, *Hist. Econ. de la Pologne avant les Partages* (Paris, 1927), pp. 91–92; L. Stone in *IX Congrès International des Sciences Historiques,* ii (1951), pp. 49–50; W. G. Hoskins, 'The Rebuilding Rural England 1570–1640', *Past and Present,* no. 4 (Nov. 1953).

[6] op. cit., p. 6. The same criticism may be made of the estimates of Urlanis, *Rost nasielenia v. Jewropie* (Moscow, 1941), p. 158, which seem rather optimistic. I am indebted to Mr. A. Jenkin for drawing my attention to these figures.

[7] S. Peller, 'Studies in mortality since the Renaissance', *Bull. Inst. Hist. of Medicine,* xiii (1943), pp. 443, 445, 452, and esp. p. 456; ibid., xvii (1947), pp. 67, 79. Meuvret and Goubert, op. cit. and the literature quoted in H. J. Habakkuk, 'English Population in the Eighteenth Century', *Econ. Hist. Rev.*, 2nd ser., vi (1953). For the epidemiology of the century, in addition to innumerable local studies, H. Haeser, *Gesch. d. Medizin u. d. epidem. Krankheiten* (Jena, 1882); C. Creighton, *Hist. of Epidemics in Britain* (Cambridge, 1891, 1894); L. F. Hirst, *The Conquest of Plague* (Oxford 1953); L. Prinzing, *Epidemics resulting from wars* (Oxford, 1916); J. Brownlee, 'Epidemiology of Phthisis in Great Britain and Ireland', *Medical Research Council* (London, 1918); Campbell, 'The Epidemiology of Influenza', *Bull. Inst. Hist. Medicine,* xiii (1943); W. J. Simpson, *A Treatise on the Plague* (Cambridge, 1905).

administrative metropoles or centres of international trade and finance grew to great size the number of great cities, which had risen in the sixteenth century, remained stable and small and medium towns frequently declined. This appears to apply in part even to the maritime countries.[8]

What happened to *production*? We simply do not know. Some areas were plainly de-industrialized, notably Italy which transformed itself from the most urbanized and industrialized country of Europe into a typical backward peasant area, most of Germany, and parts of France and Poland.[9] On the other hand there was fairly rapid industrial development in some places—Switzerland, and, in the extractive industries, England and Sweden, and an important growth of rural out-work at the expense of urban or local craft production in many areas which may or may not have meant a net increase in total output. If prices are any guide we should not expect to find a general decline in production, for the deflationary period which followed the great price-rise of the pre-1640 era is more easily explained by a relative or absolute falling-off in demand rather than by a decline in the supply of money. However, in the basic industry of textiles there may have been not only a shift from 'old' to 'new' draperies, but a decline of total output for part of the century.[10]

The crisis in *commerce* was more general. The two main areas of established international trade, the Mediterranean and the Baltic, underwent revolution, and probably temporary decline in the volume of trade. The Baltic—the European colony of the western urbanized countries—changed its staple exports from foodstuffs to products like timber, metals and naval stores, while its traditional imports of western woollens diminished. Trade as measured by

[8] W. Sombart, *Luxus u. Kapitalismus*, pp. 26–27; G. F. v. Schmoller, *Deutsches Staedtewesen in älterer Zeit* (Bonn and Leipzig, 1922), pp. 60–95; B. Bretholz, *Gesch. Boehmens u. Maehrens* (Reichenberg, 1924), iii, pp. 61–63; E. Baasch, *Hollaendische Wirtschaftsgeschichte* (Jena, 1927), pp. 24–25.

[9] C. M. Cipolla, 'The Decline of Italy', *Econ. Hist. Rev.*, 2nd ser., v (1952); Roupnel, op. cit., for reversion of Burgundy to autarky; R. Reuss, *Hist. de Strasbourg* (Paris, 1922), pp. 280–6; P. Boissonade, 'La Crise de l'industrie languedocienne 1600–1660', *Annales du Midi*, xxi (1909); G. Aubin and H. Kunze, *Leinenerzeugung . . . im oestl. Mitteldeutschland* (Stuttgart, 1940).

[10] For figures of the Dutch and Florentine production, N. W. Posthumus, *Gesch. v. d. Leidsch. Lakenindustrie* (Hague, 1932); Romano in *Annales*, loc. cit.

the Sound tolls reached its peak in 1590–1620, collapsed in the 1620s, and declined catastrophically after some recovery until the 1650s, remaining in the doldrums until 1680 or so.[11] After 1650, the Mediterranean became like the Baltic an area exchanging locally produced goods, mainly raw materials, for the Atlantic manufactures and the oriental goods now monopolized by the north-west. By the end of the century the Levant got its spices from the north, not the east. French Levantine trade halved between 1620 and 1635, sank almost to zero by the 1650s and did not really recover from depression levels until after the 1670s. Dutch Levantine trade did poorly from about 1617 to about 1650.[12] Even then the French hardly exceeded pre-depression levels much before 1700. Did the British and Dutch sales drive in the south make up for losses in the Baltic markets? Probably not. It may barely have made up for the decline in previous sales of Italian products. The international trade in foodstuffs—Baltic corn, Dutch herrings and Newfoundland fish—did not maintain its Jacobean levels. The international trade in woollen cloths may have shrunk; nor was it immediately replaced by other textiles, for the great centres of exportable linen, Silesia and Lusatia, seem to have declined somewhat after 1620. In fact it is not unlikely that a general balance of rising and declining trade would produce export figures which did not rise significantly between 1620 and 1660. Outside the maritime states it is unlikely that sales on the home markets made up for this.

As we know from the nineteenth century, the malaise of business cannot be measured simply by trade and production figures, whatever these may be. (It is nevertheless significant that the whole tone of economic discussion assumed stable markets and profit opportunities. Colbertian mercantilism, it has often been said, was a policy of economic warfare for large slices of a world trade-cake of fixed size. There is no reason why administrators and traders—for economics was not yet an academic subject—should have adopted views which were greatly at variance with appear-

[11] N. E. Bang and K. Korst, *Tabeller over Skibsfart* (København and Leipzig, 1930–53); A. Christensen, *Dutch Trade and the Baltic about 1600* (Copenhagen, 1940).

[12] G. Tongas, *Relations entre la France et l'Empire Ottoman durant la première moitié du XVIIe siècle* (Toulouse, 1942); P. Masson, *Le Commerce français dans le Levant au XVIIe siècle* (Paris, 1896), esp. pp. 130–4, App. xv, p. 236; H. Wätjen, *D. Niederländer im Mittelmeergebiet* (Berlin, 1909), pp. 145, 149.

ances.) It is certain that even in countries which did not decline there were secular business difficulties. English East India trade languished until the Restoration.[13] Though that of the Dutch increased handsomely, the average annual dividend of their East India Company fell for each of the ten-year periods from the 1630s to the 1670s (including both), except for a slight rise in the 1660s. Between 1627 and 1687 sixteen years were without dividend; in the rest of the Company's history from 1602 to 1782 none. (The value of its goods remained stable between 1640 and 1660.) Similarly the profits of the Amsterdam Wisselbank reached a peak in the 1630s and then declined for a couple of decades.[14] Again, it may not be wholly accidental that the greatest messianic movement of Jewish history occurred at this moment, sweeping the communities of the great trading centres—Smyrna, Leghorn, Venice, Amsterdam, Hamburg—off their feet with special success in the middle 1660s as prices reached almost their lowest point.

It is also clear that the *expansion of Europe* passed through a crisis. Though the foundations of the fabulous colonial system of the eighteenth century were laid mainly after 1650,[15] earlier there may actually have been some contraction of European influence except in the hinterlands of Siberia and America. The Spanish and Portuguese empires of course contracted, and changed character. But it is also worth noting that the Dutch did not maintain the remarkable rate of expansion of 1600 to 1640 and their Empire actually shrank in the next thirty years.[16] The collapse of the Dutch West India company after the 1640s, and the *simultaneous* winding-up of the English Africa Company and the Dutch West India Company in the early 1670s may be mentioned in passing.

[13] Bal Krishna, *Commercial Relations between India and England 1601–1757* (London, 1927), chaps. ii–v; S. A. Khan, *East India Trade in the Seventeenth Century* (London, 1923), pp. 74 ff.

[14] C. de Lannoy and H. Van der Linden, *Hist. de l'Expansion des Peuples Européens, Néerlande et Danemark (XVII et XVIII siècles)* (Bruxelles, 1911), pp. 334, 344–5, 363. The indebtedness of the Company was also higher than before or after; J. G. Van Dillen, *Bronnen tot d. Geschiedenis d. Wisselbanken* (Hague, 1925), ii, pp. 971 ff.

[15] Barbados began to export sugar in 1646, Jamaica started planting in 1664, Haiti re-established plantation in 1655, Martinique began it in the same year, St. Kitts's sugar exports passed its indigo exports in 1660: E. O. v. Lippman, *Gesch. d. Zuckers* (Leipzig, 1890).

[16] For a comparison of its size in 1641 and 1667, J. Saintoyant, *La Colonisation Européenne* (Paris, 1947), pp. 271–3.

It will be generally agreed that the seventeenth century was one of *social revolt* both in western and eastern Europe. This clustering of revolutions has led some historians to see something like a general social-revolutionary crisis in the middle of the century.[17] France had its Frondes, which were important social movements; Catalan, Neapolitan and Portuguese revolutions marked the crisis of the Spanish Empire in the 1640s; the Swiss peasant war of 1653 expressed both the post-war crisis and the increasing exploitation of peasant by town, while in England revolution triumphed with portentous results.[18] Though peasant unrest did not cease in the west—the 'stamped paper' rising which combined middle class, maritime and peasant unrest in Bordeaux and Brittany occurred in 1675, the Camisard wars even later[19]—those of eastern Europe were more significant. In the sixteenth century there had been few revolts against the growing enserfment of peasants. The Ukrainian revolution of 1648–54 may be regarded as a major servile upheaval. So must the various 'Kurucz' movements in Hungary, their very name harking back to Dozsa's peasant rebels of 1514, their memory enshrined in folksongs about Rakoczy as that of the Russian revolt of 1672 is in the song about Stenka Razin. A major Bohemian peasant rising in 1680 opened a period of endemic serf unrest there.[20] It would be easy to lengthen this catalogue of major social upheavals—for instance by including the revolts of the Irish in 1641 and 1689.

Only in one respect did the seventeenth century as a whole overcome rather than experience difficulties. Outside the maritime powers with their new, and experimental bourgeois régimes most of Europe found an efficient and stable form of government in *absolutism* on the French model. (But the rise of absolutism has

[17] B. Porshnev in Biryukovitch, Porshnev, Skazkin, *et al.*, *Novaya Istoriya, 1640–1789* (Moscow, 1951), p. 444. This follows a suggestion of Marx in 1850 (*Sel. Essays*, ed. Stenning [London, 1926], p. 203). The coincidence has often been noted, e.g. Merriman, *Six Contemporaneous Revolutions* (Oxford, 1938).

[18] Merriman, op. cit.; B. Porshnev, *Narodnie vosstaniya vo Frantsii pered Frondoi 1623–1648* (Moscow, 1948); O. Schiff, 'D. deutschen Bauernaufstaende 1525–1789', *Hist. Zeitschrift*, cxxx (1924), pp. 189 ff; R. Feller, *Gesch. Berns*, ii (Bern, 1953), chaps. iv and v.

[19] J. Lemoine, *La Revolte du Papier Timbré* (Paris, 1898), prints numerous documents.

[20] H. Marczali, *Hungary in the Eighteenth Century* (Cambridge, 1910), p. xxxvii; Bretholz, op. cit., pp. 57–61.

been taken as a direct sign of economic weakness.[21] The question is worth exploring further.) The great age of *ad hoc* devices in politics, war and administration vanished with the great world empires of the sixteenth century, the Spanish and Turkish. For the first time large territorial States seemed capable of solving their three fundamental problems: how to have the orders of government obeyed directly over a large area, how to have enough cash for the large lump-sum payments they periodically needed, and—partly in consequence of this—how to run their own armies. The age of the great independent financial and military subcontractors faded with the Thirty Years' War (1618–48). States still had to subcontract, as the practice of selling offices and farming taxes bears witness.[22] However, the whole business was now officially contolled by governments, not merely controlled in practice by the fact that, as the Fuggers and Wallenstein had found to their cost, the monopoly buyer can dictate terms as much as the monopoly seller. Perhaps this obvious political success of the absolutist territorial states with their pomp and splendour has in the past distracted attention from the general difficulties of the age.

If only part of this evidence holds water, we are justified in speaking of a 'general crisis' in the seventeenth century; though one of its characteristics was the relative immunity of the States which had undergone 'bourgeois revolution'. It is probable—though here we venture on the complex territory of price history[23] —that the crisis began about 1620; perhaps with the slump period from 1619 into the early 1620s. It seems certain that, after some distortion of price movements by the Thirty Years War, it reached its most acute phase between 1640 and the 1670s, though precise dates are out of order in the discussion of long-term economic movements. From then on the evidence is conflicting. Probably the signs of revival outweigh those of crisis, not only (obviously) in the Maritime States but elsewhere. However, the wild oscillations of boom and depression, the famines, revolts, epidemics and other signs of profound economic trouble in 1680–1720 should warn us against antedating the period of full recovery. If the trend was upwards from, say, the 1680s—or even earlier in *indi-*

[21] A. Nielsen, *Daenische Wirtschaftsgeschichte* (Jena, 1933), pp. 94–95.

[22] R. Mousnier, *La Vénalité des offices sous Henri IV et Louis XIII* (Rouen, 1946); K. W. Swart, *Sale of offices in the Seventeenth Century* (Hague, 1949).

[23] See the Note on Price History, below p. 28.

vidual countries—it was still liable to disastrous fluctuations.

It may, however, be argued that what I have described as a 'general crisis' was merely the result of seventeenth-century wars, particularly of the Thirty Years' War. In the past historians have in fact tended to take (or rather to imply) this view. But the crisis affected many parts of Europe not ravaged by generals and quartermasters; and conversely, some traditional 'cockpits of Europe' (e.g. Saxony and the Low Countries) did notably better than more tranquil regions. Moreover, there has been a persistent tendency to exaggerate the long-term and permanent damage done by seventeenth-century wars. We now know that (other things being equal) the losses of population, production and capital equipment of even twentieth-century wars, whose destructive capacities are much greater, can be made good within a matter of twenty to twenty-five years. If they were not in the seventeenth century, it was because wars aggravated already existing tendencies of crisis. This is not to deny their importance, though their effects were more complex than appears at first sight. Thus against the ravages of the Thirty Years' War in parts of central Europe we must set the stimulus it gave to mining and metallurgy in general, and the temporary booms it stimulated in non-combatant countries (to the temporary benefit of Charles I in the 1630s). It is also probable that, but for it, the great 'price-rise' would have ended in the 1610s and not the 1640s. The war almost certainly shifted the incidence of the crisis and may, on balance, have aggravated it. Lastly, it is worth considering whether the crisis did not to some extent produce a situation which provoked or prolonged warfare. However, this point, which is not essential to the argument, is perhaps too speculative to be worth pursuing.

THE CAUSES OF THE CRISIS

In discussing the seventeenth-century crisis we are really asking one of the fundamental questions about the rise of capitalism: why did the expansion of the later fifteenth and sixteenth centuries not lead straight into the epoch of the eighteenth- and nineteenth-century Industrial Revolution? What, in other words, were the obstacles in the way of capitalist expansion? The answers, it may be suggested, are both general and particular.

The general argument may be summarized as follows. If capitalism is to triumph, the social structure of feudal or agrarian society must be revolutionized. The social division of labour must be greatly elaborated if productivity is to increase; the social labour force must be radically redistributed from agriculture to industry while this happens. The proportion of production which is exchanged in the supra-local market must rise dramatically. So long as there is no large body of wage-workers; so long as most men supply their needs from their own production or by exchange in the multiplicity of more or less autarkic local markets which exist even in primitive societies, there is a limit to the horizon of capitalist profit and very little incentive to undertake what we may loosely call mass production, the basis of capitalist industrial expansion. Historically, these processes cannot always be separated from one another. We may speak of the 'creation of the capitalist home market' or the divorce of the producers from the means of production which Marx called 'primitive accumulation':[24] the creation of a large and expanding market for goods and a large and available free labour force go together, two aspects of the same process.

It is sometimes assumed that the development of a 'capitalist class' and of the elements of the capitalist mode of production within feudal society automatically produces these conditions. In the long run, taking the widest view over the centuries from 1000 to 1800, this is no doubt so. In the shorter run it is not. Unless certain conditions are present—it is by no means yet clear what they are—the scope of capitalist expansion will be limited by the general prevalence of the feudal structure of society, that is of the predominant rural sector or perhaps by some other structure which 'immobilizes' both the potential labour-force, the potential surplus for productive investment, and the potential demand for capitalistically produced goods, such as the prevalence of tribalism

[24] V. I. Lenin, *The Development of Capitalism in Russia*, chap. i (conclusions), chap. ii (conclusions), chap. viii (the formation of the Home Market). *Capital*, i (1938 edn.), pp. 738, 772–4. That Marx did not think primarily of the actual accumulation of resources is shown, I think, by a preparatory draft to the Critique of Political Economy: 'Eigen ist dem Kapital nichts als die Vereinigung von Haenden und Instrumente, die es vorfindet. Es agglomeriert sie unter seiner Botmaessigkeit. Das ist sein wirkliches Anhaeufen; das Anhaeufen von Arbeitern auf Punkten nebst ihren Instrumente' (*Formen die der kapitalistichen Produktion vorhergehen* [Berlin, 1952], pp. 49–50).

or petty commodity production. Under those conditions, as Marx showed in the case of mercantile enterprise,[25] business might adapt itself to operating in a generally feudal framework, accepting its limitations and the peculiar demand for its services, and becoming in a sense parasitic on it. That part of it which did so would be unable to overcome the crises of feudal society, and might even aggravate them. For capitalist expansion is blind. The weakness of the old theories which ascribed the triumph of capitalism to the development of the 'capitalist spirit' or the 'entrepreneurial spirit' is that the desire to pursue the maximum profit without limit does not automatically produce that social and technical revolution which is required. At the very least there must be mass production (that is production for the greatest aggregate profit—large profits, but not necessarily large profits per sale) instead of production for the maximum profit per unit sale. Yet one of the essential difficulties of capitalist development in societies which keep the mass of the population outside its scope (so that they are neither sellers of labour-power nor serious buyers of commodities) is that in the short view the profits of the really 'revolutionary' types of capitalist production are almost certainly less, or look less attractive, than those of the other kind—especially when they involve heavy capital investment. Christian Dior then looks a more attractive proposition than Montagu Burton. To corner pepper in the sixteenth century would seem much sounder than to start sugar plantations in the Americas; to sell Bologna silks than to sell Ulm fustian. Yet we know that in subsequent centuries far vaster profits were achieved by sugar and cotton than by pepper and silk; and that sugar and cotton contributed far more to the creation of a world capitalist economy than the other two.

Under certain circumstances such trade could, even under feudal conditions, produce large enough aggregate profits to give rise to large-scale production; for instance if it catered for exceptionally large organizations such as kingdoms or the Church; if the thinly spread demand of an entire continent were concentrated into the hands of businessmen in a few specialized centres such as the Italian and Flemish textile towns; if a large 'lateral extension' of the field of enterprise took place, for example by conquest or

[25] *Capital*, iii, pt. iv (Merchant's Capital); and esp. vol. ii, p. 63. See also R. H. Hilton, 'Capitalism, What's in a Name?', *Past and Present*, no. 1 (Feb. 1952).

colonization. A fair amount of social re-division was also possible without disturbing the fundamentally feudal structure of society—for instance the urbanization of the Netherlands and Italy on the basis of food and raw materials imported from semi-colonial territories. Nevertheless the limits of the market were narrow. Medieval and early modern society was a good deal more like 'natural economy' than we care to recall. The sixteenth- and seventeenth-century French peasant is said hardly to have used money except for his transactions with the State; retail trade in German towns was unspecialized, like that in village shops, until the late sixteenth century.[26] Except among a small luxury class (and even there changing fashion in the modern sense probably developed late) the rate of replacement of clothes or household goods was slow. Expansion was possible and took place; but so long as the general structure of rural society had not been revolutionized it was limited, or created its own limits; and when it encountered them, entered a period of crisis.

The expansion of the fifteenth and sixteenth centuries was essentially of this sort; and it therefore created its own crisis both within the home market and within the overseas market. This crisis the 'feudal businessmen'—who were the richest and most powerful just because the best adapted for making big money in a feudal society—were unable to overcome. Their unadaptability intensified it.

Before analysing these things further, it may be worth stressing that the purely *technical* obstacles to capitalist development in the sixteenth and seventeenth centuries were not insuperable. While the sixteenth century may not have been capable of solving certain fundamental problems of technique, such as that of a compact and mobile source of power which so baffled Leonardo, it was quite capable of at least as much innovation as produced the eighteenth-century revolution. Nef and others have made us familiar with the innovations which actually occurred, though the phrase 'Industrial Revolution' seems less apt for the period 1540–1640 than for the Germany of 1450–1520 which evolved the printing press, effective

[26] J. Meuvret, 'Circulation monétaire et utilisation économique de la monnaie dans la France du XVIe et du XVIIe siècle', *Etudes d'Histoire Moderne et Contemp.*, i (1947), pp. 14–29; R. Latouche, *La Vie en Bas-Quercy* (Toulouse, 1923); E. Koehler, *Der Einzelhandel im Mittelalter* (Stuttgart and Berlin, 1938), pp. 55–60.

fire-arms, watches, and the remarkable advance in mining and metallurgy summarized in Agricola's *De Re Metallica* (1556). Nor was there a crippling shortage of capital or capitalist enterprise or of labour, at least in the advanced areas. Sizeable blocks of mobile capital anxious for investment and, especially in the period of rising population, quite important reservoirs of free wage-labour of varying skill existed. The point is that neither were poured into industry of a potentially modern type. Moreover, methods for overcoming such shortages and rigidities of capital and labour supplies might have been utilized as fully as in the eighteenth and nineteenth centuries. The seventeenth-century crisis cannot be explained by the inadequacies of the equipment for industrial revolution, in any narrowly technical and organizational sense.

Let us now turn to the main causes of the crisis.

The specialization of 'feudal capitalists': the case of Italy

The decline of Italy (and the old centres of medieval commerce and manufacture in general) was the most dramatic result of the crisis. It illustrates the weaknesses of 'capitalism' parasitic on a feudal world. Thus sixteenth-century Italians probably controlled the greatest agglomerations of capital, but misinvested them flagrantly. They immobilized them in buildings and squandered them in foreign lending during the price-revolution (which naturally favoured debtors) or diverted them from manufacturing activities to various forms of immobile investment. It has been plausibly suggested that the failure of Italian manufacture to maintain itself against Dutch, English and French during the seventeenth century was due to this diversion of resources.[27] It would be ironic to find that the Medici were Italy's ruin, not only as bankers but as patrons of the expensive arts, and Philistine historians are welcome to observe that the only major city-State which never produced any art worth mentioning, Genoa, maintained its commerce and finance better than the rest. Yet Italian investors, who had long been aware that too large cathedrals harm business,[28] were acting quite sensibly. The experience of centuries had shown that the

[27] A. Fanfani, *Storia del Lavoro in Italia dalla fine del secolo XV agli inizii del XVIII* (Milan, 1943), pp. 42–49.

[28] R. S. Lopez, 'Economie et architecture médiévales', *Annales E.S.C.*, viie année (1952), pp. 443–8.

highest profits were not to be got in technical progress or even in production. They had adapted themselves to business activities in the comparatively narrow field which remained for them once one left aside the majority of the population of Europe as 'economically neutral'. If they spent vast amounts of capital non-productively, it may have been simply because there was no more room to invest it progressively on any scale within the limits of this 'capitalist sector'. (The seventeenth-century Dutch palliated a similar glut of capital by multiplying household goods and works of art[29] though they also discovered the more modern device of a speculative investment boom.) Perhaps the Italians would have been shocked into different behaviour by economic adversity; though they had made money for so long by providing the feudal world with its trade and finance that they would not have learned easily. However, the general boom of the later sixteenth century (like the 'Indian summer' of Edwardian Britain) and the suddenly expanded demands of the great absolute monarchies which relied on private contractors, and the unprecedented luxury of their aristocracies, postponed the evil day. When it came, bringing decay to Italian trade and manufacture, it left Italian finance still upright, though no longer dominant. Again, Italian industry might well have maintained some of its old positions by switching more completely from its old high-quality goods to the shoddier and cheaper new draperies of the north. But who, in the great period of luxury buying from 1580–1620, would have guessed that the future of high-quality textiles was limited? Did not the Court of Lorraine, in the first third of the century, use more textiles imported from Italy than from all other non-French countries put together?[30] (One would like to reserve judgement on the argument that Italy lost ground because of higher production costs for goods of equal quality, until stronger evidence for it is brought forward or until we have a satisfactory explanation for the failure of Italian production, after promising beginnings, to shift as wholeheartedly from towns to countryside as did the textile industries of other countries.[31])

The case of Italy shows why particular countries went down in

[29] G. Renier, *The Dutch Nation* (London, 1944), pp. 97–99.

[30] H. Roy, *La Vie, la mode et le costume au XVIIe siècle* (Paris, 1924), prints a full list of all the types of textile used at this Court.

[31] Cipolla, 'The decline of Italy' (cited above n. 9), for the high-cost argument.

the crisis, not necessarily why it occurred. We must therefore consider the contradictions of the very process of sixteenth-century expansion.

The contradictions of expansion: eastern Europe

The comparative specialization of west-European towns on trade and manufacture was to some extent achieved in the fifteenth and sixteenth centuries by the creation of a sizeable surplus of exportable food in eastern Europe and perhaps by ocean fisheries.[32] But in eastern Europe this was achieved by the creation of serf agriculture on a large scale; that is a local strengthening of feudalism. This, we may suggest, had three effects. It turned the peasant into less of a cash customer than he had been or might have been (or else it forced him off good-quality western textiles into cheap locally produced cloth). It diminished the number and wealth of the minor nobility for the benefit of a handful of magnates. In Poland the former controlled 43.8 per cent of ploughs in the mid-fifteenth century, 11.6 per cent in the mid-seventeenth; the share of the latter rose from 13.3 to 30.7 per cent in the same period. Lastly, it sacrificed the livelier market of the towns to the free trade interests of exporting landlords, or else seized much of what trade was going for the benefit of the already bloated lords.[33] The expansion thus had two results. While creating the conditions for the expansion of manufactures in western Europe, it cut down, for a time at least, the outlets of these manufactures in the Baltic area —perhaps its most important market. The desire to cash in rapidly on the growing demand for corn—the Baltic now began to feed not only northern Europe but also the Mediterranean—tempted serf-lords into that headlong expansion of their demesnes and

[32] M. Malowist in Report of *IX Congrès International des Sciences Historiques*, i (1950), pp. 305–22.

[33] For the extent of this increasing exploitation, J. Rutkowski, 'Le Régime agraire en Pologne au XVIIIe siècle', *Rev. Hist. Econ. and Soc.*, xix, xx (1926 and 1927), esp. 1927, pp. 92 ff; J. Rutkowski, 'Les Bases économiques des partages de l'ancienne Pologne', *Rev. d'Hist. Moderne*, N.S., iv (1932); R. Rosdolsky, 'The distribution of the agrarian product in feudalism', *Jl. of Econ. Hist.*, xi (1951), pp. 247 ff. For the unimportance of cash payments, Rutkowski, op. cit., 1927, p. 71 and 1926, p. 501; Malowist, op. cit., pp. 317 ff. For an example of town impoverishment due to this, F. Tremel, 'Handel d. Stadt Judenburg im 16 Jh.', *Ztschr. d. hist. Vereins fuer Steiermark*, xxxviii (1947), pp. 103–6.

intensification of exploitation which led to the Ukrainian revolution, and perhaps also to demographic catastrophes.[34]

The contradictions of expansion: overseas and colonial markets

Much of the trade between Europe and the rest of the world had, as we know, been passive throughout the ages, because Orientals did not need European goods to the same extent as Europe needed theirs. It had been balanced by bullion payments, supplemented from time to time by such exports as slaves, furs, amber or other luxuries. Until the Industrial Revolution the sales of European manufactures were not important. (African trade, which was not deficitary, may be an exception because of the staggeringly favourable terms of trade which European goods commanded among the ignorant local buyers and indeed—almost by definition—because the continent was valued chiefly as a source of bullion until late in the seventeenth century. In 1665 the Royal African Company still estimated its gain from gold at twice its gain from slaves.[35]) The European conquest of the main trade-routes and of America did not change this structure fundamentally, for even the Americas exported more than they imported. It greatly diminished the cost of eastern goods by cutting out middlemen, lessening transport charges and enabling European merchants and armed bands to rob and cheat with impunity. It also greatly increased bullion supplies, presenting us with American and African Peters to be robbed to pay the Asian Pauls. Unquestionably Europe derived immense windfall gains from this. General business activity was immensely stimulated as well as capital accumulated; but our exports of manufactures were on the whole *not* greatly expanded. Colonial powers—in good medieval business tradition—followed a policy of systematic restriction of output and systematic monopoly. Hence there was no reason why exports of home manufactures should benefit.

The benefit which Europe drew from these initial conquests was

[34] An expansion of the total area of serf export-agriculture, e.g. in the Black Sea area, might have offset this. But this did not take place until the eighteenth century, possibly owing to Turkish strength and grain policy earlier: D. Ionescu, *Agrarverfassung Rumaeniens* (Leipzig, 1909), pp. 10–19; A. Mehlan, 'D. grossen Balkanmessen in der Tuerkenzeit', *Vierteljahrschrift f. Soz-. und Wirtschaftgesch.*, xxxi (1938), pp. 2–7.

[35] *Cal. S. P. Col., 1661–8*, p. 266.

thus in the nature of a single bonus rather than a regular dividend. When it was exhausted, crisis was likely to follow. Among the colonial powers costs and overheads rose faster than profits. In both east and west we may distinguish three stages: that of easy profits, that of crisis, and with luck eventually that of a stable and more modest prosperity. In the initial phase conquest or interloping brought temporarily unchallenged profits at low costs. In the east, where profits rested on the monopoly of a restricted output of spices and the like, the crisis was probably brought on by the steep rise in 'protection costs' against old and new rivals; rising all the more steeply as the colonial power tried to screw up the monopoly price. It has been estimated that the Portuguese spice trade barely paid its way for these reasons.[36] In the west, where they rested on the cheap bulk production of bullion and other raw materials, 'protection costs' probably played a smaller part, though they also rose with piracy and competition. However, there the technical limits of the primitive 'rat-hole' mining of the Spaniards were soon reached (even allowing for the uses of the mercury process), and very possibly the labour force was virtually worked to death, being treated as an expendable asset.[37] At any rate American silver exports diminished after 1610 or so. Eventually, of course, in the east colonial powers adjusted themselves to the new level of overheads and perhaps found new sources of local taxation to offset them. In the west the familiar structure of quasi-feudal large estates came into being in the seventeenth century.[38] Since the economic basis of the Spanish colonial system was broader than the Portuguese, the results of crisis would be more far-reaching. Thus the early emigration to the Americas temporarily stimulated the export of goods from the home country; but as, inevitably, many of the colonists' wants came to be supplied locally, the expanded manufactures of Spain had to pay the price. The attempt to tighten the metropolitan

[36] F. C. Lane, 'National Wealth and Protection Costs' in Clarkson and Cochran eds., *War as a Social Institution* (New York, 1941), pp. 36 ff.

[37] C. G. Motten, *Mexican Silver and the Enlightenment* (Philadelphia and London, 1950), chaps. 2–3.

[38] Thus from the end of the seventeenth century the Dutch East India Company expanded the income from colonial taxes, previously about 9 per cent of its revenue, much more rapidly than trading profits. Lannoy and Linden, op. cit., pp. 266–7. F. Chevalier, *La Formation des grands domaines en Mexique. Terres et Société au XVI–XVIIe siècles* (Paris, 1952).

monopoly merely made matters worse by discouraging the development, among other things, of the potentially revolutionary plantation economy.[39] The effects of the influx of bullion into Spain are too well known to need discussion.

It is therefore understandable that the 'old colonial system' passed through a profound crisis; and that its effects on the general European economy were far-reaching. A new pattern of colonial exploitation which produced steadily rising exports of manufactures from Europe did indeed replace it. (Acting largely on their own the sugar planters of northern Brazil had shown the way to it from the end of the sixteenth century.) Yet the lure of the old monopoly profits was irresistible to all those who had a chance of capturing them. Even the Dutch remained resolutely 'old-fashioned' in their colonialism until the eighteenth century, though their entrepôt position in Europe saved them from the consequences of colonial inefficiency. Old colonialism did not grow over into new colonialism; it collapsed and was replaced by it.

The contradictions of the home markets

There can be little doubt that the sixteenth century came nearer to creating the conditions for a really widespread adoption of the capitalist mode of production than any previous age; perhaps because of the impetus given by overseas loot, perhaps because of the encouragement of rapidly growing population and markets and rising prices. (It is not the object of this article to discuss the reasons which caused this expansion to follow the 'feudal crisis' of the fourteenth and fifteenth centuries.) A powerful combination of forces, including even large feudal interests,[40] seriously threatened the resistance of gild-dominated towns. Rural industry, of the 'putting-out' type, which had previously been largely confined to textiles, spread in various countries and to new branches of production (for example metals), especially towards the end of the period. Yet the expansion bred its own obstacles. We may briefly consider some of them.

Except perhaps in England no 'agrarian revolution' of a capital-

[39] For the ending of sugar plantations in the early seventeenth century, E. O. v. Lippmann, op. cit.

[40] cf. H. Aubin, 'D. Anfaenge d. grossen schlesischen Leineweberei', *Vierteljahrschr. f. Soz-. und Wirtschaftgesch.*, xxxv (1942), pp. 154–73.

ist type accompanied industrial change, as it was to do in the eighteenth century; though there was plenty of upheaval in the countryside. Here again we find the generally feudal nature of the social framework distorting and diverting forces which might otherwise have made for a direct advance towards modern capitalism. In the east, where agrarian change took the form of a revival of serfdom by exporting lords, the conditions for such development were inhibited locally, though made possible elsewhere. In other regions the price-rise, the upheavals in landownership, and the growth of demand for agrarian produce might well have led to the emergence of capitalist farming by gentlemen and the kulak-type of peasant on a greater scale than appears to have occurred.[41] Yet what happened? French lords (often 'bourgeois' who had bought themselves into feudal status) reversed the trend to peasant independence from the middle of the sixteenth century, and increasingly recovered lost ground.[42] Towns, merchants and local middlemen invested in the land, partly no doubt because of the security of farm produce in an age of inflation, partly because the surplus was easy to draw from it in a feudal manner, their exploitation being all the more effective for being combined with usury; partly perhaps in direct political rivalry with feudalists.[43] Indeed, the relationship of towns and their inhabitants as a whole to the surrounding peasantry was still, as always in a generally feudal society, that of a special kind of feudal lord. (The peasants in the town-dominated cantons of Switzerland and in inland Netherlands were not actually emancipated until the French Revolution.[44]) The mere existence of urban investment in agriculture or urban influence over the countryside, therefore, did not imply the creation of rural capitalism. Thus the spread of share-cropping in France, though theoretically marking a step towards capitalism, in fact often produced merely a bourgeoisie parasitic on a peasantry increasingly exhausted by it, and by the rising demands of the

[41] P. Raveau, *L'Agriculture . . . en Poitou au XVIe s.* (Paris, 1926), p. 127; Marc Bloch, *Les Caractères Originaux de l'histoire rurale française* (new edn., Paris, 1952), pp. 148–9; but the 'gentilhomme campagnard' is not *ipso facto* a capitalist farmer.

[42] Bloch, op. cit.; Braudel, op. cit., pp. 624 ff.

[43] Bloch, op. cit., pp. 145–6; P. Raveau, op. cit., pp. 249 ff; A. Kraemer, *D. wechselnde . . . Bedeutung d. Landbesitzes d. Stadt Breslau*, op. cit., p. 48, for systematic buying of land from 1500 to the Thirty Years' War.

[44] Baasch, *Hollaend. Wirtschaftsgeschichte*, p. 50; Roupnel, op. cit.

State; and consequent decline.[45] The old social structure predominated still.

Two results may have followed from this. First, it is improbable that there was much technical innovation, though the first (Italian) handbook on crop rotation appeared in the mid-sixteenth century, and certain that the increase in agrarian output did not keep pace with demand.[46] Hence towards the end of the period there are signs of diminishing returns and food-shortage, of exporting areas using up their crops for local needs, etc., preludes to the famines and epidemics of the crisis-period.[47] Second, the rural population, subject to the double pressure of landlords and townsmen (not to mention the State), and in any case much less capable of protecting itself against famine and war than they, suffered.[48] In some regions this shortsighted 'squeeze' may actually have led to a declining trend in productivity during the seventeenth century.[49] The countryside was sacrificed to lord, town and State. Its appalling rate of mortality—if the relatively prosperous Beauvaisis is any guide—was second only to that of the domestic out-workers, also increasingly rural.[50] Expansion under these conditions bred crisis.

What happened in the non-agricultural sectors depended largely on the agricultural. Costs of manufacture may have been unduly raised by the more rapid rise of agrarian than of industrial prices,

[45] Marx, *Capital* iii, xlvii, sect. v, on *métayage*; G. de Falguérolles, 'Décadence de l'économie agricole à Lempaut (Languedoc)', *Annales du Midi*, liii (1941), pp. 142–167—an important article.

[46] Raveau, op. cit., chap. iii. For the non-innovating character of French agricultural handbooks, G. Lizerand, *Le Régime rural de l'ancienne France* (Paris, 1942), pp. 79–81. M. J. Elsas, *Umriss einer Geschichte d. Preise u. Loehne in Deutschland* (Leiden, 1949), for stable agricultural productivity.

[47] G. Coniglio, *Il regno di Napoli al tempo de Carlo V* (Naples, 1951), and Braudel, op. cit.; V. Barbour, *Capitalism in Amsterdam* (Baltimore, 1950), pp. 26–27; A. Juergens, *Z. schleswig-holsteinschen Handelsgeschichte im 16. u. 17. Jh.* (Berlin, 1914), pp. 10–12, for change from an exporting to an importing area at end of sixteenth century.

[48] Because they relied on local food supplies, while towns imported in any case, often from great distances. J. Meuvret, 'La Géographie du prix des céréales', *Revista de Economia*, iv (Lisbon, 1951), pp. 63–69. Falguérolles, op. cit., for peasants ceasing to eat wheat, which they had to sell to pay taxes.

[49] Falguérolles, op. cit., argues so.

[50] Goubert, op. cit. (above, n. 5); and below chap. 6.

Coláiste Oideachais Mhuire Gan Smál Luimneach 19768

thus narrowing the profit-margin of manufacturers.[51] (However, manufacturers increasingly used the cheap labour of rural outworkers, who were again exploited to the point of debility.) The market also had its difficulties. The rural market as a whole must have proved disappointing. Many freeholding peasants benefited from the price-rise and the demand for their goods, provided they had enough land to feed themselves even in bad years, a regular surplus for sale, and a good head for business.[52] But if such yeomen bought much more than before, they bought less than townsmen of equal standing, being more self-sufficient.[53] The experience of nineteenth-century France shows that a middle and rich peasantry is about as uninviting a market for mass manufactures as may be found, and does not encourage capitalists to revolutionize production. Its wants are traditional; most of its wealth goes into more land and cattle, or into hoards, or into new building, or even into sheer waste, like those gargantuan weddings, funerals, and other feasts which disturbed continental princes at the turn of the sixteenth century.[54] The increase in the demand from the non-agricultural sector (towns, luxury market, government demand, etc.) may for a time have obscured the fact that it grew less rapidly than productive capacity, and that the persistent decline in the real income of wage-earners in the long inflation may actually, according to Nef, have stopped 'the growth of the demand for some industrial products'.[55] However, the slumps in the export markets from the late 1610s onwards brought the fact home.

Once the decline had begun, of course, an additional factor increased the difficulties of manufacture: the rise in labour costs. For there is evidence that—in the towns at least—the bargaining

[51] Elsas, op. cit., O. Roehlk, *Hansisch-Norwegische Handelspolitik im 16. Jh.* (Neumünster, 1935), pp. 74–75 for an excellent discussion of this, though relating to the 'price-scissors' between corn and fish prices; G. D. Ramsay, 'The Report of the Royal Commission on the Clothing Industry, 1640', *Eng. Hist. Rev.*, lvii (1942), pp. 485–6.

[52] Bloch, op. cit., on this important last point.

[53] M. Campbell, *The English Yeoman* (New Haven, 1942), pp. 186–7, chap. vi *passim*, and Hoskins, *Past and Present*, no. 4 (1953).

[54] H. Widmann, *Geschichte Salzburgs* (Gotha, 1914), iii, p. 354; Feller, op. cit., ii, p. 368; H. Schnell, *Mecklenburg im Zeitalter d. Reformation* (Berlin, 1900), p. 201.

[55] 'Prices and Industrial Capitalism', *Econ. Hist. Rev.*, vii (1936–7), pp. 184–5.

power of labour rose sharply during the crisis, perhaps owing to the fall or stagnation in town populations. At any rate real wages rose in England, Italy, Spain and Germany, and the mid-century saw the formation of effective journeymen's organizations in most western countries.[56] This may not have affected the labour costs of the putting-out industries, as their workers were in a weaker position to benefit from the situation, and their piece-rate wages were more easily cut. However, it is clearly not a negligible factor. Moreover, the slackening of population increase and the stabilization of prices must have depressed manufactures further.

These different aspects of the crisis may be reduced to a single formula: economic expansion took place within a social framework which it was not yet strong enough to burst, and in ways adapted to it rather than to the world of modern capitalism. Specialists in the Jacobean period must determine what actually precipitated the crisis: the decline in American silver, the collapse of the Baltic market or some of many other possible factors. Once the first crack appeared, the whole unstable structure was bound to totter. It did totter, and in the subsequent period of economic crisis and social upheaval the decisive shift from capitalist enterprise adapted to a generally feudal framework to capitalist enterprise transforming the world in its own pattern, took place. The Revolution in England was thus the most dramatic incident in the crisis, and its turning-point. 'This nation', wrote Samuel Fortrey in 1663 in his *England's Interest and Improvement*, 'can expect no less than to become the most great and flourishing of all others.'[57] It could and it did; and the effects on the world were to be portentous.

[56] D. Knoop and G. P. Jones, *The Medieval Mason* (Manchester, 1949), pp. 207–12; Cipolla, 'The decline of Italy' (cited n. 9), p. 184; Elsas, op. cit.; E. J. Hamilton, *War and Prices in Spain 1651–1800* (Harvard, 1947), p. 219. G. Unwin, *Industrial Organisation in the Sixteenth and Seventeenth Centuries* (Oxford, 1904), chap. viii; G. Des Marez, *Le Compagnonnage des Chapeliers Bruxellois* (Bruxelles, 1909), pp. 17–21; E. Martin St. Léon, *Le Compagnonnage* (Paris, 1901); L. Guéneau, *L'Organisation de travail à Nevers au XVIIe et XVIIIe siècle 1660–1790* (Paris, 1919), pp. 79 ff; J. Gebauer, *Gesch. d. Stadt Hildesheim* (Hildesheim and Leipzig, 1922), pp. 221 ff; etc.

[57] Samuel Fortrey, *England's Interest and Improvement* (London, 1673 edn.) p.8.

A NOTE ON PRICE HISTORY

Long-term price movements have been deliberately kept outside the main argument, because other discussions of long-term economic development emphasize them so much; perhaps too much. Nevertheless, the course of prices calls for some comment.

The traditional view, as put forward by Simiand and accepted by Labrousse and others, is that the long price-rise came to an end around 1640 and was followed by a price-fall, or fluctuations round a stable trend until the second quarter of the eighteenth century. This view seems too simple. There are signs of a change in the price trend between 1605 and 1620; for instance in Spanish wheat prices. Cipolla has also noted that Milanese prices cease to rise rapidly after 1605 and continue steady or rising slowly from then until 1630 (*Mouvements monétaires dans l'état de Milan 1580–1700*, Paris, 1952). We should expect this, since Hamilton showed that the import of American bullion reached its peak in 1590–1610, though it held up quite well until 1620 or so (*American Treasure*, p. 35). If prices went on rising until 1640 (or 1635, which seems to have been the turning-point in Italy) it was probably due to debasement of coinage, to the demand for scarce goods in the Thirty Years' War, or to a combination of both. Hence it is not unlikely that, but for the war, the period of price-fall or price-stability would have begun in 1610–20. The end of the war intensified the crisis, which undoubtedly reached its most acute phase (and the lowest point of prices) in the 1660s and early 1670s. The effects of drastic post-war deflation may be studied in the typical war-profiteering country of Switzerland, where they led to the peasant war of 1653.

The course of prices differed, of course, according to regions and commodities, and some of the local and sectional phenomena are still very obscure. No attempt can be made here to account for them. In general, however, secular price-movements tally quite well with the periods of the crisis as discussed in this essay.

II

In the first part of this essay I have attempted to outline some of the evidence for the view that there was a 'general crisis' of the European economy in the seventeenth century and to suggest some reasons why it should have occurred. I have argued that it was due, in the main, to the failure to surmount certain general obstacles which still stood in the way of the full development of capitalism. The evidence also suggests that the 'crisis' itself created the conditions which were to make industrial revolution possible. In this second section I shall discuss ways in which this may have come about, that is the outcome of the crisis.

It is perhaps worth recalling that the period of difficulties lasted for about a century—say from the 1620s to the 1720s. Thereafter the general picture is rosier. The financial problems of the age of wars were more or less solved, at the expense of numerous investors, in Britain and France by means of such devices as the South Sea Bubble and Law's System. Plague and pestilence, if not famine, disappeared from western Europe after the Marseilles epidemic of 1720–1. Wherever the eye turned, it saw growing wealth, trade and industry, growing population and colonial expansion. Slow at first, the pace of economic change became precipitous from sometime between the 1760s and the 1780s. The period of industrial revolution had begun. There were indeed, as we shall see, signs of a 'crisis of growth' in agriculture, in the colonial economy and elsewhere from the third quarter of the eighteenth century, but it would be impossible to write the history of the eighteenth century in terms of a 'phase of contraction', as a recent historian has written that of the seventeenth.[58]

However, if the argument that the fundamental obstacles in the way of capitalist development disappeared sometime in the seventeenth century is right, we may legitimately ask why industrial revolution did not get into its full stride until the end of the eighteenth. The problem is a very real one. In England, at any rate, it is hard to escape the impression that the stormy pace of economic development towards the end of the seventeenth century 'ought' to have brought about industrial revolution much sooner. The gap between Newcomen and James Watt, between the time the Darbys of Coalbrookdale discovered how to smelt iron with coal and the time when the method was generally utilized, is really quite long. It is significant that the Royal Society complained in 1701 that 'the discouraging neglect of the great, the impetuous contradiction of the ignorant, and the reproaches of the unreasonable, had unhappily thwarted them in their design to

[58] R. Mousnier, *Le XVIe et le XVIIe Siècles* (Paris, 1954).

perpetuate a succession of useful inventions'.[59] Even in some other countries there are signs of economic changes in the 1690s which lead no farther, for instance agricultural innovations in Normandy and south-western France.[60] Again, a malaise hangs over British farming in the 1720s and 1730s and perhaps over some industries.[61] In the intellectual field there is an analogous gap. I do not propose to tackle this problem of the time-lag here. It must certainly be solved if we are to have a really adequate understanding of the process of modern economic development and the origins of the Industrial Revolution, but space forbids any attempt, however cursory, to discuss it here.

The obstacles in the way of industrial revolution were of two types. First, as has been argued, the economy and social structure of pre-capitalist societies simply did not leave enough scope for it. Something like a preliminary revolutionizing had to take place before they were capable of undergoing the transformations which England underwent between the 1780s and the 1840s. This had of course begun long before. We must consider how far the seventeenth-century crisis advanced it. However, there is a second problem, though a more specialized one. Even if we remove the general obstacles in the way of industrial revolution, it does not follow that a society of machines and factories will immediately result. Between 1500 and 1800 many industries evolved methods of expanding output rapidly and without limit, but with fairly primitive organization and technique; for instance the metal goods producers of Birmingham, the gun-makers of Liège, the cutlers of Sheffield or Solingen. These towns produced their characteristic wares in much the same ways in 1860 as in 1750, though in vastly greater quantities and with the use of new sources of power. What we have to explain, therefore, is not merely the rise of *Birmingham* with its subdivided craft industries, but specifically the rise of *Manchester* with its factories, for it was Manchester and its like

[59] S. F. Mason, *A History of the Sciences* (London, 1953), p. 223.

[60] H. Enjalbert, 'Le Commerce de Bordeaux et la vie écon. dans le Bassin Aquitain au XVIIe siècle', *Annales du Midi*, lxii (1950), pp. 21 ff; 'Les Études d'histoire normande de 1928 à 1951', *Annales de Normandie*, i (1951), p. 178.

[61] I owe my knowledge of this to Prof. H. J. Habakkuk, Prof. J. D. Chambers, Mr. D. C. Coleman, Mr. D. Joslin and other students of the period.

which revolutionized the world. What conditions in the seventeenth century helped, not only to sweep away the general obstacles, but to produce the conditions which gave birth to Manchester?

It would be surprising if the conditions for the development of the modern industrial economy were to arise everywhere in seventeenth- and eighteenth-century Europe. What we must show is that, as the result of seventeenth-century changes, they developed in one or two areas sufficiently largely and economically effective enough to serve as a base for revolutionizing the world subsequently. This is very difficult. Perhaps no really conclusive demonstration is possible until we have far more quantitative information about the period than we have at present. It is all the more difficult because in the most vital areas of the economy—agricultural and manufacturing production properly speaking—we not only know very little, but lack the sort of revolutionary landmarks which cheer the historian of the Industrial Revolution on his way: spinning-mills, power-looms, railways. Hence the economic historian of our period may have the very strong impression that 'somewhere about the middle of the seventeenth century European life was so completely transformed in many of its aspects that we commonly think of this as one of the great watersheds of modern history',[62] but he cannot prove it conclusively.

THE SEVENTEENTH CENTURY, AN AGE OF ECONOMIC CONCENTRATION

The main argument here may be summarized as follows. The seventeenth-century crisis resulted in a considerable concentration of economic power. In this it differed, I think, from the fourteenth-century crisis which had—at least for a time—the opposite effect. This may indicate that the old structure of European society had already been considerably undermined, for it is arguable that the normal tendency of a purely feudal society, when in difficulties, is to revert to an economy of small local producers—for example peasants—whose mode of production easily survives the collapse of an elaborate superstructure of demesne agriculture

[62] G. N. Clark, *The Seventeenth Century* (Oxford, 1929), p. ix.

and trade.[63] Directly and indirectly this concentration served the ends of future industrialization, though of course nobody intended it to do so. It did so directly, by strengthening 'putting-out' industry at the expense of craft production, and the 'advanced' economies at the expense of the 'backward' and speeding the process of capital accumulation; indirectly by helping to solve the problem of providing a surplus of agricultural products, and in other ways. Of course this was not a Panglossian process, in which everything was for the best in the best of all possible worlds. Many of the results of the crisis were sheer waste, or even regression, when considered from the point of view of an eventual industrial revolution. Nor was it an 'inevitable' process in the short run. Had the English Revolution failed, for instance, as so many other revolutions in the seventeenth century failed, it is entirely possible that economic development might have been long retarded. Nevertheless, its net effect was economically progressive.

Though the generalization may be contested, like all generalizations, there is little doubt that economic concentration took place in various forms, in east and west, under conditions of expansion, contraction or stagnation. Within the countryside large landowners gained at the expense of peasants and smaller owners, in Restoration England as in eastern Europe. (If we regard towns as special forms of feudal lords the impression of concentration is even stronger on the continent.) In non-industrial areas towns gained at the expense of the countryside, whether as a result of their greater immunity to lords, soldiers and hunger or for other reasons.[64] Administrative measures like the Prussian excise might intensify this process, but were not wholly responsible for it. The east-European areas in which towns declined, like small landowners and peasants, before the pressure of magnates, are an exception which merely confirms the general picture of concentration. Within the towns wealth may have concentrated also, at any rate where the lords were not strong enough to capture the old town rights of exploiting the countryside for themselves, as they

[63] H. Takahashi, 'The Transition from Feudalism to Capitalism', *Science and Society*, xvi (1952), p. 334.

[64] A. Girard, 'La Répartition de la population en Espagne', *Rev. Hist. Econ. et Soc.*, xxii (1929), pp. 350–1, 354; G. Roupnel, *La Ville et la campagne dijonnaises au XVIIe siècle* (Paris, 1922), pp. 89–91, 150; G. Schmoller, *Deutsches Staedtewesen in älterer Zeit* (Bonn and Leipzig, 1922), pp. 272–89.

did in eastern Europe.[65] In industrial areas we have what Espinas called 'the double orientation of production in small and large centres'[66] that is, the substitution of rural out-work controlled by great national or foreign trading groups for the medium-sized town crafts. We also have a certain re-grouping of industries which may sometimes be regarded as concentration, for example where specialized manufactures for a national or international market grew up in particular areas instead of more widespread manufactures for regional markets.[67] Everywhere the great metropolitan cities grew at the expense of town, countryside or both. Internationally trade concentrated in the maritime states, and within these in turn capital cities tended to preponderate. The growing power of centralized states also made for some economic concentration.

Agriculture

What were the effects of this process in agriculture? We have seen that there is evidence that towards the end of the sixteenth and the beginning of the seventeenth centuries the expansion of the marketable agricultural surplus was lagging behind that of non-agricultural consumption. In the long run the vast surplus essential for the development of a modern industrial society was to be achieved primarily by technical revolution—that is by raising productivity and expanding the cultivated area through capitalist farming. Only thus could agriculture produce not merely the necessary food surplus for the towns—not to mention certain industrial raw materials—but also the labour for industry. In the developed countries, notably in the Low Countries and England, signs of agricultural revolution had long been visible, and from the middle of the seventeenth century they multiply. We also find a marked increase in the cultivation of novel and rare crops such as maize, potatoes and tobacco which may be regarded as a species of agricultural revolution. Before the mid-seventeenth century maize

[65] A striking example in A. Helbok, *Bevoelkerung d. Stadt Bregenz* (Innsbruck, 1912), pp. 148, 150. Karaisl, 'Z. Gesch. d. Muenchner Patriziats', *Jb. f. Nationaloekonomie*, clii (1940), pp. 1 ff. But see F. Tremel, 'Handel d. Stadt Judenburg', *Ztschr. d. hist. Vereins f. Steiermark*, xxxviii (1947), for the levelling effect of general impoverishment.

[66] *Annales d'Hist. Econ. et Soc.*, vii (1935), pp. 186–8.

[67] G. N. Clark, op. cit., p. 76.

had only been grown in the Po delta (from 1554); soon afterwards it spread to Lombardy and Piedmont. Rice cultivation in Lombardy covered 5,000 hectares in 1550; by 1710 it covered over 150,000, about as much as today and only three-eighths below the peak acreage of 1870. Maize and cotton cultivation certainly spread in the Balkans. Potatoes appear to have made serious headway in Ireland and perhaps northern England by 1700, though virtually uncultivated elsewhere.[68] Nevertheless, it would be unwise to conclude that technical innovation contributed much to agricultural production before the mid-eighteenth century—again England and the Low Countries may be exceptions, as also the areas of maize cultivation—or that it extended much beyond gardening which, as M. Meuvret has pointed out, lent itself easily to technical experimenting.[69] It is doubtful whether in many areas of Europe the cultivated area in 1700 had extended much beyond what it had been in 1600.

Exactly what happened in western Europe is by no means clear, though we know that England exported corn increasingly from the end of the seventeenth century. It would seem, to judge from what we know of France, that the increasing demand from such large food-markets as Paris was met (a) by drawing on the reserves of proverbially rich agricultural areas which had not previously been fully tapped in normal times and (b) by increasingly 'poaching' on the preserves of other cities.[70] Since there is no obvious evidence of increases in productivity one would expect this to have meant, in the last analysis, either a transfer from food with a lower to food with a higher yield per acre (for example from cattle to corn), or a simple transfer from some Peter—probably the miserable peasant—to some Paul. There is some evidence that peasants were forced on to a worse diet, selling their wheat on the market, at any rate in the south, which had never had much of a food surplus. A decline in the dietary standard in England has also been suggested for the later seventeenth century.[71]

[68] *Encicl. Italiana*; T. Stoianovich, 'Land Tenure and Related Sectors of the Balkan Economy', *Jl. of Econ. Hist.*, xiii (1953), pp. 398–411; R. N. Salaman, *The History and Social Influence of the Potato* (Cambridge, 1949).

[69] 'Agronomie et jardinage . . .', *Hommage à Lucien Febvre* (Paris, 1953), vol. ii.

[70] A. P. Usher, *Hist. of the grain trade in France, 1400–1710* (Cambridge, Mass., 1913), pp. 56, 80–82, 180.

[71] J. C. Drummond and A. Wilbraham, *The Englishman's Food* (London, 1939), pp. 119–22.

What happened in central and eastern Europe is rather more clear.

The development of an economy of serf-estates was accelerated and accentuated in the seventeenth century, which may be regarded as marking the decisive victory of the new serfdom, or more precisely of large serf-owners ('magnates') over the lesser nobility and gentry. We need not discuss how much of this revival of feudalism was due to the increasing demand of outside food-markets—at home or abroad, how much to other factors.[72] At all events, a number of factors coincided to increase the economic and political power of the magnates, who were both the most effective and the most wholesale enserfers of the peasantry. With rare and transitory exceptions—the Swedish monarchy's peasant policy in the Baltic towards the end of the century may be one[73]—even the absolutist monarchies were unable and unwilling to interfere with it. Indeed they tended to advance it, because their victory over Estates and similar institutions generally meant the weakening of the lesser nobles (whose strongholds they were) and of the towns, and the relative strengthening of the smaller groups of magnates who gathered round the ruler's Court, which may often be regarded virtually as a mechanism for distributing the country's taxable income among them in one form or another. In any case, as in Russia and Prussia, the power of the monarch in the state was sometimes bought by renouncing all interference with the power of the lord on his estate. Where royal power was vanishing, as in Poland, or declining, as in Turkey (where non-heritable fiefs for military service gave way to heritable feudal estates), the lord's task was in any case even less complicated.

The decisive victory of the serf-estate did not lead to an increase in productivity, but it was able to create, for a time at least, a large pool of potentially saleable, and as time went on, actually sold agrarian produce. In the first place, in the most primitive areas such as the Balkans and the eastern frontier zones, it could oblige peasants to stay in the economy rather than to escape by migration or nomadism,[74] and to cultivate exportable rather than subsistence

[72] See Doreen Warriner, 'Some controversial issues in the history of Agrarian Europe', *Slavonic Review*, xxxii (1953), pp. 168 ff.

[73] O. Liiv, *D. wirtschaftl. Lage d. estnischen Gebietes am Ausgang d. 17. Jh.* (Tartu, 1935); review in *Baltic Countries*, iii (1937), pp. 129–30.

[74] Stoianovich, op. cit.

crops, or to switch from a dairying to a tillage economy. This last change was also encouraged by the Thirty Years' War, in Bohemia and elsewhere.[75] The example of eighteenth-century Ireland shows that a mere transfer from cattle to field-crops can have, for a time, the effect of an agricultural revolution. In the second place, the feudal estate could increasingly become a 'Gutsherrschaft' drawing profits from the sale of serf-produced farming rather than a 'Grundherrschaft' relying on income in money or kind from dependent peasants. Estates differed in the degree to which they did so; 69 per cent of the income from some Czech estates in 1636–7 came from demesne profits, but only between 40 and 50 per cent of that on some east German estates in the mid-eighteenth century.[76] We may assume, however, that the transfer of estates from smaller to larger owners would increase their profit-exploitation, for at the shockingly low level of serf-agriculture only the really large lord might find that the profits of running his estate as a corn-factory made the trouble of organizing and supervising the huge gangs of reluctant serfs worth while. In the neighbourhood of exporting ports merchants might encourage lords to enter the exporting economy, or force them to do so by lending money against the promise of crop-sales, as in Livonia.[77]

Admittedly this could not permanently solve the problem of capitalist growth. The serf economy was shockingly inefficient. The mere fact of forced labour tied it down to the least efficient utilization of land and manpower. Once an area had been completely 'enserfed', and forced labour intensified to its maximum—say five or six days a week[78]—production stabilized itself, unless new areas could be 'enserfed'. But difficulties of transport imposed limits. The expulsion of the Turks might open up the hinterland of the Black Sea ports, but—to take an obvious example—western

[75] W. Stark, 'Niedergang u. Ende d. landwirtsch. Grossbetriebs in d. boehmischen Laendern', *Jb. f. Nationaloekonomie*, cxlvi (1937), pp. 418, 421–2; O. Klopp, *Geschichte Ostfrieslands 1570–1751* (Osnabrück, 1856), p. 412.

[76] J. Heisig, *Die Schaffgotschen Gueterkomplexe* (Halle, 1884). W. Stark, 'Abhängigkeitsverhältnisse Boehmens im 17–18. Jh.', *Jb. f. Nationalökon.*, clxiv (1952), pp. 272–3. But in Hungary it was still only 10–15 per cent: E. Szabo, 'Les Grandes Domaines', *Rev. Hist. Comparée*, N.S., ii (1947), p. 188.

[77] U. Handrack, *Handel d. Stadt Riga* (Jena, 1932); review in *Baltic Countries*, ii (1936).

[78] R. Rosdolsky, 'The distribution of the agrarian product in feudalism' *Jl. of Econ. Hist.*, xi (1951), pp. 247 ff; Stark, op. cit., 1952, pp. 363–4.

Siberia was still bound to remain inaccessible. Hence, as soon as the effective limits of serf-agriculture had been reached, it entered upon a period of crisis. From the 1760s on this was recognized, and to some extent reflected in the projects of enlightened despotism.[79] The serf-economy was transformed between 1760 and 1861. This transformation takes us beyond the limits of our period and cannot therefore be considered here. The important thing for our purposes is that the transfer to the serf-estate economy coincided with the seventeenth-century crisis, and perhaps entered its decisive stage after the Thirty Years' War—say about 1660.[80]

The ways in which the crisis hastened this transfer are clear. Under the circumstances obtaining almost any outside event—a war, a famine, the raising of new taxes—weakened the peasant (and with him the traditional agrarian structure) and strengthened his exploiters. The crisis, moreover, encouraged all of them—landlords, provincial middle class and State in the west, lord and State in the east—to save themselves at his expense. Moreover, it has been argued that the decline in commerce and urban life over parts of the continent would encourage the rich to invest capital in the land, thus encouraging even further exploitation; as did the fall in agricultural prices. It is perhaps worth pointing out that such investment must not be confused with investment for the improvement of agriculture as in the eighteenth and nineteenth centuries. Normally it merely meant investment in the right to turn the screw on the peasant.

Industry and manufactures

The main result of the seventeenth-century crisis on industrial organization was to eliminate the crafts, and with them the craft-dominated towns, from large-scale production and to establish the 'putting-out' system, controlled by men with capitalist horizons and operated by easily exploitable rural labour. Signs of more

[79] P. Iwanow, 'Zur Frage des "aufgeklaerten Absolutismus" der 60er Jahre d. 18. Jh.', *Zur Periodisierung d. Feudalismus u. Kapitalismus in d. USSR* (Berlin, 1952), pp. 208 ff; F. Posch, 'Robotstreiks steirischer Bauern z. Zeit Josefs II', *Blaetter f. Heimatkunde*, xxv (Graz, 1951); C. Dame, *Entwicklung d. laendl. Wirtschaftslebens in d. Dresden-Meissner Elbtalgegend* (Leipzig, 1911), pp. 180–1; Stark, op. cit., 1937; A. Agthe, *Ursprung u. Lage d. Landarbeiter in Livland* (Tübingen, 1909), pp. 57, 73 ff.

[80] E. Jensen, *Danish Agriculture* (Copenhagen, 1937), pp. 41 ff; J. Rutkowski, *Hist. Econ. de la Pologne avant les partages* (Paris, 1927), pp. 119 ff.

ambitious industrial developments, 'manufactories' and the like, are not lacking, especially in the last third of the century, and in industries like mining, metallurgy and shipbuilding which required a fairly large scale of operation; but even without these the industrial changes are striking. 'Putting-out' (a protean stage of industrial development) had developed in certain textile industries in the later Middle Ages, but as a general rule the transformation of crafts into 'putting-out' industries began seriously during the boom of the later sixteenth century.[81] The seventeenth is clearly the century when such systems established themselves decisively.[82] Once again, its middle years appear to mark some sort of watershed: for instance, the large-scale export of Liège small-arms began after the 1650s.[83] This was only to be expected. Rural industries did not suffer from the high costs of urban ones, and often the small local producer of cheap goods—for example 'new draperies'—found himself able to expand sales while the high-quality and expensive goods of the old exporting industries—broad-cloth, Italian textiles—lost their markets. 'Putting-out' made regional concentration of industry possible, as it was not in the narrow town boundaries, for it made production easy to expand. But the crisis encouraged such regional concentration, for only this—for instance the concentration of European tinplate manufacture in Saxony[84]—could enable large-scale production to survive when home markets were small, and export markets perhaps not expanding. (The case of countries with a developed market will be considered below.) The negative side of this development was that towns were often left to become little islands of self-sufficiency and technical stagnation under tighter craft domination than before;[85] that is to say, since people do not live by taking in each others' washing, to batten increas-

[81] I. M. Kulischer, *Allg. Wirtschaftgesch.* (München and Berlin, 1928–9), vol. ii, chap. 9, esp. p. 117. To the works there quoted add H. Pirenne, *Hist. de Belgique*, iv (Bruxelles, 1900), pp. 427 ff; A. P. Wadsworth and J. de L. Mann, *Cotton Trade and Industrial Lancashire* (Manchester, 1931), pt. I; G. Unwin, *Studies in Economic History* (London, 1927); W. H. B. Court, *The Rise of the Midland Industries* (Oxford, 1938); U. Rottstaedt, *Besiedlung d. Thueringerwaldes* (Leipzig, 1914), p. 32, etc.

[82] Kulischer, op. cit., p. 115; Des Marez, *Le Compagnonnage des chapeliers bruxellois* (Bruxelles, 1909), pp. 13–16.

[83] C. A. Swaine, 'D. Heimarbeit in d. Gewehrindustrie v. Luettich', *Jb. f. Nationaloekonomie*, iii, Folge xii, pp. 177–8.

[84] L. Beck, *Gesch. d. Eisens (Braunschweig, 1884–1903)*, ii, pp. 979–80.

[85] E. Coornaert, *Les Corporations en France* (Paris, 1941), chap. v.

ingly on the surrounding countryside or on transit trade. This may incidentally have helped sections of the provincial middle class to accumulate capital, but this is not certain. The positive side was that 'putting-out' was a most effective dissolver of the traditional agrarian structure, and provided a means of rapidly increasing industrial production before the adoption of the factory system.

Moreover, the large-scale development of 'putting-out' normally either depends upon, or at least implies, considerable concentration of commercial and financial control. The local smith can expect to get rid of his wares on the local market. A specialized community of smiths producing scythes for an export market stretching from central Europe to Russia—as did the Styrians—depends on export merchants in some, generally a very few, trading centres.[86] (It also depends, of course, on a whole hierarchy of intermediaries.) 'Putting-out', therefore, was also likely to increase the accumulation of capital in a few centres of wealth.

The accumulation of capital

Concentration thus helped to increase the accumulation of capital in various ways. However, the problem of capital supply in the periods preceding the industrial revolution was a double one. On the one hand, industrialization probably required much greater preliminary capital accumulation than the sixteenth century was capable of achieving.[87] On the other, it required investment in the right places—where it increased productive capacity. Concentration—that is an increasingly uneven distribution of wealth within countries—almost automatically increased the capacity to accumulate, though not where the crisis led to general impoverishment.

[86] F. Tremel, 'Steirische Sensen', *Blaetter f. Heimatkunde*, xxvii (1953).

[87] It is sometimes argued that the cheap and piecemeal character of early industrial plants—for example cotton mills—enabled them to be financed with very small initial capital and by ploughing back profits. This example is misleading. We must consider not merely the investment required to start the individual firm, but the total investment required to get an industrial economy off to a flying start—roads, canals, docks, shipping, buildings of all sorts, agricultural investments, mines, etc. Really rapid industrialization needs not only this initial equipment, but continued investment of the same kind. This gives the economy with accumulated reserves—say eighteenth-century Britain—a vast advantage over the economy without them—say eighteenth-century Austria. It is too often forgotten that every government in the later eighteenth century tried to industrialize, but few succeeded.

Moreover, as we shall see, concentration in favour of the maritime economies, with their immensely effective new mechanism for capital accumulation (for example from foreign and colonial enterprise) laid the basis for accelerated accumulation such as we encounter in the eighteenth century. It did *not* automatically abolish misinvestment. But, as we have seen, this, rather than underinvestment, was the chief difficulty, and a contributory cause of the seventeenth-century crisis. Nor did it cease. In many parts of Europe the crisis diverted wealth to aristocracies and provincial bourgeoisies who were far from using it productively. Moreover, even the redistribution of capital in favour of the maritime economies might produce misinvestment, though of a different kind: for instance the diversion of capital from industry and agriculture into colonial exploitation, overseas trade and finance. The Netherlands are the standard example of such diversion, but it probably also occurred in Britain in the eighteenth century.

The crisis therefore produced no *automatic* mechanism for investing capital in the right places. However, it produced two indirect ways of doing so. First, in the continental countries, government enterprise in the new absolute monarchies fostered industries, colonies and export drives which would not otherwise have flourished, as in Colbertian France, expanded or saved from collapse mining and metallurgy[88] and laid the foundations of industries in places where the power of the serf-lords and the weakness or parasitism of the middle classes inhibited them. Second, the concentration of power in the maritime economies incidentally encouraged much productive investment. Thus the increasing flow of colonial and foreign trade, as we shall see, stimulated the domestic industries and agricultures supplying it. Home exports may, in the eyes of the great Dutch or British trading interests, have been merely a supplement to re-exports of foreign (chiefly colonial) goods, but their development was not negligible. Moreover, it is possible that the virtual Dutch monopoly of international trade may have led rival, but as yet less successful 'bourgeois' areas to invest much more of their capital at home than they would have done, had they enjoyed the Dutchmen's opportunities. Thus it seems that there was a very great deal of home investment in Britain between 1660 and 1700, which is reflected in the extremely rapid development of many British industries. In the early eigh-

[88] e.g. L. Beck, op. cit., pp. 1039–41.

teenth century this slackened off. The sluggish period of the 1720s–40s, which we noticed above, may thus be due in part to the diversion of capital overseas following the extraordinary successes of Britain in the wars of 1689–1714. Nevertheless, the basis of future industrial advance had been laid.

The commercial and financial apparatus

Little need be said about the changes in the commercial and financial apparatus which occurred during the period of the crisis. These are most obvious in northern Europe (where public finance was revolutionized), and particularly in Britain. We need not discuss how far these changes, which were, in effect, the adoption by northerners of methods and devices long known to people like the Italians, were due to the crisis itself.

Nor need we discuss the effect of the crisis on the growth of what used to be called 'the capitalist spirit' and what is now fashionably known as 'entrepreneurship'. There is no evidence that autonomous vagaries in businessmen's states of mind are as important as the German school used to think and an American school thinks now. Some of the reasons for this were suggested in the first part of this essay.

THE ORIGIN OF THE INDUSTRIAL REVOLUTION

We must now turn to the specific problem of the origin of the Industrial Revolution. Concentration and redistribution may have laid the foundations for further advance, but in themselves do not explain its precise nature. For if industrialization was to emerge from it, it had to produce two peculiar forms of expansion. First, it had to encourage manufactures in the countries with the strongest 'capitalist' base and on a scale sufficient to revolutionize (by degrees) the rest of the world. Second, it had to establish the primacy of production over consumption which is a fundamental prerequisite of capitalist industry.

The case of the Dutch

The first point is simple. Thus the development of manufactures in a country like Russia, though it heralded and prepared the eventual dissolution of feudalism there, was in fact at this period absorbed into the general feudal framework. Ural metalworkers were not proletarians, but special types of serfs. Potentially capitalist entrepreneurs like the Stroganovs, Demidovs or Yakovlevs became special types of serf-lords.[89] Russian industry eventually developed not as an extension of such enterprise but on its ruins. But the greatest beneficiary of seventeenth-century concentration, the Netherlands, was in many respects a 'feudal business' economy;[90] a Florence, Antwerp or Augsburg on a semi-national scale. It survived and flourished by cornering the world's supply of certain scarce goods and much of the world's business as a commercial and financial intermediary. Dutch profits did not depend greatly on capitalist manufacture. Hence the Dutch economy to some extent did a disservice to industrialization in the short run: to their own, by sacrificing Dutch manufactures (until 1816) to the huge vested interests of trading and finance; to that of the rest of Europe, by encouraging manufactures in feudal and semi-colonial areas where they were not strong enough to break out of the older social framework: Silesia, or west Germany. In Belgium and England the opposite was true. Thus the Belgians compensated for their loss of trade and finance to the Dutch in the late sixteenth century by developing industrial production and therefore became a major industrialized power before them. Against the free-trade and pacific policy of the Dutch, Britain upheld militant discriminatory and protectionist policies backed by aggressive wars for markets. The industrial future was more likely to be with 'modern' states like the British rather than with 'old-fashioned' ones like the United Provinces.

Indirectly, of course, the operations of the Dutch helped to advance industrial development. Theirs was an extremely powerful apparatus for dissolving feudal economies and societies, as well as bringing them more effectively into the international economy. Moreover, the mere existence of an immense mechanism for general trading and finance, at everyone's disposal, helped more progressive economies. The fact that the Dutch, the main immediate profiteers of the crisis, succeeded in cornering so much of the world's trade made it easier for rivals and successors to do the

[89] M. I. Tugan-Baranowsky, *D. Russische Fabrik* (Berlin, 1900); E. Kutaissoff, 'The Ural Metal Industry in the 18th century', *Econ. Hist. Rev.*, 2nd ser., iv (1951), pp. 252 ff; A. M. Pankratova, 'Die Rolle d. Warenproduktion', *Sowietwissenschaft*, 1954, 3, esp. pp. 439 ff.

[90] For a discussion of this type of business, see above pp. 16 ff.

same. Thus we can speak not merely of Anglo-Dutch rivalry, but also of Anglo-Dutch symbiosis. The height of Dutch commercial success in fact coincided with the rise of their rivals, 1675–1725,[91] just as the period of maximum British prosperity in the nineteenth century (1850–73) was also that of the most rapid development of Britain's future competitors. The tendency to monopoly imparted to trade by the Dutch may also have been important in another respect. It may be doubted whether before the nineteenth century the world market was large enough for the simultaneous industrialization of two or more countries on the modern scale. (In fact we know that British industrialization coincided with the British capture of virtually all the world's markets for certain manufactured goods, and the control of most of the world's colonial areas.) Dutch concentration thus proved extremely important, but it should not therefore tempt us to exaggerate the 'modernity' of the Dutch. If the only 'capitalist' economies available in the seventeenth century had been like the Dutch, we may doubt whether the subsequent development of industrial capitalism would have been as great or as rapid.

The conditions for industrial revolution

The second point is equally evident. If the cotton industry of 1760 had depended entirely on the actual demand for piece goods then existing, the railways on the actual demand of 1830, the motor industry on that of 1900, none of these industries would have undergone technical revolution. They might instead have developed like the building trade, which fluctuates roughly with the actual demand for building, sometimes running ahead, sometimes lagging, but never—until the present—pushed to the point of wholesale technical upheaval. Capitalist production therefore had to find *ways of creating its own expanding markets*. Except in rare and localized cases this is just what it could not do within a generally feudal framework. In a broad sense it achieved this end by transforming social structure. The very process which reorganized the social division of labour, increased the proportion of non-agricultural workers, differentiated the peasantry and created classes of wage-workers, also created men who depended for their needs on cash purchases—customers for goods. But this is the

[91] A. Hyma, *The Dutch in the Far East* (Ann Arbor, 1942), pp. 3–4, 170, 216.

analyst's way of looking at the matter, not the entrepreneur's, who decided whether or not to revolutionize his production. Moreover it is not at all clear whether in these early stages social transformation was rapid and vast enough to produce an expansion of demand so swift, or a prospect of further expansion so tempting and certain, as to push manufacturers into technical revolution. This is partly so because the 'developed areas' in the seventeenth and early eighteenth centuries were still relatively small and scattered, partly because the creation of the conditions for capitalist production creates markets for its goods in very different ways. At one extreme we have countries like the U.S.A., which were to develop an intense home market for their manufactures. At the other end—and this was, for various reasons, much more likely in our period—we have countries in which the *per capita* demand for goods was extremely low, at any rate among the mass of peasants and labourers. If there was to be industrial revolution, a number of countries or industries therefore had to operate within a sort of 'forced draught', which fanned the entrepreneurs' cupidity to the point of spontaneous combustion.

How was this 'forced draught' generated? The following answers may be suggested. First (as we have seen) the trade of all countries was largely concentrated in the hands of the most industrially advanced, directly or indirectly. Second, these countries—England in particular—generated a large and expanding demand within their home markets. Third, and perhaps most crucial, a new colonial system, based mainly on the slave-plantation economy, produced a special 'forced draught' of its own, which was probably decisive for the British cotton industry, the real industrial pioneer. All three were probably essential. Which of them provided the main incentive may be debated. But if the argument of this article is correct, we should expect to find signs of fundamental change and advance in the world's markets in the latter part of the seventeenth century, though these should be more marked in the markets controlled by 'advanced' capitalist economies than in others.

The undeveloped markets

We know very little about home markets (that is the demand of the mass of citizens in any country) before the twentieth century. We know even less about that characteristic phenomenon of the modern era, the rise of demand for unprecedented goods and services like radio (or, in our period, tobacco, tea, coffee, chocolate), as distinct from the demand for new goods substituting for old needs—nylons for silk stockings (or, in our period, sugar for older sweetening agents). Hence we can only speak about market developments with extreme caution. However, it is most unlikely that demand increased greatly in the bulk of continental countries, even among the comfortable urban middle classes who were the most intensive buyers of standardized manufactures before the nineteenth century. Tea and coffee remained luxury articles until the eighteenth century, and sugar production remained sluggish between 1630 and 1670.[92] There was as yet little substitution of glass and pottery for metal even among prosperous middle class families.[93] The Swiss watch-making districts (with the exception of Geneva, which produced luxury articles) did not get into their stride until the eighteenth century.[94] Retailing remained unspecialized in many German towns and until the mid-seventeenth century even Parisians still drew much of their corn from farmers rather than traders.[95] There may have been a growth of rural retailing in the late sixteenth century, where towns and lords did not prevent it. However, complaints about the growth of hawking may indicate a weakening of town monopolies rather than an increase in rural cash purchases,[96] and in any case rural trade slumped during the crisis. Certainly Rennes and Dijon in our century were no longer the markets they had once been.[97] Only the demand for some goods, often monopolized by states and lords and farmed out by them, may have increased: tobacco and alcohol.[98] On balance the crisis can therefore hardly have favoured the

[92] Simonsen's estimate, quoted in N. Deerr, *History of Sugar* (London, 1949), i, p. 112.

[93] J. M. Richard, *La Vie privée à Laval aux XVIIe et XVIIIe siècles* (Paris, 1922), pp. 59–75.

[94] A. Pfleghardt, *D. Schweizerische Uhrenindustrie* (Leipzig, 1908).

[95] Usher, op. cit. For a general bibliography of retail trade, W. Sombart, *D. moderne Kapitalismus* (München, 1916), ii (I), pp. 421–35; also E. Koehler, *D. Einzelhandel im Mittelalter* (Stuttgart and Berlin, 1938), pp. 55–60.

[96] J. H. Gebauer, *Gesch. d. Stadt Hildesheim* (Hildesheim and Leipzig, 1922), p. 227; R. Scholten, *Z. Gesch. d. Stadt Cleve* (Cleve, 1905), p. 412; E. v. Ranke, 'Koeln u. d. Rheinland', *Hans. Gesch. Blaetter*, xxvii (1922), p. 29.

[97] H. Sée, *Hist. Econ. de la France* (Paris, 1939), i, p. 232.

[98] For the importance of alcohol in the seignorial economy, Stark, op. cit., 1952 (above, n. 76); Szabo, op. cit. (above, n. 76).

spontaneous development of capitalist industry for continental home markets. It might have favoured (a) craft production for a series of local markets, which retarded the progress of industry or (b) the rise of very cheap manufacturers, by-products of peasant leisure or oppression.

The most available market in most such countries was also the least suitable for capitalist development—that of states and aristocracies. The fact that aristocrats were the greatest savers did not prevent them from also being great spenders. Thus the Counts Czernin lent the Emperor 4 million gulden between 1690 and 1724, yet had enough left over for the most sumptuous building and spending.[99] But much of this did not lubricate the wheels of industry half so effectively as middle class purchases. Thus a medium-sized Holstein Junker in 1690 employed forty-five lackeys and servants in addition to serfs about the house; more than the regular staff of the Duke of Bedford in the mid-eighteenth century.[100] Yet the future industrialist required not an infinite willingness to keep scores of chefs, stucco artists and perruquiers employed, but mass demand.

Some of this the states and aristocracies did provide, rather inefficiently.[101] First, they did so by means of direct orders for standardized army equipment, uniforms—a seventeenth-century innovation—and the like. Probably the effect of this was greatest in the metal industries for which, before the Industrial Revolution, war was the chief customer. Second, they passed on purchasing power to classes with a higher propensity to buy standardized goods than theirs: to soldiers, and the publicans and shopkeepers who battened on them, to small and medium rentiers, and to the mass of civil and personal servants and minor dependents. Indeed in many areas the prospects of a good market depended largely on the efficiency with which valets robbed their masters. Most of these methods found expression in the 'great city', a much more efficient market for goods than the small and medium-sized town, let alone the miserable village. In Paris or Vienna a simulacrum of

[99] B. Bretholz, *Gesch. Boehmen's u. Maehrens* (Reichenberg, 1921–4), iii, pp. 52–53.

[100] G. Hanssen, *Agrarhistorische Abhandlungen* (Leipzig, 1880), p. 457; G. Scott Thompson, *The Russells of Bloomsbury* (London, 1940), p. 238.

[101] These have been discussed, but their importance exaggerated, by Sombart, *Krieg u. Kapitalismus, Luxus u. Kapitalismus.*

a capitalist home market, with a mass demand for food,[102] household goods, middle class textiles, building materials, etc., could come into being—encouraged by the concentration of wealth during the crisis period—though perhaps it stimulated semi-craft expansion like that in the building trades more than industry.[103]

Absolutist states did, of course, also provide financial, political and military backing for risky commercial undertakings such as wars and new industries, and acted as agents for the transfer of wealth accumulated from the peasantry and others to entrepreneurs. It is possible that this may have led to a more efficient tapping of home demand, though, as we know, the main effort of continental mercantilist states was for exports: or at any rate for a combination of various home markets, the country's own and the captured ones of others. In this task, however, the entrepreneurs of undeveloped states, even with state backing, were at a great disadvantage compared to the developed ones which really did possess a growing home market. Over part of Europe, therefore, the seventeenth-century crisis, unlike that of 1815–48, proved economically sterile; or at any rate, the seeds then sown did not germinate until very much later.

In the maritime areas the home market unquestionably grew greatly. In England at least one is tempted to see the seventeenth century as the decisive period in the creation of a national market. Here we can claim with some confidence that, by 1700, all sections of the population apart from the most remote were, to some extent, cash customers for goods produced outside their area, and that goods of common consumption were manufactured in specialized areas for national or for wide regional sale. The giant size of London, of course, gave the home market a great advantage. No other country (barring the Dutch) possessed so vast a proportion of its people concentrated in a single urban block. Professor Fisher has illuminated the effect of this London market on the English economy as a whole.[104] However, if the rise of the Tyneside

[102] For the Viennese meat market, H. Hassinger, 'D. erste Wiener orientalische Handelskompanie 1667–83', *Vierteljahrschr. f. Soz-. und Wirtschaftgesch.*, xxxv (1942).

[103] G. des Marez, 'La Transformation de la ville de Bruxelles au XVIIe siècle', *Etudes Inédites* (Bruxelles, 1936), pp. 129–31.

[104] F. J. Fisher, 'London's Export Trade in the Early Seventeenth Century', *Econ. Hist. Rev.*, 2nd ser., iii (1950–1), pp. 151–61; 'Commercial Trends

collieries—to take one example—is almost entirely due to London, that of the other coalfields, which expanded almost as rapidly, is not.[105] By the beginning of the eighteenth century, if Defoe is to be believed, 'there are shopkeepers in every village, or at least in every considerable market town,'[106] and a nation of shopkeepers implies a nation of customers. Equally important, hawkers were by this time wholesalers or commercial travellers as much as direct retailers of textiles and hardware.[107] The second half of the seventeenth century saw the rise of some important semi-industrialized cheap consumer goods industries. The sudden growth of specialized areas for making popular pottery began then: no potters are reported from the Bristol apprenticeship lists before 1671. The Midland hardware trades also began their rise about this time.[108] Most significant of all, even the rural population became, to some extent, customers. Earthenware (instead of the more durable pewter) occurs in Essex farms and cottages from the middle of the century.[109] The growth of the home market certainly exceeded that of population at this period. If we take Harper's estimates of the tonnage of coastal shipping as an index, we find that the combined coastwise and collier tonnage increased by an average of less than 1,000 tons per year from 1582 to 1609/15 and by an average of over 1,100 tons per year from then on till 1660; the number of London's coastwise ships trebled between 1628 and 1683.[110] Similarly the rise of imports in this period appears to have been greater than that of exports.[111] At any rate we can see why seventeenth-century English

[105] J. U. Nef, *The Rise of the British Coal Industry* (London, 1932).

[106] *The English Tradesman* (1727), p. 334.

[107] ibid.; R. B. Westerfield, *Middlemen in British Business* (New Haven, 1915), p. 313.

[108] W. Burton, *English Earthenware and Stoneware* (London, 1904), pp. 7, 28, 30–32, 58; W. Pountney, *Old Bristol Potteries* (Bristol, 1920), App. i, p. 3; W. H. Court, op. cit.; H. Hamilton, *The English Brass and Copper Industries to 1800* (London, 1926).

[109] F. Steer, *Farm and Cottage Inventories of Mid-Essex* (Chelmsford, 1950); G. E. Fussell, *The English Rural Labourer* (London, 1949).

[110] L. A. Harper, *The English Navigation Laws* (New York, 1939), p. 339; T. S. Willan, *The English Coasting Trade 1600–1750* (Manchester, 1938), esp. chap. vii, pp. 203–5.

[111] E. Lipson, *Econ. Hist. of England*, 4th edn. (London, 1947), ii, p. 189; Harper, op. cit., p. 343.

---

and Policy in Sixteenth-Century England', *Econ. Hist. Rev.*, x (1940), pp. 95–117.

economists congratulated themselves on possessing a large home market for 'middling' goods, unlike the chief continental states.

In certain respects, moreover, all the maritime states may be considered as one large, diversified home market, lying as they did close to one another. Within this area international trade could be, and was, far more intense than trade between each maritime state and its (non-colonial) export markets.[112] Thus English coal was sold almost entirely to the home market, the Dutch and their dependencies, and the colonies. Again, the trade in beer between Hamburg and the United Provinces[113] can count virtually as trade within such an extended 'home market'.

Three results would follow the development of such home markets. First, it would assist the disintegration of the old economy, progressively turn citizens into cash purchasers and cash earners, and encourage the increasing import of food and raw materials, thereby stimulating the growth of exports. Indeed, the development of an intensive home market was itself a sign that social transformation had gone quite a long way. Moreover, as Marx has shown, the home market demands not only consumer but also capital goods.[114] Second, it provided a large and fairly steady reservoir of demand for goods, and hence of productive capacity—a stable foundation for rapid expansion, and a cushion against the chanciness of the export market. Moreover, the maritime home markets with their millions of inhabitants were vastly larger than the medieval city markets at their greatest. Third, it might under specially favourable conditions expand so rapidly as to produce within itself the impetus to revolutionize certain industries. The mining industry had clearly by 1700 got to the verge of industrial revolution mainly by such means. Perhaps industries like brewing and soap-making benefited in a similar manner. Nevertheless this was probably not normal. The really headlong and limitless prospects of expansion which encouraged, and indeed compelled, technical revolution were probably most easily achieved in the export markets, though it is doubtful whether any country

[112] This problem is discussed in League of Nations, *Industrialization and Foreign Trade* (Geneva, 1945), p. 118.

[113] Nef, op. cit., App. D; W. Vogel, 'Ueber d. Groesse d. Handelsflotten', *Forschungen u. Versuche z. Gesch. d. Mittelalters u. d. Neuzeit . . . Festschrift f. D. Schaefer* (Jena, 1915), pp. 274–5.

[114] *Capital*, i (1938 edn.), p. 772.

not possessed of a developed home market could, in the seventeenth and eighteenth centuries, have been in a position to seize export opportunities. We must therefore consider export prospects.

Colonial and export markets

The major achievement of the seventeenth-century crisis is the creation of a new form of colonialism. As we have seen, under the sixteenth-century colonial system—which, by the way, the Dutch took over virtually unchanged—the colonial market for home manufactures was unimportant, though a large colonial undertaking or the state, considered as an employer of labour and a buyer of capital and consumer goods, stimulated the home economy in addition to bringing in profits for accumulation. Between 1660 and 1681 the East Indies traffic is said to have been only one twelfth of the total Dutch traffic.[115] Traders seemed to show little enthusiasm for the consumer demand in Latin America.[116] However the possibilities of colonial markets were transformed with the foundation of plantation colonies which produced without systematic restriction of output, and of European colonies of settlement. The middle of the seventeenth century, here again, marks a turning point.[117] At any rate such quantitative information as we have about the slave-trade demonstrates how incomparably smaller the imports before the Restoration were than in the golden age of the trade in the eighteenth century. We may, summarizing the scattered information,[118] estimate the average annual import of live slaves

[115] C. de Lannoy and H. Linden, *Hist. de l'expansion coloniale: Néerlande et Danemark* (Bruxelles, 1911), p. 334; I. J. Brugmans, 'D. oost-Ind. Compagnie . . .', *Tijdschr. v. Gesch.*, lxi (1948), pp. 225–31.

[116] Savary, *Le Parfait Négociant* (Paris, 1675), ii, p. 78.

[117] cf. the dates of the beginning of sugar plantation and exports in the West Indies above p. 11, n. 15; cf. also W. Borah, *New Spain's Century of Depression* (Ibero-Americana 35, Berkeley, 1951), a very suggestive study.

[118] This passage is based on the following authorities, and calculations derived from them; there is no space to discuss the methods of arriving at the estimates: Lippmann, op. cit.; the materials in N. Deerr, op. cit. (i, pp. 123–4, 132–3, ii, pp. 266, 278–9); U. B. Phillips, *American Negro Slavery* (New York and London, 1918), p. 18; E. Donnan, *Documents Illustrative of the History of The Slave Trade to America* (Washington, 1930), i—I cannot accept her estimate; G. Freyre, *The Masters and the Slaves* (New York, 1946), p. 463 n.; C. R. Boxer, *Salvador de Sá* (London, 1952), p. 225 n.; Calogeras-Martin, *History of Brazil* (Chapel Hill, 1939),

into the Americas in the 1640s—the peak of Brazilian sugar production—as of the order of 10,000, between the 1730s and the 1780s as of the order of 50–100,000. By the time the British Africa Company had been reconstituted, and two French Companies, the Senegal and the Guinea, had been founded specifically for the slave-trade in 1673 and 1685, the stage was set for the great colonial boom.

The new types of colony were to some extent 'captive markets' which depended on home supplies. Half of the planter's profit, it was estimated, returned to the West Indies in the form of merchandise:[119] nails and ironware, saddlery, a variety of ordinary textiles, bricks for ballast, pots for molasses, in fact just the sort of merchandise to encourage the future industrialist and perhaps the progressive farmer.[120] The rising supply of slaves set up a rising demand for goods in Africa—always a market for European exports; the growing supply of increasingly cheap plantation goods like sugar and tobacco, a rising demand for European goods in the plantations and elsewhere. Political control by European powers enabled them to cope with any unwelcome competition from the colonies, as well as to rob their unhappy natives with remarkable efficiency. This was very much the kind of expansion which manufacturers needed, though the self-expanding market was bound to fluctuate with the vagaries of war and politics, not to mention economic difficulties. Indeed, as Marx argued that they must, they relied largely upon it in these early stages.[121] By 1700 something like 20 per cent of English exports may have gone to areas which could be described as colonial (including the colonies of other states).[122]

[119] J. Oldmixon, *The British Empire in America* (London, 1708), ii, p. 163.

[120] Wadsworth and Mann, op. cit., p. 72 n.; Enjalbert, op. cit. The demand of settlement colonies like New England would be even better.

[121] *Capital*, i (1938 edn.), pp. 775, 778–9.

[122] From the figures in 'An Essay Towards Finding the Ballance of Our Whole Trade', in G. N. Clark, *Guide to English Commercial statistics, 1696–1782* (London, 1938); L. A. Harper, op. cit., p. 266; Sir C. Davenant, *Works* (London, 1771), ii, p. 17, v, pp. 356, 403.

---

p. 27; Waetjen, 'D. Negerhandel in Westindien u. Suedamerika', *Hans. Gesch. Blaetter* (1913), pp. 417 ff; J. Saintoyant, *La Colonisation française sous l'ancien régime* (Paris, 1929), i, p. 252; D. Macpherson, *Annals of Commerce* (London, Edinburgh, 1805); E. Williams, *Capitalism and Slavery* (Chapel Hill, 1945).

In 1759–60 and 1770 over one third went to British colonies alone, not counting direct exports to Spanish and Portuguese colonies. Moreover, if one can judge by the statistics of 1784, when exports first came to be distinguished from re-exports, the colonies were even better customers than these figures imply. Half our exports then went to them (including the recently emancipated U.S.A.). The importance of the colonial market for cotton piece-goods exports is even more striking. Until 1770—that is to say in the crucial period leading up to the industrial revolution—it (including Ireland) never took less than some 90 per cent of them.[123]

However, like the new serf-economies, the new colonial economies were not capable of permanent expansion, and for the same reasons: their use of land and labour was essentially extensive and inefficient. Moreover, the supply of slaves (who rarely reproduced themselves on a sufficient scale) could not be increased fast enough, as is suggested by the rapidly rising trend of slave-prices. Hence exhaustion of the soil, inefficiencies of management and labour difficulties led to something like a 'crisis of the colonial economy' from the 1750s.[124] This found various forms of expression—for instance anti-slavery sentiment, and the Home Rule movements of local white settler oligarchies which grew up rapidly in the last third of the eighteenth century in Latin America, in the West Indies, North America and Ireland, and contributed to the development of revolution in western Europe. However, we cannot here discuss the difficulties of the new colonialism. It is sufficient to remind ourselves that its adoption gave the 'advanced' economies several precious decades of dizzy economic expansion from which they drew inestimable benefits.

None of these developments was wholly new, yet all were greatly advanced by the seventeenth-century crisis. Absolutism and its great capital cities on the continent were strengthened by it. The triumph of the English Revolution hastened the social transformation of England, and thereby the formation of an active home market. Lastly, the new colonialism developed where the old was impossible or no longer profitable, and when the old colonialists had grown too weak to fight off interlopers, though remaining strong enough to stop them from capturing bullion and spices. On

[123] Macpherson, op. cit., vol. iv; Wadsworth and Mann, op. cit., pp. 146–7.

[124] Well discussed in L. Dermigny, 'Saint Domingue au XVIIe et XVIIIe siècles', *Rev. Hist.*, cciv (1950), pp. 237–8.

the other hand none of them was the result of planning. Brazil had grown up as a plantation colony while Portugal was looking elsewhere, and flourished greatly as a result, resisting Dutch attempts to detach it from Portugal.[125] The Dutch, on the other hand, had all the old-fashioned distaste for expanded production and lowered prices, as is shown by their attitude to sugar—and to a lesser extent coffee—production in their empire and to overseas settlement.[126] The Brazilians turned their eyes to gold and diamonds as soon as they discovered them on their territory at the end of the century. In a sense, therefore, the progressive 'new' economies established themselves because of the partial ruin of the old, which the seventeenth-century crisis brought about.

CONCLUSION

The second part of this essay has attempted to show two things, first, that the seventeenth-century crisis provided its own solution, and second, that it did so in indirect and roundabout ways. But for the existence of countries capable of wholeheartedly adopting the new—and as it turned out, revolutionary and economically progressive—economic systems, it might well have led to far greater stagnation or regression than it did. But of all the economies the most 'modern', the most wholehearted in its subordination of policy to the capitalist entrepreneur was England: the country of the first complete 'bourgeois revolution'. Hence, in a sense, the economic history of the modern world from the middle of the seventeenth century hinges on that of England, which began the period of crisis—say in the 1610s—as a dynamic, but a minor power, and ended it in the 1710s as one of the world's masters. The English Revolution, with all its far-reaching results, is therefore in a real sense the most decisive product of the seventeenth-century crisis.

These, then, are some suggestions about the economic development of Europe in a crucial, but still surprisingly obscure period. They may not resist criticism. However, it is to be hoped that they

[125] J. L. De Azevedo, *Epocas de Portugal Econômico* (Lisbon, 1929); C. R. Boxer, op. cit.; G. Freyre, op. cit., p. 253, for an interesting argument of 1573 for the superiority of the plantation economy.

[126] Lannoy and Linden, op. cit., pp. 264 ff, 360; A. N. Coombes, *Evolution of Sugar Cane Culture in Mauritius* (Port Louis, 1937).

will serve to stimulate further work on the origins of modern capitalism.

III: POSTSCRIPT

It is always a risky thing to attempt a synthesis towards the beginning rather than the end of a historical debate, and it may therefore be worth noting briefly how the argument of my essay on the General Crisis, which was one of the first contributions to this discussion in Britain, has fared since 1954. It is not possible here to discuss, or even to list, the very ample literature which has appeared on the subject in the past ten years.[127]

The existence of such a general crisis in the European economy is not now widely disputed. It has lately been admirably illustrated in Slicher van Bath's study of crop-yields from the ninth to the nineteenth centuries, which clearly brings out the breaks in the secular upward trend in the fourteenth to fifteenth and seventeenth centuries.[128] Purely extraneous explanations of the phenomenon in terms of climatic change, suggested by Utterström, have been specifically rejected by Le Roy Ladurie and Slicher van Bath.[129] Though recent work has tended to re-emphasize the independent economic devastation caused by seventeenth-century wars such as the Thirty Years War, few would disagree with the contention that an unsatisfactory economic conjuncture certainly inhibited recovery, or even that in many areas of Europe decline clearly

[127] For an immensely valuable survey of statistical data, and a more up-to-date bibliography, see R. Romano, 'Tra XVI e XVII secolo. Una crisi economica: 1619–1622', *Riv. Stor. Ital.*, lxxxiv (1962), pp. 480–531. Dr. Romano's general agreement with my basic argument that the seventeenth century is the last phase of the general transition from a feudal to a capitalist economy, makes his monograph particularly welcome to the present author.

[128] B. H. Slicher van Bath, 'De oogstopbrengsten van verschillende gewassen . . . ca. 810–1820', *A.A.G.Bijdragen* 9 (Wageningen, 1963), esp. pp. 74–85. cf. also the same author's *Agrarian History of Western Europe A.D. 850–1850* (London, 1963), which also accepts the concept of the seventeenth-century crisis.

[129] G. Utterström, 'Climatic Fluctuations and Population Problems in Early Modern History', *Scand. Econ. Hist. Rev.*, iii (1955); E. Le Roy Ladurie, 'Histoire et climat', *Annales E.S.C.*, xive année (1959); Slicher van Bath, loc. cit. (*A. A. G. Bijdragen*, ix).

antedated the wars.[130] The case for regarding the mid-seventeenth century as the beginning of the secular upswing which led to the Industrial Revolution is less easy to establish, but remains plausible, especially in view of the recent emphasis on agrarian change in the period 1660–1760, the rising competition after 1660 from imported oriental textiles which led to the growth of the European cotton industries,[131] and such figures as the English tin production series to which attention has lately been drawn.[132] The rapid spurt of the English economy after the Restoration is common knowledge. In brief, the main factual thesis of my article appears to stand up, and has indeed been reinforced.

However, my attempt to suggest a general chronology of the crisis was mistaken, or at least premature, in view of the wide variation of the periods of maximum disturbance in different parts of Europe between 1620 and 1720. (It is also possible that, as F. Mauro has argued for Portugal, certain areas ought to be excluded from the decline, at least in part.)[133] I also think that my neglect of financial and monetary phenomena, though deliberate and polemically justifiable—modern views have increasingly stressed real rather than monetary factors in price-movements—was excessive.

There has been relatively little discussion of possible explanations of the crisis. Among the few general essays on the subject R. Romano's (referred to in note 127) runs broadly parallel to my own. Strangely enough the question of Italy's decline has attracted less attention than one might suppose, Italian historians having been recently preoccupied above all with the post-risorgimental economy.[134] The contradictions of the East-European economy

[130] A. Mączak, 'Polnische Forschungen auf dem Gebiet der Agrargeschichte', *Acta Poloniae Historica*, i (1958), p. 46; Jerzy Topolski, 'La Régression economique en Pologne du XVIe au XVIIIe siècle', ibid., vii (1962), pp. 45–46—this also contains references to Czech and German material.

[131] Slicher van Bath, loc. cit., pp. 66, 68; C. Wilson, 'Cloth production and international competition in the seventeenth century', *Econ. Hist. Rev.*, 2nd ser., xiii (1960), p. 220.

[132] P. Deane and W. A. Cole, *British Economic Growth 1688–1959* (Cambridge, 1962), p. 60.

[133] cf. F. Braudel, P. Jeannin, J. Meuvret, R. Romano, 'Le Déclin de Venise au XVIIe siècle', *Aspetti e Cause della Decadenza economica veneziana nel secolo XVII, Civiltà Veneziana, Studi*, ix (Venezia-Roma, 1961), esp. pp. 23–35. For Portugal, see note 137 below.

[134] But the school of Prof. Braudel in France has devoted attention to the problem, and the decline of Venice has been fairly intensively studied.

have been studied much more intensively, notably in Poland, generally in terms of the revival of agrarian feudalism. A variety of factors (all, I think, consistent with my argument) have been mentioned: for instance the tendency of growing export monocultures to impoverish the soil even by 1615,[135] the changing relations between seignorial and peasant holdings and labours, and in general the tendency for crop-yields to diminish with the imposition of heavier serfdom. The crisis in turn intensified this: 'The East-European countries after 1650 were in something like the position of primary producers in a period of long depression of their export markets; rather like the Latin American countries in 1929–39. Their only possibility of competing was to lower costs. This led to a sharp increase in the system of large estates cultivated by unfree labour.'[136]

The crisis of an 'old' and the emergence of a 'new' colonial system, which contained the seeds of self-generating economic expansion, have been studied for Spain and Portugal, chiefly by French scholars, but the rise of the West Indies remains in some obscurity.[137] I would place an even greater emphasis on this aspect of the crisis than I did ten years ago. On the other hand the contradictions of the home markets have not been systematically or seriously studied for western Europe. R. Romano attempts to do so in terms of a general 'refeudalization' of agriculture (outside Holland and England) from the later sixteenth century, which, with the concurrent and consequent impoverishment of the peasantry, restricted the basic home market for industry and commerce, leaving only the limited market of the rich:[138]

From the end of the sixteenth century European agriculture presents evident signs of weariness: refeudalization begins to make itself felt. The agrarian structure of almost all Europe begins to creak and bend,

[135] A. Wyczański, 'Le Niveau de la récolte . . . en Pologne du XVIe au XVIIIe siècle', *First. Int. Conf. Economic History* (Stockholm, 1960), p. 589.

[136] Slicher van Bath, op. cit., p. 84.

[137] cf. esp. F. Mauro, *Le Portugal et l'Atlantique au XVIIe siècle* (Paris, 1960), esp. pp. 496–502, 511–13, and the monumental work of the Chaunus.

[138] cf. M. Malowist, 'Evolution industrielle en Pologne du XIVe au XVIIe siècle', *Studi in Onore di Armando Sapori* (Milano-Varese, 1957), pp. 573–603.

---

cf. D. Sella, *Commerci e industrie a Venezia nel secolo XVII* (Venezia-Roma, 1961).

not only in terms of the quantity of production, but in terms of its social as well as economic relationships. The phenomenon is general. Amid this faltering of agriculture, commerce and industry, benefiting by their earlier impetus, continue to advance. They overcome the pre-crisis of 1609–13 and resume their progress, but this time under the stimulus of a special 'drug': credit. . . . In spite of such stimulation, commerce and industry fail to recover from the crisis of 1619–22. A normal cyclical depression is transformed into a structural crisis, because the economy increasingly lacks the sustenance of agriculture.[139]

The argument is tempting, especially to this writer, though the generality of refeudalization doubtless requires further investigation. One would also guess that recent research, which has emphasized the importance of population movements as determinants of demand, might favour a more specific Malthusian mechanism such as I suggested at one point as a partial explanation.[140]

A highly suggestive observation by M. Malowist (who has contributed much to our understanding of this problem) may be noted in passing. It is to the effect that the inability of 'feudal' economies to achieve economic development led, in the conditions of population growth of the sixteenth century, to emigration and politico-military expansion, i.e. to the colonial system in the west, the rise of Sweden and the feudal colonization in the East.[141]

The second part of my argument dealt with the outcome of the crisis, that is the origins of the Industrial Revolution. British and U.S. studies have very much revived in this field, and apart from agrarian and demographic studies, the relative roles of the home and foreign markets have attracted most attention. My own argument was to the effect that a large 'home market' (which was in effect the collective home market of several adjacent 'developed' areas) was an essential condition for the Industrial Revolution, but that the dynamic element came from exports, and especially from the British capacity to monopolize foreign markets.[142] In the light

[139] Romano, op. cit., p. 518.

[140] e.g. the articles by Y. S. Brenner on the inflation of prices in England 1450–1650 in *Econ. Hist. Rev.*, 2nd ser., xiv (1961), pp. 225–40, and xv (1962), pp. 266–85.

[141] M. Malowist, 'Un Essai d'histoire comparée: les mouvements d'expansion en Europe au XVe et XVIe siècles', *Annales E.S.C.*, xviie année (1962), pp. 923–9.

[142] 'The concentration of trade and manufactures in a single country, England, which developed irresistibly during the seventeenth century, gradually

of subsequent discussion this view remains perfectly tenable, though some of my incidental observations on the early eighteenth century are clearly in need of revision. However, while the British case has been much discussed, the general European situation of which it was a special element, has not.

My essay dealt only very incidentally with the problem of the seventeenth-century revolutions, which has attracted discussion, especially in *Past and Present*. I do not wish to add anything to my observations in that journal, no. 18 (November 1960), on this point. However, it may be legitimate to note a recent restatement of the argument of my article in *Science and Society*.[143]

To sum up. The fact of the seventeenth-century crisis may be regarded as established. An explanation of it which would meet with general agreement still remains to be found, and its place in the genesis of modern industrialism also awaits more discussion. I would suggest that it will be found to fit most readily into some elaborated or modified version of the Marxist model of economic development.

[143] E. J. Hobsbawm, 'The Seventeenth Century in the Development of Capitalism', *Science and Society*, xxiv (1960), pp. 97–112.

---

created a relative world market for the manufactured products of that country, which could no longer be supplied by the hitherto available forces of industrial production.' Marx–Engels, *The German Ideology* (*Werke*, iii [Berlin, 1958], p. 59). The passage, of which I was not aware at first writing, is worth rescuing from relative obscurity.

III

THE GENERAL CRISIS OF THE SEVENTEENTH CENTURY*

H. R. Trevor-Roper

THE middle of the seventeenth century was a period of revolutions in Europe. These revolutions differed from place to place, and if studied separately, seem to rise out of particular, local causes; but if we look at them together they have so many common features that they appear almost as a general revolution. There is the Puritan revolution in England which fills the twenty years between 1640 and 1660, but whose crisis was between 1648 and 1653. In those years of its crisis there was also the series of revolts known as the Frondes in France, and in 1650 there was a *coup d'état* or palace revolution, which created a new form of government in the United Provinces of the Netherlands. Contemporary with the troubles of England were those of the Spanish Empire. In 1640 there was the revolt of Catalonia, which failed, and the revolt of Portugal, which succeeded; in 1641 there was nearly a revolt of Andalusia too; in 1647 there was the revolt of Naples, the revolt of Masaniello. To contemporary observers it seemed that society itself was in crisis, and that this crisis was general in Europe. 'These days are days of shaking . . .' declared an English preacher in 1643, 'and this shaking is universal: the Palatinate, Bohemia, Germania, Catalonia, Portugal, Ireland, England.'[1] The various countries of Europe seemed merely the separate theatres upon

[1] Jeremiah Whittaker, *Εἰρηνοποιός*, *Christ the Settlement of Unsettled Times*, a fast sermon before the House of Commons, 25 Jan. 1642–3.

* From no. 16 (1959).

which the same great tragedy was being simultaneously, though in different languages and with local variations, played out.

What was the general cause or character of this crisis? Contemporaries, if they looked beyond mere surface parallels, tended to find deep spiritual reasons. That there was a crisis they felt sure. For a generation they had felt it coming. Ever since 1618 at least there had been talk of the dissolution of society, or of the world; and the undefined sense of gloom of which we are constantly aware in those years was justified sometimes by new interpretations of Scripture, sometimes by new phenomena in the skies. With the discovery of new stars, and particularly with the new comet of 1618, science seemed to support the prophets of disaster. So also did history. It was at this time that cyclical theories of history became fashionable and the decline and fall of nations was predicted, not only from Scripture and the stars, but also from the passage of time and the organic processes of decay. Kingdoms, declared a Puritan preacher in 1643, after touching lightly on the corroborative influence of the comet of 1618, last for a maximum period of 500 or 600 years, 'and it is known to all of you how long we have been since the Conquest'.[2] From our rationalist heights we might suppose that the new discoveries of science would tend to discredit the apocalyptic vaticinations of Scripture; but in fact this was not so. It is an interesting but undeniable fact that the most advanced scientists of the early sixteenth century included also the most learned and literal students of Biblical mathematics; and in their hands science and religion converged to pinpoint, between 1640 and 1660, the dissolution of society, the end of the world.[3]

This intellectual background is significant because it shows that the crisis of the mid-seventeenth century did not come by surprise, out of sudden accidents: it was deep-seated and anticipated, if only vaguely anticipated, even before the accidents which launched it.

[2] William Greenhill, *'Αξίνη πρὸς τὴν 'Ρίζαν*, a sermon preached before Parliament, 26 April 1643.

[3] It is enough here to refer to J. H. Alsted, the great scholar and educationalist of Herborn, who was also 'the standard-bearer of millenaries in our age'; to his pupil, the great Bohemian educator, J. A. Comenius; to the English disciple of Bacon, Joseph Mede, the author of *Clavis Apocalyptica;* and to the Scottish mathematician Napier of Merchistoun, who invented logarithms in order to speed up his calculations of the Number of the Beast.

No doubt accidents made revolution longer or deeper here, shorter or more superficial there. No doubt, too, the universality of revolution owed something to mere contagion: the fashion of revolution spreads. But even contagion implies receptivity: a healthy or inoculated body does not catch even a prevailing disease. Therefore, though we may observe accidents and fashions, we still have to ask a deeper question. We must ask what was the general condition of western European society which made it, in the mid-seventeenth century, so universally vulnerable—intellectually as well as physically—to the sudden new epidemic of revolution?

Of course there are some obvious answers. Most obvious of all is the Thirty Years' War, which began in 1618, the year of the comet, and was still raging in the 1640s, the years of revolution. The Thirty Years' War, in the countries affected by it, undoubtedly prepared the ground for revolution. The burden of war taxation, or military oppression, or military defeat, precipitated the revolts in Catalonia, Portugal, Naples. The dislocation of trade, which may have been caused by the Thirty Years' War, led to unemployment and violence in many manufacturing or commercial countries. The destructive passage or billeting of soldiers led to regular peasant mutinies in Germany and France. One need only look at M. Roupnel's study of Burgundy in those years, or at the reports sent to the chancellor Séguier describing the constant risings of the French peasants under the stress of war-taxation, or at the grim etchings of Callot, to realize that the Thirty Years' War was a formidable factor in the making of that discontent which was sometimes mobilized in revolution.[4]

And yet it is not a sufficient explanation. After all, the European wars of 1618–59 were not new phenomena. They were a resumption of the European wars of the sixteenth century, the wars of Charles V against Francis I and Henry II, of Philip II against Elizabeth and Henry of Navarre and the Prince of Orange. Those sixteenth-century wars had ended with the century, in 1598, in 1604, in 1609: in 1618 and 1621 and 1635 they had been resumed, consciously resumed. Philip IV looked back constantly to the

[4] See G. Roupnel, *La Ville et la Campagne au XVIIe Siècle dans le pays dijonnais* (Paris, 1955); Séguier's documents are printed, in French, in the Appendix to B. F. Porshnev, *Narodnie Vosstaniya vo Frantsii pered Frondoi, 1623–48* (Moscow, 1948).

example of Philip II, 'mi abuelo y mi señor'; Prince Maurice and Prince Frederick Henry to William of Orange, their father; Oliver Cromwell to 'Queen Elizabeth of glorious memory'. Richelieu and Mazarin sought to reverse the verdict of Câteau Cambrésis in 1559. And yet, in the sixteenth centuries these wars had led to no such revolutions. Moreover, the seventeenth-century revolutions were sometimes independent of the war. The greatest of those revolutions was in England which was safely—some said ignominiously—neutral. In the country which suffered most from the war, Germany, there was no revolution.

I have said that the sixteenth-century wars had led to no such revolutions. Of course there had been revolutions in the sixteenth century: famous, spectacular revolutions: the religious revolutions of Reformation and Counter-Reformation. But we cannot say that those revolutions had been caused by those wars. Moreover, those revolutions, however spectacular, had in fact been far less profound than the revolutions of the next century. They had led to no such decisive breach in historical continuity. Beneath the customary wars of Habsburg and Valois, beneath the dramatic changes of the Reformation and Counter-Reformation, the sixteenth century goes on, a continuous, unitary century, and society is much the same at the end of it as at the beginning. Philip II succeeds to Charles V, Granvelle to Granvelle, Queen Elizabeth to Henry VIII, Cecil to Cecil; even in France Henry IV takes up, after a period of disturbance, the mantle of Henry II. Aristocratic, monarchical society is unbroken: it is even confirmed. Speaking generally, we can say that for all the violence of its religious convulsions, the sixteenth century succeeded in absorbing its strains, its thinkers in swallowing their doubts, and at the end of it, kings and philosophers alike felt satisfied with the best of possible worlds.[5]

How different from this is the seventeenth century! For the seventeenth century did not absorb its revolutions. It is not continuous. It is broken in the middle, irreparably broken, and at the end of it, after the revolutions, men can hardly recognize the beginning. Intellectually, politically, morally, we are in a new age, a new climate. It is as if a series of rainstorms has ended in one

[5] This point—the growing social insensitivity of the sixteenth-century thinkers as monarchical, aristocratic society becomes more self-assured—is made by Fritz Caspari, *Humanism and the Social Order in Tudor England* (Chicago, 1954), pp. 198–204.

final thunderstorm which has cleared the air and changed, permanently, the temperature of Europe. From the end of the fifteenth century until the middle of the seventeenth century we have one climate, the climate of the Renaissance; then, in the middle of the seventeenth century we have the years of change, the years of revolution; and thereafter, for another century and a half we have another, very different climate, the climate of the Enlightenment.

Thus I do not believe that the seventeenth-century revolutions can be explained merely by the background of war, which had also been the background of the previous, unrevolutionary century. If we are to find an explanation, we must look elsewhere. We must look past the background, into the structure of society. For all revolutions, even though they may be occasioned by external causes, and expressed in intellectual form, are made real and formidable by defects of social structure. A firm, elastic, working structure—like that of England in the nineteenth century—is proof against revolution however epidemic abroad. On the other hand a weak or over-rigid social structure, though it may last long in isolation, will collapse quickly if infected. The universality of revolution in the seventeenth century suggests that the European monarchies, which had been strong enough to absorb so many strains in the previous century, had by now developed serious structural weaknesses: weaknesses which the renewal of general war did not cause, but merely exposed and accentuated.

What were the general, structural weaknesses of the western monarchies? Contemporaries who looked at the revolutions of the seventeenth century saw them as political revolutions: as struggles between the two traditional organs of the ancient 'mixed monarchy'—the Crown and the Estates. Certainly this was the form they took. In Spain, the Crown, having reduced the Cortes of Castile to insignificance, provoked the Catalan revolution by challenging the Cortes of the Kingdom of Aragon. In France, after the meeting of the Estates General in 1614, Richelieu contrived to discontinue them, and they never met again till 1789; the Parlement of Paris struck back in the Fronde, but only to be defeated by Mazarin and reduced to the insignificance which was afterwards so bluntly rubbed in to it by Louis XIV. In Germany the Emperor challenged and reduced the Electoral college, even though the electors, as individual princes, reduced their own Diets to insignificance. In England the Parliament challenged and defeated the King. At the same time the Kings of Denmark and Sweden, struggling with or within their Diets, ended by establishing a personal monarchy, while the King of Poland, unable to imitate them, became the puppet of his. Altogether, we may say, the universal casualty of the seventeenth century was that Aristotelian concept, so admired in 1600, so utterly extinct in 1700, 'mixed monarchy'. The position was described summarily by the English political philosopher, James Harrington who, in 1656, diagnosed the general crisis which had produced such violent results in his own country of *Oceana*. 'What', he asked, 'is become of the Princes of Germany? Blown up. Where are the Estates or the power of the people in France? Blown up. Where is that of the people of Aragon and the rest of the Spanish kingdoms? Blown up. Where is that of the Austrian princes in Switz? Blown up. . . . Nor shall any man show a reason that will be holding in prudence why the people of Oceana have blown up their king, but that their kings did not first blow up them.'

Now there can be no doubt that politically Harrington was right. The struggle was a struggle for power, for survival, between crowns and estates. But when we have said this, have we really answered our question? If revolution was to break out otherwise than in hopeless rural *jacqueries*, it could only be through the protest of estates, parliaments, cortes, diets; and if it was to be crushed, it could only be through the victory of royal power over such institutions. But to describe the form of a revolution is not to explain its cause, and today we are reluctant to accept constitutional struggles as self-contained or self-explanatory. We look for the forces or interests behind the constitutional claims of either side. What forces, what interests were represented by the revolutionary parties in seventeenth-century Europe—the parties which, though they may not have controlled them (for everyone would agree that there were other forces too) nevertheless gave ultimate social power and significance to the revolts of cortes and diets, estates and parliaments?

Now to this question one answer has already been given and widely accepted. It is the Marxist answer. According to the Marxists, and to some other historians who, though not Marxists, accept their argument, the crisis of the seventeenth century was at bottom a crisis of production, and the motive force behind at least some of the revolutions was the force of the producing bourgeoisie, hampered in their economic activity by the obsolete, wasteful, restrictive, but jealously defended productive system of 'feudal' society. According to this view, the crisis of production was general in Europe, but it was only in England that the forces of 'capitalism', thanks to their greater development and their representation in parliament, were able to triumph. Consequently while other countries made no immediate advance towards modern capitalism, in England the old structure was shattered and a new form of economic organization was established. Within that organization modern, industrial capitalism could achieve its astonishing results: it was no longer capitalist enterprise 'adapted to a generally feudal framework': it was capitalist enterprise, from its newly-won island base, 'transforming the world'.

This Marxist thesis has been advanced by many able writers, but, in spite of their arguments, I do not believe that it has been proved or even that any solid evidence has been adduced to sustain it. It is of course easy to show that there were economic changes in the seventeenth century, and that, at least in England, industrial capitalism was more developed in 1700 than in 1600; but to do this is not the same as to show either that the economic changes precipitated the revolutions in Europe, or that English capitalism was directly forwarded by the Puritan 'victory' of 1640–60. These are hypotheses, which may of course be true; but it is equally possible that they are untrue: that problems of production were irrelevant to the seventeenth-century revolutions generally, and that in England capitalist development was independent of the Puritan revolution, in the sense that it would or could have occurred without that revolution, perhaps even was retarded or interrupted by it. If it is to be shown that the English Puritan revolution was a successful 'bourgeois revolution', it is not enough to produce evidence that English capitalism was more advanced in 1700 than in 1600. It must be shown either that the men who made the revolution aimed at such a result, or that those who wished for such a result forwarded the revolution, or that such a result would not have been attained without the revolution. Without such evidence, the thesis remains a mere hypothesis.

Now in fact no advocate of the Marxist theory seems to me to have established any of these necessary links in the argument. Mr. Maurice Dobb, whose *Studies in the Development of Capitalism* may be described as the classic textbook of Marxist history, consistently assumes that the English Puritan revolution was the crucial 'break-through' of modern capitalism. It bears, he says, 'all the marks of the classic bourgeois revolution': before it, capitalism is cramped and frustrated, never progressing beyond a certain stage, a parasite confined to the interstices of 'feudal' society; in it, the 'decisive period' of capitalism reaches its 'apex'; after it, the bonds are broken and the parasite becomes the master. Similarly, Mr. E. J. Hobsbawm, in his two articles on 'The Crisis of the Seventeenth Century',[6] consistently maintains the same thesis. 'Had the English Revolution failed', he writes, 'as so many other European revolutions in the seventeenth century failed, it is entirely possible that economic development might have been long retarded.' The results of the Puritan 'victory' were 'portentous': nothing less than the transformation of the world. But it is to be observed that although Mr. Dobb assumes this position throughout his book, he nowhere gives any evidence to prove it. As soon as he reaches the 'decisive period' of capitalism, he suddenly becomes vague. 'The lines of this development', we learn, 'are far from clearly drawn'; 'the details of this process are far from clear and there is little evidence that bears directly upon it.' In fact, not a single piece of documented evidence is produced for what is throughout assumed to be the crucial event in the whole history of European capitalism. And Mr. Hobsbawm is even more summary. He dwells at length upon the economy of Europe at the time of the revolutions. He assumes the 'portentous' importance of the Puritan revolution in changing the economy. But of the actual connexion between the two he says not a word.[7]

[6] In *Past and Present,* no. 5 (May 1954) and no. 6 (Nov. 1954); repr. above, ch. 2—the quotation is at p.32.

[7] As far as I can see, Mr. Dobb's only arguments of such a connexion are the statements (1) that agricultural capitalists supported the Parliament while old-fashioned 'feudal' landlords supported the Crown; (2) that 'those sections of the bourgeoisie that had any roots in industry . . . were wholehearted supporters of the parliamentary cause'; and (3) that the industrial towns, particularly the clothing towns, were radical. None of these statements seems to me sufficient. (1) is incorrect: the only evidence given consists in undocumented statements that Oliver Cromwell was an improving agriculturalist (which is untrue: in fact having—in his own words—'wasted his estate', he had declined from a landlord to a tenant farmer), and that 'Ireton his chief lieutenant was both a country gentleman and a clothier' (for which I know of no evidence at all). In fact some of the most obvious 'improving landlords', like the Earl of Newcastle

Altogether, it seems to me that the Marxist identification of the seventeenth-century revolutions with 'bourgeois' 'capitalist' revolutions, successful in England, unsuccessful elsewhere, is a mere *a priori* hypothesis. The Marxists see, as we all see, that, at some time between the discovery of America and the Industrial Revolution, the basis was laid for a new 'capitalist' form of society. Believing, as a matter of doctrine, that such a change cannot be achieved peacefully but requires a violent 'break-through' of a new class, a 'bourgeois revolution', they look for such a revolution. Moreover, seeing that the country which led in this process was England, they look for such a revolution in England. And when they find, exactly half-way between these terminal dates, the violent Puritan revolution in England, they cry *εὕρηκα*! Thereupon the other European revolutions fall easily into place as abortive bourgeois revolutions. The hypothesis, once stated, is illustrated by other hypotheses. It has yet to be proved by evidence. And it may be that it rests on entirely false premises. It may be that social changes do not necessarily require violent revolution: that capitalism developed in England (as industrial democracy has done) peacefully, and that the violent Puritan revolution was no more crucial to its history than (say) the fifteenth-century Hussite and Taborite revolutions in Bohemia, to which it bears such obvious resemblances.

If the crisis of the seventeenth century, then, though general in western Europe, is not a merely constitutional crisis, nor a crisis of economic production, what kind of a crisis was it? In this essay I shall suggest that, in so far as it was a general crisis—i.e. ignoring inessential variations from place to place—it was something both wider and vaguer than this: in fact, that it was a crisis in the relations between society and the State. In order to explain this, I shall try to set it against a longer background of time than is sometimes supposed necessary. For general social crises are seldom explicable in terms of mere decades. We would not now seek to explain the communist revolution in Russia against a background merely of

---

and the Marquis of Worcester, were royalists. (2) is unsubstantiated and, I believe, incorrect; wherever the industrial bourgeoisie has been studied —as in Yorkshire and Wiltshire—it has been found to be divided in its loyalty. (3) is correct, but inconclusive; the radicalism of workers in a depressed industry may well spring from depression, not from 'capitalist' interest.

Colaiste Oideachais Mhuire Gan Smal

the twelve years since 1905, nor the great French Revolution against the background merely of the reign of Louis XVI. For such a purpose, we would think it necessary to examine the whole *ancien régime* which came to an end here in 1917, there in 1789. Similarly, if we are to seek an explanation of the general European crisis of the 1640s, we must not confine ourselves to the preceding decade, ascribing all the responsibility (though we must undoubtedly ascribe some) to Archbishop Laud in England or the Count-Duke of Olivares in Spain. We must look, here too, at the whole *ancien régime* which preceded the crisis: the whole form of State and society which we have seen continually expanding, absorbing all shocks, growing more self-assured throughout the sixteenth century, and which, in the mid-seventeenth century, comes to an end: what for convenience we may call the State and society of the European Renaissance.

The Renaissance—how loose and vague is the term! Defining it and dating it has become a major industry among scholars, at international congresses and in learned papers. But let us not be deterred by this. All general terms—'*ancien régime*', 'capitalism', 'the Middle Ages'—are loose and vague; but they are nevertheless serviceable if we use them only generally. And in general terms we know well enough what we mean by the European Renaissance. It is the sudden expansion of our civilization, the excited discovery of world upon world, adventure upon adventure: the progressive enlargement of sensitivity and show which reached its greatest extension in the sixteenth century and which, in the seventeenth century, is no more. Expansion, extension—these are its essential characteristics. For the sixteenth century is not an age of structural change. In technology, in thought, in government, it is the same. In technology, at least after 1520, there are few changes. The expansion of Europe creates greater markets, greater opportunities, but the machinery of production remains basically constant. Similarly, in culture, the great representatives of the European Renaissance are universal but unsystematic. Leonardo, Montaigne, Cervantes, Shakespeare, take life for granted: they adventure, observe, describe, perhaps mock; but they do not analyse, criticize, question. And in government it is the same too. The political structures of Europe are not changed in the sixteenth century: they are stretched to grasp and hold new empires, sometimes vast new empires, vaster than they can contain for long without internal change. Nevertheless, as yet, there is no such change. The Renaissance State—up to and beyond 1600—expands continuously without as yet bursting its old envelope. That envelope is the medieval, aristocratic monarchy, the rule of the Christian prince.

It is a fascinating spectacle, the rise of the princes in sixteenth-century Europe. One after another they spring up, first in Italy and Burgundy, then all over Europe. Their dynasties may be old, and yet their character is new: they are more exotic, more highly coloured than their predecessors. They are versatile, cultivated men, sometimes bizarre, even outrageous: they bewilder us by their lavish tastes, their incredible energy, their ruthlessness and *panache*. Even when they are introverted, bigoted, melancholic, it is on a heroic scale: we think of Charles V solemnly conducting his own funeral at Yuste or Philip II methodically condemning millions of future lives to the treadmill of ceaseless prayer for his own soul. Undoubtedly, in the sixteenth century, the princes are everything. They are tyrants over past and future; they change religion and divine truth by their nod, even in their teens; they are priests and popes, they call themselves gods, as well as kings. And yet we should remember, if we are to understand the crisis at the end of their rule, that their power did not rise up out of nothing. Its extraordinary expansion in the early sixteenth century was not *in vacuo*. Europe had to make room for it. The princes rose at the expense of someone or something, and they brought in their train the means of securing their sudden, usurped new power. In fact, they rose at the expense of the older organs of European civilization, the cities; and they brought with them, as the means of conquest, a new political instrument, 'the Renaissance Court'.

Not much has been written about the eclipse of the European cities on the eve of the Renaissance; but it is an important phenomenon.[8] For how can we think of the Middle Ages without thinking of the cities, and yet who thinks of them after 1500? In the Middle Ages the free communes of Flanders and Italy had been the founders of Europe's trade and wealth, the centres of its arts and crafts, the financiers of its popes and kings. The German cities had been the means of colonizing and civilizing the barbarous north, the pagan east of Europe. These cities, moreover, had had

[8] Fernand Braudel has touched on it in his great work, *La Méditerranée et le Monde Méditerranéen au Temps de Philippe II* (Paris, 1949), pp. 285–91.

their own way of life and had imposed upon Europe some of their own methods of government and standards of value. In its earliest form, the Renaissance itself had been a city phenomenon: it had begun in the cities of Italy, Flanders and south Germany before it was taken over, and changed, by princes and popes. And this early Renaissance had the character of the cities within which it was still contained. Like them it was responsible, orderly, self-controlled. For however great their wealth, however splendid their town halls and hospitals, their churches and squares, there is always, in the cities, a trace of calculation and self-restraint. It is the virtue of civic self-government, however oligarchically controlled: a spirit very different from the outrageous, spendthrift, irresponsible exhibitionism of the princes which was to come.

For between the fifteenth and the sixteenth century the princely suitors came, and one after another the cities succumbed. The rich cities of Flanders gave in to the magnificent dukes of Burgundy, the rich cities of Lombardy and Tuscany to the magnificent princes of Italy. The Baltic cities of the Hanse were absorbed by the kings of Poland or Denmark or ruined themselves by vain resistance. Barcelona yielded to the King of Aragon, Marseilles to the King of France. Even those apparent virgins, Genoa and Augsburg, were really 'kept cities', attached by golden strings to the King of Spain and the Emperor. The Doge of Venice himself became a prince, ruling over lesser cities in the *terra ferma*. Only a few, like Geneva, remained obstinate spinsters; and that sour, crabbed city missed the gaiety of the Renaissance. Even the exceptions prove the rule. Accidental princely weakness, or indirect princely patronage, lie behind the new prosperity of Frankfurt, Ragusa, Hamburg, Danzig.

For as a rule surrender was the price of continued prosperity: how else could the cities survive, once the princes had discovered the secret of State? By subduing the Church, extending their jurisdiction, mobilizing the countryside, the princes had created a new apparatus of power, 'the Renaissance State', with which they could tax the wealth of the cities, patronize and extend their trade, take over and develop their art and architecture. If the cities hope to thrive now, it must be by new methods. It must not be through independence: those days are past. It must be through monopoly, as the sole grantees of princely trade in these expanding dominions; as Lisbon and Seville throve on the grants of the Kings of

Portugal and Spain. Or they might thrive as centres of extravagant princely consumption, as royal capitals. For in some of the old cities the victorious princes would establish their new courts: courts which sucked up the wealth of the whole country and rained it down on the city of their residence. Essentially the sixteenth century is an age not of cities but of courts: of capital cities made splendid less by trade than by government. It was not as industrial or commercial cities, but as courts, that Brussels, Paris, Rome, Madrid, Naples, Prague achieve their splendour in the sixteenth century. And the brilliance of these courts is not the discreet, complacent self-advertisement of great merchants out of their calculated profits: it is the carefree magnificence of kings and courtiers, who do not need to count because they do not have to earn.

Of course the cities wriggled at first. Ghent resisted its Burgundian dukes. The old cities of Spain struck back against their foreign King. Florence sought to throw out the Medici. Genoa and Augsburg surrendered only after doubt and strife. But in the end each in turn was overpowered, subdued, and then—if lucky—rewarded with the golden shower which fell not from trade, or at least not directly from trade, but from the Court. And with the cities the old city culture was transformed too. Erasmus, preaching peace and civic justice and denouncing the heedless wars and wasteful magnificence of princes, is a true figure of the first, the city Renaissance, cultivated, pious, rational; but he is swept up in the princely embrace and made a mascot of royal courts, until he flees to die in a free city on the Rhine. Sir Thomas More, whose *Utopia* was a league of virtuous, independent cities, is captured and broken by the splendid, cannibal Court of Henry VIII. Soon after 1500 the age of independent city culture is over. So is the age of careful accountancy. We are in the age of the Field of Cloth-of-Gold, of heroic conquests and impossible visions and successive state bankruptcies: the age of Columbus and Cortés, of Leonardo da Vinci and St. Francis Xavier, each, in his way, like Marlowe's hero, still climbing after knowledge infinite, or, like don Quixote, pursuing unattainable mirages, heedless of mortal limitations. It is the age, also, whose fashionable handbooks were no longer civic nor clerical but were called *The Courtier, The Governour, The Prince, The Institution of a Christian Prince, The Mirror* (or *the Horologe*) *of Princes*.

How was this miracle possible? When we look back at that age, with its incredible audacities, its contemptuous magnificence in speculation and spending, we are amazed that it lasted so long. Why did not European civilization burst in the sixteenth century? And yet not only did it not burst, it continued to expand, absorbing all the time the most fearful strains. The Turks in the east wrenched away the outposts of Europe; Christendom was split asunder by religious revolution and constant war; and yet at the end of the century the kings were more spendthrift, their courts more magnificent than ever. The Court of Spain, once so simple, had been changed to a Burgundian pattern; the Court of England, once so provincial, had become, under Queen Elizabeth, the most elaborate in Europe; and the princes of Italy and Germany, with palaces and libraries, picture-galleries and *Wunderkammer*, philosophers, fools and astrologers, strove to hold their own. As the century wore on, social conscience dwindled, for social change seemed impossibly remote. Was ever an architect more effortlessly aristocratic than Palladio, or a poet than Shakespeare, or a painter than Rubens?

How indeed was it possible? One answer is obvious. The sixteenth century was an age of economic expansion. It was the century when, for the first time, Europe was living on Asia, Africa and America. But there was also another reason. The reason why this expansion was always under the princes, not at their expense, why the princes were always carried upwards, not thrown aside by it, was that the princes had allies who secured their power and kept them firmly in place. For the princes could never have built up their power alone. Whatever weaknesses in society gave them their opportunity, they owed their permanence to the machinery of government which they had created or improved, and to the vested interests which that machinery fostered. This machinery, the means and result of princely triumph, is the Renaissance State, and it is to this that we must now turn: for it was the Renaissance State which, in so much of Europe, first broke or corroded the old power of the cities and then, in its turn, in the seventeenth century, faced its own crisis and dissolved.

We often speak of the Renaissance State. How can we define it? When we come down to facts, we find that it is, at bottom, a great and expanding bureaucracy, a huge system of administrative centralization, staffed by an ever-growing multitude of 'courtiers' or 'officers'. The 'officers' are familiar enough to us as a social type. We think of the great Tudor ministers in England, Cardinal Wolsey, Thomas Cromwell, the two Cecils; or of the *letrados* of Spain, Cardinal Ximénez, the two Granvelles, Francisco de los Cobos, Antonio Pérez; and we see their common character: they are formidable administrators, machiavellian diplomats, cultivated patrons of art and letters, magnificent builders of palaces and colleges, greedy collectors of statues and pictures, books and bindings. For of course these men, as royal servants, imitated their masters, in lavishness as in other matters. But what is significant about the sixteenth century is not merely the magnificence of these great 'officers', it is the number—the ever-growing number—of lesser officers who also, on their lesser scale, accepted the standards and copied the tastes of their masters. For all through the century the number of officers was growing. Princes needed them, more and more, to staff their councils and courts, their new special or permanent tribunals which were the means of governing new territories and centralizing the government of old. It was for this reason that the Renaissance Princes and their great ministers founded all those schools and colleges. For it was not to produce scholars, or to advance learning or science, that old colleges were reorganized or new founded by Cardinal Ximénez or Cardinal Wolsey, by Henry VIII of England or John III of Portugal, or Francis I of France. The new learning, it is notorious, grew up outside the colleges and universities, not in them. The function of the new foundations was to satisfy the royal demand for officers—officers to man the new royal bureaucracies—and, at the same time, the public demand for office: office which was the means to wealth and power and the gratification of lavish, competitive tastes.

Thus the power of the Renaissance Princes was not princely power only: it was also the power of thousands of 'officers' who also, like their masters, had extravagant tastes and, somehow, the means of graitfying them. And how in fact were they gratified? Did the princes themselves pay their officers enough to sustain such a life? Certainly not. Had that been so, ruin would have come quicker: Cobos and Granvelle alone would have brought Charles V to bankruptcy long before 1556, and Henry VIII would have had to dissolve the monasteries fifteen years earlier to sustain the economic burden of Cardinal Wolsey. The fact is, only a fraction of the cost of the royal bureaucracy fell directly on the Crown:

three-quarters of it fell, directly or indirectly, on the country.

Yes, three-quarters: at least three-quarters. For throughout Europe, at this time, the salaries paid to officers of State were small, customary payments whose real value dwindled in times of inflation; the bulk of an officer's gains came from private opportunities to which public office merely opened the door. 'For the profits of these two great offices, the Chancellor and the Treasurer', wrote an English bishop, 'certainly they were very small if you look to the ancient fees and allowances; for princes heretofore did tie themselves to give but little, that so their officers and servants might more depend upon them for their rewards.'[9] What Bishop Goodman said of Jacobean England was true of every European country. Instances could be multiplied indefinitely.[10] Every officer, at every court, in every country, lived by the same system. He was paid a trivial 'fee' or salary and, for the rest, made what he could in the field which his office had opened to him. Some of these profits were regarded as perfectly legitimate, for no man could be expected to live on his 'fee' alone: it was taken for granted that he would charge a reasonable sum for audiences, favours, signatures, that he would exploit his office to make good bargains, that he would invest public money, while in his hands, on his own account. But of course there were other profits which were generally regarded as 'corruption' and therefore improper. Unfortunately the line dividing propriety from impropriety was conventional only: it was therefore invisible, uncertain, floating.

[9] Godfrey Goodman, *The Court of King James I* (London, 1839 edn.), i, p. 279.

[10] On this subject generally see Federico Chabod's essay 'Y a-t-il un Etat de la Renaissance?' in *Actes du Colloque sur la Renaissance, Sorbonne, 1956* (Paris, 1958), and also, for Milanese instances, his 'Stipendi Nominali e Busta Paga Effettiva dei Funzionari nell' Amministrazione Milanese alla Fine del Cinquecento' in *Miscellanea in Onore di Roberto Cessi II* (Rome, 1958) and 'Usi e Abusi nell' Amministrazione dello Stato di Milano a mezzo il 1500' in *Studi Storici in Onore di Gioachino Volpe* (Florence, n.d.). For Naples, see G. Coniglio, *Il Regno di Napoli al Tempo di Carlo V* (Naples, 1951), pp. 11–12, 246, etc. For France see R. Doucet, *Les Institutions de la France au XVIe Siècle* (Paris, 1948), pp. 403 ff; cf. Menna Prestwich, 'The Making of Absolute Monarchy, 1559–1683' in *France: Government and Society*, ed. J. M. Wallace-Hadrill and J. McManners (London, 1957). I have given some English instances in *The Gentry, 1540–1640* (Econ. Hist. Rev., Suppl. no. 1, 1953). See also J. E. Neale, 'The Elizabethan Political Scene', *Proceedings of the British Academy*, xxiv (1948); K. W. Swart, *The Sale of Offices in the Seventeenth Century* (The Hague, 1949).

It differed from person to person, from place to place. It also differed from time to time. As the sixteenth century passed on, as the cost of living rose, as the pressure of competition sharpened and royal discipline slackened, there was a general decline of standards. The public casuists became more indulgent, the private conscience more elastic, and men began to forget about that conventional, invisible line between 'legitimate profits' and 'corruption'.

Let us consider a few instances which illustrate the system. In England, the Master of the Wards had a 'fee' of £133 p.a., but even Lord Burghley, a conscientious administrator, made 'infinite gains'—at least £2,000 p.a.—out of its private opportunities, quite apart from its non-financial advantages. His son did far better. The Lord Treasurer's fee was £365 p.a., but in 1635 even Archbishop Laud, a notable stickler for administrative honesty, reckoned that that great officer had 'honest advantages' for enriching himself to the tune of over £7,000 p.a. The Archbishop made this calculation because he had been shocked by the much larger sums which recent Lord Treasurers had been making at the expense of king and subject alike. In 1600 the Lord Chancellor's fee was £500 p.a., but in fact the office was known to be 'better worth than £3,000 p.a.' To Lord Chancellor Ellesmere this did not seem enough, and, like many great men, he sighed that he could not make ends meet. He was thought conscientious: perhaps (like Burghley) he was also hypocritical. At all events, his successors had no such difficulty. 'How have the Lord Chancellors lived since', exclaimed Bishop Goodman, 'how have they flowed with money, and what great purchases have they made, and what profits and advantages have they had by laying their fingers on purchases! For if my Lord desired the land, no man should dare to buy it out of his hands, and he must have it at his own price; for any bribery or corruption, it is hard to prove it: men do not call others to be witnesses at such actions.'[11] All writers of the early seventeenth century agree that the casual profits of office had grown enormously; and these casual profits were multiplied at the expense of the consumer, the 'country'.

[11] See, for the Master of the Wards, J. Hurstfield, 'Lord Burghley as Master of the Court of Wards', *Trans. Roy. Hist. Soc.*, 5th ser., xxxi (1949); for the Lord Treasurer, P. Heylin, *Cyprianus Anglicus* (1668), p. 285; for the Lord Chancellor, Goodman, loc. cit.; *Manningham's Diary* (Camden Soc., 1868), p. 19.

Thus each old office granted, each new office created, meant a new burden on the subject. Royal parsimony made little difference. Our Queen Elizabeth, we all know, was judged very parsimonious: far too parsimonious by her own officers. But she was not praised for her parsimony in her own time. For what in fact did it mean? 'We have not many precedents of her liberality', says a contemporary, 'nor of any large donatives to particular men. . . . Her rewards consisted chiefly in grants of leases of offices, places of judicature; but for ready money, and in any great sums, she was very sparing.'[12] In other words, she gave to her courtiers not cash but the right to exploit their fellow subjects: to Sir Walter Ralegh the right to despoil the bishops of Bath and Wells and Salisbury and to interpose his pocket between the producer and consumer of tin; to the Earl of Essex the right to lease the monopoly of sweet wines to merchants who would recoup themselves by raising the cost to the consumer. All European sovereigns did likewise. They had no alternative. They had not the ready money, and so, if they were to gratify their servants, reward their favourites, service their loans, they had to raise it at a discount or pay excessively in kind. They leased Crown lands at a quarter (or less) of their true value in order that 'officers' or 'courtiers' could live, as lessees, on the difference. They granted monopolies which brought in to the Crown less than a quarter of what they cost the subject. They collected irrational old taxes, or even irrational new taxes, by imposing, fourfold, irrational burdens on the tax-payers. The King of France obliged his peasants to buy even more salt than they needed, in order to raise his yield from the *gabelle*. We all know what a burden wardship and purveyance became in the reigns of Queen Elizabeth and King James. Both visibly cost the subject four times what they brought to the Crown. Invisibly—that is, beyond that invisible line—they cost far more.[13] Nor was it only

[12] Sir R. Naunton, *Fragmenta Regalia* (ed. A. Arber, 1870), p. 18.

[13] For the cost of monopolies see W. R. Scott, *The Constitution and Finance of . . . Joint-Stock Companies to 1720*, vol. i (London, 1911). The cost of wardship appears clearly from Mr. Joel Hurstfield's studies. He concludes that 'the unofficial profits from fiscal feudalism taken as a whole, were at least three times as high as the official ones': 'The Profits of Fiscal Feudalism, 1541–1602', *Econ. Hist. Rev.*, 2nd ser., viii (1955–6), p. 58. Of purveyance, Bacon wrote, 'There is no pound profit which redoundeth to Your Majesty in this course but induceth and begetteth £3 damage upon your subjects, besides the discontentment' (*Works*, ed. Spedding, iii, p. 185). The truth

the Crown which acted thus. The practice was universal. Great men rewarded their clients in exactly the same way. The Church, which was now everywhere a department of State, was similar. It was burdened with its sinecures: absentee clergy, tithe-eating laity; with its 'officers': the swollen number of ecclesiastical officers—'caterpillars of the Commonwealth'—was one of the great complaints against the Anglican Church in the 1630s; with its lessees: Church lands, like Crown lands, were regularly leased at absurd under-rents. It was not only the State, the whole of society was top-heavy.

Moreover, and increasingly as the seventeenth century succeeded to the sixteenth, this multiplication of ever more costly offices outran the needs of State. Originally the need had created the officers; now the officers created the need. All bureaucracies tend to expand. By the process known to us as Parkinson's Law, office-holders tend to create yet more offices beneath them in order to swell their own importance or provide for their friends and kinsmen. But whereas today such inflation is curbed by the needs of the Treasury, in the sixteenth century the needs of the Treasury positively encouraged it. For offices, in the sixteenth century, were not granted freely: they were sold, and—at least in the beginning—the purchase-price went to the Crown. If the Crown could sell more and more offices at higher and higher prices, leaving the officers to be paid by the country, this was an indirect, if also a cumbrous and exasperating way of taxing the country. Consequently, princes were easily tempted to create new offices, and to profit by the competition which forced up the price. As for the purchaser, having paid a high price, he naturally sought to raise his profits still higher, in order to recoup himself, with a decent margin, for his outlay: a decent margin with which an ambitious man might hope, in the end, to build a house like Hatfield or Knole, entertain royalty to feasts costing thousands, retain

of this last statement is clearly demonstrated in Miss Allegra Woodworth's excellent study, *Purveyance in the Reign of Queen Elizabeth* (Philadelphia, 1945). For Crown lands, Bacon told King James that, properly administered, they 'will yield four for one' (*Works*, iv, p. 328): others put the proportion far higher, sometimes twenty to one. Cf. E. Kerridge, 'The Movement of Rent', in *Econ. Hist. Rev.*, 2nd ser., vi (1953–4), pp. 31–32. The Earl of Bedford similarly, in 1641, calculated that in some places the proportion was twenty to one (Woburn Abbey, Duke of Bedford's MSS.).

and reward an army of clients, plant exotic gardens, and collect *objets d'art* and pictures.

So 'the Renaissance State' consisted, at bottom, of an ever-expanding bureaucracy which, though at first a working bureaucracy, had by the end of the sixteenth century become a parasitic bureaucracy; and this ever-expanding bureaucracy was sustained on an equally expanding margin of 'waste': waste which lay between the taxes imposed on the subject and the revenue collected by the Crown. Since the Crown could not afford an absolute loss of revenue, it is clear that this expansion of the waste had to be at the expense of society. It is equally clear that it could only be borne if society itself were expanding in wealth and numbers. Fortunately, in the sixteenth century, the European economy was expanding. The trade of Asia, the bullion of Africa and America, was driving the European machine. This expansion may have been uneven; there may have been strains and casualties; but they were the strains of growth, which could be absorbed, individual casualties which could be overlooked. Occasional State bankruptcies clear off old debts: they do not necessarily affect new prosperity. War increases consumption: it does not necessarily consume the sources of wealth. A booming economy can carry many anomalies, many abuses. It could even carry—provided it went on booming—the incredibly wasteful, ornamental, parasitic Renaissance Courts and Churches.

Provided it went on booming. . . . But how long would it boom? Already, by 1590, the cracks are beginning to appear. The strains of the last years of Philip II's wars release everywhere a growing volume of complaint: complaint which is not directed against constitutional faults—against the despotism of kings or the claims of estates—but against this or that aspect or consequence of the growth and cost of a parasitic bureaucracy. For of course, although war has not created the problem, war aggravates it: the more the costs of government are raised, the more the government resorts to those now traditional financial expedients: creation and sale of new offices, sale or long lease, at undervalues, of Crown or Church lands, creation of monopolies, raising of 'feudal' taxes: expedients which, on the one hand, multiply the already overgrown bureaucracy and thus the cost to the country, and, on the other hand, further impoverish the Crown.

But if the strains are already obvious in the 1590s, they are, as yet, not fatal: for peace comes first. A few opportune deaths—Philip II in 1598, Queen Elizabeth in 1603—hasten the process, and throughout Europe war after war is wound up. And then, with peace, what relief! The overstrained system is suddenly relaxed, and an era of pleasure and renewed extravagance follows. Was there ever an era of such lavishness as the time between the end of Philip II's wars and the outbreak of the Thirty Years' War, the time when the world was ruled, or at least enjoyed, by Philip III and the Duke of Lerma in Spain, James I and the Duke of Buckingham in England, 'The Archdukes' in Flanders, Henry IV and Marie des Médicis in France? It is a world of giddy expenditure, splendid building, gigantic feasts and lavish, evanescent shows. Rubens, when he came to the Duke of Buckingham's England, marvelled at such unexpected magnificence 'in a place so remote from Italian elegance'. No nation in the world, said a contemporary Englishman, spent as much as we did in building. We built houses, said another, thinking of Hatfield and Audley End, 'like Nebuchadnezzar's'. All 'the old good rules of economy', said a third, had gone packing. But the Spanish ambassador, reporting to his king these costly Jacobean festivals, would only say that no doubt they would seem very impressive 'to anyone who had not seen the grandeur and state with which we do such things in Spain'—as well he might, in the days when the Duke of Lerma, the courtier of the almost bankrupt King of Spain, went forth to meet his future queen with 34,000 ducats' worth of jewels on his person, and another 72,000 ducats' worth carried behind him.[14]

Such is the character of the Renaissance Courts in their last Indian summer after the close of the sixteenth century. And even this, of course, is only the conspicuous, still sunlit tip of the iceberg whose sides are hidden from us by intervening oblivion and whose greater base was always, even at the time, submerged. How, we may ask, could it go on? Even in the 1590s, even a far less expensive, more efficient bureaucracy had only been saved by peace: how could this much more outrageous system survive if

[14] *Corespondencia Oficial de . . . Gondomar* (Madrid, 1944), iii, p. 232. P. Mantuano, *Casamientos de España y Francia* (Madrid, 1618), pp. 124–5, quoted in Agustín Gonzales de Amezúa, *Lope de Vega en sus Cartas* (Madrid, 1935), i, pp. 70–71.

the long prosperity of the sixteenth century or the saving peace of the seventeenth, should fail?

In fact, in the 1620s they both failed at once. In 1618 a political crisis in Prague had set the European powers in motion, and by 1621 the wars of Philip II had been resumed, bringing in their train new taxes, new offices, new exactions. Meanwhile the European economy, already strained to the limit by the habits of peace-time boom, was suddenly struck by a great depression, the universal 'decay of trade' of 1620. Moreover, in those twenty years, a new attitude of mind had been created: created by disgust at that gilded merry-go-round which cost society so much more than it was willing to bear. It was an attitude of hatred: hatred of 'the Court' and its courtiers, hatred of princely follies and bureaucratic corruption, hatred of the Renaissance itself: in short, Puritanism.

In England we naturally think of our own form of Puritanism: extreme Protestantism, the continuation, to unbearable lengths, of the half-completed sixteenth-century Reformation. But let us not be deceived by mere local forms. This reaction against the Renaissance Courts and their whole culture and morality was not confined to any one country or religion. Like the thesis, the antithesis also is general. In England there is an Anglican Puritanism, a 'Puritanism of the Right'. What greater enemy had English Puritanism, as we know it, than Archbishop Laud, the all-powerful prelate who drove it to America till it returned to destroy him? And yet he too illustrates this same reaction. Did English Puritans denounce 'the unloveliness of lovelocks', gay clothes, the drinking of toasts? The Archbishop forbade long hair in Oxford, reformed clerical dress, waged war on alehouses. In Roman Catholic countries it was the same. Did the English Puritans first denounce, then close the London theatres? In Spain—even the Spain of Lope de Vega—*pragmática* after *pragmática* denounced stage-plays. In France the Jansenist Pascal disliked them hardly less. In Bavaria there was a Catholic prudery, and a police enforcement of it, as disagreeable as the worst form of English Puritanism. There was the same war against luxury too. In 1624 Philip IV of Spain cut down his household, published sumptuary laws, and banished the ruff—that symbol of sartorial magnificence—from Spain by decree, from Europe by example. In France, Cardinal Richelieu was doing likewise. It was a sudden war, almost a crusade, against the old

Renaissance extravagance. In Flanders, Rubens would find himself surviving his old Court patrons and would turn to country landscapes. Literature reflects the same change. Of Castiglione's famous manual, *The Courtier*, at least sixty editions or translations were published between 1528 and 1619; after the latter date, for a whole century, none.

In the 1620s Puritanism—this general mood of Puritanism—triumphs in Europe. Those years, we may say, mark the end of the Renaissance. The playtime is over. The sense of social responsibility, which had held its place within the Renaissance Courts of the sixteenth century—we think of the paternalism of the Tudors, the 'collectivism' of Philip II—had been driven out in the early seventeenth century, and now it had returned, and with a vengeance. War and depression had made the change emphatic, even startling. We look at the world in one year, and there we see Lerma and Buckingham and Marie des Médicis. We look again, and they have all gone. Lerma has fallen and saved himself by becoming a Roman cardinal; Buckingham is assassinated; Marie des Médicis has fled abroad. In their stead we find grimmer, greater, more resolute figures: the Count Duke of Olivares, whose swollen, glowering face almost bursts from Velázquez's canvases; Strafford and Laud, that relentless pair, the prophets of Thorough in Church and State; Cardinal Richelieu, the iron-willed invalid who ruled and re-made France. In literature too it is the same. The fashion has changed. After Shakespeare, Cervantes, Montaigne, those universal spirits, with their scepticism, their acceptance of the world as it is, we are suddenly in a new age: an age here of ideological revolt, Milton's 'jubilee and resurrection of Church and State', there of conservative pessimism, cynicism and disillusion, of John Donne and Sir Thomas Browne, of Quevedo and the Spanish Baroque: for the baroque age, as Mr. Gerald Brenan says, '—one cannot say it too often—was a tight, contracted age, turned in on itself and lacking self-confidence and faith in the future'.[15]

Such was the mood of general, non-doctrinal, moral Puritanism which, in the 1620s, launched its attack—here from within, there from without—on the Renaissance Courts. There are differences of incidence, of course, differences of personality from place to place, and these differences could be crucial—who can say what would

[15] Gerald Brenan, *The Literature of the Spanish People* (Cambridge, 1951), p. 272.

have happened if Archbishop Laud had really been, as Sir Thomas Roe thought, 'the Richelieu of England'? There were also differences in society itself. But if we look closely we see that the burden on society is the same even if the shoulders which creak under it are different. For instance, in England the cost of the Court fell most heavily on the gentry: they were the tax-paying class: wardships, purveyance and all the indirect taxes which were multiplied by the early Stuarts fell heaviest on them. On the other hand in France the *noblesse* was exempt from taxation, and the *taille* and *gabelle*, which were multiplied by the early Bourbons, fell heaviest on the peasants. No doubt English landlords could pass some of their burdens on to their tenants. No doubt impoverishment of French peasants diminished the rents of their landlords. But the difference is still significant. It was a commonplace in England, where 'the asinine peasants of France', with their 'wooden shoes and canvas breeches' were regularly contrasted with our own, more prosperous yeomen. It is illustrated by the ultimate result: in England, when revolution came, it was a great revolution, led and controlled by the gentry; in France, there were, every year for the same twenty years, revolts—little but serious revolts—of the peasants. Nevertheless, if the rebels were different, the general grievance against which they rebelled—the character and cost of the State—was the same.

For wherever we look, this is the burden of all complaints. From 1620 to 1640 this is the cry of the country, the problem of the Courts. We can hear the cry from the back-benches of the English parliaments in the 1620s. We can see the problem in Bacon's great essays, written between 1620 and 1625, on 'Sedition and Troubles' and 'The True Greatness of Kingdoms'. We hear the cry in Spain in the protests of the Cortes, see the problem in the pamphlets of the *arbitristas*, in Fernández Navarrete's *Conservación de Monarquías* with its wonderful analysis of the social ills of Spain, and in Olivares's long memorandum to Philip IV, outlining his new programme for the country,[16] both written in the 1620s. We see it in France, above all, in the *Testament Politique* of Richelieu, written in 1629 and the early 1630s, the period when governments everywhere were facing these problems, or trying to face them, before it was too late. And these demands, these problems, are not con-

[16] Published in Valladares, *Semanario Erudito*, vol. xi (Madrid, 1788). (I owe this reference to Mr. J. H. Elliott.)

stitutional, they are not concerned with monarchy or republic, Crown or Parliament. Nor are they economic: they are not concerned with methods of production. Essentially they are demands for emancipation from the burden of centralization; for reduction of fees; reduction of useless, expensive offices, including—even in Spain—clerical offices; abolition of the sale of offices ('for whosoever doth farm or buy offices doth bind himself to be an extortioner', and 'they which buy dear must sell dear'); abolition of heredity of offices; abolition of those wasteful, indirect taxes which yield so little to the Crown but on whose superabundant 'waste' the ever-expanding fringe of the Court is fed.

Thus the tension between Court and country grew, and the 'revolutionary situation' of the 1620s and 1630s developed. But revolutionary situations do not necessarily lead to revolutions—nor (we may add) are violent revolutions necessary in order to create new forms of production or society. Society is an organic body, far tougher, far more resilient, than its morbid anatomists often suppose; the frontiers between opposing classes are always confused by a complex tissue of interests;[17] and if a country is to pass from a revolutionary situation to a revolution, a whole series of political events and political errors must intervene. Therefore if we are to carry this study further, from crisis to revolution, we must take account of these intervening events and errors: events and errors which, by definition, must vary from place to place, and whose variation will explain, in part, the difference between the revolutions in those different places.

Perhaps we can see the problem best if we consider the means of avoiding revolution. If the Renaissance Courts were to survive, it was clear that at least one of two things must be done. On the one hand the parasitic bureaucracies must be cut down; on the other hand the working bureaucracy must be related to the economic capacity of the country. The first programme was one of administrative, the second of economic reform. The first was easy enough to define—any country gentleman could put it in two words—but difficult to carry out: it meant the reduction of a parasitic, but living and powerful class; and although this can be done without

[17] e.g. in this instance, the interpenetration of 'bourgeoisie' and office-holders, which paralysed the Spanish cortes, the French parlements and even the English parliament.

revolution, as it was done in nineteenth-century England—one only has to read the *Extraordinary Black Book* of 1831 to see the huge parasitic fringe which had grown again around the eighteenth-century Court—it is at best a delicate and difficult operation. The second was far more difficult to define: it meant the discovery, or re-discovery, of an economic system. Nevertheless, such a definition was not beyond the wit of seventeenth-century thinkers, and in fact several thinkers did point out, clearly enough, the kind of economic system which was required.

What was that system? It was not a 'capitalist' system—or at least, if it was capitalist, there was nothing new about it. It did not entail revolution or a change in method of production or in the class structure. Nor was it advocated by revolutionary thinkers: in general, those who advocated it were conservative men who wished for little or no political change. And in fact the economic programme which they advocated, though applied to modern conditions, looked back for its example. For what they advocated was simply the application to the new, centralized monarchies of the old, well-tried policy of the medieval communes which those monarchies had eclipsed: mercantilism.

For what had been the policy of the medieval cities? It had been a policy of national economy—within the limits of the city-State. The city had seen itself at once as a political and as an economic unit. Its legislation had been based on its trading requirements. It had controlled the price of food and labour, limited imports in the interest of its own manufactures, encouraged the essential methods of trade—fishing and shipbuilding, freedom from internal tolls—invested its profits not in conspicuous waste or pursuit of glory, or wars merely of plunder, but in the rational conquest of markets and the needs of national economy: in technical education, municipal betterment, poor relief. In short, the city had recognized that its life must be related to its means of livelihood. In the sixteenth-century eclipse of the cities, in their transformation into overgrown, overpopulated capitals, centres merely of exchange and consumption, much of this old civic wisdom had been forgotten. Now, in the seventeenth-century eclipse of the spendthrift Renaissance Courts, it was being remembered. The economists wished to go farther: to re-apply it.

Of course, they would re-apply it in changed circumstances, to different national forms. The princes, it was agreed, had done their work: it could not be reversed. The new nation-states had come to stay. But, said the Reformers, having come, let them now apply to their different conditions the old good rules of the cities. Let them not merely pare down the parasitic fringe that had grown around them, but also relate their power, in a positive sense, to economic aims. Let them favour a gospel of work instead of aristocratic, or pseudo-aristocratic *hidalguía*. Let them protect industry, guarantee food-supplies, remove internal tolls, develop productive wealth. Let them rationalize finance and bring down the apparatus of Church and State to a juster proportion. To reverse the Parkinson's law of bureaucracy, let them reduce the hatcheries which turned out the superfluous bureaucrats: grammar schools in England, colleges in France, monasteries and theological seminaries in Spain. Instead, let them build up local elementary education: skilled workers at the base of society now seemed more important than those unemployable university graduates, hungry for office, whom the new Renaissance foundations were turning out. 'Of grammar-schools', declared that great intellectual, Sir Francis Bacon, 'there are too many'; and he and his followers advocated a change in the type of education or the diversion of funds to elementary schools. Of colleges, declared the founder of the French Academy, Cardinal Richelieu, there are too many: the commerce of letters would banish absolutely that of merchandise 'which crowns states with riches' and ruin agriculture 'the true nursing-mother of peoples'. Of monasteries, declared the Catholic Council of Castile in 1619, there are too many, and it prayed that the Pope be asked to authorize their reduction, for although the monastic state is no doubt, for the individual, the most perfect, 'for the public it is very damaging and prejudicial'. So, in country after country, the protest was raised. It was the backswing of the great educational impulse of the Renaissance and Reformation, the great religious impulse of the Counter-Reformation.[18]

To cut down the oppressive, costly sinecures of Church and State, and to revert, *mutatis mutandis*, to the old mercantilist policy of the cities, based on the economic interest of society—such were

[18] For Bacon's proposal see his *Works*, ed. Spedding, iv, pp. 249 ff; for Richelieu, his *Testament Politique* (ed. Louis André, Paris, 1947), pp. 204–5; for Spain the *Consulta del Consejo Supremo de Castilla*, published in P. Fernández Navarrete, *Conservación de Monarquías* (Madrid, 1947, Biblioteca de Autores Españoles, vol. xxv), p. 450.

the two essential methods of avoiding revolution in the seventeenth century. How far were either of them adopted in the states of western Europe? The answer, I think, is instructive. If we look at those states in turn, we may see, in the extent to which either or both of these policies were adopted or rejected, some partial explanation of the different forms which the general crisis took in each of them.

In Spain neither policy was adopted. In spite of the *arbitristas,* in spite of the wisdom of influential statesmen, including the greatest of Spanish ambassadors, Gondomar, whose letters show him a perfect mercantilist,[19] in spite of the Council of Castile, in spite even of Philip IV and Olivares, the system remained basically unchanged. Whatever projects of reform he may once have entertained, whatever beginnings of reform or paper-reforms he may even have carried out,[20] Olivares, like Richelieu, soon surrendered to necessity and the fact of war. On the other hand Spain—that is, Castile—lacked the organs of effective protest. The middle class was weak and penetrated by office-holders; the old Cortes towns had been suppressed in their last rising against the Burgundian state; and the Cortes of Castile were now an aristocratic body which hardly sought to do more than demur. In spite of constant demands for reduction and disendowment, the wealth and number of churches and monasteries constantly grew; so did Court offices and the sale of offices. In 1621—the first year of crisis and reforming zeal—the number of royal officers had been fixed by law. In 1646 the Cortes of Castile pointed to the factual consequences: instead of one president and three councillors of the Treasury, there were now three presidents and eleven councillors; instead of three *contadores* and a *fiscal,* there were now fourteen *contadores*; instead of four councillors at war there were now more than forty; and all these, salaried or unsalaried (for their salaries, their 'fees', were anyway trifles), had entertainment, expenses, lodgings, privileges and perquisites at the expense of the subject.[21] The weight of this

[19] See, in particular, Pascual Gayangos, *Cinco Cartas Politico-Literarias de D. Diego Sarmiento, Conde de Gondomar* (Madrid, 1869), *Sociedad de Bibliófilos,* vol. iv.

[20] For a summary of these reforms, see H. Bérindoague, *Le Mercantilisme en Espagne* (Bordeaux, 1929), pp. 85–104.

[21] *Consulta* of the Cortes of Castile, 18 Aug. 1646, printed in Alonso Núñez de Castro, *Libro Historio-Político, Solo Madrid es Corte,* 2nd edn. (Madrid, 1669), pp. 84 ff. This whole book, written by the royal chronicler and first published in 1658, illustrates the process I am describing.

burden might have been redistrubuted a little within the country, but it had certainly not been reduced.[22] Nor had the Spanish economy been enabled to bear it. For meanwhile the national wealth of Spain had not increased: it had diminished. The voices of the mercantilists were stifled. The trade of Spain was taken over almost entirely by foreigners. The vitality of the country was crushed beneath the dead weight of an unreformed *ancien régime*. It was not till the next century that a new generation of *arbitristas* —philosophers inspired by English and French examples—would again have the strength and spirit to urge on a new dynasty the same reforms which had clearly but vainly been demanded in the days of Philip III and Philip IV.[23]

Very different was the position in the emancipated northern Netherlands. For the northern Netherlands was the first European country to reject the Renaissance Court, and the Court they rejected was their own court, the greatest, most lavish court of all, the Burgundian Court which had moved and made itself so fatally permanent in Spain. The revolt of the Netherlands in the sixteenth century was not, of course, a direct revolt of society against the Court. That is not how revolutions break out. But in the course of the long struggle the Court itself, in those provinces which freed themselves, was a casualty. There the whole apparatus of the Burgundian Court simply dissolved under the stress of war. So did the Burgundian Church, that huge, corrupt department of State which Philip II unskilfully sought to reform and whose abuses the great patrons of revolt, in the beginning, were seeking to preserve. Whatever the causes or motives of the revolution, the United Provinces emerged from it incidentally disembarrassed of that top-heavy system whose pressure, a generation later, would create a revolutionary situation in other countries. Consequently, in those provinces, there was no such revolutionary situation. The new Court of the Princes of Orange might develop some of the

[22] For the factual (though not legal) redistribution of fiscal burdens in Spain under Philip IV, see the interesting article of A. Domínguez Ortiz, 'La desigualidad contributiva en Castilla en el siglo XVIII', *Anuario de Historia del Derecho Español*, 1952.

[23] For these *arbitristas* of the eighteenth century see M. Jean Sarrailh's excellent work, *L'Espagne eclairée* (Paris, 1954): which does not, however, bring out the extent to which Ward, Jovellanos, Campomanes, etc., were repeating the programme of the early seventeenth-century Spanish mercantilists.

characteristics of the old Court, but only some: and as it started lean, it could better afford a little additional fat. There were crises no doubt in seventeenth century Holland—the crises of 1618, of 1650, of 1672: but they were political crises, comparable with our crisis not of 1640 but of 1688; and they were surgically solved for the same reason: the social problem was no longer acute: the top-heavy apparatus of the State had been purged: society beneath was sound.

Moreover, if accident rather than design had rid the United Provinces of the Renaissance State, policy had also achieved there the other, economic reform of which I have written. It was not that there was a 'bourgeois' or 'capitalist' revolution in Holland.[24] Dutch industry was relatively insignificant. But the new rulers of Holland, seeking the means of guarding their hard-won freedom, set out to imitate the fortune and the methods of those older mercantile communities which had preserved their independence through centuries by rationally combining commercial wealth and maritime power. By adopting the techniques of Italy, welcoming the *émigré* experts of Antwerp, and following the old good rules of Venetian policy, Amsterdam became, in the seventeenth century, the new Venice of the north. The economic originality of seventeenth-century Holland consisted in showing that, even after the victory and reign of the Renaissance Princes, whom they alone had driven out, the mercantilism of the cities was not dead: it could be revived.

Midway between completely unreformed Spain and completely reformed Holland lies what is perhaps the most interesting of all examples, Bourbon France. For France, in the seventeenth century, was certainly not immune from the general crisis, and in the Frondes it had a revolution, if a relatively small revolution. The result was, as in Spain, a victory for the monarchy. Triumphant over its critics and adversaries, the monarchy of the *ancien régime* survived in France, and survived for another century and a half. On the other hand the French monarchy of Louis XIV was

[24] That the economy of the United Provinces was not a new, revolutionary form of capitalism, but a return to the system of the medieval Italian cities is argued by Mr. Jelle C. Riemersma in his article 'Calvinism and Capitalism in Holland, 1550–1650', *Explorations in Entrepreneurial History*, i (1), p. 8, and is admitted even by Marxists like Mr. Dobb and Mr. Hobsbawm, who calls the Dutch economy 'a feudal business economy' (*Past and Present*, no. 6, 1954, repr. above at p. 42).

not like the Spanish monarchy of Philip IV and Charles V. It was not economically parasitic. Industry, commerce, science flourished and grew in France, in spite of the 'failure' of the 'bourgeois revolution', no less than in England, in spite of its 'success'. To all appearances, in 1670, in the age of Colbert, absolutism and the *ancien régime* were perfectly compatible with commercial and industrial growth and power.

And indeed, why not? For what had hindered such growth in the past, what had caused the crisis in society, was not the form of government, but its abuses; and though these abuses might be removed by revolution, or might fall as incidental casualties of a revolution, their removal did not necessarily require revolution. There was always the way of reform. It is not necessary to burn down the house in order to have roast pig. And although France (like Holland) had had a fire in the sixteenth century, in which some of its burden of waste matter had been incidentally consumed, it did also, in the years thereafter, achieve some measure of reform. The fire, indeed, had prepared the ground. The French civil wars of the sixteenth century, if they had done much harm, had also done some good. They had burnt up the overgrown patronage of the great nobles and reduced the patronage of the Court to the patronage of the King. Henry IV, like the Prince of Orange, like Charles II of England after him, found himself at his accession disembarrassed of much ancient parasitism: he could therefore afford to indulge a little new. And on this basis, this *tabula partim rasa*, he was able to achieve certain administrative changes. The *Paulette*, the law of 1604 which systematized the sale of offices, did at least regulate the abuses which it has often, and wrongly, been accused of creating. Sully, by his *économies royales*, did keep down the waste around the throne. And Richelieu, in the 1630s not only meditated a complete mercantilist policy for France, but also, even in the midst of war, succeeded—as Laud and Olivares, whether in peace or war, did not—in regulating that most expensive, most uncontrollable of all departments, the royal household.[25] Thanks to these changes, the *ancien régime* in France was repaired and strengthened. The changes may not have been

[25] For Richelieu's mercantilism see H. Hauser, *La Pensée et l'Action Economique du cardinal de Richelieu* (Paris, 1944). For his reform of the royal household, see M. R. Mousnier's article in vol. i of *Histoire de France,* ed. M. Reinhard (Paris, 1955). (I owe this reference to Mr. J. P. Cooper.)

radical, but they were enough. Richelieu and Mazarin no doubt had other advantages in their successful struggle to maintain the French *ancien régime* in the era of the Huguenot revolt and the Frondes. They had an army absolutely under royal control; they had taxes whose increase fell not on gentry, assembled and vocal in parliament, but on scattered, inarticulate peasants; and they had their own political genius. But they had also an apparatus of state which had already undergone some salutary reform: a State which, in the mind of Richelieu and in the hands of his disciple Colbert, could become a mercantilist State, rationally organized for both profit and power.

Finally there is England. In England the Crown had not the same political power as in France or Spain, and the taxes fell on the gentry, powerful in their counties and in parliament. In England therefore, it was doubly important that the problem be faced and solved. How far was it in fact faced? To answer this question let us look in turn at the two sides of the problem, administrative and economic.

In the sixteenth century the apparatus of the English State had neither suffered nor benefited from any such destructive accident as had befallen Holland or France. The Renaissance Court of the Tudors, whose parsimony under Elizabeth had been so unreal and whose magnificence and ceremony had so impressed foreign visitors, survived intact into the new century, when its cost and show were magnified beyond all measure by King James and his favourites. Already in 1604 Francis Bacon warned the new King of the danger. The Court, he said, was like a nettle: its root, the Crown itself, was 'without venom or malignity', but it sustained leaves 'venomous and stinging where they touch'.[26] Two years later, King James's greatest minister, Robert Cecil, Earl of Salisbury, apprehended revolution against the same burden of the Court; and in 1608, on becoming Lord Treasurer, he applied all his energies to a large and imaginative solution of the whole problem. He sought to rationalize the farming of taxes and the leasing of Crown lands, to reform the royal household, liberate agriculture from feudal restrictions, and abolish archaic dues in exchange for other forms of income whose full yield, or something like it, instead of a mere fraction, would come to the Crown. In 1610 Salisbury staked his political career on this great programme of

[26] Francis Bacon, *Works* (ed. Spedding), iii, p. 183.

reorganization. But he failed to carry it through. The 'courtiers', the 'officers' who lived on the 'waste', mobilized opposition, and the King, listening to them, and thinking 'not what he got but what he might get' out of the old, wasteful, irritant sources of revenue, refused to surrender them. Within two years of his failure, Salisbury died, out of favour with the King, completely unlamented, even insulted by the whole Court which he had sought to reform and, by reform, to save.[27]

After Salisbury, other reformers occasionally took up the cause. The most brilliant was Francis Bacon. He had been an enemy of Salisbury, but once Salisbury was dead he sang the same tune. He diagnosed the evil—no man, perhaps, diagnosed it so completely in all its forms and ultimate consequences—but he could do nothing to cure it except by royal permission, which was refused, and he was overthrown. After his fall, in the years of the great depression, even the Court took alarm, and a new reformer seemed to have obtained that permission. This was Lionel Cranfield, Earl of Middlesex, who set out to carry through some at least of Salisbury's proposals. But permission, if granted, was soon, and conspicuously withdrawn. Cranfield, like Bacon, was ruined by Court-faction, led from above by the royal favourite, the Duke of Buckingham, the universal manager and profiteer of all those marketable offices, benefices, sinecures, monopolies, patents, perquisites and titles which together constituted the nourishment of the Court. Thus when Buckingham was murdered and Strafford and Laud, the 'Puritans of the right', came to power, they inherited from him an utterly unreformed Court.[28]

[27] Public justice has never been done to Salisbury's programme of reform in 1608–12, although the 'Great Contract', which was only part of it, is well-known. The evidence of it is scattered among the official papers of the time. Of contemporaries, only Sir Walter Cope and Sir William Sanderson, both of whom had been employed in it, sought to make it known and understood, but neither Cope's *Apology for the Late Lord Treasurer* (which was given to the King in MS.) nor Sanderson's *Aulicus Coquinariae* was published at the time. Bishop Goodman and Sir Henry Wotton also appreciated it, but also did not publish their appreciation. See L. Pearsall Smith, *Life and Letters of Sir Henry Wotton* (London, 1907), vol. ii; Goodman, op. cit., i, pp. 36–42, 487–9.

[28] Bacon's projects are scattered through his writings which Spedding collected. One only has to compare his various proposals for reform of the court, the law, education, the Church, the Crown estates, etc., with the demands of the radical party in the 1640s, to see the truth of Gardiner's

Did they do anything to reform it? Ostensibly they did. 'The face of the court', as Mrs. Hutchinson wrote, 'was changed'. King Charles was outwardly frugal compared with his father: but such frugality, as we have seen in the case of Queen Elizabeth, was relatively insignificant. Laud and Strafford waged war on the corruption of the Court, whenever they perceived it; but they left the basic system untouched. Whenever we study that system we find that, in their time, its cost had not been reduced: it had grown. The greatest of Court feasts in Buckingham's days had been his own entertainment of the King in 1626, which had cost £4,000; the Earl of Newcastle, in 1634, went up to £15,000. An office which was sold for £5,000 in 1624 fetched £15,000 in 1640. Wardships, which had brought in £25,000 to the Crown when Salisbury had sought to abolish them in 1610, were made to yield £95,000 in 1640. And the proportion that ran to waste was no smaller. For every £100 which reached the Crown, at least £400 was taken from the subject. As Clarendon says, 'The envy and reproach came to the King, the profit to other men.'

Thus in 1640 the English Court, like the Spanish, was still unreformed. But what of the English economy? Here the parallel no longer holds. For in England there was not that absolute divorce between Crown and *arbitristas* that was so obvious in Spain. The early Stuart governments did not ignore matters of trade. They listened to the City of London. By their financial methods, whether deliberately or not, they encouraged the formation of capital, its investment in industry. There were limits of course to what they did: they did not satisfy the systematic mercantilist theorists; they paid less attention to the base of society than to its summit. Nevertheless, in many respects, they favoured or at least allowed a mercantilist policy. They sought to naturalize industrial processes; they sought to protect supplies of essential raw-materials; they sought to monopolize the herring-fisheries; they protected navigation; they preferred peace abroad and looked to their moat. The years of their rule saw the growth of English capitalism, sponsored by them, on a scale unknown before. Unfortunately such growth entailed dislocation, claimed victims; and when political crisis increased the dislocation and multiplied the victims, the stiff and

statement (in *Dict. Nat. Biog.*, s.v. Bacon) that his programme, if carried out, might have prevented the revolution. For Cranfield's work see R. H. Tawney, *Business and Politics under James I* (London, 1958).

weakened structure of government could no longer contain the mutinous forces which it had provoked.

For in 1640 the leaders of the Long Parliament did not seek—they did not need to seek—to reverse the economic policy of the Crown. They sought one thing only: to repair the administration. The Earl of Bedford as Lord Treasurer, John Pym as Chancellor of the Exchequer, intended to resume the frustrated work of Salisbury: to abolish monopolies, wardships, prerogative taxes, cut down the 'waste', and establish the Stuart Court on a more rational, less costly basis. Having done this, they would have continued the mercantilist policy of the Crown, perhaps extending it by redistribution of resources, rationalization of labour, at the base of society. They would have done for the English monarchy what Colbert would do for the French. All they required was that the English monarchy, like the French, would allow them to do it.

For of course monarchy itself was no obstacle. It is absurd to say that such a policy was impossible without revolution. It was no more impossible in 1641 than it had been in the days of Salisbury and Cranfield. We cannot assume that merely human obstacles—the irresponsibility of a Buckingham or a Charles I, the reckless obscurantism of a Strafford—are inherent historical necessities. But in fact these human obstacles did intervene. Had James I or Charles I had the intelligence of Queen Elizabeth or the docility of Louis XIII, the English *ancien régime* might have adapted itself to the new circumstances as peacefully in the seventeenth century as it would in the nineteenth. It was because they had neither, because their Court was never reformed, because they defended it, in its old form, to the last, because it remained, administratively and economically as well as aesthetically, 'the last Renaissance Court in Europe', that it ran into ultimate disaster: that the rational reformers were swept aside, that more radical men came forward and mobilized yet more radical passions than even they could control, and that in the end, amid the sacking of palaces, the shivering of statues and stained-glass windows, the screech of saws in ruined organ-lofts, this last of the great Renaissance Courts was mopped up, the royal aesthete was murdered, his spendid pictures were knocked down and sold, even the soaring gothic cathedrals were offered up for scrap.

So, in the 1640s, in war and revolution, the most obstinate and yet, given the political structure of England, the frailest of the

Renaissance monarchies went down. It did not go down before a new 'bourgeois' revolution. It did not even go down before an old 'mercantilist' revolution. Its enemies were not the 'bourgeoisie'—that bourgeoisie who, as a Puritan preacher complained, 'for a little trading and profit' would have had Christ, the Puritan soldiers, crucified and 'this great Barabbas at Windsor', the King, set free.[29] Nor were they the mercantilists. The ablest politicians among the Puritan rebels did indeed, once the republic was set up, adopt an aggressive mercantilist policy; but in this they simply resumed the old policy of the Crown and, on that account, were promptly attacked and overthrown by the same enemies, who accused them of betraying the revolution.[30] No, the triumphant enemies of the English Court were simply 'the country': that indeterminate, unpolitical, but highly sensitive miscellany of men who had mutinied not against the monarchy (they had long clung to monarchist beliefs) nor against economic archaism (it was they who were the archaists), but against the vast, oppressive, ever-extending apparatus of parasitic bureaucracy which had grown up around the throne and above the economy of England. These men were not politicians or economists, and when the Court had foundered under their blows, they soon found that they could neither govern nor prosper. In the end they abdicated. The old dynasty was restored, its new mercantilist policy resumed. But the restoration was not complete. The old abuses, which had already dissolved in war and revolution, were not restored, and, having gone, were easily legislated out of existence. In 1661 Salisbury's 'Great Contract', Bedford's excise, were at last achieved. The old prerogative courts—whose offence had been not so much their policy as their existence—were not revived. Charles II began his reign free at last from the inherited lumber of the Renaissance Court.

Such, as it seems to me, was 'the general crisis of the seven-

[29] The preacher was Hugh Peters, as quoted in *State Trials*, v (1), pp. 129–30.

[30] Those who regard the whole revolution as a bourgeois revolution on the strength of the mercantile policy of the Rump between 1651 and 1653 might well reflect (a) that this policy, of peace with Spain, navigation acts, and rivalry with Holland over fishery and trade, had been the policy of Charles I in the 1630s, and (b) that it was repudiated, emphatically and effectively, by those who had brought the revolution to a 'successful' issue—the Puritan Army—and only revived at the Restoration of the monarchy.

teenth century'. It was a crisis not of the constitution nor of the system of production, but of the State, or rather, of the relation of the State to society. Different countries found their way out of that crisis in different ways. In Spain the *ancien régime* survived: but it survived only as a disastrous, immobile burden on an impoverished country. Elsewhere, in Holland, France and England, the crisis marked the end of an era: the jettison of a top-heavy superstructure, the return to responsible, mercantilist policy. For by the seventeenth century the Renaissance Courts had grown so great, had consumed so much in 'waste', and had sent their multiplying suckers so deep into the body of society, that they could only flourish for a limited time, and in a time, too, of expanding general prosperity. When that prosperity failed, the monstrous parasite was bound to falter. In this sense, the depression of the 1620s is perhaps no less important, as a historical turning-point, than the depression of 1929: though a temporary economic failure, it marked a lasting political change. At all events, the princely Courts recognized it as their crisis. Some of them sought to reform themselves, to take physic and reduce their bulk. Their doctors pointed the way: it was then that the old city States, and particularly Venice, though now in decadence, became the admired model, first of Holland, then of England. And yet, asked the patient, was such reform possible, or even safe? Could a monarchy really be adapted to a pattern which so far had been dangerously republican? Is any political operation more difficult than the self-reduction of an established, powerful, privileged bureaucracy? In fact, the change was nowhere achieved without something of revolution. If it was limited in France, and Holland, that was partly because some of the combustible rubbish had already, in a previous revolution, been consumed. It was also because there had been some partial reform. In England there had been no such previous revolution, no such partial reform. There was also, under the early Stuarts, a fatal lack of political skill: instead of the genius of Richelieu, the suppleness of Mazarin, there was the irresponsibility of Buckingham, the violence of Strafford, the undeviating universal pedantry of Laud. In England therefore the storm of the mid-century, which blew throughout Europe, struck the most brittle, most overgrown, most rigid Court of all and brought it violently down.

IV

TREVOR-ROPER'S 'GENERAL CRISIS'
Symposium*

I: Roland Mousnier

IT is a great pleasure to read Professor H. R. Trevor-Roper's brilliant essay, so sparkling with intelligence. To reduce his rich and luxuriant elaborations to a few dry propositions is to run the risk of distorting his ideas. But in a brief comment, the risk must be taken. According to Trevor-Roper, between 1640 and 1660 Europe witnessed a series of political revolutions. Whether successful or not, they mark a watershed: on the one side is the Renaissance and on the other the Age of Enlightenment. Indeed these revolutions are themselves the apogee of a prolonged crisis in the structure of society. The Renaissance State, with its Court and its bureaucratic apparatus of officials remunerated in part by their own hands, laid too heavy a burden on society. This burden became unbearable during the economic recession of the seventeenth century, when different social groups tried to throw it off through revolt and revolution. The *Stände* rose against the Court. The Court not only tried to quell the rebellions, but also to suppress their cause by adjusting through mercantilism the levies of the bureaucrats to the resources of the country.

Let us examine the validity of these suggestions in the case of France.

Now Trevor-Roper has grasped a vital point: that there was a general crisis in the seventeenth century. I have discussed this

* From no. 18 (1960). Because of shortage of space, not all the contributions to the original Symposium are reprinted here.

crisis in various books and articles published since 1945; and as far back as 1953, I devoted the second part (208 pages) of the fourth volume of the *Histoire Générale des Civilisations* (3rd edn., Paris, 1961) to the European crisis of the seventeenth century.

How far is it true that the revolts of the seventeenth century and the revolution of the Fronde can be interpreted in France as a rising of the country against the Court and against the bureaucratic apparatus of the State? It is clear that the office-holders provoked discontent. Throughout the troubles, nobles and bourgeois complained of the pullulation of office-holders and of the way they drained the public revenues. But they complained just as loudly of the excessive price of offices and the difficulty of acquiring them. They regarded offices as an evil, but strove to lay hands on one. However it must be pointed out that the office-holders helped to provoke the revolts and also played an outstanding part in the attempted revolution of the Fronde. And this seems to me to go directly against the theory of Trevor-Roper.

The part played in the Fronde by the Parlements and by certain groups of office-holders is already well known.[1] In a recent article[2] and more lately I have analysed the movements of peasant revolt, so numerous in France, from about 1625 until the Fronde and beyond. Broadly speaking, this is what seems to have happened in most cases: the landlords, whether gentry or royal officials or municipal magistrates, incited the peasants not to pay the *tailles* or the numerous new taxes imposed by the Government, because if the peasants paid these royal taxes they would be unable to pay their feudal dues or their rents, and also because it was a lord's duty to protect his peasants; the peasants then violently drove off the bailiffs with their warrants or the agents of the tax-farmers; the Government sent *commissaires* to obtain payment; officials and gentry stirred up the peasantry; gentry joined together to help their peasants to resist; in the towns, the royal officials and the *échevins* provoked risings among the urban population to help the peasants by paralysing the movements of the royal *commissaires*;

[1] R. Mousnier, 'Recherches sur les Syndicats d'officiers pendant la Fronde. Trésoriers généraux de France et Elus dans la Révolution', *XVIIe Siècle* (Bulletin de la Société d'Etude du XVIIe Siècle), no. 42 (1959); 'Quelques raisons de la Fronde. Les Causes des journées révolutionnaires parisiennes de 1648', ibid., no. 2 (1949).

[2] R. Mousnier, 'Recherches sur les soulèvements populaires en France avant la Fronde', *Revue d'histoire moderne et contemporaine*, v (1958).

then, as happened with the *Croquants* of Villefranche-de-Rouergue in 1643 and with other movements, the peasants sent some of their men into the towns; or the royal officials made the peasants come from their *seigneuries* and make up bands or companies of insurgents, as in Paris during the Fronde, in Aix and elsewhere; or sometimes the peasants themselves seized a town. Thus in most cases we do not find a revolt of the country against an oppressive public service, but the revolt of a public service which considered itself oppressed and which dragged in its wake those social groups over which the structure of society gave it influence. Is not this exactly the opposite of what Trevor-Roper thinks?

What did the office-holders complain of? *That they contributed too much to the expenses of the State*; that they were being deprived of their power. It is a theoretical concept to think of this bureaucratic structure of office-holders in terms of pure gain. Sometimes the King made new offices so that existing office-holders would have to buy them up in order to keep away eventual competitors, or would have to pay for their suppression. Sometimes the King decreed an increase in the salaries and fees of officials, but only in return for a cash sum which constituted the capital of which these benefits were merely the interest. The officials often had to borrow the money at interest from others, in which case the whole operation merely turned them into intermediaries in the movement of money, without any personal benefit accruing.[3] Moreover after 1640 the King gradually reduced the salaries and many of the fees of his officials, who now were only getting a minute interest or none at all, in return for a capital investment which was immobilized, or lost. The *Elus*, who were finance officers, alleged in 1648 that they had paid over 200 million *livres* since 1624, including 60 million paid since 1640 'for confirmation of an imaginary right or grant of a fictitious increment'.[4] The officials considered themselves robbed.

On the other hand, in the throes of the Thirty Years' War the Government found their administrative routine too slow. It accused them of favouring in the assessment of taxes their lessees and sharecroppers and those of their relatives, associates and friends, and of causing deficiencies by shifting the burden on to others. The Government farmed out to *traitants* or *partisans*, not

[3] R. Mousnier, *La Vénalité des Offices en France sous Henri IV et Louis XIII* (Rouen, 1945). See pp. 365–86.

[4] See n. 1.

only the *aides*, but also the direct taxes such as the *tailles*. It handed over to *commissaires*, of whom the most important were the *intendants*, not only the supervision of officials, but also often the execution of their duties.[5] At the same time, when dealing with corporate bodies of officials the royal Government increasingly ignored the *remontrances* which traditionally they were in duty bound to present to the King for the better ordering of the service. Wounded in their honour, their prestige and their interests, the officials revolted. Are Trevor-Roper's views really in keeping with these facts?

Can one say that this bureaucratic apparatus of officers imposed an unbearable burden on the country? Trevor-Roper should have distinguished more clearly between the great officers of the Crown and the courtiers, some of whom became very rich thanks to the privileges of their offices or their relations with tax-farmers, and those officials who were not of the Court but who nevertheless held a high rank in society and exercised important functions: members of the sovereign courts (Parlements, *Chambres des Comptes, Cours des Aides, Grand Conseil*); officials of the *Présidiaux*, the *baillages* and the *senéchaussées*; *Trésoriers Généraux de France, Elus*, etc. In spite of what Trevor-Roper believes, these officials were on the whole men of simple tastes, who had nothing to do with the opulent way of life of princes and a handful of great courtiers. Plain practitioners learned in the law and in the rules of their profession, rarely humanists and with little interest in the arts, save perhaps at the third generation,[6] they made their money less as office-holders than as landowners and feudal lords, as moneylenders and creditors of peasants and artisans. Their salaries and fees, the fortunes built up by the courtiers, could have upset the balance neither of the budget nor of society. In seventeenth-century France the expenses of the Court never represented more than a small fraction of the expenses of the State. The same applies to the salaries and fees of the office-holders. The sums levied by officials in the form of judicial bribes, fees, *taxes de finances*, do not

[5] R. Mousnier, 'Etat et commissaire. Recherches sur la création des Intendants des provinces (1634–1648)', *Forschungen zu Staat und Verfassung: Festgabe für Fritz Hartung* (Berlin, 1958).

[6] See ' "Serviteurs du Roi". Quelques aspects de la fonction publique dans la société française du XVIIe siècle' (Etudes sous la direction de R. Mousnier), *XVIIe Siècle*, nos. 42–43 (1959).

strike me as affecting more than a modest part of the resources of the King's subjects. The great expenses of the State, the heavy burdens on the unprivileged were those of the army and of war, pay, munitions and billeting for the troops. It would therefore be necessary to prove that these huge armies, these long wars, were merely of interest to the Court, and not to the nation, and this would be a difficult task.

Would it be possible, however, to say that in fact this opposition on the part of the office-holders was an aspect of the struggle of the country against the Court? On the one hand there were the officials, owners of their offices, irremovable, given security of tenure by the *Paulette*, landowners and often feudal lords in the district where they practised, linked with many local families, themselves with local roots, convinced that if office demanded fidelity to the King, it required them equally faithfully to serve justice and protect the rights of the King's subjects; they were thus simultaneously notables representing the districts and provinces in their dealings with the King, and instruments of the royal will. On the other hand there were the *commissaires* used by his Council, his Household, his Court. Is it not then a struggle of officials against the Court rather than (as in Trevor-Roper's view) of the country against the Court and its bureaucratic apparatus?

But one cannot simplify things in this way. The royal *commissaires* came from the same social stratum as the royal officials. A *maître des requêtes* was also an official. Before becoming one he might have been *conseiller au Parlement*. Many *conseillers d'Etat* came from the sovereign courts. The King's *commissaire* would have been powerless in the provinces if he had not always found among the officials, judges to help him pass judgement, finance officers to help him with their technical skill, and in the country barristers to act as Public Prosecutors. Nor must we forget that it is at Court that the worst revolts occurred. It was when magnates such as Monsieur, the King's brother, or Condé, a prince of the blood royal, withdrew from the Court and rallied their supporters, that provincial risings took a particularly serious turn. Is it not a little artificial to oppose the Court and the rest of the country? Trevor-Roper could obviously answer that what matters is not so much the origins of the *commissaires* and those who helped them as their obedience to the will of the King, in his Council, in his Court.

But what did all their followers want? Monsieur and Condé

wanted to turn absolute monarchy to their own ends. They wanted an aristocratic monarchy, not a *Ständestaat*. Other princes and other magnates dreamed of a quasi-independence in their provinces and in their *seigneuries*, of a return to the French institutions of the time of Hugh Capet 'and better still if possible'. They were followed by many feudal lords, many towns, many provinces, who looked back with regret to their days of autonomy or independence, and feared their increasing subjection. As contemporaries saw very clearly, in most of France it was undoubtedly a struggle of feudal elements against the State.[7] It was less an opposition between the country and the Court, than between what remained feudal in society and what was new, *étatique*, progressive, 'modern' in the King's Council and its dependent organs.[8] Since the time of Henry IV, it was lawyers and no longer landed gentry who formed the majority in the King's Council. If we ask to what extent the Council was part of the Court we raise yet another question: to what extent had society ceased to be feudal and become penetrated by commercial capitalism?[9] This brings us back again to the economic aspect of the problem.

It is doubtful whether one can say that mercantilism represented an attempt to adapt the capacity of the country to support the burdens imposed by the bureaucratic apparatus of officials. Mercantilism was first and foremost a weapon in the struggle against the foreigner, a tool of war and of foreign policy. Already a royal tendency in the days of Louis XI, it became doctrine under Chancellor Duprat in the reign of Francis I. It was taken up once more by the States General of 1576 during the great inflation in the latter half of the wars of religion. In the seventeenth century, Laffemas, Richelieu, Colbert saw it as a means of ensuring French hegemony. The great economic recession of the seventeenth century made it more necessary, without it appearing to be any more closely tied to internal politics.

Nor does it seem that the revolts and the revolutionary attempt

[7] R. Mousnier, 'Comment les Français voyaient la Constitution', ibid., nos. 25–26 (1955).

[8] R. Mousnier, 'Le Conseil du Roi, de la mort de Henri IV au gouvernement personnel de Louis XIV', *Etudes d'Histoire moderne et contemporaine* (publ. by 'La Société d'histoire moderne'), i (1947).

[9] R. Mousnier, 'L'Opposition politique bourgeoise à la fin du XVIe siècle et au debut du XVIIe. L'Oeuvre de Louis Turquet de Mayerne', *Revue Historique*, ccxiii (1955).

of the Fronde mark any sort of watershed in France. Political and social problems are not essentially different before and after. In their nature, they do not seem to change. All that happened was that, for a while, the King was the victor. By the end of the century a process of social change was under way, but this had no connection with the revolts and revolutions of the mid-century. The wars of religion of 1572–98 were certainly of greater importance for France. For these conflicts represent a revolt against the office-holders on the part of those social groups who were thwarted of office, such as barristers, doctors, *procureurs fiscaux*, etc. The victory of Henry IV was, in part, a victory of those in office.[10] It is perhaps to the wars of religion that Trevor-Roper's ideas would best apply.

He appreciates, though perhaps without attaching sufficient importance to it, the strain imposed by the Thirty Years' War, coinciding as it did with the great economic recession of the century. It is a pity that he pays no attention to the increase, during the seventeenth century, in the number of bad harvests, of subsistence crises, of famines, of plagues, which killed off artisans and peasants, and begot a long series of cumulative economic crises. They were so numerous in the seventeenth century that some historians have thought to ascribe them to a change in the climate, which is improbable.[11] After the plague of 1629–30 two thirds of the kingdom was in a state of endemic economic and social distress. In these circumstances it is understandable that the struggle between royal taxes and feudal dues should have worsened, that peasants and artisans should have been more willing to listen to incitements to rid themselves of the agents of the tax-farmers, or the bailiffs with their warrants. A number of revolts coincide with price rises due to subsistence crises.[12] Trevor-Roper would do well to look into these matters.

Trevor-Roper is aware that the use of the word 'crisis' for the seventeenth century would be less justified if we considered only its political and social aspects. A great crisis of ideas and feeling, a revolution in the manner of thinking and of understanding the

[10] Henri Drouot, *Mayenne et la Bourgogne, Etude sur la Ligue* (1587–96) (Thèse de Lettres, Sorbonne, 1937), 2 vols.

[11] E. Leroy-Ladurie, 'Climat et récoltes aux XVIIe et XVIIIe siècles', *Annales E.S.C.*, xve année (1960).

[12] R. Mousnier, 'Etudes sur la population de la France au XVIIe siècle', *XVIIe Siècle*, no. 16 (1952).

Universe, almost an intellectual mutation took place at that time in Europe. It marks the end of Aristotelianism, the triumph of quantitative rationalism, of the notion of mathematical function, of experimental rationalism, with Descartes, the *Mécanistes* and Newton; it is present in the 'Catholic Renaissance' and the mystical movement, in all that the words classical and baroque signify, in the growth of witchcraft, and in so many other aspects which would need to be studied, if we really want to talk of the crisis of the seventeenth century. None of these matters is totally divorced from politics. Is it pure chance that in France the kings were 'classical' in taste, while the rebel princes favoured the *libertins* and the baroque?

If we stick strictly to Trevor-Roper's brief, his point of departure is a sound one: the political crisis of the seventeenth century represents a crisis in the relations between the State and society. His attempt at synthesis seems to me to rest on inadequate analysis, but there is considerable merit in having presented the problem as a whole. What emerges is the necessity, which I pointed to in 1958,[13] of studying afresh the revolts and revolutions in seventeenth-century Europe, through a rigorous social analysis of these movements, which in turn implies a study in depth of social structures, and methodical comparisons with the social structures and the revolts of the preceding and following centuries.

II: J. H. Elliott

IN his dazzling and ingenious interpretation of the crisis of the seventeenth century, Professor Trevor-Roper calls it 'not merely a constitutional crisis, nor a crisis of economic production' but 'a crisis in the relations between society and the State'. In the context, the point is well worth making, but it does not take us very much farther, for what revolution does not represent a 'crisis in the relations between society and the State'? The real problem is to discover what caused the divorce between the two, and it is in Trevor-Roper's answer to this problem that the main interest of his interpretation lies. The clue, he suggests, is to be found in the

[13] See n. 2.

expansion and the wastefulness of a parasitic State apparatus; in the size and cost of the Court.

It may be suspected that Trevor-Roper's placing of the problem of the Court at the centre of the revolutionary crisis was originally inspired by his inquiries into the origins of the English Civil War. Can the idea be satisfactorily carried across the Channel and still retain such validity as it may have for England? Can it, for instance, help the historian of seventeenth-century Spain to understand the Catalan and Portuguese revolutions—for presumably the object of the exercise is to make these and other revolutions comprehensible? 'These days are days of shaking', and even if Catalonia and Portugal virtually disappear from the scene after the first page, we hope by the last to have a better understanding of the seismic movements that shook them.

Trevor-Roper's thesis, applied to Spain, would seem to be that the Court and the State apparatus had become grossly top-heavy by the end of Philip III's reign; that Olivares tried, but failed, to introduce the reforms of the *arbitristas*; that (from this point the stages of the argument have to be reconstructed by reference to France, England and the United Provinces) as the result of his failure, 'the tension between Court and country grew, and the "revolutionary situation" of the 1620s and 1630s developed'; and that the 'revolutionary situation' failed to develop into actual revolution in Castile because it lacked the organs of effective protest, but did lead to revolution in Catalonia and Portugal, presumably because they did possess such organs.

If this summary represents his argument correctly, it raises two important questions. First, how far did the Court and the State apparatus absorb the royal revenues and divert the national wealth into unproductive channels? Second, how far is the problem of an unreformed Court really the 'cry of the country' from 1620 to 1640, and in particular the cry of the Catalans and the Portuguese?

The first of these questions—as to the real cost of the Court to the country—is virtually unanswerable and is likely to remain so, for, as Trevor-Roper points out, we see only the sun-lit tip of the submerged iceberg. Even in the ostentatious reign of Philip III, however, this is rather less impressive than one might have imagined. If we take the year 1608 as being reasonably representative for the reign of Philip III, we find that ordinary expenditure for the first ten months of the year is expected to be rather over

7 million ducats.[14] Of these 7 million, some 1½ are reserved for miscellaneous expenses and the payment of interest on the Crown's outstanding debts, and another 1½ for the expenses of the Court and the salaries of officials. What happens to the remaining 4 million ducats? They are all devoted to military and naval expenditure.

It is, I think, the proportion of revenues devoted to military purposes—even in the 'peaceful' reign of Philip III—rather than to the expenses of Court and government, which is likely to strike anyone who looks at the papers of the Council of Finance. It is, of course, true that real expenditure on the Court always exceeded the anticipated expenditure, since Philip III bestowed an enormous number of pensions and *mercedes* which do not appear in the budget figures. Between 1 January 1619 and 1 December 1620, for instance, he gave away something like 400,000 ducats in pensions and *ayudas de costa*, besides many other unrecorded gifts.[15] Yet military expenditure was just as likely as Court expenditure to outrun the estimated provisions, as the Council of Finance was always lamenting.

If the visible cost of Court and government is well under half, and often nearer a quarter, the cost of military and naval preparations, what of the relative *invisible* costs to the national economy? In discussing the burden of the Court, Trevor-Roper is presumably thinking in particular of the diversion of national resources away from economically productive channels into the stagnant backwater of office in Church and State. Here we are hampered by the lack of any adequate study of the sale of offices in Spain, but from Mr. K. W. Swart's comparative study of the sale of offices in the seventeenth century, it would seem that offices in Spain were not created and sold on quite the same scale as in France, and that there was a good deal less willingness to buy.[16] My own feeling is that, to explain the diversion of money away from economically productive fields of investment, we must look not so much to the sale of offices as to the crippling difficulties that attended industrial development and commercial expansion in Castile, and to the

[14] A(rchivo) G(eneral de) S(imancas) Hacienda leg(ajo). 345–474 f. 405. *Relación*, 22 Dec. 1607.

[15] AGS Hacienda leg. 414–573 *Relación de . . . mercedes* (1621).

[16] K. W. Swart, *Sale of Offices in the Seventeenth Century* (The Hague, 1949), chap. 2.

growth of the highly elaborate system of *censos* and *juros* which, unlike trade and industry, provided a safe form of investment and assured rates of interest. In fact, we are driven back again to the appallingly expensive foreign policy of the sixteenth-century rulers of Spain—a foreign policy which led to heavy taxes falling on the most productive members of the community, and to the creation of a vast national debt, in which it was easy and profitable to invest.

Naturally, nobody would dispute the enormous weight of a top-heavy bureaucracy on Castile. This is one of the most frequent complaints of the Spanish *arbitristas*. But we must also remember the burden imposed by Castile's military commitments. One of the principal reasons for the depopulation of Castilian villages must be sought in the activities of the recruiting sergeant and the quartermaster, and I should hesitate to put the scourge of billeting below the plague of officers among the many misfortunes that dogged seventeenth-century societies.

In spite of its intolerable burdens, Castile did not revolt. Trevor-Roper attributes this, with a good deal of justice, to the lack of 'effective organs of protest' in Castile. But let us now turn to the two parts of the peninsula which *did* revolt—Catalonia and Portugal. How far was the 'general grievance against which they rebelled' the 'character and cost of the State'? Catalans who visited Madrid in the reign of Philip III had no illusions about the 'character' of the State, and wrote home the most devastating accounts of the extravagance and corruption of life at Court. The Catalans could well afford to be critical of the ways of the Court, since they themselves were excluded from all the delights traditionally associated with living in the royal presence. This ambivalent attitude—half hatred, half jealousy—fits well enough into Trevor-Roper's general framework. But it is difficult to see that the Catalans or the Portuguese had any real cause for complaint about the *cost* of the State, at least to themselves. *They* did not pay for Castile's large bureaucracy or for the lavish Court festivities. They did not even pay for the cost of their own defence, for (like the English gentry?) they were not over-taxed but under-taxed—at least in relation to Castile. Between 1599 and 1640 the King received from the Catalan Cortes one subsidy of 1 million ducats, and no other taxes except ecclesiastical dues and a number of minor taxes which did not even suffice to cover the costs of the small viceregal administration in the Principality. Castile, over the same forty years, was paying over 6 million ducats *a year* to the Crown in secular taxes alone. Nor was money raised in Catalonia by the sale of offices, for the Crown could neither create nor sell offices in the Principality. As a result, the royal administration in Catalonia consisted of only a handful of officials, and there simply did not exist a vast parasitic bureaucracy like the one that lay so heavy on Castile.

We have, then, revolutions in two provinces which admittedly possess effective organs of protest, but which—since the cost of Court and bureaucracy is hardly any concern of theirs—do not seem, on the Trevor-Roper principle, to have much to protest about. Why, then, do they revolt? For the answer to this, we must look primarily to the policies of Olivares. Trevor-Roper rightly points to the 'puritanical' character of Olivares's reforming movement in the 1620s—his anxiety to curb the extravagance of the Court, and cut down on the multitude of *mercedes* and offices so lavishly bestowed by the profligate régime that preceded his own. Yet the problem of the Court, serious as it was, can hardly be considered the Conde Duque's principal anxiety. His real problem was the high cost of war. With the expiry of the truce with the Dutch in 1621, the annual provision for the Flanders Army was raised from 1½ to 3½ million ducats, and the sum earmarked for the Atlantic fleet went up to 1 million.[17] And this was only the beginning. It was primarily the needs of defence and the cost of war which imposed on Olivares the urgent need for reform; and this reform necessarily entailed much more than tinkering with the Court or reducing the number of offices in Castile. It demanded a radical reorganization of the fiscal system within the Spanish Monarchy.

It does not, therefore, seem to me that, even if Olivares had succeeded in doing what Richelieu did in the way of household reform, he would have gone very far towards solving his fundamental problem—that of defence (a problem, incidentally, in which the shortage of manpower was to loom as large as the shortage of money). It was his determination to solve this problem which led him to devise schemes for the more effective exploitation of the resources of the Crown of Aragon and Portugal, and these schemes eventually brought him into conflict with the Catalans and the Portuguese. No doubt the knowledge that the Court was still

[17] AGS Hacienda leg. 414–573 f. 303 *Consulta*, 10 Dec. 1621.

spending lavishly on *fiestas* strengthened their resolve to refuse payment, but I do not believe that 'the character and cost of the State', in the sense used by Trevor-Roper, figured very prominently in their calculations. At the time of their revolutions, the apparatus of the State still lay lightly on them, and such money as had been squeezed out of them was being used, not to subsidize the Court, but to improve the very inadequate defences of their own territory. Their principal purpose in rebelling was to escape the imminent threat to their national identities and to their economic resources implied in the Conde Duque's demands that they should play a fuller part in the war.

While, then, Trevor-Roper has performed a valuable service in drawing attention to the size and cost of the State apparatus, this seems to be of use mainly in explaining the troubles of the part of Spain which did *not* rebel—Castile. And even here it is very doubtful whether it should be allowed to occupy the centre of the stage, for Court extravagance and the inflation of the bureaucracy would hardly seem to rank in the same class among the causes of Castile's decline as the burden imposed on the Castilian economy and Castilian society by a century of Habsburg wars. Indeed, the proliferation of offices is best regarded, alongside the rise of taxation or the development of *juros*, as one among the many natural consequences of that intolerable burden. To say simply that 'war aggravates' the problem of the growth of a parasitic bureaucracy is surely rather a remarkable understatement. Admittedly, 'the sixteenth-century wars had led to no such revolutions' but they had bequeathed a terrible inheritance to the seventeenth century; and, on top of this, seventeenth-century wars were fought on a very different scale. Philip II's army consisted of perhaps 40,000 men, while Philip IV's was probably at least twice as large. This new scale of warfare created problems of an entirely new magnitude and order for the rulers of seventeenth-century States. It placed an additional enormous burden on economies already subjected to heavy strain.

How was the strain to be eased? By relating the State's life, as Trevor-Roper says, to its means of livelihood. This meant a programme of austerity and of 'puritanical' reforms; it meant more rational economic policies. But it also meant extending the power of the King over his subjects, in order to draw on the resources of provinces and of social classes hitherto under-taxed or exempt.

This was the acid test that faced seventeenth-century ministers. Richelieu may perhaps have met with rather more success than Olivares in his household reforms, but can this really have made any significant difference to the relative fortunes of France and Spain? The most obvious difference stems from the fact that Olivares's fiscal demands provoked revolution first. Otherwise, it is the similarities, not the differences, that impress. Both Richelieu and Olivares came to power with the best intentions of putting their own house in order; these intentions were frustrated by the exigencies of war; both were compelled by the cost of the war effort to tighten their grip on the resources of their States, and, in so doing, *they unwittingly precipitated revolution.* This, I believe, is the real moral of the story. The reforming movement of the 1620s, so far from showing the way of escape from revolution, in fact hastened its approach, because real reform included a fiscal, constitutional and social reorganization so radical that it inevitably brought the power of the Crown into head-on collision with those who had hitherto enjoyed special liberties and immunities. The essential clue to the revolutionary situation of the 1640s is, I suspect, to be found in the determination of governments to exercise fuller control over their States without yet having the administrative means or fiscal resources to ensure obedience to their will; and that determination sprang in the first instance from something which could not be gainsaid and brooked no delay—the imperious demands of war.

III: H. R. Trevor-Roper

IN some ways, in my essay, I have doubtless sacrificed clarity to brevity. Let me try to reverse the process by some further explanations. First, let me make it clear that by the words 'office' and 'Court' I have never meant only the offices directly under the Crown, or the Court in its narrow sense, as the group of metropolitan officials and courtiers around the sovereign. By 'office' I mean all the offices, metropolitan and local, which formed the bureaucratic machine of government, including offices in the law and the State-Church; and by 'Court' I mean the sum of such offices. Consequently any reform of the system was not merely 'household reform', it was social reform. Secondly, when writing of the cost to society of such offices, I am not referring merely to the cost paid by the Crown out of taxes but to the whole cost of maintaining this apparatus, the greater part of which fell not on the Crown but directly upon the country. I think that I may have made this latter point more clearly than the former, but it may be that I did not make either of them clearly enough. If they are made, a significant change in emphasis follows. For instance, it could be argued that in England in the 1630s the cost of the Court, in the narrow sense of the word, was reduced; but in the wider sense, in which I used it, I believe that it can be shown to have risen.

The same distinction must be made in Spain. Mr. Elliott quotes Mr. K. W. Swart's view that offices were not created and sold in Spain on the same scale as in France. This may be so—although until someone gives as much attention to Spain as M. Mousnier has done to France, I would prefer to suspend judgement. But even if it is so, is creation and sale by the Crown a sufficient criterion, and does Mr. Swart use 'office' in the same wide sense as I do? I believe that it is a good rule that the foot knows where the shoe pinches, and the literature of complaint shows every sign of multiplication of office in the reigns of Philip III and Philip IV. These offices may not all have been sold by the Crown, but if they (or their reversions, which was perhaps more usual in Spain) were sold from person to person, the effect upon society would be the same. So in 1619 Philip III was urged to abolish, as a burden to society, the 100 *receptores* created six years earlier, even though that should mean repaying the price at which they had bought their offices. In 1622 Philip IV, in his brief reforming period, declared that since an excessive number of offices is pernicious in the State ('most of them being sold, and the officers having to make up the price they have paid'), and since a great number of *escribanos* is prejudicial to society ('and the number at present is excessive, and grows daily') the number of *alguaciles, procuradores*, and *escribanos* in Castile must be reduced to one-third, and recruitment must be discouraged by various means. Such demands are regular in Spain; they are repeated in the submissions of the Cortes, the *consultas* of the Councils, the programmes of the *arbitristas*, the letters of statesmen; they were officially granted in the famous *Capítulos de Reformación* of 1623; but their constant repetition thereafter shows how ineffective were the measures taken to satisfy them.[18]

Moreover, whatever the case of lay offices, it is certain that offices in the Church grew enormously. Socially, superfluous idle monks and friars had exactly the same effect as superfluous, parasitic officials, and in this sector Spain probably suffered more than France. Philip III and the Duke of Lerma were praised by devout writers for their foundations and privileges (Lerma alone founded eleven monasteries as well as other *obras pias*), and those years were praised as a revival of 'the golden age of St. Jerome'; and yet all the time Philip III and Philip IV were being repeatedly begged to reduce these foundations, which contained many persons 'rather fleeing from necessity to the delights of indolence than moved by devotion'. Thus, using 'office' in the wide sense, as I have used it, it does not seem to me that Spain was less burdened than other western monarchies. As Gondomar wrote to Philip III, the monarchy was imperilled by 'two powerful enemies: first, all the princes of the world, and secondly, all us officers and courtiers who serve your Majesty (*todos los ministros y criados que servimos a V. Magd.*)'.[19]

The point about the Church as a department of State is important and I regret that I did not express myself more fully. It seems to me that in the sixteenth and seventeenth centuries the Church should be regarded, sociologically, as an element in the bureaucratic structure. The Reformation movement, Catholic as well as Protestant, was in many respects a revolt against the papal 'court' in the widest sense: the indecent, costly, and infinitely multiplied personnel, mainly of the regular orders, which had overgrown the working episcopal and parish structure. One only has to read the records of the Council of Trent to see this: the exclusion of the Protestants from that assembly merely shows that, socially, Catholic demands were identical. The difference is that, in Catholic countries, such demands were ultimately defeated: the 'Catholic Reform' may have been a moral and spiritual reform, but structurally it was a positive aggravation. On the other hand this

[18] Archivo Histórico Español, *Colección de Documentos Inéditos para la Historia de España y de sus Indias*, vol. v (Madrid, 1932), pp. 28, 381, etc. *Actas de las Cortes de Castilla*, vol. xxii, pp. 434, etc.

[19] *Correspondencia Oficial de D. Diego Sarmiento de Acuña, Conde de Gondomar*, ed. A. Ballesteros y Beretta (*Documentos Inéditos para la Historia de España*), vol. ii (Madrid, 1943), p. 146.

aggravated clerical bureaucracy could also, if it were reanimated, be made socially palliative, and this is what happened in Catholic countries after the Counter-Reformation. The new orders then created may on the one hand have doubled and trebled the burden of 'the Court' upon society, but, on the other hand, by evangelization, they reconciled society to the burden which they increased. They also physically strengthened the Court. It was partly for this reason, I suspect, that in the Mediterranean countries the Court was able to survive and stifle the forces of change, so that Queen Henrietta Maria could regard Popery, and Italian princes could regard the Jesuits, as the sole internal preservative of monarchy. It was partly for this reason, also, that I described the English Court as the most 'brittle' of all. There the oppressive class of 'courtiers', 'monopolists', lawyers who composed 'the Court' lacked the massive support of the preaching orders. The English friars, the lecturers, were on the other side. Hence, in part, the relative fragility of the English Court. It lacked the costly, but also effective outworks which the Counter-Reformation was able to build up around the Catholic thrones.

I agree with Mr. Elliott that the final strain, perhaps even the greatest strain, was war. But can one separate the impact and burden of war from the form of the society which sustains it? In the arguments in the Spanish Council of State before 1621, those who advocated a renewal of war against the Netherlands regularly appealed to a social fact: the fact that whereas the Dutch had constantly gained strength and wealth throughout the years of peace, the Spanish economy, even in peace, had as constantly declined; and this decline, they admitted, was due to social, structural reasons. War to these men was an expedient—a desperate, and as it proved, a fatal expedient—to remedy a disease which was already perceptible in peacetime. Although clearly there are many factors to consider, I would still prefer to say that in the monarchies of western Europe there was a structural crisis which was general, although the transition from structural crisis to revolution, which is not natural or inevitable but *requires* the intervention of a political event, was effected here by war, there without it.

Moreover, there is a further point to be made about war and structure. Since my article was published, the late J. Vicens Vives published the communication he proposed to make to the Eleventh

International Historical Congress at Stockholm.[20] In this he argued that the European Renaissance monarchies, as I have defined them, were created by and for the necessities of war. In other words, it was in order to make war and survive the burden of war, that they developed their peculiar social structure. But if this is so, and if war in fact imposed too great a strain upon them, then it follows not that war was an unexpected burden to them, but that their social structure was inadequate within their own terms of reference. And if war created the burden of the Renaissance Courts, equally it developed and overdeveloped that burden. M. Mousnier, in his great work *La Vénalité des Offices sous Henri IV et Louis XIII*, has shown how the French Government, again and again, considered reform of that venality of office which was the basic mechanism of the monarchy, but on each occasion, faced by the threat of war, postponed its projects and, instead of reforming, positively strengthened the system. Richelieu at first (like Olivares in Spain) sought to combine war and reform, but in the end (again like Olivares) sacrificed reform to war. Marillac would have sacrificed war to reform. In both countries, we may say that war not only created but extended the system, until not war but its own weight overwhelmed it.

At one point I evidently over-simplified my argument, and I regret that, in the cause of brevity, I omitted two paragraphs which would perhaps have clarified it. This passage concerned the point, or rather the social area, within which the opposite pressures of 'Court' and 'country' met. By excessive economy I have here exposed myself, as I believe, to misunderstanding by M. Mousnier. He points out that in many cases, and particularly in the French Fronde, the antithesis of Court *v.* country is not at all clear, and seems to ask me in which category, 'Court' or 'country', I place the French Parlements. But this is precisely what cannot be done. If Court and country were absolutely separable, then, I submit, there would not have been a social crisis. Social crises are caused not by the clear-cut opposition of mutually exclusive interests but by the tug-of-war of opposite interests *within one body*. Figuratively, they are to be represented not by a clean split, but by an untidy inward crumbling: the result of complex pressures on a complex body.

[20] J. Vicens Vives, 'Estructura administrativa estatal en los siglos XVI y XVII', *XIe Congrès International des Sciences Historiques* (Stockholm, 1960), Rapports iv.

And this complexity is caused by the complexity of human interests. 'Court' and 'country' in the seventeenth century, like bureaucrats and tax-payers, or producers and consumers today, constantly overlap. A man feels himself part of the 'country', a tax-payer, in one respect, and then discovers that, in another hitherto forgotten respect, he too is of 'the Court', dependent on taxes. The history of all revolutions is full of such painful discoveries, leading occasionally to painful apostasies. Sometimes they prevent revolution from breaking out; sometimes, when it has broken out, they entangle its course, making it bloody and indecisive: instead of performing a neat, surgical operation upon society, men find themselves hacking blindly among unpredicted organs. It is not only in the Fronde that one sees this. The English Parliament, which represented many of the grievances of the country, consisted also of 'officials' with a vested interest in the system against which they complained. Even the Spanish Cortes were similarly divided; the representatives of the towns might be mere functionaries, 'courtiers', aristocrats, but they did also, at times, represent 'country' grievances. The spokesmen of a society in crisis represent not its separate compartments, but its inmost contradictions.

M. Mousnier remarks that the general crisis of the seventeenth century was a crisis of ideas as well as of structure. Of course I agree with him. But to embark on this topic would be another task and any summary might prove grossly simplified. So I will only say that whereas I believe that experimental science, mysticism and the witch-craze can all be related to the social and structural revolution, I do not believe that they can be equated with any single social force or party in that revolution. I believe that here too they are to be related rather to the formation or disintegration of the Church-State than to any particular interest which contributed to either process. I believe that the sociologists who (for instance) equate experimental science with Puritan opposition are guilty of over-simplification only a little less gross than those who equate the witch-cult with Protestantism. I hope I may some time say something on this subject, but not here.

Finally, a point made by Mr. Elliott. I quoted contemporaries to illustrate the sense of universal revolution, and those contemporaries included, in their catalogues, Catalonia and Portugal. But I did not myself pursue the cases of Catalonia and Portugal because I do not consider them to be comparable. In Catalonia and Portugal local separatism and particular forces exploited the weakness of Castile; but it is the structural weakness of the Castilian Crown, not the forces which exploited it, which is relevant to my analysis. A better comparison is between Catalonia and Portugal on the one hand and Scotland on the other: Scotland, which I also omitted, as largely irrelevant, from my analysis.

For of course no one would suggest that the crisis of society in the seventeenth century was *only* a social crisis: many other stresses were involved in it. In particular there was the stress of 'provincial' opposition, caused by the federal structure of the great monarchies. In response, no doubt, to social or economic pressures, the Kings of Spain, France, England all sought to impose the bureaucratic system, which had been established in their greater kingdoms, upon the different societies of those lesser realms which their ancestors had ruled as independent kingdoms but which were now without resident princely Courts. In consequence they provoked risings which the very absence of a local Court and local patronage made it more difficult to suppress, and to which the historic national identity of the revolting provinces gave an added ideological strength. The revolt of the Netherlands had been such a revolt in the sixteenth century; the revolts of Béarn, Scotland, Catalonia and Portugal illustrate the similar but greater pressures of the period in which I have placed 'the general crisis of the seventeenth century'.

V

FOREIGN MERCENARIES AND ABSOLUTE MONARCHY*

V. G. Kiernan

WHEN Alexander invaded Asia in 334 B.C. his army included 5,000 mercenaries, and the Persian army that faced him at Issos contained 10,000 Greeks.[1] The foreign soldier enlisting for pay is a ubiquitous type in history. One of the epochs in which he may be seen most hard at work is the one that links medieval and modern Europe, when absolute monarchy and the modern state were taking shape. Underlying this political development was a re-organization—rather than a transformation—of the social structure of Europe. The feudal order, the rule of the landowning aristocracy, was in the later Middle Ages divided and demoralized. It was meeting with growing resistance from below, and its military resources for coping with both internal and external challenges were obsolescent. In the fifteenth century the knight on horseback who had dominated Europe for a millennium was being driven to shut himself up inside a load of armour that made him clumsy and ineffective. Under the auspices of absolute monarchy, by what might be described as a sort of 'managerial revolution', the aristocratic order achieved a remarkable recovery, though it had of course to undergo important changes.

The new state rested on a new kind of army, and to this the

[1] P. Jouquet, *Macedonian Imperialism and the Hellenization of the East* (English edn., London, 1928), pp. 12–14. Greek mercenaries served as far away as southern India; see Sir M. Wheeler, *Rome beyond the Imperial Frontiers* (London, 1955 edn.), p. 160.

* From no. 11 (1957).

foreign mercenary contributed so much that his services can be regarded as an indispensable condition of all that happened.

'A prince ought to have no other aim or thought', said Machiavelli, 'nor select anything else for his study, than war and its rules and discipline'.[2] A good army was the *summum bonum*, the vehicle of salvation. The awkward problem lay in finding the soldiers to fill it. Every ruler would have echoed Henry V, who wished his yeomen to imitate the action of the tiger when abroad, and to be quiet and docile at home. It was a difficult combination of qualities for any martial breeder to produce, in an age when popular jingoism had hardly begun to stir; he was more likely to have to complain with Coriolanus that his men were mutinous at home, timid on the field. Recruitment from the mass of ordinary peasants and burghers might have for the Crown the advantage of counterbalancing the strength of the nobility. Norman kings had thought of preserving a Saxon fyrd. For this very reason, however, it would be obnoxious to the nobility, without whose participation no army could be put together. In Castile, for instance, the nobles objected strongly to an ordinance made by Ximénez, when Regent in 1516, on military training for the burgher class.[3] And rulers could not fail to share this reluctance to put arms into the hands of the people. The State was growing out of conditions of civil war; often violent class warfare, as in several provinces of Aragon under John II, Ferdinand, and Charles V in turn. Four years after Ximénez's ordinance the burghers of Castile were in rebellion against their king.

Of military thinking about the end of that century Hanotaux writes: 'Tous les contemporains sont d'accord pour déclarer, qu'en France, on ne donnait plus d'armes au peuple, de peur qu'il ne se soulevât contre ses oppresseurs.'[4] Often, it may be added, the common man was positively unwilling to be armed. Many detested

[2] *The Prince* (Everyman edn.), chap. xiv. K. Brandi, *The Emperor Charles V* (English edn., London, 1939), p. 465, reckons that of the Spanish revenue of over 2 million ducats in 1543, four-fifths went on war expenses. Cf. H. Koenigsberger, *The Government of Sicily under Philip II of Spain* (London, 1951), p. 124: 'Compared with military and naval expenses the charges of the civil administration were relatively insignificant'.

[3] W. H. Prescott, *The History of the Reign of Ferdinand and Isabella the Catholic*, ed. J. F. Kirk (London, 1879), ii, p. 516; cf. the militia experiment of 1496, ibid., p. 69.

[4] G. Hanotaux, *Tableau de la France en 1614* (Paris, 1898), p. 109.

the senseless wars in whose fires new chains were being forged for them. One of the leading principles of Anabaptism was refusal of military service. A vast amount of popular feeling in Europe was distilled by Shakespeare into the great scene in which his English soldiers argue about war on the night before Agincourt. Recruits of a less disputatious sort were no doubt available. With feudal society cracking and crumbling there was a plentiful human debris at every level. In a later period the 'scum of the earth' would be effectively handled by the drill-sergeant. But that could only be after army cadres had been organized and habits of command and obedience evolved. The problem was where to begin. A further objection was that drumming up volunteers had to be left, until the growth of the State was far advanced, to nobles who might turn it to their own political as well as pecuniary ends. Even Richelieu, well on in the seventeenth century, might prefer on this account to look for an army in Germany rather than in France.[5]

A glance at the French army of the fifteenth and sixteenth centuries will illustrate the problem. In 1445 towards the end of the Hundred Years War Charles VII took the first step towards a standing army by embodying, out of the old feudal mass that had answered the *ban* and *arrière-ban*, the *compagnies d'ordonnance*: each company made up of 100 'lances', units of one heavy-armed horseman (*gendarme*) with two or three footmen or mounted infantry. Of the original fifteen companies the first in order and precedence was composed of Scots;[6] otherwise the gendarmes of this picked force were normally Frenchmen, all (until 1584) were gentlemen, all were permanently in the royal pay. Technically they suffered from a certain aristocratic conservatism,[7] and politically the civil wars of the late sixteenth century revealed the instability of the class from which they were drawn. In their day they were the finest heavy cavalry in Europe; but no cavalry could make an army by itself now that the long-bow was being followed by the pike and the arquebus. A reliable infantry was needed as well. In the fourteenth century employment of footmen from the town militias had been

[5] C. V. Wedgwood, *The Thirty Years War* (London, 1938), p. 401.

[6] E. Fieffé, *Histoire des Troupes Etrangères au service de la France* (Paris, 1854), i, p. 41.

[7] R. Doucet, *Les Institutions de la France au XVIe siècle* (Paris, 1948), ii, p. 627.

hindered by 'the sharp new hostility of the feudal nobles towards the lower social strata from which infantry was recruited'.[8] Only sporadically, under pressure of critical circumstances, did the monarchy now try to form bodies of soldiers out of ordinary Frenchmen. In 1448 the *francs-archers* were raised in the countryside, each parish having to find and equip one man. By this time the long-bow was getting out of date, and these rustic reserves, practising at their targets on Sundays, soon dropped out of sight.[9] Political hesitations on the government's part may have helped to keep the experiment futile, as well as the similar ones planned by Louis XII in 1513 and by Francis I in 1534. The fear that the people inspired in the King was, as Lot remarks, a hindrance to any success with infantry.[10]

Only along the troubled and shifting frontiers were regular French infantry formations slowly taking shape, beginning with the *Bande de Picardie*, first of the 'old four' regiments of the later army, and that of Piedmont. But most of the *aventuriers* recruited from these borderlands in the sixteenth century were a mere mob of pilferers. They came from populations mostly more poverty-stricken than those of France proper, and only half French. Gascony, which with Picardy and Brittany furnished a high proportion of France's infantry, was the old 'Vasconia' or Basque land, and had been under English rule until the mid-fifteenth century. Brittany was an autonomous duchy until 1491; Commines mentions a large contingent of Breton gendarmes in Louis XI's service a little before this date, who deserted him at an awkward moment, and Bretons were to be found in the service of Burgundy too.[11] Picardy extended into the Netherlands, and Picards fought for Habsburg as well as Valois.[12]

Frenchmen were seldom eager to serve their king, and their king

[8] O. L. Spaulding, N. Nickerson and J. W. Wright, *Warfare; a Study of Military Methods from the Earliest Times* (London, 1925), p. 370.

[9] See e.g. *The 'Instructions sur le Faict de la Guerre' of Raymond de Beccarie de Pavie Sieur de Fourquevaux*, ed. G. Dickinson (London, 1954), p. xxviii.

[10] F. Lot, *L'Art Militaire et les Armées au Moyen Age* (Paris, 1946), ii, p. 436; cf. p. 433. The 'francs-archers' were so called because they were released from various tax obligations.

[11] *The Memoirs of Philip de Commines*, ed. A. R. Scoble (London, 1855), Bk. i, chaps. iii, iv.

[12] See e.g. *The Scandalous Chronicle* of Jean de Troyes, in Commines, ed. cit., ii, p. 390.

was not eager to employ Frenchmen. Despots have often chosen to surround themselves with bodyguards of aliens: we see Byzantine emperors with their Varangians, French kings with their Scots and then their Swiss Guard, Napoleon with his Poles, Franco with his Moors. In this spirit Charles the Bold of Burgundy 'entertained strangers rather than his own subjects', of whom he felt 'strange jealousies', in his army.[13] Sixteenth-century France came to depend to a very remarkable degree on foreign mercenaries. A patriot like Fourquevaux might lament this,[14] and Machiavelli had condemned the practice;[15] but the Florentine was often anything but a realist. Use of foreign troops, while it suffered from various drawbacks, had the great merit of being politically safe. It had several secondary advantages. Since as a rule only the king could afford to hire mercenaries in bulk they strengthened him against his nobles; they strengthened both king and nobles against the people, with whom they had no ties of sympathy. While much more expensive than native troops, they left no troublesome widows and orphans; and at the end of a campaign they could be sent away, unlike a country's own men coming home from the wars. Professional fighting-men competing for employment were more likely than others to keep up with technical progress.[16] Experts from the industrially advanced regions played a leading part in spreading the use of firearms. In England the first hand-gun soldiers were Flemings and Germans hired for the Wars of the Roses.[17]

Long before absolute monarchy arose, soldiers offering themselves for hire had constituted a major export trade of the Middle Ages, and one of the first to establish a European market. Byzantium, the Crusades, and the rich cities of Italy and Flanders had all helped to set it going. It had been, in its way, as vital to the formation of the feudal state as it was now to the new monarchy of the sixteenth century. Feudal rulers had made use of foreign troops both at home and abroad, up to the limit of their purses. John Lackland leaned so heavily on his Flemish mercenaries that Magna Carta prohibited their employment. Flemings assisted in the

Colaiste Oideachais Mhuire Gan Smal, Luimneach

[13] Commines, Bk. v, chap. i.
[14] Dickinson, op. cit., p. xxxi, chap. i.
[15] *The Prince*, chap. xii.
[16] Doucet, op. cit., ii, p. 632.
[17] C. W. C. Oman, *A History of the Art of War in the Middle Ages* (rev. edn., London, 1925), ii, p. 229.

conquest of South Wales and then of Ireland.[18] Capetian kings imitated their Plantagenet rivals.

Like the 'Brabançons' of the thirteenth century, the 'Armagnacs', 'Écorcheurs', and similar professionals in the disorderly Companies of Adventurers of the fourteenth and fifteenth were largely pauperized or bastard gentlemen, offscourings of feudality.[19] Not so the men who wielded the long-bow, the weapon which revolutionized warfare for a century. They came from Wales. 'It was the South Welsh archers of Strongbow and his fellow-adventurers . . . who made the Norman Conquest of Ireland possible'.[20] With the North Welsh spearmen they 'gradually became famous all over Europe for their courage and skill', while their removal from Wales made that country more easily governed by its foreign masters.[21] Of 12,500 foot in the army Edward I led to Scotland in 1298, 10,000 were Welsh.[22] Wales was only one of a series of recruiting-bases lying outside the settled limits of feudal Europe; and these held far more significance for the future than feudal Europe's internal sources of supply. Besides Welshmen, Henry II and Richard I of England had hired Basques, Navarrese, and Galloway 'kerns'.[23] Most of the 'Genoese' crossbowmen who served everywhere from London to Constantinople, and were the staple infantry of medieval France, must have been drawn from Genoa's possessions, the Ligurian hills and Corsica and Sardinia. Venice got many of its best men from Dalmatia.[24] Altogether, a striking number of these recruiting-grounds lay in mountainous regions on the fringes of Europe, inhabited by alien peoples such as Celts or Basques. In an age when the cultivators of the settled plains had been disarmed by their noble 'protectors', and ravaged by famine and pestilence, these sturdy, needy hillmen were still ready for war.

One may find analogies in the reliance of Byzantine rulers on Anatolian mountaineers, or in the armies of the Persian kings, always until the nineteenth century drawn from the nomad hill and

[18] E. Curtis, *A History of Medieval Ireland from 1086 to 1513* (enlarged edn., London, 1938), pp. 39, 48.

[19] Lot, op. cit., i, p. 366; ii, p. 432.

[20] Oman, op. cit., ii, p. 59.

[21] E. Inglis-Jones, *The Story of Wales* (London, 1955), pp. 81–82.

[22] Oman, op. cit., ii, p. 77; cf. on Welshmen in the Hundred Years War, Lot, op. cit., i, p. 346; A. H. Burne, *The Crecy War* (London, 1955), p. 34.

[23] Lot, op. cit., i, p. 306.

[24] B. Dudan, *Il Dominio Veneziano di Levante* (Bologna, 1938), pp. 255, 257.

desert tribes of neighbouring Kurdistan, Luristan, or Makran.[25] The absolute monarchs followed the same policies, though on a grander scale than in the Middle Ages, for they needed more men, for whom they paid out of the increasing output of the central European silver mines in the late fifteenth century, and even more, out of the stocks of gold and silver which reached Europe from the Americas in the sixteenth.

Salvation for paymasters came from the Andes; for recruiting-officers from the Alps. A new race of hill-folk was coming to market, the Swiss, for two centuries the mercenary soldiery of Europe *par excellence*. It is a striking paradox that the old ruling groups were now, in great measure, saved by the mountaineers who had most resolutely defied feudalism in their Alpine strongholds, and whose revolutionary example had not gone unnoticed in central Europe. 'They want to become Swiss' was the proverbial expression in Germany for all those who wished to throw off allegiance to their lawful lords.[26] Luckily for their aristocratic neighbours the Swiss were as poverty-stricken as they were liberty-loving—'no people in the world could be poorer', Commines says of them in 1476 when they put an end to Charles the Bold and his ambitions[27]—and they found offers of pay and plunder irresistible. A nation of armed peasants, afflicted with the chronic over-population of the barren uplands, numerous enough to form massive columns of pikemen, they acquired by incessant practice the 'extraordinary perfection of skill and discipline' demanded by their system of warfare,[28] and they did this at home in their valleys, at no cost to their employers. True, they were too democratic to be easily handled, and if the pay-chest gave out they changed sides or marched off home. *Pas d'argent, pas de Suisse.* While money lasted they fought like Trojans, local and professional pride giving them a high morale. Altogether they gave their employers the benefits without the drawbacks of a free citizen army.

These Swiss set new standards to Europe's martial classes, and in doing so inaugurated a new epoch. Naturally rulers sought for equivalent mercenaries. Towards 1500 the Emperor Maximilian

[25] Sir A. T. Wilson, *Persia* (London, 1932), pp. 68–69.

[26] W. Oechsli, *History of Switzerland 1499–1914* (English edn., Cambridge, 1922), p. 7.

[27] Bk. v, chap. i.

[28] Spaulding *et al.*, *Warfare*, p. 339.

began to recruit their neighbours, the Swabians, who came from an area with many trading towns and few big territorial princes, which retained a large number of free peasants, at any rate until the aftermath of the Peasants' War. Modelled on the Swiss formations, and intended for use against them, the Swabians were never quite equal to them as soldiers and soon merged into the ordinary mass of German mercenaries or *Landsknechts*.[29] While the Swiss had a special link with France, *Landsknechts* served everywhere indiscriminately, and may have been preferred by some employers because, having less solidarity among themselves, they could be got cheaper and cheated more easily. However, Germany was industrially more advanced than Switzerland and therefore produced professionals who took to fire-arms more readily, such as the mounted arquebusier and the *Schwartzreiter*, a mounted pistoleer.

Soldiers from Germany, which had no national army, helped to build up almost every organized state in Europe, acquiring meanwhile the conscientious ferocity of modern German warfare long before the first Prussian drill-ground was laid out. Italy was also without a national army. Unlike their fourteenth-century predecessors, the mercenaries of fifteenth-century Italian cities, whose elaborate shadow-boxing Machiavelli derided, were mainly Italians. Yet men of their nationality were to make very respectable cut-throats in the service of foreign and strong governments. Absolute monarchies also utilized much other cannon-fodder in their long series of wars. After their defeat in Bohemia, the Taborites straggled over Germany and into Poland as mercenaries, often armed with the hand-guns in whose use they had been pioneers;[30] they were to be followed in later days by many others who, defeated in the struggle for freedom at home, had to earn their bread by fighting against freedom abroad. By way of the Venetian possessions swordsmen came into circulation from the Balkans, where the collapse of Byzantium and the turmoil of Turkish conquest coincided with the crisis of the medieval order in the west. Albanians fled in large numbers to Venetia. Old followers of Scanderbeg were the first *Stradiots* or *Estradiots*, a wild type of light cavalry that figures largely in sixteenth-century annals;

[29] Commines defines *landsknechts* as 'a collection from all the countries upon the Rhine, Suabia, the Pays de Vaux in Sequania, and Guelderland' (Bk. viii, chap. xxi).

[30] Lot, op. cit., ii, p. 209; Oman, op. cit., ii, p. 366.

another type was represented by the *Argoulets*, originally Greek horsemen from Epirus. Most of these military trade-names were soon borrowed by men of other nationalities.[31]

In France, whose example was decisive for Europe, Louis XI inaugurated a system destined to survive down to the Revolution when, in 1474, he enlisted Swiss auxiliaries by treaty arrangement with the Cantons. From now on Switzerland, conveniently close at hand, was to the French kings what Wales had been to the English. Sluggish in social evolution compared with England, France had hitherto been unable to make effective use of such auxiliaries. More than once on the battlefield the haughty knights had ridden down their own Genoese crossbowmen, as contemptible plebeians. The Swiss were ostentatiously plebeian, but the bluest-blooded gendarme could not fail to respect their prowess, all the more perhaps because they fought hand to hand, not with long-range missiles like the Genoese. To a Louis XII they were barbarians, but they provided an almost ideal answer to the problem of how to build a solid French infantry without Frenchmen.

Within a few years after the treaty of 1474, a certain number of Swiss came to form part of the new permanent army of the French monarchy, along with its gendarmerie and artillery; while much bigger numbers were imported in wartime. Charles VIII started the Italian Wars in 1494 with 10,000 Swiss and Germans in his army, whose native infantry was merely 'a hastily raised force, poorly armed and equipped . . .; there was still the fear of arming the people'.[32] At Ravenna in 1512 during a brief estrangement from the Cantons Louis XII had 5,000 allied Italians (partly under Scots officers), 6,000 Germans, 8,000 Gascons and Picards, some Flemish archers, miscellaneous light horse, and 1,200 'lances' of gendarmerie.[33] In 1543 there were 19,000 Swiss in France.[34] They were the backbone of the infantry; and from Francis I to Henry IV they and the gendarmerie were brigaded together and fought in

[31] C. W. C. Oman, *A History of the Art of War in the Sixteenth Century* (London, 1937), p. 41; Dickinson, op. cit., pp. xxxix–xl. The name 'Croat' for a type of light horse was similarly made free with; F. Watson, *Wallenstein: Soldier under Saturn* (London, 1938), p. 164.

[32] Spaulding *et al.*, op. cit., p. 416.

[33] J. S. C. Bridge, *A History of France from the Death of Louis XI*, vol iv, *The Reign of Louis XII 1508–1514* (Oxford, 1929), p. 151; Fieffé, *Histoire des Troupes Etrangères*, i, p. 71.

[34] Doucet, *Institutions de la France*, ii, p. 638.

close co-operation.[35] Vacancies in the French ranks were filled up with smaller numbers of Englishmen, Scots, Italians, Corsicans, Poles, Greeks. A body of Albanians first enrolled by Charles VIII became 'the nucleus and foundation of the French light cavalry'.[36] Ships and crews were often hired from abroad, especially from Genoa.

In Spain several factors combined to give the army a more 'national' character than any other of the sixteenth century, and this undoubtedly helped it to dominate the battlefield from about 1520, when the Swiss pike by itself ceased to carry all before it, down to the battle of Rocroy in 1643. For one thing Castile—and more particularly the Basque provinces—had been less rich and less heavily feudalized than France, and a gentleman could serve on foot without derogation. For another, Spain's many dependencies required permanent garrisons; this fostered the growth of the *tercios*, regiments with a continuous tradition and with the special morale of occupation forces. What also counted was that Spanish troops stationed far away in Sicily or Flanders would not cause their government the same uneasiness that they might have done at home in Spain. None the less, foreign ingredients were needed here too, from the conquest of Granada (1481–91) onward. In the campaigns of Naples, Gonzalvo de Córdoba began operations in 1496 with a very small army including some Germans, as well as many Basques, and he had to hire Italian heavy cavalry.[37] For the battle of Cerignola in 1503 he acquired another 2,000 Germans, making about one-third of his total; there is a symbolic touch about the anecdote of the Great Captain himself riding to the field with a German behind him on the crupper.[38] As the century wore on the Spanish army, much the greatest part of it stationed abroad, was increasingly diluted with non-Spanish elements; until in the end only five out of the twenty infantry regiments at Rocroy were Spanish, five being Walloon, five German, three Italian, and two Franc-Comtois.[39]

[35] Fieffé, op. cit., i, p. 53, n. 1.

[36] G. T. Denison, *A History of Cavalry* (London, 1877), p. 243.

[37] Hon. J. W. Fortescue, *A History of the British Army* (London, 1899, etc.), i, p. 97; Oman, *Sixteenth Century*, p. 54.

[38] Prescott, *Ferdinand and Isabella*, ii, pp. 239, 250 ff; U. R. Burke, *The Great Captain* (London, 1877), p. 120; L. M. de Lojendio, *Gonzalvo de Córdoba (El Gran Capitán)* (Madrid, 1942), p. 214.

[39] Lot, op. cit., ii, p. 318; Spaulding *et al.*, op. cit., p. 489.

Henry VIII of England relied on foreign mercenaries throughout his adventures on the Continent: German or Burgundian pikemen, Netherlands or Burgundian heavy cavalry.[40] In 1545 he gave offence to Charles V by enticing into his service a body of some 700 Spanish arquebusiers who happened to land on his coasts (Spaniards and Frenchmen seldom served in other armies), and sending them up under a notable Basque *condottiere* named Pedro de Gamboa to strengthen the garrisons along the border, where the Scots, says the Spanish chronicler, 'were very frightened when they got to know them'.[41] Also stationed on the border were Albanian horsemen and a company of Italians under the Marquis Palavicino:[42] nearly as heterogeneous an array as Rome had once sent to this frontier to defend the Wall. Elizabeth, unable to multiply taxes or plunder a wealthy church as her father had done, could not make war in this high-spirited style, and her army was in general a mere wretched militia. Of the pressed men sent with Leicester to the Netherlands many deserted: 'the Spaniards had a whole regiment of English renegades under William Stanley'.[43] In the conquest of Ireland liberal use was made of cheap but very unreliable Irish mercenaries: 'kerns', the lowest sort of foot-soldiers, and 'gallowglasses' or 'bonaghts' who had long been coming into Ireland from the Scottish Highlands as mercenaries in the pay of tribal chiefs.[44] For Scotland the Highlands were a valuable if turbulent reservoir of manpower. At Pinkie in 1547 8,000 Highlanders, along with 4,000 Irish archers, made up a considerable part of the Scots army defeated by Somerset with the help of his Spaniards and Italians.[45] In 1640 Leslie marched into England with forces which included a large contingent of 'Redshanks', or Highlanders.

[40] Oman, *Sixteenth Century*, pp. 288–90, and Bk. iv *passim*.

[41] *Chronicle of King Henry VIII of England*, trans. M. A. S. Hume (London, 1899), chap. lviii. See also M. Hume, *Españoles é Ingleses en el Siglo XVI* (Madrid, 1903), chap. i, 'Los mercenarios españoles'.

[42] *The Hamilton Papers*, ed. J. L. Bain (Edinburgh, 1890–2), i, pp. 578–80, 592–3.

[43] Oman, *Sixteenth Century*, pp. 376, 549. On Elizabeth's financial embarrassments over the hiring of continental troops to aid the Dutch in 1578, see L. Stone, *An Elizabethan: Sir Horatio Palavicino* (Oxford, 1956), chap. 3.

[44] C. Falls, *Elizabeth's Irish Wars* (London, 1950), pp. 41, 68–69, 76 ff, 84; C. G. Cruickshank, *Elizabeth's Army* (London, 1946), p. 12.

[45] J. A. Froude, *History of England*, vol. iv (London, 1872), pp. 291 ff; Oman, *Sixteenth Century*, p. 359.

European governments thus relied very largely on foreign mercenaries. One of the employments for which they were particularly well suited was the suppression of rebellious subjects, and in the sixteenth century, that age of endemic revolution, they were often called upon for this purpose. 'Where are my Switzers?' was the cry of many a harassed monarch besides Claudius. Military technique has always evolved in response to the requirements of internal pacification as well as of external war. Thus fire-arms, which were improved into practical weapons during the crisis of feudalism, were essential to the rise of the modern state, not only because cannon could batter feudal strongholds, but even more because fire-arms could deal with peasant revolts more effectively than any earlier equipment. And such arms (like crossbows earlier) were more safely entrusted to foreign than to native troops. France was the last country to adopt hand-guns for its own troops,[46] though it had led the way with artillery. It is thus not really as 'curious' as Oman suggests 'that among the many results of the growing importance of fire-arms was the fact that popular risings became progressively more impotent against trained soldiery'.[47]

Faced with internal rebellion, local regular troops or tenants collected from noble estates might be unreliable, as the King of Spain found in 1520, when the revolt of the Comuneros in Castile and the Germanias in Valencia and Majorca broke out. Governments thus had to look either to backward areas for honest, simple-minded fellows untainted by political ideas—as to the hills of Aragon and the Basque provinces in 1520–1—or to foreigners. Charles V, who had been caught with few troops in 1520, learned the lesson. When he returned to Spain in 1522 it was with three or four thousand Germans and seventy-four guns. 'Foreign soldiers and foreign cannon were henceforth often employed by Charles V to forestall and put down rebellion in his different dominions'.[48] Gueldrians, Italians, and bloodthirsty Albanians and Stradiotes crusaded against the rebels of 1525 in Alsace, under the pious Duke of Lorraine;[49] Czech, Croat and Magyar soldiery against them in Upper Austria, Styria and Carinthia. Three hundred Italian

[46] Fieffé, *Histoire des Troupes Etrangères*, i, p. 78.

[47] Oman, op. cit., p. 288.

[48] R. B. Merriman, *The Rise of the Spanish Empire* (New York, 1925), iii, p. 120.

[49] E. B. Bax, *The Peasants' War in Germany 1525–1526* (London, 1899), p. 313.

arquebusiers and some hundreds of *Landsknechts* under Lord Grey de Wilton were sent to reinforce Lord Russell in Cornwall in 1549; a thousand Welsh hillmen were also drafted. At the fight at Sampford Courtenay the government side could hardly have carried the day without its artillery and foreign professionals.[50] In Norfolk, Italians and a thousand German matchlockmen were also thrown in. Warwick was saved, and the battle in August decided, by the arrival of the Germans.[51] Their very foreignness ensured their loyalty, for 'every foreigner who fell out of rank was instantly killed';[52] a strong inducement to the mercenaries *not* to fall out of rank.

Naturally professionalism cut both ways. In the insurgent areas of Austria and south-west Germany during the Peasants' War many peasants had seen military service, and were thus much better armed and organized than in Thuringia, where there were few ex-soldiers. 'The Allgaeu peasants counted in their ranks a host of foreign soldiers and experienced commanders and possessed numerous well-manned cannon'.[53] (On the other hand much of the 'demoralization' among the peasants may be traceable to the infection of habits learned while fighting and plundering abroad.) Rebellions headed by moneyed men could hire their own mercenaries. If the Huguenots in the French Wars of Religion were worn down by government forces composed largely of Swiss, Germans and Italians (including Protestants), they themselves, mostly gentlemen-cavalry, hired *Landsknechts* and others to make up infantry, as well as numbers of the disorderly *Reiter*. In the decisive year of 1590, when Henry IV won the battle of Ivry, he owed his success to the loyalty of the 13,000 Swiss in his camp.[54] However, in general, governments could outbid rebels at this game. Only in the exceptional case of the Netherlands did mercenaries turn the scales *against* absolutism, because the rebels were the better paymasters. They fought Philip II throughout with a force as polyglot as his own. William of Orange's first attempts in 1568 and 1572

[50] Froude, op. cit., iv, pp. 411–36. At the time of the Pilgrimage of Grace a shortage of matchlockmen had been complained of on the government side (Oman, *Sixteenth Century*, p. 350).

[51] ibid., pp. 445–53; cf. Oman, op. cit., p. 369.

[52] Froude, op. cit., iv, p. 432.

[53] F. Engels, *The Peasant War in Germany* (English trans., Moscow, 1956), chaps. v and vi.

[54] Oechsli, *History of Switzerland*, pp. 182–3.

were made with riotous bands sharked up in Germany.[55] The new element contributed by the thrifty Dutch as the war went on was regular pay and careful accounting, rather than native soldiers. It was in the sea-fighting that authentic Dutch glory was won; apart from heroic defence of some besieged towns, 'the warfare on land, with the foreign auxiliaries, the innumerable foreigners even in the States' pay, the foreign noblemen surrounding the princely commander, could never create a really national tradition—not during the whole period of the Republic's existence'.[56] Much the same had been true of Venice, and was to be true of England.

However, the mercenary system also militated against revolution in a subtler way. The reservoirs of mercenary recruitment remained politically stagnant, compared with their neighbours, somewhat as Nepal and the Punjab, two great recruiting-grounds for the British army, long did. For Switzerland the three centuries of symbiosis with despotic France had evil consequences. Cantonal politics were corrupted by the fees received for licensing the export of soldiers, and rings of patricians increased their power at the expense of the common people.[57] In vain had Zwingli tried to put an end to the traffic along with prostitution and adultery. For Europe as well as for themselves the corruption of the Swiss was a misfortune. As Alfieri was to remark bitterly, these free men of the hills became the chief watch-dogs of tyranny.[58] European history might have taken a different turn if the Swiss had still been as revolutionary a force in 1524, when the Peasants' War was fought, as fifty years earlier. The German rebels had close contacts with Switzerland, and were hoping for help from across the border. Many of the *Bundschuh* agitators of previous decades had fled there. But already the old democracy was in decay; a century later the Swiss peasants in their turn were goaded into rebellion and crushed by the united strength of the cantonal governments. And professional rivalry had stirred up violent animosities between Swiss and Swabians. Altogether the mercenary system had a considerable

[55] P. Geyl, *The Revolt of the Netherlands, 1559–1609* (London, 1932), pp. 107, 117 ff.

[56] ibid., p. 235.

[57] Oechsli, op. cit., pp. 23 ff, 62.

[58] 'E per una strana contraddizione, che molto disonora gli uomini, gli Svizzeri, che sono il popolo quasi il piu libero dell' Europa, si lasciano prescegliere e comprare, per servir di custodi alla persona di quasi tutti i tiranni di essa' (*Della Tirannide*, 1789, chap. vii).

share in diverting the danger that might have threatened the aristocratic order of society from popular forces outside the limits of feudal Europe.

Inside those limits, moreover, it provided a safety-valve, drawing away from social revolt unnumbered multitudes who, like the murderer hired by Macbeth, were so incensed by the vile blows and buffets of the world that they were reckless what they did to spite the world. The common soldier was almost the first proletarian. He had his wage disputes, his strikes and lock-outs. A Swiss contingent, especially, was a trade union, and one that would not put up with any breach of contract.[59] But this haggling over pence, compared with the old epic struggle for Swiss freedom, was a sad falling away. The social conflicts of the age were in part transmuted and diluted into such professional disputes. Even the New Model was a craft union of skilled workers with grievances, though it was much else too. War had become the biggest industry in Europe. Every officer, collecting recruits for a government and making what he could out of their pay, was an entrepreneur, a businessman great or small. Profits and pickings from war—still in the sixteenth century including ransoms[60]—helped the gentry to recoup the deficiencies in its feudal income.

All these tendencies reached a disastrous climax in the Thirty Years' War. In one sense we can think of this as a mechanism diverting the energies of common men who, on the sixteenth-century continent as in seventeenth-century Britain, would have 'fought for religion' as rebels or revolutionary soldiers, into pillage and the strengthening of absolute monarchies. Peasants still revolted, as in Upper Austria in 1626, with many old soldiers in their bands, but they were easily put down by the now swarming armies, composed of men for whom war was the alternative to poverty or starvation. From each ravaged area the common man drifted along the well-worn path to the camp, to prey on others in his turn. Women also found the vast baggage trains their most accessible refuge.[61] The demoralization, already visible in 1525,

[59] See Oman, *Sixteenth Century*, p. 36.

[60] 'Do you think', Henry VIII's Spanish captains once said to their general, 'we are in the King's service for the four ducats a month we earn? Not so, my lord; on the contrary we serve with the hope of taking prisoners and getting their ransom' (*Chron. of King Henry VIII of England*, chap. lvi).

[61] Armies then conventionally reckoned one woman and boy to each soldier (Wedgwood, *Thirty Years War*, p. 132). On peasant resistance, see O.

grew to enormous proportions; the German people never fully recovered from it. The war got out of hand—but it never seriously imperilled the governing classes. On the contrary, they emerged from it with a new and powerful political and military implement: the 'standing army' composed of mercenaries, but permanently attached to a given government.

The Thirty Years' War thus brings us from the discussion of mercenaries as weapons against rebellion to consideration of the more general problem of mercenaries and the growth of the modern state apparatus. We must first look at western Europe, for, as we shall see, eastern Europe followed a rather different course. In the west independent mercenary forces were still, at the outbreak of the Thirty Years' War, essential to governments which had not yet built a regular army framework of their own. Mansfeld, Tilly, Wallenstein, heirs of the sixteenth-century *Landsknecht*-contractors, were indispensable to states like England, Bavaria and above all Austria, whose hotch-potch of territories only really coagulated into an empire under the pressure of this war; while even France and Sweden, which possessed the foundations of national armies, used foreign professionals to build on them. Wallenstein in particular brought the freelance private sub-contract army to its point of highest development, after which nothing remained but for it either to disintegrate or to be permanently attached to some state. His army, which, with its camp-followers, was comparable in numbers to a good-sized modern city, was the biggest and best organized private enterprise seen in Europe before the twentieth century, and its structure mirrored that of contemporary society. All the officers had a financial stake in it, and counted on a rich return on their investment; the rank and file, dredged up from all over Europe and incapable of solidarity, were poorly and irregularly paid, which resulted in a rapid turnover of the 'labour force'.[62] But the commander himself claimed unlimited authority, as though in virtue of a Hobbesian social contract. The day of the free democratic Swiss phalanx had ended, that of the modern regular army was about to begin. 'Midway between them Wallenstein introduced the principle of uncondi-

[62] G. Pagès, *La Guerre de Trente Ans 1618–1648* (Paris, 1939), pp. 115–16.

Schiff, 'Die Deutschen Bauernaufstände von 1525 bis 1789', *Hist. Zeitschrift*, cxxx (1924), pp. 189–209.

tional military obedience that made possible the construction of the modern type of command'.[63] So vast a force could no longer sell itself to all buyers, for few could afford it. It could either attempt to become the basis of a state itself—as Wallenstein was accused of wishing—or pass to the paymaster by whose support it had grown, and who had grown by its support. Austria inherited what Wallenstein had built up.

As usual it was France which perfected the new type of national-mercenary army organization. Louis XIV and Louvois set on foot an army which found more room than before for native recruits, though it drew its volunteers from the least 'national', most nondescript types, the dregs of the poorest classes. Because foreign troops had by now given France a solid military framework and tradition, this 'scum' could be put to reasonably good use. Military tactics could be based largely on an infantry force, though the riff-raff was officered by gentlemen. Even now, bullying or deception were often needed to persuade the humblest Frenchman to join the colours; paupers, convicts, drunkards, boys of fifteen had to be accepted, and desertion was rampant.[64] In 1677 the Maréchal de Vivonne found that 4,000 of his 7,000 men had absconded. Hence an extremely high proportion of foreign stiffening was still requisite. 'Les victoires de Louis XIV seront souvent dues autant à des soldats d'autres nations qu'à des soldats français'.[65]

These foreigners were now being incorporated into standardized units of the army, some of them kept permanently on the list. Once more the Swiss stood first, though not in France alone for in other lands too they were 'the lineal ancestors of the modern regiments of Europe'.[66] In France they, unlike the common run of mercenaries, retained their own rights of citizenship and worship.[67] One of Louis XIV's first acts was to raise four more permanent

[63] Watson, *Wallenstein*, p. 161.

[64] L. André, *Michel le Tellier et Louvois*, 2nd edn. (Paris, 1943), pp. 329–41. See also J. U. Nef, *War and Human Progress* (London, 1950), pp. 206–7 and E. J. Hamilton, *War and Prices in Spain, 1651–1800* (Harvard U.P., 1947), p. 134 n. 58.

[65] P. Sagnac and A. de Saint-Léger, *La Prépondérance française: Louis XIV (1661–1715)*, 2nd edn. (Paris, 1944), p. 232. In 1688 there was another attempt, again of limited value, to form a militia.

[66] Oman, *Art of War*, ii, p. 236.

[67] Fieffé, *Histoire des Troupes Etrangères*, i, p. 284.

Swiss regiments.[68] Twenty-five thousand Swiss, including Protestants, took part in the invasion of Holland.[69] Another source of raw material that could be turned to good account was the mass of refugees flooding Europe after the religious wars. Prominent among them were the Irish. At the battle of the Dunes in 1658 Turenne's army contained a Scottish regiment previously in Swedish service and one of Irish driven out of their homes by Cromwell; the Spanish army he was fighting contained one Scottish, one English and three Irish regiments.[70] After the battle of the Boyne in 1690 about 14,000 of the defeated Irish came over to France to join the 6,000 already in Louis's service. With no homes to return to they were in a poor bargaining position, and were only paid the same 'petite solde' as the French soldier, less than the Swiss or Germans got.[71] From 1693 down to 1789 an Irish brigade formed a part of the French Army.

The first permanent regiment of Germans in France was enrolled in 1654, and survived to 1789. More nationalities than ever before had been laid under contribution by Richelieu and Mazarin; and Spanish, Italian, Corsican, Walloon, Swedish, Danish, Polish, Hungarian and Croat regiments could all be counted on the pay-roll of Louis XIV. In 1748 foreign troops totalled 52,000. Still more exotic ingredients were being added to the mixture: Turks, Wallachians, Tartars, even a brigade of negroes drawn from various parts of Africa and Asia. Germans fought in America for France as well as for England in the War of Independence; and vacancies in foreign regiments tended to be filled up with German-speaking volunteers from France's eastern provinces.[72]

This Bourbon army, not less multifarious than Napoleon's, was available for police work as well as for war, in an age when revolt was always smouldering among the French masses who had to pay for all the glory. When for instance the peasantry of the Boulonnais broke out in 1662, the infantry section of the force concentrated by the Governor of Picardy consisted of ten companies of French and

[68] ibid., i, pp. 164–5.

[69] Oechsli, *History of Switzerland*, p. 224.

[70] Fortescue, *History of the British Army*, i, pp. 270–1.

[71] D. C. Boulger, *Battle of the Boyne* (London, 1911), pp. 288–90; cf. Fieffé, op. cit., i, pp. 176–8.

[72] Fieffé, op. cit., i, pp. 180, 183 ff, 278–81, 279, 282, 284, 414.

five of Swiss guards.[73] In the later years of Louis XIV's reign Swiss troops were among those fighting the Camisard rebels in the Cevennes. During the eighteenth century the government looked on its foreign detachments as among its chief props, and took pains to keep them contented and loyal.[74] In May 1789 the monarchy mustered them round Paris in an attempt to cling to power. Even in 1830 Swiss troops made the last stand for the restored Bourbons.

Sweden's army, for a brief spell the best in Europe, came to the forefront in alliance with the French. It was also to verify the lesson learned by Machiavelli from the fate of the Italian communes: 'It is more difficult to bring a republic, armed with its own arms, under the sway of one of its citizens than it is to bring one armed with foreign arms.'[75] Gustavus Adolphus started with a provincial militia; as soon as foreign conquests and French subsidies gave him the means he went into the market for foreign troops. Only a little more than half of the men with whom he entered the Thirty Years' War were Swedish or Finnish—part of Finland being Sweden's first colony.[76] War losses were made good chiefly with Germans. And as the military machine and the Baltic empire expanded, the Vasa dynasty, originally put on the throne by the people, lost its fear of antagonizing its subjects. War burdens pressed the mass of the people down, while the landed nobles, now prosperous generals and ministers of the Crown, achieved an ascendancy over the peasantry they had never had before.

War is an equalizer, and Holland and England, whose seventeenth- and eighteenth-century evolution led far away from absolute monarchy, differed from France in their methods of recruitment much less than might have been expected. Holland's commercial oligarchy after the struggle for independence had no more taste than its anointed enemy at Paris for a citizen army. Independence had been born out of intense class struggle, and divisions between rich and poor were still bitter. Besides, it was more profitable for rich Dutchmen that poor Dutchmen should work for them than fight for them. Out of the profits foreign

[73] André, op. cit., pp. 107 ff.

[74] Fieffé, op. cit., i, pp. 245, 283.

[75] *The Prince*, chap. xii.

[76] C. Hallendorff and A. Schück, *History of Sweden* (London, 1929), p. 238. One odd influx into Sweden's army was of Irish *bonaghts*, exiled by James I's conquest (Falls, *Elizabeth's Irish Wars*, p. 69).

muskets could be hired. In 1629, for instance, there were three British regiments in service, with Dutch, French and German officers, and 'a mixture of deserters and out-casts from all nations' to fill up gaps.[77] A Scots brigade was retained down to the French Revolution.[78] It was a system that at times set national security in hazard, but was always good for the security of the governing class. England was working meanwhile on even more Carthaginian lines. At the height of the Civil War the parliamentary leaders (much like the Regent class in the revolt of the Netherlands) looked askance at enrolment of armed Saints, and preferred to subsidize a less disturbing army from Scotland. After the Restoration the memory of the Ironsides lingered on as a bogy to England's rulers as well as enemies: the plutocracy wanted soldiers, but not soldiers who read pamphlets and debated affairs of Church and State. William III fought the battle of the Boyne with a gallimaufry of Englishmen, Ulstermen, Dutchmen, Scots, Huguenots, Danes, Swedes and Prussians,[79] an army whose ideology, at any rate, left nothing to be deplored. A splendid new vista opened about the end of the century when Hesse-Cassel began jobbing off troops to foreign governments, chiefly to England, for whom Hessians became the counterpart of France's Swiss. They were sometimes useful inside Britain. In February 1746 the Prince of Hesse landed at Leith with 5,000 men. Not many years later the Hessians were on their way to uphold law and order in America. In 1701 Frederick IV of Denmark had similarly disposed of 20,000 soldiers to England, including 6,000 Norwegians.[80] After the 'Forty-five' a very important recruiting-ground was opened up in the Highlands. During the Napoleonic wars all comers were welcome to the British ranks;[81] as late as the Crimean War a foreign legion was enrolled.

Eastern Europe after 1648 followed a rather different path. Unlike the west, it developed not voluntary but conscript service (though England had her Hessian conscripts, her press-ganged sailors, and Highlanders who were often volunteers in name rather

[77] F. Grose, *Military Antiquities respecting a History of the English Army* (London, 1786–8), ii, App. vi.

[78] Fortescue, op. cit., i, p. 294.

[79] T. A. Jackson, *Ireland Her Own* (London, 1947), p. 63.

[80] K. Gjerset, *History of the Norwegian People* (New York, 1927), ii, p. 305.

[81] See e.g. C. W. C. Oman, *Wellington's Army 1809–1814* (London, 1912), pp. 220–33.

than in fact).[82] Volunteers were linked with personal freedom, conscripts with serfdom. In the west the reorganization of feudal society by absolutism involved the disappearance of most serfdom. Eastern imitators of Versailles, however, could only come by the military resources they needed by abetting their nobles in imposing serfdom on their peasantry, often for the first time. When the people had been made accustomed to this it became safe to force guns into their hands and conscript them into standing armies for life—a very different system from the old casual militia service of the west.

But in the east too the foreign mercenary, a familiar figure long before 1648, still had an important part to play. Often he was the first bearer of fire-arms; gunpowder helped to destroy peasant freedom as it spread eastward. An illustration of some earlier phases can be found in Estonia. Here from the early thirteenth century German feudal lords were confronted by masses of Russian and Lithuanian footmen, and needed infantry support more urgently than did the chivalry of the west. For this purpose the Teutonic Order had to utilize its conquered Estonian peasants, and allow them to retain arms. Thereby it also allowed them to go on rebelling, as they did on a great scale in 1343. When fire-arms came in it would have been too dangerous as well as costly to supply them to the rank and file, and in 1498 the Diet ended peasant service in the army and replaced it with a tax designed to meet the cost of mercenaries from Germany. From 1507 peasants had no right to bear arms. 'This made them completely defenceless against their masters, and their legal and economic welfare began to deteriorate rapidly.'[83]

The next stages can be traced in the story of Brandenburg-Prussia. Stretched out between Poland and Holland, this State combined the military systems of east and west and drew from the fusion its peculiar strength. Beginning his reign in 1640 with a scanty 2,500 mercenaries, the Great Elector left 30,000 at his death in 1688. Nursing this force carefully, with the aid of revenues from their richer western provinces, he and his heirs were able to coerce their Estates into paying more taxation, and at the same time to join hands with the nobility in subjugating the peasantry. By 1713

[82] See Earl of Selkirk, *Observations on the Present State of the Highlands of Scotland* (London, 1805), chap. v.

[83] E. Uustalu, *The History of the Estonian People* (London, 1952), pp. 55–61, 62.

it was safe to impose regular conscription.[84] Mercenaries, however, continued to form a good proportion of the army, where they provided a countercheck to the native serfs. As late as the eve of Jena Prussia was paying 80,000 foreign—mainly German—troops.[85]

If Prussia combined the strength of east and west, Poland ended by falling between two stools and having neither.[86] For a very long time, and very closely, Polish military evolution paralleled French; until Poland's political and economic structure diverged so far from that of France that her army had to seek another path. In the Middle Ages its backbone was the feudal cavalry of the *szlachta*, which in the sixteenth century became a paid force like the gendarmerie; but from as early as the thirteenth century the kings had looked for soldiers more dependent on themselves, and found them by hiring men from outside. Moravians and Bohemians, Lithuanians, Ruthenians and Tartars, fought in the Polish ranks at Tannenberg in 1410. Germans, Hungarians, Serbs, Wallachians were gathered in; Cossacks were first enlisted for the defence of the south-east in 1524.[87] Precisely as in France there were sporadic attempts at times of crisis to form a national infantry. Stephen Bathory (1575–86), the King imported from Hungary, started a system of recruiting peasants from Crown estates, and there was a vain effort to expand it just before the great catastrophe of the invasions of 1655. But with a social order moving steadily in the sixteenth and seventeenth centuries towards the reduction of the peasantry to serfdom, reliance on mercenaries was easier and safer. Wladislaw IV (1632–48) hired Cossacks to fight Russia and Sweden; later he planned to use a Cossack army against the Sejm, exactly as Strafford may have

[84] See G. A. Craig, *The Politics of the Prussian Army 1640–1945* (Oxford, 1955), pp. 3–9.

[85] W. O. Shanahan, *Prussian Military Reforms 1786–1813* (New York, 1945), p. 56.

[86] My colleague Mr. A. J. A. Malkiewicz was good enough to translate and discuss with me the relevant passages of M. Kukiel, *Zarys Historji Wojskowosci w Polse* (Military History of Poland) (London, 1949).

[87] 'Cossack' was a vague term, at first perhaps occupational. One element among the Cossacks came from the Circassians, who were prominent in Turkish military life after having been so among the Mamelukes in Egypt. See W. E. D. Allen, *The Ukraine: A History* (Cambridge, 1940), pp. 68–69; cf. Denison, *History of Cavalry*, pp. 273–5.

planned to use an Irish army against Parliament.[88] He instituted a permanent division between 'Polish' and 'foreign' units; in the latter, though some of the foot might in fact be Polish, the drill and word of command were German. The fatal debility of government and treasury however prevented further development of a professional army. A change-over to a conscript army was also out of the question. Living comfortably off the labour of the peasants, and finding no need of an army to keep them in order, the nobles refused to allow the state either to tax or to conscript their serfs. Poland came to an end—Polish aristocracy went on.

It was in Russia that the East-European system came to full flower, producing the only army capable of standing up to Revolutionary and Napoleonic France on something like equal terms. Russia's long-continuing poverty and backwardness limited the possibility both of an armoured feudal cavalry in the Middle Ages and of a strong professional force in the sixteenth and seventeenth centuries. Originally soldiers were drawn from the small gentry, and from the poorer townsfolk who came to provide the semi-regular body of *streltsi*, one easily infected with the political grievances of the class to which it belonged.[89] In addition to these national contingents, foreign mercenaries were employed here too —Lithuanians and Tartars, for example.[90] In the last years of Boris Godunov (1598–1605) it was noticeable that his small guard of Germans stood by him to the end when all his other supporters had gone over to Dmitri and the Poles. This hint was not lost on the Romanovs, who now mounted the shaky throne. Like many other rulers, they made good use of the prodigious glut of soldiers of fortune produced by the Thirty Years' War. And presently it was realized that a still stronger as well as much cheaper alloy could be produced by mingling foreign professionals with native peasants conscripted for life and drilled by German officers or on German lines. The Romanov Army, while enabling Russia to intervene in Europe, found, as Pokrovsky points out, its first and fundamental task at home.[91] During the seventeenth and eigh-

[88] Allen, op. cit., p. 105.

[89] M. N. Pokrovsky, *Brief History of Russia* (English edn., London, 1933), i, p. 85.

[90] Lot, *L'Art Militaire*, ii, p. 389.

[91] Pokrovsky, op. cit., i, pp. 85–86, 89. Peter the Great's navy was officered as well as built for him by foreigners. In the Baltic fleet in 1713 only two out

teenth centuries serfdom was being imposed on a steadily expanding area, and the nobles accepted the necessity of a strong State and army to crush the strong resistance they met. As the peasants of each province were cowed, they could be enrolled and used to break resistance in others. The Tsarist Empire's size and heterogeneity, characteristic of all the States that survived in eastern Europe, facilitated this.

By the close of the seventeenth century one small corner of north-western Europe was committed to a new road of change and progress; but taking Europe as a whole, far more of its people were serfs than at the end of the fifteenth century, and its landlords were richer and more secure. Absolute monarchy had cauterized the continent with war and famine, and left it exhausted, but safe for the landowning aristocracy. Everywhere kings owed this success at least as much to the services of their foreign soldiers as to those of their own subjects.

---

of eleven commanders and seven out of seventy other officers were Russians (M. Mitchell, *The Maritime History of Russia 848–1948* [London, 1949], p. 63). Cf. the picture of foreign officers running away from their own Russian soldiers in A. Tolstoy, *Peter the First* (English edn., London, 1956), chap. iii, section 4.

VI

THE FRENCH PEASANTRY OF THE SEVENTEENTH CENTURY: A REGIONAL EXAMPLE[1]

Pierre Goubert

'THE seventeenth century is *terra incognita* as far as the land is concerned', wrote Marc Bloch in 1942, to explain a 'sad deficiency' in his *Caractères Originaux*.[2] For England and the Netherlands this is no longer true. But Marc Bloch was thinking only of France, and there his remark remains valid—and will do so until Jean Meuvret publishes his great work on *Le Problème des Subsistances au temps de Louis XIV*, the first volume of which will deal with agriculture and rural society throughout the kingdom of France.[3]

[1] This article (translated by G. Rudé was originally published in no. 10 (1956) and was by way of a preface to my thesis which was published in 1960 (below, note 4). We now know a good deal more about the French peasantry in the seventeenth century. But with two exceptions, we still await major studies: P. de Saint-Jacob, *Les Paysans de la Bourgogne du Nord au dernier siècle de l'Ancien Régime* (Paris, 1960); and R. Baehrel, *Une Croissance; la Basse-Provence rurale* (Paris, 1961). And it will be some years before we can get an overall view and precise knowledge of the problems.

[2] Letter by Marc Bloch published in *Annales E.S.C.*, iie année (1947), p. 365. M. Bloch's masterpiece, *Les Caractères Originaux de l'Histoire Rurale Française* (Paris and Oslo, 1931), was republished in 1952 and 1956 (Paris, edn. Armand Colin, two vols.). This work should serve as the basic text-book for any study of French rural history.

[3] Jean Meuvret's important work is still unpublished, and reference should be made to his numerous articles. Among those bearing on French rural history, the following should be noted: 'L'Histoire des prix des céréales en France dans la seconde moitié du XVIIe siècle, sources et publications', *Mélanges d'Histoire Sociale*, v (1944); 'Les Mouvements des prix de 1661 à

My intention in the present study is more modest and more limited in scope. I propose to examine rural society in a fairly small region, the Beauvaisis.[4] The Beauvaisis forms a link between the great cereal producing plains of Picardy, semi-pastoral Normandy, and the rich and varied lands of the Ile-de-France. This region had already by the seventeenth century acquired a degree of unity, by virtue of its past history (it corresponds to the old *civitas Bellovacorum*), and of the predominating influence exerted on it by the town of Beauvais, its regional capital, which was then of some importance.

In this type of research the historian's scope is strictly limited by the sources at his disposal. Among the most fruitful of these are the probate records relating to peasant properties, similar to those in England, the considerable interest of which has been repeatedly stressed by Dr. W. G. Hoskins. Equally valuable are the lawsuits

[4] All place-names cited in this article are in the western part of the present department of the Oise, most of them in the *arrondissement* of Beauvais. See P. Goubert, *Beauvais et le Beauvaisis de 1600 à 1730, contribution à l'histoire sociale de la France du XVIIe siècle*, 2 vols. (Paris, 1960).

1715 et leurs répercussions', *Jl. de la Société de Statistique de Paris*, May 1944; 'Les Crises de subsistances et la démographie de la France d'Ancien Régime', *Population* (Institut National d'Etudes Démographiques), i (1946); 'Circulation monétaire et utilisation économique de la monnaie dans la France du XVIe et du XVIIe siècle', *Etudes d'Histoire moderne et contemporaine*, i (1947); 'La Géographie des prix des céréales et les anciennes économies européennes: prix méditerranéens, prix continentaux, prix atlantiques à la fin du XVIIe siècle', *Revista de Economia*, iv (Lisbon, 1951); 'Agronomie et jardinage au XVIe et au XVIIe siècle', *Hommage à Lucien Febvre. Eventail de l'Histoire Vivante* (Paris, 1953), vol. ii; 'Manuels et traités à l'usage des commerçants aux premières époques de l'âge moderne', *Etudes d'Histoire moderne et contemporaine*, v (1953); 'Conjoncture et crise au XVIIe siècle. L'exemple des prix milanais', *Annales E.S.C.*, viiie année (1953); 'L'Agriculture en Europe aux XVIIe et XVIIIe siècles', *X Congresso internazionale di scienze storiche. Relazioni* (Florence, 1955), vol. iv; 'Comment les Français du XVIIe siècle voyaient l'impôt', *XVIIe siècle*, nos. 25–26 (1955); 'Le Commerce des grains et des farines à Paris et les marchands parisiens à l'époque de Louis XIV', *Rev. d'Histoire moderne et contemporaine*, iii (1956); 'Circuits d'échanges et travail rural dans la France du XVIIe siècle', *Studi in onore di Armando Sapori* (Milan, 1957), vol. ii; 'Les Prix des grains à Paris au XVe siècle et les origines de la mercuriale', *Paris et Ile-de-France, Mémoires*, xi (1960). Also M. Baulant and J. Meuvret, *Prix des céréales extraits de la mercuriale de Paris (1520–1698)*, 2 vols. (Paris, 1960–2).

involving appeals against over-assessment for the *taille*, in the course of which experts gave a complete analysis and valuation of the real estate (either owned or leased), the livestock, debts and credits of the tax-paying peasants who were challenging the amounts for which they were being assessed.[5] Also of prime interest are the field maps,[6] giving a dated analysis of landed property in the various parishes and lordships (*seigneuries*). Other sources of interest are the private papers, accounts, and leases of the *seigneurs* and other landowners—whether noble, bourgeois, or (as very frequently) clergy. This constitutes our basic documentary material.

For reasonably serious study to be possible such documentation must be fairly abundant and—perhaps even more important—sufficiently concentrated. In the case of the Beauvaisis neither requirement is fulfilled before the 1660s or 1670s, so I am not in a position to present a thorough social analysis, based on solid foundations, until the assumption of personal power by Louis XIV. In the preceding period the surviving sources are distinctly inferior in both quantity and quality: there are no field-maps or appeals against over-assessment; the inventories drawn up after death, though numerous enough, are brief, slipshod, carelessly drafted, and often incomplete. It is by no means impossible to present a picture of certain aspects of peasant society before 1660, but it would be dishonest to lay claim to any strict accuracy of analysis; general ideas, impressions, and hypotheses must, for this period, take the place of hard facts.

That is why I shall confine myself largely to presenting a picture of rural society as it appears in the last quarter of the seventeenth century, based on an abundance of source material which is both detailed and (I believe) sound. I shall then attempt a brief sketch

[5] The best study of the *taille* is by E. Esmonin, *La Taille en Normandie au temps de Colbert* (Paris, 1913). The documents used here are in Series C of the Departmental Archives.

[6] For land surveys and field maps see, above all, Marc Bloch's articles in the first numbers of *Annales* (1929). Paul Guichonnet has drawn attention to the exceptional character and interest of the Savoy land survey, in 'Le Cadastre savoyard de 1738 et son utilisation pour les recherches d'histoire et de géographie sociales', *Revue de géographie alpine*, xliii (1955), pp. 255–78. E. Le Roy-Ladourie will shortly publish his important thesis, *Les Paysans du Bas-Languedoc, XV*[e]*–XVIII*[e] *siècles*, in which land surveys of southern France are extensively used.

of a social evolution ranging over the whole of the seventeenth century and the early part of the eighteenth; but I fully admit that in the latter part of this project there will be an element of personal speculation, the extent of which I shall indicate as precisely as I can.

I

A detailed survey of 38 parishes of the *Election de Beauvais* was carried out in 1717. This survey was initiated by the Government and was not peculiar to this corner of France. The intention of the *Conseil Royal du Commerce* was to consider a fresh imposition of the *taille*, the principal direct tax of the day.[7] The division of the landed property in these 38 parishes was as follows: 22 per cent of the land belonged to the Church, 22 per cent to the nobility, 13 per cent to the bourgeoisie of Beauvais, and 43 per cent to the peasants. The peasants owned only a very small part of the vineyards, woods, and meadows (these being, incidentally, the most profitable form of cultivation). For our present purpose the important thing to notice in this government survey is the proportion of land held by the various groups: the peasants did not own half the land they tilled; their portion did not include the best lands; further, their holdings were more widely scattered than the lands of the privileged orders.

Forty years earlier a few large abbeys in the Beauvaisis had carried out a complete, careful, and accurate survey of the numerous parishes of which they held the lordship (*seigneurie*).[8] These abbeys did not concern themselves exclusively with their own estates (*domaines*) which their tenant-farmers cultivated; they also surveyed and charted the lands of their 'vassals'—the peasants who paid them seigneurial dues (and often tithes as well, which the large abbeys had generally taken over from the parish priests). Most of the maps made between 1670 and 1680 are accompanied by separate tables of proprietots and parcels of land. An examination of this complex of documents yields results similar to those which we have just quoted for 1717. Between 1670 and 1680 the peasants nowhere owned as much as half the land; sometimes, as

[7] This point is dealt with in *Beauvais et le Beauvaisis*, i, pp. 156–7.

[8] These documents are in Series G and H of the Departmental Archives of the Oise. The most complete set is that relating to the Benedictine Abbey of Saint-Germer. See *Beauvais et le Beauvaisis*, i, pp. 154–5 and 158.

in the neighbourhood of Beauvais, they owned only a quarter. In addition, at this date too, peasant land was the most scattered and the poorest in quality.

The field maps prepared by the abbeys have an additional advantage: they show how the lands were divided among the peasants themselves. To take a few examples—at Goincourt, of 98 peasant proprietors, 3 owned 10, 12, and 18 *hectares* respectively (a French *hectare* = nearly $2\frac{1}{2}$ acres); 94 owned less than 2 *hectares*. At Espaubourg, of 148 peasant proprietors, not one held as much as 10 *hectares*, and 125 held less than 2 *hectares*. At Coudray-Saint-Germer, 106 out of 125 held less than 2 *hectares*; only one owned as much as 30 *hectares*. These examples fall in the period 1672–80; they are all drawn from that part of the Beauvaisis which comes within the *Pays du Bray*, a region of great common pastures, where one might expect the peasants to be able to rear livestock at low cost. We shall see how far this possibility was, in fact, realized.

Two distinctive features, then, emerge. The peasants did not own half the land they cultivated, and among the peasants themselves holdings were extremely unevenly distributed. At least 80 per cent of the peasantry of the Beauvaisis owned only tiny plots; only a small minority of them owned more than 10 *hectares* (i.e. more than 25 acres). Were we to erect a social pyramid of peasant property, it would have a very broad base and an absurdly slender apex.

As the lands of the nobles, Church, and bourgeoisie were leased to peasants, it is clear that the latter were working that large proportion of the land of which they were not themselves the owners. It is not as easy to chart tenancy as landownership, nor as easy to compile a statistical analysis of tenants as of owners. To do so it would be necessary to assemble a wide range of documents that are, of course, scattered through a multiplicity of records and archives. Even so, the result would not correspond closely to reality. A general point does, however, emerge: the scattered parcels of land owned by the privileged orders and bourgeoisie were let out to small peasants, whereas the lands concentrated in large units (especially those belonging to the Church) were leased *en bloc* to enterprising tenants, such as the *laboureurs-fermiers* (substantial tenant-farmers) or *receveurs de seigneurie* (receivers for the lords of the manors): the latter formed the peak of the peasant social pyramid. But as these substantial people took on lease considerable estates (estates of 80, 100, 150 *hectares*, or more), they were only to be found in the villages in ones and twos; in some villages they were not to be found at all. Therefore, a general examination of tenancy in the Beauvaisis leads to both a confirmation and a correction of the conclusions arrived at from the study of the ownership of land. It leads to a confirmation in the sense that the small leases (of 1, 2, or 3 *hectares*) go to the small proprietors, and that these remain 'small men' (there are, however, a few exceptions to this rule). But it also leads to a correction, because we shall now have to place at the summit of the economic and social hierarchy of the peasants the great *fermiers-receveurs* of the nobility and clergy, and not the ordinary *laboureurs* who, as we shall see, rarely owned and exploited holdings of more than 30 *hectares*.

We shall, therefore, not be tempted to base the rest of our account on the antithesis *laboureur* (peasant)—*manouvrier* (wage-worker), which expresses almost the sum total of what is generally known about French peasant society. If this oversimplified antithesis remains roughly true, it is far from expressing the whole graded complexity of social relations in the village. It has, however, the merit of stressing the interest in social terminology which prevailed in the French countryside. Like the town-dwellers the French peasants were very conscious of titles and dignities. One has only to look through the registers of baptisms, marriages, and burials (the most abundant of all French documents of the seventeenth century), or to peruse the tax-rolls to see that Jacques Bonhomme or Pierre Durand is only too glad to assume a title to express his position in society. If he can do no better, he is merely 'Jacques Bonhomme, manouvrier'. If he tenderly cultivates three rows of bad vine-stock, he styles himself 'vine-grower'. If, in the course of the winter, he repairs three pairs of wheels, he becomes 'wheelwright'. Should he sell a few sacks of wheat or a few fleeces in the neighbouring market, he proudly calls himself 'merchant'. Should he happen to own that great wooden instrument bound with a few pieces of iron, which in the Beauvaisis was the usual plough, and the two horses required to pull it, he becomes 'laboureur'. But if he holds lands of the Prince de Conti, of the nuns of the Abbaye Royale de Saint-Paul, or of Jacques-Bénigne Bossuet, Bishop of Meaux and Abbot of Saint-Lucien-les-Beauvais, Jacques Bonhomme flaunts the title of 'laboureur, fermier, et receveur de Monseigneur'.

In fact, the host of *manouvriers* constituted, in nearly every village, the majority—the overwhelming majority—of the inhabitants. In the Beauvaisis it was rare for a *manouvrier* to be a fully-fledged proletarian. Doubtless there existed a few wretched families, dependent more or less on begging, who eked out their lives in hovels of wood, straw, and dried mud, which could scarcely be called houses. These poor wretches appear in the tax-rolls as 'propertyless', 'destitute', 'impotent', taxed symbolically at a farthing. Except in times of plague and famine, however, these social outcasts remain the exception.

The typical *manouvrier* owns a few acres, a cottage, and a small garden—for the *manouvriers* of the Beauvaisis were almost all very small proprietors. The garden yielded hemp, beans, cabbages, and a few apples. Their few acres produced some sacks of maslin (a mixture of wheat and rye): in short, enough to feed a family for a few months or a few weeks a year. Could the *manouvriers* count on their cattle to improve their situation? Poultry and pigs, though providing tasty dishes, are ravaging, scavenging, and marauding beasts, that compete with human beings in their greed for grain. The Beauvaisis *manouvrier* generally kept three or four hens, but rarely a pig. The regular habit of eating salt bacon and 'chicken in the pot' was, to all intents and purposes, impossible for him. Could he not at least get milk from his cow, seeing that our best writers commonly speak of the cow as the 'poor man's beast'? Our documents bring to light a few skinny cows: for lack of a meadow or even common pasture, young lads would drive them along the lanes and occasional thickets on the edge of the fields. But one *manouvrier* in two had no cow of his own. The real 'poor man's beast' was the sheep, whose fleeces and lambs helped to pay his taxes. It fed as best it could—on the stony plots they call *riez* in Picardy; on the fallow-land four months in the year, between gleaning and the first ploughing; in winter, in the stall, grazing off its straw litter for want of real hay (for it is certain that what they called 'fodder' in Picardy was straw).

It is understandable, then, that the *manouvrier* should often hire himself out to the *laboureurs* and large farmers. He was the all-round countryman who worked for others at trivial, seasonal, and occasional jobs: at haymaking, harvesting, gathering grapes, threshing, clipping hedges, sawing wood, or cleaning out ditches. The larger farms, especially in summer, had need of this cheap and abundant labour. The *manouvrier* received for his pains a bowl of soup, a jug of wine, a few ears of corn, a few pence; and often he did not actually receive any money since he was already in debt to his employer. By working for the man who had ploughed a field for him, advanced him seed, peas, or wood, the *manouvrier* paid back his creditor and might hope for new loans, new advances, new services, which might help him to get through the year.

To get through it without too much hardship and to supplement the meagre resources provided by his few acres and insufficient wages, the *manouvrier* often tried to set up as a tenant-farmer himself, or to take up some kind of subsidiary occupation, generally of a seasonal nature.

Having no horses and insufficient cattle to provide an abundance of manure, and being without capital reserves, the peasant smallholder could not be other than a small tenant-farmer. The owner of three acres, he could hardly hope to take on the cultivation of more than another three. He would find land to lease among the small plots belonging to country churches or *fabriques*—small religious institutions in the parishes. Again, he might lease a few scattered fields that a stranger to the village had inherited or a townsman had acquired from a mortgaged debtor. In any event, these snippets of land cost the *manouvrier* dear in return for a meagre, sometimes non-existent, profit. In a bad year the rent swallowed up the yield; in a plentiful year, when the price of corn was low, the harvest represented a poor return for a heavy expenditure of toil; but at least it then helped to feed his household.

It was better, in fact, to try to take up a secondary occupation. The coopers, wheelwrights, tailors, and weavers, that one finds in such large numbers in every village, were really *manouvriers* seeking additional means of livelihood. Their village clients, however, were not sufficient to keep them in full employment: they would work at their trade from time to time, at the most favourable seasons of the year. But always they were peasants rather than artisans. Yet there is one exception—if indeed it is an exception—which is to be found in the plains of Picardy: that is the countrymen who worked wool in the south and west of Picardy, and linen in the east and north-east. On the outskirts of Beauvais a dozen villages were engaged in carding and combing the wool produced locally or imported from neighbouring districts. The carders and combers were also spinners, for they did not always leave the handling of the spinning-wheel and winder to their womenfolk. Very often, too, they prepared the serge-warp, which they sold to the manufacturers of Beauvais. Farther north, towards Amiens and Abbeville, we find serge-weavers rather than carders and combers, who wove their heavy, coarse Picard cloths on crude looms—cloths ranging over every conceivable type of serge, whose names are taken from such villages as Blicourt, Aumale, and Tricot. These country weavers owned neither their raw materials nor their tools; these they hired from Amiens and Beauvais merchants, who paid them by the piece, in kind more often than in cash. Most of the villages were peopled with a host of these 'sergers' and carders, and looms were more in evidence than ploughs. All these textile-workers are, of course, *manouvriers* and smallholders, who would interrupt their weaving to tend their garden of beans and their acre of maslin: in the summer they would hire themselves out for the harvest. And so, in this almost pastureless plateau of Picardy, which yielded nothing but grain, its dense population was often saved from starvation by its occupation in the various processes of woollen manufacture. So it was in the case of the *mulquiniers* who wove linen cloth in the region of Clermont, Péronne, and Saint-Quentin: these men, working in damp and gloomy cellars, were also peasants—tiny proprietors, small graziers, in fact *manouvriers*.

It is clear that, generally speaking, numerous imperceptible gradations lead from the mass of *manouvriers* to the favoured, restricted group of *laboureurs*. But these shades of social distinction and transitional stages are not to be found on the plateau of Picardy. In that bleak countryside, with its monotonous type of farming, peasant society appeared only in brutal contrasts. At the social peak was the large farmer, flanked by five or six *laboureurs*; down below was the wretched mass of *manouvriers*; between them, nothing.

The southern part of the Beauvaisis, however, affords a sharp contrast. Here we find rolling pastures, reminiscent of Normandy, cut by the fertile banks of the Oise and the Thérain; its hillsides covered with vines and crowned with woods, on the borders of the Ile-de-France. The charm, freshness, and diversity of the landscape seem in themselves to give rise to a rural society in which finer gradations and distinctions abound. Here we no longer find serge-weavers tied to town manufacturers or merchants, but one or two weavers in every village who work up, for all, the hemp which everyone grows in his garden. There are still *manouvriers*, but they often possess their own cow and half a dozen sheep, sometimes even their own sow, for here it is easier to feed livestock. These *manouvriers* are not only a little less poor, they are also far less numerous, and rarely a majority in their village. The largest proportion of the population is composed of the most 'French' of all the peasants:[9] these were not the village poor, still less were they proletarians, nor were they ever prosperous members of the community; they were gardeners rather than farmers, vine-growers rather than corn-growers: skilled enough in the use of their hands to make remarkable craftsmen, artists even, though unrecognized: intelligent and adaptable enough to vary their occupation according to the season, the year, local urban demand, or the whims and fashions emanating from 'the big city', Paris, which lay ten or fifteen leagues away. These were the *airiers*, a kind of market-gardener who supplied the neighbouring markets with fresh vegetables: those of Bresles grew artichokes and asparagus for Paris; others tended high-grade apple trees which they imported from Normandy. On the slopes overlooking the Oise and the Thérain, in the near vicinity of Beauvais, vine-growers forced, from a soil too heavy and starved of warm sunshine, a few hogsheads of dry, bitter, harsh wine that was either drunk immediately or sent north, especially to Amiens. They were makers of the *blondes* and *noires*, the names given to a species of linen-thread lace which 'invaded' Paris in Louis XIV's time and, in the eighteenth century, 'conquered' Spain and the West Indies. Among them, too, were the makers of fans and fancy wear in the district of Meru, skilled in working ivory for sale to Paris dealers. Less prosperous were the *blatiers* (corn chandlers) peasants furnished with a donkey or mule, on which they carried, one sack at a time, corn to the mills of Pontoise or flour to the bakers of Gonesse. Or there were those who drove Norman cattle to the plains of Poissy to be fattened up before being handed over to the butchers of Paris.

Of course, all these peasants tended their gardens and a few fields, became haymakers, reapers, and threshers, and periodically

[9] 'France', in the strict meaning of the word, is the small fertile plain extending to the north of Paris from Saint-Denis 'en France'. The term 'province of the Ile-de-France' is an early extension of this meaning. The northern limit of the Ile-de-France is the Forest of Chantilly.

hired themselves out as wage-workers pure and simple; but they refused to call themselves *manouvriers*.

Very close to these social types were the so-called *haricotiers* (kidney bean growers), found in the district of Bray in the Oise valley and occasionally in the Soissonnais. Not that they specialized in growing kidney beans: indeed what we now call kidney beans were called peas in the seventeenth century. The *haricotiers* with whom I am most familiar—those of the Bray district—owned a few more acres than the ordinary *manouvrier*: they normally farmed about 20 acres, of which they owned at least half. They kept one or two cows, five or six sheep, and sometimes a mule. They sold apples, eggs, and cheese. They made vine-props and worked in wicker, flax, or wood. Yet these humble peasants rarely hired out their labour to rich farmers: their own occupations kept them too busy. Were we to adopt a modern, colloquial, yet reasonably appropriate term, we might call them *bricoleurs* (jacks-of-all-trades).

None of these different types of peasant—*haricotiers*, craftsmen, vine-growers, corn chandlers, gardeners—had the pretension to call themselves by the exalted title of *laboureur*.

In other provinces—in Poitou for example—there existed *laboureurs à bras*, that is *laboureurs* who did not possess a plough or a horse. In the Beauvaisis such a thing would have been impossible. In fact no social term had so clear and concise a meaning: a *laboureur* was, almost by definition, a man who owned a plough and a pair of horses. (Oxen were quite unknown, both as draught animals and for stock raising.) The social importance of people who possessed so precious and rare a capital may be appreciated: a simple plough-horse, fully grown and in good health, was worth at least 60 *livres*. This corresponded to the price of three fatted cows, or 20 sheep, or twenty *hectolitres* (55 bushels) of corn in a good year. The *laboureur*, therefore, took a pride in ploughing, three or four times a year, his own land with his own horses. He could take on lease other lands and plough them when he wished; he could use his horses for carting manure, crops, straw, hay, wood, or wine. He would hire out his horses to the *manouvriers* and *haricotiers*, who were incapable of engaging in the humblest form of farming without the essential aid of the *laboureur*'s horses. Thus the *laboureurs* became the creditors of the mass of small peasants and, when occasion demanded, their employers at low wages.

How much better the *laboureur* lived than the mass of the peasants! He ate off pewter, sometimes laid out on a table-cloth. His cupboards were stocked with pairs of sheets, towels, shirts—some of fine embroidered cloth. He had reserves of corn, peas, beans, and even a whole pig in his earthen salting-tub. His Sunday-clothes were of stout serge. To attend mass or the village ball his wife and daughters would deck themselves out in linen bodices, bright-coloured skirts and petticoats, and a small golden cross at their necks. All of which was in glaring contrast with the manner of living of the bare-footed *manouvrier*, clad in coarse hempen cloth, often without bed- or table-linen, without even a table or provisions, eating a thick soup from an earthen bowl with a wooden spoon.

But the *labourewr* is a fairly rare social specimen. At Loueuse, out of 86 householders, only 3 were *laboureurs*; in Saint-Omer en Chaussée, 10 out of 93; at Crillon, 6 out of 70; at Glatigny, 3 out of 90; at Litz, 6 out of 43; at La Houssaye, only 1 out of 46 payers of the *taille*.

Yet even within this strictly limited social class, so clearly cut off from the mass of the peasantry, there were many grades both in the size of landholding and in social position. There were genuine *laboureurs* who farmed no more than 35–40 acres and kept only three cows. Others were the owners, apart from their horses and cattle, of a mere two or three pieces of land; they farmed chiefly as tenants. Such a man might keep a fair number of pigs, perhaps twenty or more—because he had bought from the lord of the manor the *droit de glandée*, the right to graze his pigs in the lord's wood when the acorns fell. At Loueuse, in 1694, François Andrieu had the distinction of not renting any land: he farmed his own land, nearly 100 acres, with five horses and two ploughmen. This large peasant-proprietor, however, owned no more than three cows, two pigs, and twenty-three sheep—an indication of the small amount of livestock owned by even the largest farmers in this province at this period. In a better grazing district, Charles Bournizien of Villers-Vermont, in 1683, kept thirteen cows and eighty-five sheep: he had a few enclosed pastures of his own, was a tenant of a noble lady, and had the use, in the Bray district, of the common pastures of his village, which, though not yielding grass of the highest quality, were extremely spacious. Bournizien and Andrieu are the most substantial *laboureurs* that I have come across in the Beauvaisis between 1670 and 1700. They both possessed the enviable privilege of never having to fear hunger and of always having a surplus of produce for sale—grain, calves, or fleeces: yet even they are not at the top of the peasant social hierarchy.

That position, without any doubt, is occupied by the big tenants and receivers of the *seigneuries*. Claude Dumesnil, tenant and receiver of the Abbaye Royale de Saint-Paul at Goincourt, worked 100 *hectares* of land, 12 *hectares* of meadow, a large vineyard, and two woods, with the aid of twelve horses, two carters, two ploughmen, and an abundant supply of seasonal workers. Tenant of the abbey lands, he also farmed the seigneurial rights, the tithes (which the Abbey had appropriated from the local priest), and the monopoly of the wine-press. For all this he paid the 'Ladies of Saint-Paul' 1,200 *livres tournois* and 40 *hectolitres* of best wheat a year. He had leased out his own property (a house and a few fields) for 100 *livres*. At Goincourt he owned twenty-five cows, six sows, and 225 sheep. These are the highest figures I have come across. The seigneurial dovecot on his farm housed 160 pigeons; 180 fowl fed in his backyard: among them were a couple of dozen turkeys, and as many ducks—birds that are seldom found at all, even among the wealthiest *laboureurs*. His reserves of grain, beans, peas, liquor, and timber, were considerable: there were more than 8,000 sheaves, over 100 barrels of wine and cider, and 200 fleeces in his barn. Half the villagers of Goincourt were in his debt, and 41 families in the adjoining parishes owed him a total of 1,700 *livres*. Dumesnil lent out horses, wagons, corn, hay, timber, and even money. It was this role of creditor that made him a figure of economic, social, and political importance. In short, he was a power in the land. Dumesnil even had a small library, composed of pious works and stories of travel: many a merchant in the neighbouring town possessed no more than a prayer-book.

Such persons were to be found in every parish where the *seigneur* owned a large, compact domain. They usually appear to be the tenants of bishops, canons, and large abbeys. The tenant of the Ursulines of Beauvais at Moyenneville lent money to the convent, where his two daughters were inmates. The tenant of the Benedictine monastery of Saint-Germer at Coudray-Saint-Germer had ruined the petty noblemen of the neighbourhood by lending them money at heavy rates of interest on mortgages. By the end of the seventeenth century the large *fermiers-receveurs* constituted a closed caste. They intermarried, succeeded one another from father to son, or from father to son-in-law, entered into agreements to reserve for themselves the best leases, and left no tenancies available for those outside their circle. During the Revolution they frequently bought up the lands which their old masters, now expropriated, had for many years been renting to their families. Even today it is not uncommon to find established on former ecclesiastical lands, sold at the time of the Revolution, the descendants of the powerful receivers of the *ancien régime*. It is these receivers, placed high above the common peasant, who form the apex of the peasant hierarchy of the Beauvaisis.[10]

II

A precise answer must now be attempted to the question: how many of all these peasants were able to enjoy economic independence—to feed their families from that portion of the harvest left at their disposal?

First, let us consider the most vital product of all, wheat. It represents the staple food of the people of the north and centre of France, whether in the shape of bread, soup, or gruel. M. Labrousse has shown that a daily ration of 2 to 2½ pounds of bread was essential to the maintenance of each adult, and that the value of this amount of bread represented at least half the poor man's budget.[11] These calculations apply to the more prosperous part of the eighteenth century, from 1733 to the Revolution. There are good reasons for supposing that these figures are not high enough for the seventeenth century; nevertheless, let us accept them as a basis. The most common type of peasant household consisted of six persons—father, mother, three children, and a grandparent. Even if it included two very young children (fed from an early age on gruel and bread), it is unlikely that a family of this size consumed less than 10 pounds of bread per day. To produce this amount of bread for a whole year required 18 quintals of wheat. From extensive documentary evidence it appears that the yield of

[10] See above, n. 3.

[11] cf. E. Labrousse, *Esquisse du Mouvement des Prix et des Revenus en France au XVIIIe siècle*, 2 vols. (Paris, 1933); and *La Crise de l'Economie Française à la Fin de l'Ancien Régime et au Début de la Révolution* (Paris, 1944).

the best lands in the Beauvaisis, even with the most favourable harvests, rarely exceeded 9 quintals per *hectare*, or six times the outlay of seed.[12] In years when harvests were bad, the yield barely reached 4 quintals per *hectare*.

Yet we cannot conclude from the above that 2 *hectares* of land in good years and 4½ in bad were sufficient to feed a household of peasants. For one thing, the whole of the Beauvaisis belonged to the great region of triennial rotation: usually a field would be under wheat for only one year in three. We shall therefore need to treble the areas just quoted, which will give us a minimum of 6 *hectares* and a maximum of 13½. Secondly, we must remember that the peasant-proprietor could not possibly retain his whole crop. What deductions had first to be made from it?

In the first place, he had to deduct his future seed—one-sixth of his crop, and a larger proportion in bad years. He had to pay the *taille* to the King. An average peasant—let us say a fair-sized *haricotier* or small *laboureur*—would have to pay at least 20 *livres tournois* a year, the equivalent of 4 quintals of wheat in a year when prices were low, or the output of half a *hectare* of land. He was subject to other royal taxes as well, such as the *gabelle* (salt tax), which, though their incidence is hard to compute, amounted to at least as much as the *taille*. So the King took from our small *laboureur* the equivalent of the full yield of a *hectare* of wheat, corresponding to 3 *hectares* of land. The ecclesiastical tithe-owner had been the first to appear on the scene and had already carried off from six to nine in every hundred sheaves. The *seigneur*, of course, had his share as well: what he exacted varied widely from place to place. In the northern Beauvaisis, the *droits de champart* (tributes in kind) took a heavy toll: nine sheaves in every hundred on top of the tithe. A further charge was the grain paid as wages to the reapers and threshers, whose services were generally required. If we total up these various initial charges—seed, sundry expenses, royal taxes, ecclesiastical and seigneurial dues—they amount to at least half of the wheat-crop. (Similar charges also applied to spring-sown cereals, such as oats, and even to wine.) In fact, the peasant proprietor who aimed to feed his family on the produce of his land would need to grow twice the amount he required for this purpose. To run over the figures again: the peasant who aspired to

[12] cf. P. Goubert, 'Les Techniques agricoles dans les pays picards aux XVIIe et XVIIIe siècles', *Rev. d'Histoire économique et sociale,* xxxv (1957), pp. 24–40.

a state of economic independence had to farm a minimum of 12 *hectares* (nearly 30 acres) in years of plenty, and 27 *hectares* (65 acres) in years of shortage. Thus, not a single *manouvrier*, not a single *haricotier* or average *laboureur*, could be economically independent. The large *laboureurs*, the owners of at least 27 *hectares*—considerably less than one-tenth of the peasantry—alone were assured of being able to feed their families comfortably under all circumstances. Those owning less than 12 *hectares* of land could not provide from the produce of their own fields the means to feed their families: they would have to buy additional wheat—that is, sell their labour in exchange.

Leaving aside the large tenant-farmers, whose lot need arouse no pity, the position of the majority of the tenant-farmers was even more precarious. Indeed, in their case, the rent has to be added to all the other charges already mentioned. In the northern part of the Beauvaisis the rent usually amounted to 1½ quintals of wheat per *hectare*. So the annual charge of the landlord amounted to a proportion varying from one-sixth to one-third of the crop, according to the nature of the harvest.

In short, the small peasant who was least severely affected by the complex system of initial charges on the yearly produce was the proprietor who farmed his own land; the most severely affected was the small tenant-farmer who owned but few acres. By heavy toil, the *manouvriers, haricotiers,* and small *laboureurs* were able, in favourable years, to extract from a good deal of rented land, a fair proportion of the food required for their family's upkeep, which their own fields were unable to provide. In years of bad harvest small farms were more of a burden than a support. In no case could a holding of less than 12 *hectares* assure its occupant of the slightest trace of economic independence. As our documents amply illustrate, the great majority of peasants—three-quarters or more—remained well below that level. Were they, then, condemned to suffer hunger, or even starve to death?

The answer is most definitely in the affirmative. Three facts emerge beyond dispute. In the first place, the majority of the peasants of the Beauvaisis suffered from almost continuous undernourishment. Secondly, they devoted considerable courage and imagination to attempts to procure that extra food which their own lands could not produce. Thirdly, they did not always succeed in doing so: during lean years, which were not exceptional, they had to resign themselves to dying in their thousands for lack of food.

The first fact, the most difficult to prove beyond all doubt, emerges from the study of a large number of inventories drawn up after death. The almost total absence of meat from the *manouvrier*'s diet was due, as we have seen, to his lack of livestock. He hardly ever had bacon since he had not the means to feed pigs. His vegetables were those of low food value: apart from cabbages, green vegetables were little known, and certainly rarely grown, except just outside the towns. There was a general absence of fruit, except in autumn: soft fruit was scarce since it takes a long time to ripen. The wild berries picked in the hedges were mostly used in drinks; the cider-apples and pears were crushed to make weak cider, heavily diluted with water. A little fruit of better quality was sold in the town markets: the income derived from it helped to pay the taxes. On the plateau of Picardy only the wealthier *laboureurs* and the larger tenant-farmers had milk and cheese: in the pastoral district of Bray, milk was made into butter and cheese and sold to Parisians at Gournay. As for whey, we know that the great bleaching establishments of Beauvais had a considerable demand for it between March and September.[13] What we know for certain is that the basis of the diet was formed by bread, soup, gruel, large peas (called *bizaille*), and beans—a diet both heavy and lacking in nutrition, insufficient during winter and increasingly so as spring approached, despite the seasonal addition of the first green vegetables, gathered in fields, meadows, and ditches. Nor did his pale cider or bitter, green wine (that quickly spoiled) have any nutritional, or even medicinal, value.

In our analysis of peasant society we have repeatedly stressed the incessant search for other forms of income, for piece-work and such like, that is characteristic of all the *manouvriers*, of almost all the *haricotiers*, and of most of the smaller *laboureurs*. This search, which was absolutely essential in order to feed their families, to pay the *taille*, and to survive at all, took the form of hunting for vacant leases, for wool to spin, for lace to manufacture, for wood to chop, carve, or sell, for any small job on the larger estates. If need be, should ordinary work fail, they would resort to all sorts

[13] I hope that the importance of the part played by the cloth-bleaching establishments of Beauvais and elsewhere is clear from my *Familles Marchandes sous l'Ancien Régime: les Danse et les Motte de Beauvais* (Paris, 1959).

of alternatives—picking leaves, herbs, acorns, berries, which every forest-owner forbade, royal, noble, or episcopal. The result was a considerable crop of offences against the forest laws, not to mention breaches of the laws relating to fishing and hunting. (It is a striking fact that nearly every peasant went armed.) It was but a small step from this to a profusion of minor thefts, or even to open begging. This was a particularly distinctive feature of those dreadful years when, as the saying went, 'the times were out of joint', and harvests shrank to a half, or even to a third, of their normal yield.

At such times that considerable majority of peasants whose farms were too small went short of everything: of wheat, first of all, and then of all those subsidiary foods just mentioned, which formed part of their basic subsistence. In fact the larger *laboureurs* and farmers reduced the number of their hands and cut their wages. The weavers, too, lacked work; in times of high prices the woollen cloth bought by the poor of the Beauvaisis found no sale, and merchants, fearful of adding to the stocks already in their hands, compelled the town and country craftsmen to stop their looms.[14] Everything fell off at the same time—crops, work in the fields, and work in industry.

Some of the peasants, normally tied to the soil, would then take to the road in search of bread. They would beg at the doors of the rich farmers and the *curés*; but even if the latter were charitably disposed they could not help everybody. They would go knocking at the gates of the wealthy abbeys, some of which would organize a free distribution of bread; but then thousands of poor wretches would appear, bringing with them the inevitable accompaniment of contagious disease. Most of the impoverished peasants would try to enter the towns, where there was always some provision of relief organized by a variety of charitable bodies. But the towns would turn away these 'foreigners', by force if need be: they were already bearing the heavy burden of their own poor.

Very swiftly the weaker elements of the rural (and urban) population would begin to die off—old folk, infants, adolescents. In September or October, two months after the harvest, the names entered in the parochial burial registers would begin to mount up. There would be no fall in the mortality rate during the winter, and

[14] M. Labrousse's *Esquisse du Mouvement des Prix* clearly showed the connection between agricultural and textile crises. I have observed the same in the Beauvaisis in the seventeenth century.

it would reach its peak in the spring, when dwindling stocks of food would be exhausted, and epidemics, thriving on weakened physiques, would spread among the poorer classes and, eventually, strike the rich, who, till then, had suffered nothing. At the same time there would be fewer marriages and even births would fall far below their accustomed figure; the very fertility of the population would be severely affected. In ten or twelve months—between 1661 and 1662, between 1693 and 1694, and again between 1709 and 1710—ten to fifteen per cent of the inhabitants of a village would disappear, carried off by famine or epidemic. Some townships of the Beauvaisis lost as much as a quarter of their population in this manner. The *manouvriers* were always the hardest hit, both relatively and absolutely. After such a blood-letting there followed a few years of comparatively prosperous existence; there was more work for fewer hands, there was more land to let, and the people of the countryside could breathe a little more freely, until the next disastrous harvest, which inevitably brought in its train, at least until 1740, the same or similar misfortunes.

There can be little doubt that these phenomena—and they are amply proven—express a kind of periodical disequilibrium between an irregular food-supply and a prolific population, subject to fitful and uncontrolled increase. It seems likely that they left a deeper mark on a cereal-producing region like Picardy than on a fertile and varied region such as Normandy and the Ile-de-France: and this difference suggests that small-scale farming, so roundly condemned by the Physiocrats in the eighteenth century, had certain solid advantages. Above all, we must not forget that, in those years of endurance, the memory of which remained deeply imprinted on the popular mind, the villages suffered as much as or perhaps more than the towns, and that the social structure of the peasantry was then brutally laid bare: those who died in their thousands were the *manouvriers*, the small peasants who owned a few acres and a cow and could not find work to supplement their incomes.

Although every adult had had some experience of such years, these years of heavy mortality were fairly rare—not more than one in ten. During the years of respite the Beauvaisis peasants managed, in one way or another, to make a living; yet it was under a growing burden of debt.

It would require a whole volume on its own to study the

question of peasant indebtedness in any detail—an important question, though little explored. Here we can only indicate its diversity, inevitability, and intensity. Every small peasant was indebted to one or more *laboureurs*, who lent him horses and working stock, carted his produce, sold or advanced him a lamb, timber, beans, wheat. Every small peasant owed his landlord arrears of rent and for advances of seed or money. His debts to the *seigneur* were not so great; but he always owed substantial amounts to the tax-collector, since he found difficulty in having the necessary ready cash available. Then, less onerous, but a burden nevertheless, there were his debts to the blacksmith, wheelwright, tailor, weaver, village shepherd, the religious confraternity, the schoolmaster, not to mention the innkeeper of the nearest township. Finally, there were the usual rural money-lenders—lawyers, innkeepers, large farmers, magistrates—whose activities extended over a large part of the countryside. They often acted as 'covers' for the wealthy bourgeois of Beauvais. This type of lender was the most dangerous: he held contracts for loans drawn up by lawyers, and they always involved a mortgage on the debtor's property. When the debtor defaulted his land passed to the creditor. The courts automatically returned a verdict in favour of such transfers, all the more readily since the creditors were often themselves the judges. The study of peasant indebtedness is, in fact, one of the main clues that make it possible to trace the evolution of the condition of the peasantry throughout the seventeenth century.

III

Available sources do not enable one to trace the development of the peasantry of the Beauvaisis, Picardy, or the northern Ile-de-France between 1600 and 1635. An historian of excessive ingenuity—and there are such—could, of course, use isolated examples to invent a social pattern corresponding to his own pet theories or the fashion of the moment. For 1635 to 1660 the documentary material is more abundant and makes it possible to put forward certain tentative hypotheses, some of which appear to have fairly solid foundations, even if they do not accord with traditional ideas on the subject. For the period after 1660 it will be possible, in a few years' time, when extensive archival research has been completed, to present a study that is solidly based on reliable source material. No conclusion of general validity can, of course, be advanced with any confidence until comparative studies have been carried out in a number of strictly limited and defined regions of seventeenth-century France. What follows is, therefore, no more than a number of hypotheses, of uncertain validity for the earlier periods and, in any case, not claiming to be applicable to any region other than the Beauvaisis.

The general economic atmosphere prevalent in the Beauvaisis and Picardy during the years 1600 to 1635 may be defined as follows: in spite of occasional temporary falls the general trend of prices during these years was a rise of about 25 per cent. This may seem surprising as some historians have claimed that prices began to fall from 1620, or even from 1600. In the region covered by our study (including Picardy), however, the movement of prices followed the trend just noted.[15] A study of successive and comparable lists of farm-leases shows that rents in no way lagged behind the upward movement of agricultural prices; in fact, rather the contrary. From what statistics there are available of textile production at Beauvais—and Amiens, too—it appears that the highest urban output of the whole century took place between 1624 and 1634; but we know nothing about rural output for this period, and seem never likely to. If the long-term trend of baptisms, marriages, and burials can be taken as a reliable indication of the movement of population, it may be established with reasonable certainty that the population noticeably increased between 1600 and 1635, despite a number of disasters of varying magnitude, such as a plague between 1620 and 1630 and a great food crisis in 1630–1. The sum total of these symptoms—economic, social and demographic—reveals a phase of economic expansion, an 'A phase', to adopt the terminology in vogue since Simiand's day. But this expansive phase is slight and its significance is not easy to estimate; perhaps it was peculiar to the north of France. During such a period it may be suggested that the conditions of the peasantry were not at their worst.

But this evidence is only indirect. My own direct knowledge of the peasantry—very scanty for this period—boils down to a few impressions. The small, 'average' *laboureurs* seem relatively numerous; their post-mortem inventories suggest a fair standard

[15] For prices, incomes, etc., see *Beauvais et le Beauvaisis*, i, *passim*, and ii, 'Cartes et graphiques'.

of prosperity; some even amassed a little ready cash. On the other hand there are few really rich *laboureurs*. The great abbeys had trouble in finding tenants for their larger estates—those of over 60 *hectares*: they were compelled to divide them into three or four plots and lease each one to a fair-sized *laboureur*, and each of the tenants found it difficult to pay his yearly rent. I know next to nothing about the *manouvriers*, and I have found no trace of peasant revolts, although they are frequent in the neighbouring provinces, such as Normandy.[16] If we leave aside a number of terrible disasters, the peasantry probably did not suffer at this time from exceptional poverty; and it seems likely that the contrasts between the various social groups were less marked than they became later.

The subsequent period is notorious for the military disasters of 1636, twenty-five years of war, bringing every sort of fiscal imposition in their train, a weak regency, and five years of civil war. Few years of French history are in such need of being studied afresh; the results are likely to be surprising.

Between 1635 and 1660 the peasants of the Beauvaisis and southern Picardy suffered a few months of panic in 1636, followed in 1647 to 1653 by a crisis—economic, social, demographic, physiological, and moral—of an intensity and duration hitherto unknown. The panic of 1636 resulted from the Spanish invasion. A few villages were burned down, some of the crops plundered. The peasants fled before the troopers, carrying with them their livestock, food-supplies, savings, and families. We find the Picards encamped in the Bray district in August and September; many took refuge with their belongings behind the solid walls of Beauvais and there awaited liberation. They had set out after the harvest and returned to their farms in time for the autumn ploughing. In Alsace and Lorraine, as we know, the results for the countryside of the events of 1636 were extremely serious;[17] but in

[16] These peasant revolts have been stressed by V.-L. Tapié, *La France de Louis XIII et de Richelieu* (Paris, 1952), following B. F. Porshnev, *Narodnie Vosstaniya vo Frantsii pered Frondoi* (Moscow, 1948). See also R. Mousnier, 'Recherches sur les soulèvements populaires en France avant la Fronde', *Rev. d'Histoire moderne et contemporaine*, v (1958), p. 81; and R. Mandrou, 'Les Soulèvements populaires et la société française du XVIIe siècle', *Annales E.S.C.*, xive année (1959), p. 756.

[17] G. Livet, *L'Intendance d'Alsace sous Louis XIV, 1648–1715* (Strasbourg–Paris, 1956), must serve as the basis for all future studies of eastern France in the seventeenth century.

our region they were comparatively slight. From 1636 to 1647 prices remained fairly high, rents continued to rise, and the population figures resumed their upward course (a cause for lamentation rather than rejoicing). There followed a series of disasters, of which the complex phenomena called the Fronde is only an aspect.[18] In the Beauvaisis—as, no doubt, in other provinces—the key is probably to be found in an unusually prolonged series of bad harvests. For five consecutive years, from 1647 to 1651, agriculture was the victim of bad weather; the most disastrous harvests being those of 1649 and 1651. The usual food crisis was therefore carried over (generally with increased intensity) from one year to the next; the result was a steep rise and heavy extension of poverty and mortality, and a sharp fall in births. As usual the crisis in industry followed close on the heels of the agricultural crisis. The population of the Beauvaisis (and, maybe, of the whole of France) experienced in these years a succession of misfortunes the like of which did not recur in the following years. It seems probable that it was at this point that the general structure of peasant society that we have analysed took firm shape. Crushed by debt the small peasants had to give up a large part of their land to their creditors.

This was the moment chosen by the bourgeoisie of Beauvais, by a series of easy transactions, to appropriate hundreds of *hectares* of land. At the same time this bourgeoisie was completing the ruin of a part of the old rural nobility. For paltry sums, on terms that were little short of scandalous, they bought up manors, noble domains, whole *seigneuries*. And these new lords, former bourgeois who quickly acquired titles of nobility, pressed far more heavily on the mass of the subject peasantry than the old. Simultaneously, in these crucial years of 1647 to 1653, the more substantial *laboureurs*, those who had surplus crops to sell, sold them at considerable profit, since the prices of cereals had risen two, three, or even four times. Thus enriched they bought up lands from their debtors among the small peasants; and, most important of all, they were able to take

[18] E. H. Kossmann's *La Fronde* (Leiden, 1954), deserves to be better known; despite some questionable conclusions it is probably the best work available on the subject. Further work on the Fronde is urgently needed (but based on archive material: Kossmann's essay is based on printed sources only). Several research workers are engaged on the subject, in Paris and elsewhere.

out leases on the great ecclesiastial domains, of which there was an abundance in the Beauvaisis, and set up as *fermiers-receveurs* of the *seigneuries*. Meanwhile taxation, which had increased as the result of foreign and civil war and the incompetent management of the treasury, and whose main weight fell on the peasantry, seemed more oppressive than ever to the *manouvriers* and small *laboureurs* during this period of hardship. In short, the terrible years of 1647 to 1653, which decimated the Beauvaisis, left a profound mark on peasant society and decisively widened social differences. It was then that the chasm appeared separating the so-called 'rural bourgeoisie'[19] from the growing mass of *manouvriers* and smallholders.

The subsequent period is far better known to us. The whole period 1660–1730 is characterized by a general fall in prices and incomes. This fall, sometimes gradual, sometimes abrupt, with occasional brief moments of stabilization, is the symptom of a prolonged economic depression. It is certain that the production and prices of textiles in Picardy and the Beauvaisis both fell disastrously at this time and there was a feverish search for new markets; such symptoms in industry are in no sense the mark of a period of prosperity. In terms of population, the losses incurred in 1647 to 1653, followed by another heavy drain in 1661 to 1662, were to have serious consequences for a number of age-groups over the next twenty years or more. After the decade 1680–90, when normal fertility was about to lead to another upward movement, the heavy mortalities of 1691–4 and 1709–10 intervened; then the number of burials increased three- or fourfold above normal and the birth-rate was gradually depressed, leading to a profound disturbance of the age-composition of the population for nearly fifty years to come. Except in the first years of Colbert's ministry the tax burden on the countryside continually increased, particularly after 1690. During the same period the French coinage became progressively debased. It is true that the peasantry, into whose economy money scarcely entered, suffered only indirectly from successive devaluations; but the drastic reorganization of the

[19] The expression is Georges Lefebvre's in *Les Paysans du Nord pendant la Révolution Française* (Paris–Lille, 1924). It is a term used by a historian in relation to a social situation; but it is an anachronism: Frenchmen of the *ancien régime* never gave the name 'bourgeois' to persons engaged in agriculture.

seigneuries held by the bourgeoisie and clergy, accompanied by a general overhaul of the registers of landed property and more accurate land surveys, led, in practice, to an increase in seigneurial dues, which fell mainly on the countryside. The condition of the peasantry under Louis XIV is, in fact, the product of an exceptional convergence of unfavourable factors. Those writers who were aware of economic developments and had a direct knowledge of the country as a whole—men like Hévin and Boisguilbert, and reformers, Vauban above all—pointed to, and even exaggerated, the fall in agricultural incomes, the decline of ground-rents, the stagnation of industry, and the general impoverishment of the peasantry. By and large this was the picture presented by the Beauvaisis, which never quite recovered from the long crisis of the mid-century. One is tempted to talk of an atrophy or general stagnation of the countryside. Suddenly, around 1694 and 1710, catastrophic increases in prices and poverty, which drove up still further the endemic burden of peasant debt, led to yet another transfer of thousands of acres of plough-land to the bourgeoisie, who, at the same time, completed the ruin of the last remnants of the old nobility of the Beauvaisis. This time, too, the great abbeys took part in the kill. It is true that the reign of Louis XIV ended, for the majority of the peasantry of the Beauvaisis, in the unhappy manner described in the orthodox textbooks. But, in the midst of the general distress, the powerful caste of the big *fermiers-receveurs* attained its highest point of wealth, social power, and arrogance. More sharply than before, peasant society became split into distinctive groups with conflicting interests and outlooks. Though the general picture is one of decline, the privileged few rose to new heights.

VII

THE DECLINE OF SPAIN[1]

J. H. Elliott

BY the winter of 1640, the Empire which had dominated the world scene for the best part of a century seemed at last, after many a false alarm, to be on the verge of collapse. In October of that year, after the revolt of Catalonia but before the revolt of Portugal, the English ambassador in Madrid wrote home of 'the state of Christendom, which begins already to be unequally balanced'.[2] Six months later he was writing: 'Concerning the state of this kingdom, I could never have imagined to have seen it as it now is, for their people begin to fail, and those that remain, by a continuance of bad successes, and by their heavy burdens, are quite out of heart.'[3] Olivares's great bid between 1621 and 1640 to turn back the pages of history to the heroic days of Philip II had visibly failed; and, like everything about Olivares, his failure was on the grand scale. The man whom eulogists had portrayed in the days of his greatness as Atlas, supporting on his shoulders the colossal

1 An earlier version of this essay (originally published in no. 20, 1961) was read as a paper to the Stubbs Society at Oxford, and I have deliberately left it as a contribution to discussion, based on a general survey of the present state of knowledge, rather than attempting to transform it into a detailed analysis. I have treated the period 1598–1648 in closer detail in a chapter on the Spanish peninsula in the forthcoming vol. iv of the *New Cambridge Modern History*. Any reader of this article will appreciate how much I, in company with other historians of Spain, owe to the ideas of M. Pierre Vilar in his 'Le Temps du Quichotte', *Europe* (Paris), xxxiv (1956), pp. 3–16.

2 P(ublic R(ecord) O(ffice, London) SP 94.42 f. 51, Hopton to Windebank, 22 Sept./2 Oct. 1640.

3 PRO SP 94.42 f. 144, Hopton to Vane, 3/13 April 1641.

structure of the Monarchy, was now, Samson-like, bringing it crashing down with him in his fall.

The dissolution of Spanish power in the 1640s appears so irrevocable and absolute that it is hard to regard it as other than inevitable. The traditional textbook approach to European history of the sixteenth and seventeenth centuries has further helped to establish the idea of the inevitability of Spain's defeat in its war with France. Spanish power is first presented at its height under Philip II. Then comes, with the reign of Philip III, the *decline of Spain*, with the roots of decline traced back to Philip II, or Charles V, or even to Ferdinand and Isabella, depending upon the nationality, or the pertinacity, of the writer. After the lamentable scenes that have just been portrayed, the early years of Philip IV come as something of an embarrassment, since the ailing patient not only refuses to die, but even shows vigorous and unexpected signs of life. But fortunately the inexplicable recovery is soon revealed as no more than a hallucination. When a resurgent France under Richelieu at last girds itself for action, Spain's bluff is called. Both diagnosis and prognostication are triumphantly vindicated, and the patient dutifully expires.

It is not easy to reconcile this attractively simple presentation of early seventeenth-century history with our increasing knowledge of the discontent and unrest in Richelieu's France.[4] If Spain may still be regarded as a giant with feet of clay, France itself is coming to seem none too steady on the ground. This naturally tends to cast doubt on the validity of any concept of a French triumph in the first half of the century as being a foregone conclusion. Yet the lingering survival of the traditional view is easily understood. France had a population of some sixteen million, as against Spain's seven or eight, and it is commonly argued that, in the end, weight of numbers is bound to tell. It is also argued that the fact of Spain's decline is notorious and irrefutable, and that a power in decline will not win the final battle.

The argument from the size of populations is notoriously dangerous when used of a period when governments lacked the resources and the techniques to mobilize their subjects for war.

[4] See B. P. Porshnev, *Die Volksaufstände in Frankreich vor der Fronde* (Leipzig, 1954) and R. Mousnier, 'Recherches sur les Soulèvements Populaires en France avant la Fronde', *Revue d'Histoire Moderne et Contemporaine*, v (1958), pp. 81–113.

Victory in war ultimately depended on the capacity of a state to maintain a continuing supply of men (not necessarily nationals) and of credit, and this capacity was by no means the exclusive prerogative of the large state. But the decisive argument in favour of an inevitable French victory is obviously the second: that Spain was in a state of irrevocable decline.

The phrase *decline of Spain* automatically conjures up a series of well-known images. Most of these are to be found in Professor Earl J. Hamilton's famous article,[5] which remains the classic statement of the theme: 'the progressive decline in the character of the rulers'; mortmain and vagabondage, the contempt for manual labour, monetary chaos and excessive taxation, the power of the Church and the folly of the Government. These so-called 'factors' in the decline of Spain have a long and respectable ancestry, and both their existence and their importance are irrefutable. Most of them can indeed be traced back to the writings of seventeenth-century Spaniards themselves—to the treatises of the economic writers or *arbitristas*, of whom Hamilton says that 'history records few instances of either such able diagnosis of fatal social ills by any group of moral philosophers or of such utter disregard by statesmen of sound advice'. The word *decline* itself was used of Spain at least as early as 1600 when González de Cellorigo, perhaps the most acute of all the *arbitristas*, discussed 'how our Spain . . . is subject to the process of decline (*declinación*) to which all other republics are prone'.[6] Vigorously as González de Cellorigo himself rejected the determinist thesis, the condition of Spain seemed to his contemporaries graphic evidence of the validity of the cyclical idea of history, of which the concept of decline formed an integral part.

The skilful dissection of the Spanish body politic by contemporary Spaniards, each anxious to offer the patient his own private nostrum, proved of inestimable value to writers of later generations: to Protestants of the later seventeenth century, and to rationalist historians of the eighteenth and nineteenth, who saw in the decline of Spain the classic instance of the fatal consequences

[5] 'The Decline of Spain', *Econ. Hist. Rev.*, 1st ser., viii (1938), pp. 168–79.

[6] Martín González de Cellorigo, *Memorial de la Política necesaria y útil Restauración a la República de España* (Valladolid, 1600), p. 1. I am indebted to Manchester University Library for the loan of a microfilm of this important work, of which I have been able to find no copy in this country.

Coláiste Mhuire Gan Smál Luimneach

of ignorance, sloth and clericalism. Apart from its important additions on Spanish wages and prices, and its rejection of the traditional thesis about the grave results of the expulsion of the Moriscos, Hamilton's article would seem to belong, in content as in approach, to the eighteenth- and nineteenth-century historiographical tradition.

It would be pleasant to be able to record that, in the twenty years since Hamilton's article was published, our knowledge and understanding of seventeenth-century Spain have been significantly enlarged. But, in most of its aspects, our picture of the reigns of Philip III and IV remains very much as it was drawn by Martin Hume in the old *Cambridge Modern History* over fifty years ago. The one significant exception to this story of historiographical stagnation is to be found in Hamilton's own field of monetary history. Whatever the defects either of Hamilton's methods or of his generalizations, both of them subject to growing criticism, historians now possess a vast amount of information on Spanish monetary history which was not available to Hume; and the work of a generation of historians, culminating in the monumental study of Seville and the Atlantic by M. and Mme Chaunu,[7] has revealed much that is new and important about the character of Spain's economic relations with its American possessions.

It could, however, be argued that these advances in the fiscal and commercial history of Habsburg Spain have been achieved only at the expense of other equally important aspects of its economic life. Hamilton's pioneering example has encouraged an excessive concentration on the *external* influences on the Spanish economy, such as American silver, to the neglect of *internal* economic conditions.[8] Little more is known now than was known fifty years ago about Spanish forms of land tenure and cultivation, or about population changes, or about the varying fortunes of the different regions or social groups in the peninsula. It could also be argued that Hamilton's lead, together with the whole trend of contemporary historical writing, has produced a disproportionate concentration on *economic* conditions. Explanations of the decline

[7] H. and P. Chaunu, *Séville et l'Atlantique (1504–1650)*, 8 vols. (Paris, 1955–9).

[8] This point is well made in the useful bibliographical survey of recent work on this period of Spanish history: J. Vicens Vives, J. Reglá and J. Nadal, 'L'Espagne aux XVIe et XVIIe Siècles', *Revue Historique*, ccxx (1958), pp. 1–42.

in terms of Spanish religious or intellectual history have become unfashionable. This is understandable in view of the naïveté of many such explanations in the past, but it is hard to see how an adequate synthesis can be achieved until detailed research is undertaken into such topics as the working of the Spanish Church, of the Religious Orders and the educational system. At present, we possess an overwhelmingly economic interpretation of Spain's decline, which itself is highly arbitrary in that it focuses attention only on certain selected aspects of the Spanish economy.

If this leads to distortions, as it inevitably must, these become all the greater when, as so often happens, the decline of Spain is treated in isolation. The very awareness of crisis among late sixteenth- and early seventeenth-century Spaniards prompted a flood of pessimistic commentaries which helped to make the subject exceptionally well documented. The extent of the documentation and the critical acuteness of the commentators, naturally tended to encourage the assumption that Spain's plight was in some ways unique; and this itself has led to a search for the origins of that plight in specifically Spanish circumstances and in the dubious realm of allegedly unchanging national characteristics. But considerably more is known now than was known twenty or thirty years ago about the nature of social and economic conditions in seventeenth-century western Europe as a whole. Much of the seventeenth century has come to be regarded as a period of European economic crisis—of commercial contraction and demographic stagnation after the spectacular advances of the sixteenth century—and certain features which once seemed peculiarly Spanish are now tending to assume a more universal character. The impoverished *hidalgos* of Spain do not now seem so very different from the discontented *hobereaux* of France or the gentry of England. Nor does the contempt for manual labour, on which historians of Spain are prone to dwell, seem any longer an attitude unique to the peninsula. A study like that by Coleman on English labour in the seventeenth century[9] suggests how 'idleness', whether voluntary or involuntary, was a general problem of European societies of the time, and can be regarded as the consequence, as much as the cause, of a backward economy: as the outcome of the inability of a predominantly agrarian society to

[9] D. C. Coleman, 'Labour in the English Economy of the Seventeenth Century', *Econ. Hist. Rev.*, 2nd ser., viii (1956), pp. 280–95.

offer its population regular employment or adequate remuneration for its labour.

Seventeenth-century Spain needs, therefore, to be set firmly back into the context of contemporary conditions, and particularly conditions in the Mediterranean world, before recourse is had to alleged national characteristics as an explanation of economic backwardness. It may be that idleness *was* in fact more widespread, and contempt for manual labour more deep-rooted, in Spain than elsewhere, but the first task must be to *compare*: to compare Spanish conditions with those of other contemporary societies, and then, if it is possible to isolate any features which appear unique to Spain, to search for their origins not only in the realm of national character, but also in the conditions of the soil and the nature of land-holding, and in the country's social and geographical structure.

Some of the difficulties in breaking free from traditional assumptions about the decline of Spain must be ascribed to the powerful connotations of the word 'decline': a word which obscures more than it explains. Behind the phrase *decline of Spain* there lurk different, although interrelated, phenomena. The decline of Spain can, in the first place, be regarded as part of that general setback to economic advance which mid-seventeenth-century Europe is said to have experienced, although the Spanish regression may well prove to have been more intense or to have lasted longer. Secondly, it describes something more easily measured: the end of the period of Spanish hegemony in Europe and the relegation of Spain to the rank of the second-rate powers. This implies a deterioration in Spain's military and naval strength, at least in relation to that of other states, and a decrease in its ability to mobilize the manpower and credit required to maintain its traditional primacy in Europe.

Any attempt to analyse the reasons for the decline of Spanish *power* in the middle decades of the seventeenth century must obviously begin with an examination of the foundations of that power in an earlier age. Olivares, between 1621 and 1643, was pursuing a foreign policy which recalls that of Philip II in the 1580s and 1590s. The general aims of that policy were the same: the destruction of heresy and the establishment of some form of Spanish hegemony over Europe. The nominal cost of the policy was also the same, though the real cost was greater. Philip III's ministers maintained that Philip II was spending nearly 13 million ducats a year between 1593 and 1597; Philip IV's ministers in 1636 estimated an expenditure of just over 13 million for the coming year,[10] and estimates were always liable to prove too conservative, in view of the rising premium on silver in terms of Castilian *vellón* (copper coinage), and of the sudden emergency expenses that invariably arose in time of war.

While the policy, as well as its nominal cost, remained the same under Philip IV as under Philip II, the basis of Spanish power under the two kings was also unchanged. It was, as it had always been, the resources of the Crown of Castile. Philip IV's best troops, like Philip II's, were Castilians. Philip IV's principal revenues, like Philip II's, came from the purse of the Castilian taxpayer, and Philip IV relied, like his grandfather, on the additional income derived from the American possessions of Castile.

The primacy of the Crown of Castile within the Spanish Monarchy, stemming as it did from its unique value to its kings, was obvious and acknowledged. 'The King is Castilian and nothing else, and that is how he appears to the other kingdoms', wrote one of the most influential ministers at the Court of Philip III.[11] Olivares found himself as dependent on Castile as Philip II had been. But the assistance that Castile could render Olivares proved to be less effective than the assistance it rendered Philip II, and was extracted at an even greater expense. From this, it would seem that we are faced with a diminution of Castile's capacity to bear the cost of empire, and consequently with the problem, in the first instance, not so much of the decline of Spain as of the *decline of Castile*, which is something rather different.

Three principal foundations of Castile's sixteenth-century primacy were its population, its productivity and its overseas wealth. If the process by which these foundations were slowly eroded could be traced in detail, we should have a clearer picture of the chronology of Castile's decline. But at present our knowledge is fragmentary and inadequate, and all that is possible is to suggest

[10] A(rchivo) G(eneral de) S(imancas) Hacienda leg(ajo) 522–750 no. 231, Consulta, 23 Aug. 1636.

[11] AGS Cámara de Castilla leg. 2796 Pieza 9 Inquisición f. 329, Don Pedro Franqueza to Dr. Fadrique Cornet, 22 Jan. 1605.

something of what has been done, and the areas still to be investigated.

Spain's great imperial successes of the sixteenth century had been achieved primarily by the courage and vitality of the surplus population of an overcrowded Castile. Figures for the population of sixteenth-century Spain are scanty and unreliable, but it would probably now be generally agreed that Castile's population increased during much of the century, as it increased elsewhere in Europe, with the fastest rate of increase in the 1530s. The population of the peninsula, excluding Portugal, in the middle of the sixteenth century, is thought to have been about 7½ million, of which 6½ million were to be found in Castile.[12] But perhaps even more significant than the overwhelming numerical predominance of the Castilian population is its superior density. As late as 1594 there were 22 inhabitants to the square kilometre in Castile, as against only 13.6 in the Crown of Aragon. The great empty spaces of modern Castile seem so timeless and so inevitable, that it requires an effort of the imagination to realize that Castile in the sixteenth century was relatively more populous than the rich Levantine provinces; and here, indeed, is to be found one of the fundamental changes in the structure of Spanish history. In the early 1590s the central regions of Castile accounted for 30.9 per cent of the population of Spain, whereas they now account for only 16.2 per cent. The political preponderance of Castile within Spain therefore rested in the sixteenth century, as it now no longer rests, on a population that was not only larger but also more densely settled.

This relatively dense Castilian population, living in an arid land with a predominantly pastoral economy—a land which found increasing difficulty in feeding its rising numbers—provided the colonists for the New World and the recruits for the *tercios*. It is not known how many Castilians emigrated to America (a figure of 150,000 has been suggested for the period up to 1550), nor how many died on foreign battlefields; nor is it even known how many were required for the armies of Philip II. Although foreign troops

[12] For this and the following information about population figures, see J. Vicens Vives, *Historia Económica de España* (Barcelona, 1959), pp. 301 ff; Ramón Carande, *Carlos V y sus Banqueros*, i (Madrid, 1943), p. 43; and J. Ruiz Almansa, 'La Población Española en el Siglo XVI', *Revista Internacional de Sociología*, iii (1943), pp. 115–36.

already represented an important proportion of the Spanish Army under Philip II, the contrast between military conditions under Philip II and Philip IV is none the less striking. Native Castilians, who formed the *corps d'élite* of the army, were increasingly difficult to recruit. By the 1630s, Olivares was desperate for manpower. Provincial governors were reporting the impossibility of raising new levies, and the majority of the recruits were miserable conscripts. 'I have observed these levies', wrote the English ambassador in 1635, 'and I find the horses so weak as the most of them will never be able to go to the rendezvous, and those very hardly gotten. The infantry so unwilling to serve as they are carried like galley-slaves in chains, which serves not the turn, and so far short in number of what is purposed, as they come not to one of three.'[13]

The explanation of this increased difficulty in recruiting Castilian soldiers may be found to lie primarily in changed military conditions. Philip IV had more men under arms than Philip II, and the demand on Castile was correspondingly greater; better chances of earning good wages or of obtaining charity at home may have diminished the attractions of military service abroad; the change from the warrior Charles V to a sedentary, bureaucratic monarch in Philip II, no doubt had its influence on the Castilian nobles, whose retreat from arms would in turn add to the difficulty of recruiting their vassals for war. All these problems deserve investigation,[14] but, in the search for the origins of Olivares's troubles over manpower, it would be natural to look also to the exhaustion of Castile's demographic resources.

Here, contemporary accounts may be misleading. There are numerous complaints of depopulation in late sixteenth-century Castile, but some of these can be explained by movements of population within the peninsula rather than by any total fall in numbers. There was a marked drift of population from the countryside to the towns, most of which grew considerably between 1530 and 1594; and there was also, during the course of the century, a continuous migration from *north* Castile—the most

[13] B(ritish) M(useum) Egerton MS. 1820, f. 474, Hopton to Windebank, 31 May 1635.

[14] Some of them are in fact now being examined by Mr. I. A. A. Thompson of Christ's College, Cambridge, who is researching into the Spanish military system in the late sixteenth and early seventeenth centuries.

dynamic part of the country under Ferdinand and Isabella—into central Castile and Andalusia. This southwards migration, which may be regarded as a continuation by the populace of the *reconquista*,[15] was not completed before 1600. For all those Castilians who could not themselves cross the Atlantic, Andalusia became the El Dorado. The population of Seville, the gateway to the Atlantic, rose from 45,000 in 1530 to 90,000 in 1594, and, between those dates, the populations of all but two of the larger towns of the southern half of Spain increased, while several of the northern towns, like Medina del Campo, recorded a marked decline.

A survey of conditions in north Castile alone might therefore provide a false picture of the state of the population in the Crown of Castile as a whole, and it does not seem on present evidence that an overall decline in population can be established before the end of the 1590s. All that *can* be said is that Castile's population became concentrated in the towns, particularly those of the centre and south, and that it lost some of its most vital elements through emigration and military service. Then, in 1599 and 1600, famine and plague swept up through Andalusia and Castile, causing fearful ravages in the countryside and in the densely packed cities. Unfortunately, there are no figures for the losses of these years. One village, near Valladolid, reported that no more than eighty inhabitants survived out of 300,[16] but it is impossible to say how this figure compares with others elsewhere.

Although the traditional view of its importance has recently been questioned,[17] it is hard to avoid the conclusion that the plague of 1599–1600 marks the turning-point in the demographic history of Castile. Hamilton's figures, while too unsatisfactory as a series for the immediate years of the plague to allow of any comprehensive statistical deductions, do at least point to a very sharp increase of wages over prices in the following decade, and suggest something of the gravity of the manpower crisis through which Castile was passing.

This crisis was exacerbated by the expulsion of the Moriscos ten years after the plague. The figures of the expelled Moriscos used to range to anything up to 1 million. Hamilton reduced them to 100,000. The recent meticulous study of the size and distribution

[15] Chaunu, *Séville et l'Atlantique*, viii (1), pp. 257–8 and 265.
[16] AGS Hacienda leg. 293–409 no. 222, Consulta, 27 Aug. 1601.
[17] Chaunu, op. cit., viii (2), pt. 2, pp. 1267–8.

of the Morisco population by M. Lapeyre,[18] shows that between 1609 and 1614 some 275,000 Moriscos were expelled from Spain. Of these 275,000 perhaps 90,000 came from Castile and Andalusia, and the rest from the Crown of Aragon—above all, Valencia, which lost a quarter of its population. If Hamilton underestimated the number of the Moriscos, he also underestimated the economic consequences of their expulsion. The consequences to the Valencian economy were very grave,[19] but it is important to remember that the Valencian and Castilian economies were distinct, and that Castile would be only marginally affected by the disruption of the economic life of Valencia. But Castile also lost 90,000 Moriscos of its own. These Moriscos, unlike those of Valencia and Aragon, were predominantly town-dwelling, and they undertook many of the more menial tasks in Castilian life. Their disappearance would naturally produce an immediate dislocation in the Castilian economy, which is reflected in the relationship between prices and wages for the crucial years of the expulsion, but it is not known how far this dislocation was remedied by Old Christians taking over the jobs previously occupied by Moriscos.

The present picture of the Castilian population, therefore, suggests a rapid increase slackening off towards the end of the sixteenth century, and then a catastrophic loss at the very end of the century, followed by the further loss of 90,000 inhabitants through the expulsion of the Moriscos. After that, almost nothing is known. Figures available for towns in 1646 show heavy losses, and there was another disastrous plague between 1647 and 1650. Where Hamilton suggests a 25 per cent decline during the course of the seventeenth century, there are others who believe that the population remained stationary rather than actually diminishing. All that can be said at present with any certainty is that Olivares was making heavy demands on the manpower of a country whose population had lost its buoyancy and resilience, and had ceased to grow.

In so far, then, as Castile's primacy rested on its reserves of manpower, there was a marked downward turn in its potentialities after the 1590s. Castile's national wealth, on which the Habsburgs relied for the bulk of their revenues, also shows signs of depletion.

[18] Henri Lapeyre, *Géographie de l'Espagne Morisque* (Paris, 1959).

[19] See J. Reglá, 'La Expulsión de los Moriscos y sus Consecuencias', *Hispania*, xiii (1953), pp. 215–67 and 402–79.

One of the principal difficulties involved in measuring the extent of this depletion is our ignorance of economic conditions in Castile in the first half of the sixteenth century. It is hard to chart the descent when one is still trying to locate the summit. But the researches of Carande and of Lapeyre[20] have gone far to confirm that the first half of the sixteenth century is a period of quickened economic activity in Castile and Andalusia, presumably in response to a growing demand. This was a time of population increase and of sharply rising prices. Indeed, Dr. Nadal has recently shown, on the basis of Hamilton's own figures, that there was a faster proportional rise of prices in the first half of the century than in the second, although American silver shipments were much greater in the second half than in the first.[21] The average annual rise in prices from 1501–62 was 2.8 per cent, as against 1.3 per cent from 1562–1600, and the highest maximum rise in any decade occurred between 1521 and 1530, long before the discovery of Potosí. This sharp upswing in prices during Charles V's reign may be attributable to a rising scale of aristocratic expenditure, to the dramatic growth of Charles V's debts, which he financed by the distribution of *juros*, or credit bonds, and to a vastly increased demand: an increased demand for food from Castile's growing population, an increased demand in north Europe for Castilian wool, and an increased demand for wine and oil and textiles, and for almost all the necessities of life, from the new American market. This was the period which saw the development of large-scale wine and oil production in Andalusia, and of cloth production in the towns of Castile, to meet the needs of the New World; and it was also the great age of the Castilian fairs—international institutions which linked the Castilian economy to that of Italy and northern Europe in a complicated network of reciprocal obligation.

If it is accepted that the reign of Charles V represents a period of economic expansion for Castile, the first clear signs of a check to this expansion appear in 1548, when the country was experiencing one of the five-year periods of highest price increase for the entire

[20] Carande, op. cit.; Henri Lapeyre, *Une Famille de Marchands: les Ruiz* (Paris, 1955); and see Ladislas Reitzer, 'Some Observations on Castilian Commerce and Finance in the Sixteenth Century', *Journal of Modern History*, xxxii (1960), pp. 213–23 for a detailed bibliography.

[21] Jorge Nadal Oller, 'La Revolución de los Precios Españoles en el Siglo XVI', *Hispania*, xix (1959), pp. 503–29.

sixteenth century. In that year the Cortes of Valladolid, moved by the general complaint of high prices, petitioned the Crown to forbid the export of Castilian manufactures, even to the New World, and to permit the import of foreign goods, which would be less expensive for the Castilian consumer than Castile's own products.[22] The assumption that the export trade was pushing up Castilian prices above the general European level appeared sufficiently convincing for the Crown to agree to the Cortes' request in 1552, except in so far as Castilian exports to the Indies were concerned. The consequences of the new anti-mercantilism were exactly as might have been expected, and six years later the prohibition on exports was lifted at the request of the Cortes themselves. The whole episode, brief as it was, augured badly for the future of Spanish industry.

During the reign of Philip II foreign merchants succeeded in forcing wider and wider open the door that they had suddenly found so obligingly ajar in the 1550s, and Castile's industries proved unable to resist the pressure. Professor Hamilton gave the classic explanation of this industrial failure in his famous argument that in Spain, unlike France or England, wages kept pace with prices, and that therefore Spain lacked the stimulus to industrial growth which comes from a lag between wages and prices in an age of price revolution.[23] This argument, if correct, would naturally furnish a vital clue to the *decline of Spain*; but the evidence behind it has recently been critically examined, and the whole argument has been increasingly questioned.[24] Professor Phelps Brown has shown how Hamilton's own figures would indicate that a Valencian mason's wages by no means kept pace with the rising cost of living, and indeed lagged farther behind prices than those of his English equivalent[25] (although, if comparisons of this

[22] José Larraz López, *La Epoca del Mercantilismo en Castilla (1500–1700)* (Madrid, 1943), pp. 31 ff.

[23] Hamilton, 'The Decline of Spain', and 'American Treasure and the Rise of Capitalism (1500–1700)', *Economica*, ix (1929), pp. 338–57.

[24] David Felix, 'Profit Inflation and Industrial Growth', *The Quarterly Journal of Economics*, lxx (1956), pp. 441–63. See also for criticisms of Hamilton: Pierre Vilar, 'Problems of the Formation of Capitalism', *Past and Present*, no. 10 (1956), pp. 15–38; Docent Ingrid Hammarström, 'The "Price Revolution" of the Sixteenth Century', *Scandinavian Econ. Hist. Rev.*, v (1957), pp. 118–54; and Jorge Nadal, 'La Revolución de los Precios'.

[25] E. H. Phelps Brown and Sheila V. Hopkins, 'Builders' Wage-rates, Prices

kind are to be really satisfactory, they require a knowledge of comparative diets and household budgets such as we do not yet possess). Hamilton does not provide sufficiently connected series to allow similar calculations for other parts of the peninsula, but his hypothesis that Spanish wages kept abreast of prices would seem so far to be quite unfounded. Indeed, further investigation may well show a marked deterioration in the living standards of the mass of the Castilian population during the first half of the century. Such a deterioration, combined with the high level of Castilian prices in relation to those of other European states, would go a long way towards explaining the peculiar structure of Castile's economy by the end of the century: an economy closer in many ways to that of an East-European State like Poland, exporting basic raw materials and importing luxury products, than to the economies of West-European states. In so far as industries survived in Castile they tended to be luxury industries, catering for the needs of the wealthy few and subject to growing foreign competition.

Castile's industrial development, then, would seem to have been hampered not only by the Crown's fiscal policies and by unfavourable investment conditions, but also by the lack of a sufficiently large home market. This lack of a market for cheap manufactures points to an economy in which food prices are too high to leave the labourer and wage-earner with anything more than the bare minimum required for their housing, fuel and clothing. One of the most important reasons for the high price of food is to be found in the agrarian policies pursued by the kings of Castile even before the advent of the Habsburgs. Their traditional practice of favouring sheep-farming at the expense of tillage—a practice vigorously continued by Ferdinand and Isabella—meant that Castile entered the sixteenth century with a dangerously unbalanced economy. While the demand for corn increased as the population grew, the sheep-owners of the *Mesta* continued to receive the benefits of royal favour. The corn-growers, on the other hand, were positively hampered, not only by the presence of the ubiquitous and highly privileged sheep, but also by the *tasa del trigo*—a fixed maximum for grain prices, which, after being sporadically applied in the first

---

and Population: Some Further Evidence', *Economica*, xxvi (1959), pp. 18–38.

years of the century, became a permanent feature of the Crown's economic policy from 1539.[26]

The consequences of this short-sighted policy towards the agricultural interest, at a time of rapid population increase, require no comment. Professor Braudel has shown how, in the last decades of the century, Castile, in common with other south-European states, became heavily dependent on grain supplies from northern and eastern Europe.[27] Castilian agriculture was simply incapable of meeting the national demand for food. What is not clear is whether agriculture was expanding, but not expanding fast enough to keep pace with the population, or whether agricultural production for the home market was actually falling off in the later sixteenth century. There are indications that more land was being cultivated in south Spain after the middle years of the century, but this may have been more to meet the needs of the American market than to satisfy home demand. The debates of the Castilian Cortes under Philip II give an impression of mounting agrarian crisis, characterized by large-scale rural depopulation, but unfortunately, apart from the tentative pioneering survey by Viñas y Mey,[28] agrarian questions in this period remain unstudied. There are signs that the smaller landowners in Castile were being squeezed out in the later sixteenth century: it was harder for them than for the large landowners to survive the misfortunes of bad years, and they were liable to run into debt and find themselves compelled to sell out to their more powerful neighbours. This still further encouraged the concentration of land in the hands of a small number of powerful landowners, at a time when mortmain and the entail system were working powerfully in the same direction. It is customary to find historians frowning upon this process, as if the consolidation of estates in a few hands was in itself necessarily inimical to agrarian progress. But a large landlord is not automatically debarred from being an improving landlord. It would be very useful to know how far, if at all, improving landlords *were* to be found among the great lay and ecclesiastical landowners, and also to what extent they were

[26] See Eduardo Ibarra y Rodriguez, *El Problema Cerealista en España durante el Reinado de los Reyes Católicos* (Madrid, 1944), and Carande, op. cit., i. pp. 78–79.

[27] F. Braudel, *La Méditerranée et le Monde Méditerranéen à l'époque de Philippe II* (Paris, 1949), pp. 447–70.

[28] C. Viñas y Mey, *El Problema de la Tierra en la España de los Siglos XVI–XVII* (Madrid, 1941).

diverted from corn-growing by the profits of sheep-farming, or by the production of wine and oil for the American market.

The discussion in the Castilian Cortes of 1598 on agrarian conditions suggests that by this time the crisis was acute,[29] and certainly the movement of the great Castilian nobles to take up residence at Court after the accession of Philip III did nothing to lessen it. Philip III's Government found itself vainly legislating against absentee landlords, in the hope that an overcrowded Court could be cleared overnight, and the lackeys and servants who thronged the streets of Madrid would be compelled to return to the land. But much more than legislation against absentee landlordism was required to save Castilian agriculture. If the real causes of rural depopulation are to be found, they must be sought, in the first instance, at the level of village life. It is here that the dearth of good local histories in Spain becomes particularly serious. Apart from what can be learnt from the discussions of the Cortes, and from one useful but necessarily general article by Professor Domínguez Ortiz,[30] little can so far be said about the exact nature of the crisis that was overwhelming Castilian rural communities in the late sixteenth and early seventeenth centuries.

It is, however, clear that the Castilian village was pitifully unprotected. There was, for instance, the little village of Sanzoles, which in 1607 addressed to the Crown a petition that has survived at Simancas.[31] It raised a loan for municipal purposes, to place itself under royal jurisdiction instead of that of Zamora cathedral, and then, as the result of a series of bad harvests, found itself unable to pay the annual interest. The creditors moved in on the village and so harassed its inhabitants that eventually, out of ninety householders, no more than forty remained. Communal indebtedness was frequent among Castilian villages, and it obviously became particularly grave when even a handful of villagers moved away, and the reduced population found itself saddled with obligations that it was now even less able to meet. But the moneylender and the powerful neighbour were only two among the many natural enemies of Castilian villages. They were exposed also to the merciless attentions of the tax-collector, the recruiting-

[29] *Actas de las Cortes de Castilla*, xv (Madrid, 1889), pp. 748 ff.

[30] 'La Ruina de la Aldea Castellana', *Revista Internacional de Sociología*, no. 24 (1948), pp. 99–124.

[31] AGS Hacienda leg. 345–473, Consulta, 25 Mar. 1607.

sergeant and the quartermaster. Unfortunately we do not yet possess the information to tell us what proportion of a seventeenth-century villager's income went in taxes. A speaker in the Cortes of 1623 suggested that, in a poor man's daily expenditure of 30 maravedis, 4 went in the *alcabala* and *millones* alone;[32] and besides these and other taxes paid to the Crown—taxes which the peculiar fiscal structure of Castile made particularly heavy for the peasant—there were also dues to be paid to landlords and tithes to the Church. Then, in addition to the purely fiscal exactions, there were all the vexations and the financial burdens connected with the quartering and recruiting of troops. Villages along the principal military routes, particularly the road from Madrid to Seville and Cadiz, were dangerously exposed, and billeting could be very expensive—100 ducats a night for a company of 200 men, according to a report made in the 1630s.[33]

The persistence of these many afflictions over a long period of time left the villager of Castile and Andalusia very little inducement to remain on the land. He would therefore either move with his family and become swallowed up in the blessed anonymity of the great towns, or he would join the army of vagabonds that trudged the roads of Castile. We have, then, the spectacle of a nation which, at the end of the sixteenth century, is dependent on foreigners not only for its manufactures but also for its food supply, while its own population goes idle, or is absorbed into economically unproductive occupations. Accusing fingers are commonly pointed at Church and bureaucracy as important agents of decline, in that they diverted the population from more useful employment. But is it not equally likely that the growth of Church and bureaucracy was itself a consequence of contemporary conditions: of the lack of incentive to agricultural labour at the village level, and of the inability of the Castilian economy to provide its population with adequate employment? The nature of the economic system was such that one became a student or a monk, a beggar or a bureaucrat. There was nothing else to be.

What could be done to revitalize a flagging economy, and increase national productivity? There was no shortage of ideas. The *arbitristas*—the economic writers—of the early seventeenth century, men like González de Cellorigo, Sancho de Moncada,

[32] *Actas de las Cortes*, xxxix, p. 142.

[33] BM Add. MS. 9936, Papeles tocantes a las Cortes, f.2.

Fernández Navarrete, all put forward sensible programmes of reform. Royal expenditure must be regulated, the sale of offices halted, the growth of the Church be checked. The tax system must be overhauled, special concessions be made to agricultural labourers, rivers be made navigable and dry lands irrigated. In this way alone could Castile's productivity be increased, its commerce be restored, and its humiliating dependence on foreigners, on the Dutch and the Genoese, be brought to an end.

The ideas were there; and so also, from the truce with the Dutch in 1609, was the opportunity. This opportunity was thrown away. The ineptitude of the Lerma régime, its readiness to dissipate the precious years of peace in a perpetual round of senseless gaiety, is one of the tragedies of Spanish history, and goes far to explain the fiasco that finally overwhelmed the country under the government of Olivares. But behind this inert government, which possessed neither the courage nor the will to look its problems squarely in the face, lay a whole social system and a psychological attitude which themselves blocked the way to radical reform.

The injection of new life into the Castilian economy in the early seventeenth century would have required a vigorous display of personal enterprise, a willingness and ability to invest in agrarian and industrial projects, and to make use of the most recent technical advances. None of these—neither enterprise, nor investment, nor technical knowledge—proved to be forthcoming. 'Those who can, will not; and those who will, cannot', wrote González de Cellorigo.[34] Why was this?

The conventional answer, useful so far as it goes, is that the social climate in Castile was unfavourable to entrepreneurial activity. The Castilians, it is said, lacked that elusive quality known as the 'capitalist spirit'. This was a militant society, imbued with the crusading ideal, accustomed by the *reconquista* and the conquest of America to the quest for glory and booty, and dominated by a Church and an aristocracy which perpetuated those very ideals least propitious for the development of capitalism. Where, in Castile, was that 'rising middle class', which, we are told, leavened the societies of northern Europe until the whole lump was leavened? 'Our republic', wrote González de Cellorigo, 'has come to be an extreme contrast of rich and poor, and there is no means of adjusting them one to another. Our condition is one in which

[34] *Memorial de la Política*, p. 24 v.

there are rich who loll at ease or poor who beg, and we lack people of the middle sort, whom neither wealth nor poverty prevents from pursuing the rightful kind of business enjoined by Natural Law.'[35]

These words were published in 1600, and accurately describe Castilian society at that time, but they cannot be said to describe it in 1500. For, however uncapitalistic the dominant strain in sixteenth-century Castilian life, there *were* vigorous 'people of the middle sort' in the Castile of Ferdinand and Isabella and of Charles V. The towns of north Castile at that time could boast a lively bourgeoisie—men like Simón Ruiz, willing to engage their persons and their fortunes in commercial enterprise. But the decay of commercial and financial activity in north Castile, which is patent by 1575, suggests the disappearance of such people during the course of the century. What happened to them? Doubtless they acquired privileges of nobility. The passion for *hidalguía* was strong in Castile, and a title secured not only enhanced social standing, but also exemption from taxation. Yet it is hard to believe that this is an adequate explanation for the disappearance from the Castilian scene of men like Simón Ruiz. All over Europe it was the practice of merchants to buy their way into the nobility, and yet it was not everywhere so economically stultifying as it proved to be in Castile.

It would seem desirable to press farther than this, and to turn away for a time from repeating the conventional arguments about contempt for commerce and the strength of the aristocratic ideal, to the technical and neglected subject of investment opportunities.[36] What was happening to wealth in sixteenth-century Castile? Much of it was obviously going, as it was going elsewhere, into building and jewelry, and all the expensive accoutrements connected with the enjoyment of a superior social status. But it was also being invested, and unproductively invested, in *censos*, or personal loans, and in *juros*, or government bonds. Sixteenth-century Castile saw the development of a highly elaborate credit system—a system which no doubt received much of its impetus

[35] ibid., p. 54.

[36] An indication that this question may at last be arousing attention is provided by the pioneering article of Bartolomé Bennassar, 'En Vieille-Castille: Les Ventes de Rentes Perpétuelles', *Annales E.S.C.*, xve année (1960), pp. 1115–26.

from the exigencies of the Crown's finances. Anyone with money to spare—a noble, a merchant, a wealthy peasant—or institutions, like convents, could lend it to private persons, or municipal corporations, or else to the Crown, at a guaranteed 5, 7 or 10 per cent. A proper study of *censos* and *juros* in Spain could tell us much about the reasons for its economic stagnation, especially if related to similar studies for other parts of Europe. *Censos* and *juros* might almost have been deliberately devised to lure money away from risky enterprises into safer channels, of no benefit to Castile's economic development. Indeed, in 1617 the Council of Finance complained that there was no chance of a Castilian economic revival as long as *censos* and *juros* offered better rates of interest than those to be gained from investment in agriculture, industry or trade.[37]

To this unwillingness to engage one's person and one's money in risky entrepreneurial undertakings, there must also be added Castile's increasing technological backwardness, as an explanation of its failure to stage an economic recovery. This backwardness is suggested by the failure of Spanish shipbuilders between the 1590s and the 1620s to keep pace with the new techniques of the north-European dockyards.[38] It was commented upon by foreign travellers, like the Frenchman Joly, who remarked in 1603 on the backwardness of the Spaniards in the sciences and the mechanical arts,[39] and Olivares himself in the 1630s was complaining of the Spanish ignorance of modern engineering techniques: 'I am certain that no man who comes from abroad to see Spain can fail to blame us roundly for our barbarism, when he sees us having to provision all the cities of Castile by pack-animal—and rightly so, for all Europe is trying out internal navigation with great profit.'[40]

While these technical deficiencies can presumably be attributed in part to the general lack of business enterprise in Castile, they should also be related to the whole climate of Castilian intellectual life. Here we are seriously hampered by the lack of a good study of the Castilian educational system. Why was it that science and tech-

[37] AGS Hacienda leg. 395–547 no. 58, Consulta, 3 Sept. 1617.

[38] See A. P. Usher, 'Spanish Ships and Shipping in the Sixteenth and Seventeenth Centuries', *Facts and Factors in Economic History for E. F. Gay* (Harvard University Press, 1932), pp. 189–213.

[39] 'Voyage de Barthélemy Joly en Espagne (1603–1604)', ed. L. Barrau-Dihigo, *Revue Hispanique*, xx (1909), p. 611.

[40] BM Add. MS. 25,689 f. 237, Consulta del Conde Duque a SM.

nology failed to take root in Spain, at a time when they were beginning to arouse considerable interest elsewhere in Europe? It may be that further investigations will show a greater degree of scientific interest in Spain than has hitherto been assumed, but at present there is no evidence of this.[41] Indeed, such evidence as does exist points in an opposite direction—to the gradual separation of Habsburg Spain from the mainstream of European intellectual development. Early sixteenth-century Spain was Erasmian Spain, enjoying close cultural contacts with the most active intellectual centres of Europe. From the 1550s there was a chilling change in the cultural climate. The *alumbrados* were persecuted, Spanish students were forbidden to attend foreign universities, and Spain was gradually sealed off by a frightened monarch from contact with the contagious atmosphere of a heretical Europe. The conscious transformation of Spain into the redoubt of the true faith may have given an added intensity to Spanish religious experience under Philip II, but it also served to cut Spain off from that powerful intellectual current which was leading elsewhere to scientific inquiry and technical experiment.[42]

The period between 1590 and 1620, then, sees a rapid erosion of two of the principal foundations of Castile's sixteenth-century primacy, and consequently of Spain's imperial power: a decline both in Castile's demographic vitality and in its productivity and wealth. Recent investigations have also confirmed that it sees the erosion of the third foundation of Castile's primacy, in the form of a drastic reduction in the value, both to the Crown and to Castile, of Castile's possessions overseas. The great convoy of volumes launched by M. and Mme Chaunu has brought home to us the enormous significance of trade between the port of Seville and Spanish America. It is, they suggest, in the 1590s that the *Carrera de las Indias* shows its first signs of serious strain. In 1597 it became clear for the first time that the American market for European goods was overstocked, but already from about 1590 the upward trend of Seville's trade with the Indies was losing speed. Although

[41] A collection of essays on Spanish science, of very varying quality, was published in Madrid in 1935 under the title of *Estudios sobre la Ciencia Española del Siglo XVII*, but they have not been followed up.

[42] For the intellectual isolation of Spain as a factor in the decline, see especially Santiago Ramón y Cajal, *Los Tónicos de la Voluntad*, 5th edn. (Buenos Aires, 1946), pp. 203 ff; and Claudio Sánchez-Albornoz, *España, Un Enigma Histórico* (Buenos Aires, 1956), ii, p. 553.

the trade fluctuated round a high level between the 1590s and 1620, its whole character was changing to the detriment of the Castilian economy. As Mexico developed its industries and Peru its agriculture, the colonies' dependence on the traditional products of the mother country grew less. There was a decreased demand in America for the Spanish cloth, and for the wine, oil and flour which bulked so large in the transatlantic shipments of the sixteenth century. The consequences of this were very serious. The galleons at Seville were increasingly laden with foreign goods, although unfortunately we do not know the relative proportions of Spanish and non-Spanish cargoes. With less demand in America for Castilian and Andalusian products, less of the American silver carried to Seville is destined for Spanish recipients, and it is significant that Spanish silver prices, which had moved upwards for a century, begin their downward movement after 1601. Moreover, the changes and the stresses in the transatlantic system began to undermine the whole structure of credit and commerce in Seville.

The principal beneficiaries of this crisis were the foreigners—the hated Genoese ('white Moors' as an irate Catalan called them[43]), the Portuguese Jews and the heretical Dutch. Foreign bankers ran the Crown's finances; foreign merchants had secured a stranglehold over the Castilian economy, and their tentacles were wrapping themselves round Seville's lucrative American trade. Castile's sense of national humiliation was increased by the truce with the Dutch in 1609, and bitterness grew as the Dutch exploited the years of peace to prise their way into the overseas Empires of Spain and Portugal. The humiliating awareness of the sharp contrast between the dying splendour of Castile and the rising power of the foreigner is one of the most important clues to the psychological climate of Philip III's Castile. It helps to accentuate that sense of impending disaster, the growing despair about the condition of Castile which prompts the bitter outbursts of the *arbitristas*; and it turns them into fierce patriots, of whom some, like Sancho de Moncada, betray a hysterical xenophobia.

The resulting mental climate goes far to explain some of the more baffling characteristics of the age of Olivares. Insufficient attention has been paid to the many signs of a revival of aggressive Castilian nationalism between 1609 and 1621—a nationalism that

[43] Acadèmia de Bones Lletres, Barcelona. Dietari de Pujades i, f. 135, 1 Dec. 1602.

would seem to have been inspired by Castile's growing sense of inferiority. Consciously or subconsciously Castilians were arguing that peace with heretics, itself deeply humiliating, was politically and economically fruitless, since it had done nothing to check the advance of the English and the Dutch. Yet, if the foreigner triumphed in the contemptible arts of commerce, Castile could at least evoke the spirit of its former greatness—its military prowess. The answer to its problems was therefore a return to war.

This appears to have been the attitude of the great Castilian Viceroys of Philip III's reign, the Osunas and the Alcalás, and it was in this climate of aggressive Castilian nationalism, with its strong messianic overtones, that Olivares came to power in 1621. In the person of Olivares one finds curiously blended the two dominant strains of thought of the reign of Philip III: the reforming idealism of the *arbitristas* and the aggressive nationalism of the great Castilian proconsuls. With his boundless confidence in his own powers, Olivares determined to combine the programmes of both. He would restore Castile to economic vigour, and simultaneously he would lead it back to the great days of Philip II when it was master of the world.

But the ambitious imperial programme of the Conde Duque depended, as the imperial programme of Philip II had depended, on the population, the productivity and the overseas wealth of Castile, and each of these had undergone a serious crisis between 1590 and 1620. It would conventionally be argued also that Philip II's imperialism was dependent, and indeed primarily dependent, on the flow of American silver coming directly to the Crown; and in so far as that flow had diminished by the second and third decades of the seventeenth century, the attempt to revive Spain's imperial greatness was in any event doomed. Here, however, the popular conception of the role played by the King's American silver supplies can be misleading. The silver remittances to the Crown at the end of Philip II's reign averaged about 2 million ducats a year. This was little more than the annual sum raised by ecclesiastical taxation in the King's dominions, and under a third of the sum which Castile alone paid the Crown each year in its three principal taxes.[44]

The American remittances were important, in the long run, less

[44] This can be deduced from papers and *consultas* of the Council of Finance in AGS Hacienda for the years 1598–1607, and particularly leg. 271–380.

for their proportionate contribution to the Crown's total income than for the fact that they were one of the few sources of revenue not pledged for many years in advance. Their existence assured a regular supply of silver which was necessary if the bankers were to continue to provide the King with credit. During the decade 1610–20 the remittances began to fall off. Instead of the 2 millions of the early 1600s, the President of the Council of Finance reported in December 1616 that 'in the last two years hardly a million ducats have come each year',[45] and by 1620 the figure was as low as 800,000. It recovered in the 1620s, but between 1621 and 1640 1½ million ducats represented an exceptional year, and not more than a million ducats could be expected with any degree of confidence; in fact, about half the sum that Philip II could expect.

This was serious, but it was not crippling in relation to the overall revenues of the Crown. Under Philip IV, as under Philip II, it was not America but Castile that bore the main burden of Habsburg imperialism, and Castile was still paying its 6, 7, or 8 million ducats a year in taxation. But during the 1620s it became increasingly expensive for Castile to raise these sums. Since 1617 large new quantities of *vellón* coinage had been manufactured, and by 1626 the premium on silver in terms of *vellón* had risen from 4 per cent in 1620 to some 50 per cent.[46] This meant in practice that a tax collected in *vellón* would now buy abroad only half the goods and services for which it was nominally supposed to pay.

Olivares tried to compensate for the disastrous drop in the purchasing power of Castilian money by raising the level of taxation in Castile and inventing a host of ingenious fiscal devices to extract money from the privileged and the exempt. In many ways he was extremely successful. The Castilian aristocracy was so intensively mulcted that a title, so far from being a badge of exemption, became a positive liability, and the Venetian ambassador who arrived in 1638 reported Olivares as saying that, if the war continued, no one need think of possessing his own money any more since everything would belong to the King.[47] While this

[45] AGS Hacienda leg. 391–542 no. 1, Don Fernando Carillo to King, 23 Dec. 1616.

[46] Earl J. Hamilton, *American Treasure and the Price Revolution in Spain, 1501–1650* (Harvard University Press, 1934), Table 7, p. 96.

[47] *Relazioni degli Stati Europei*, ed. Barozzi and Berchet. Serie 1. Spagna, ii (Venice, 1860), p. 86.

fiscal policy, when applied to the Castilian nobles, caused no more than impotent rumblings of discontent, it proved to be self-defeating when adopted towards what remained of the Castilian merchant community. The long series of arbitrary confiscations of American silver remittances to individual merchants in Seville, who were 'compensated' by the grant of relatively worthless *juros*, proved fatal to the town's commercial life.[48] Olivares's tenure of power saw the final alienation of Spain's native business community from its king, and the final defeat of native commercial enterprise in the name of royal necessity. The crumbling of the elaborate credit structure of Seville and the collapse of Seville's trading system with the New World between 1639 and 1641,[49] was the price that Olivares had to pay for his cavalier treatment of Spanish merchants.

In spite of Olivares's ruthless exploitation of Castile's remaining resources, there was never enough to meet all his needs. Castile's growing inability to meet his demands for manpower and money naturally forced him to look beyond Castile for help. To save his beloved Castile, it became imperative for him to exploit the resources of the peripheral provinces of the Iberian peninsula, which had been under-taxed in relation to Castile, and which were under no obligation to provide troops for foreign service. It was this determination to draw on the resources of the Crown of Aragon and Portugal which inspired Olivares's famous scheme for the Union of Arms: a device which would compel all the provinces of the Spanish Monarchy to contribute a specified number of paid men to the royal armies.[50]

Olivares's scheme of 1626 for the Union of Arms was in effect an implicit admission of a change in the balance of economic power within the Spanish peninsula. Behind it lay the contemporary Castilian assumption that Castile's economic plight was graver

[48] See Antonio Domínguez Ortiz, 'Los Caudales de Indias y la Política Exterior de Felipe IV', *Anuario de Estudios Americanos*, xiii (1956), pp. 311–83. The same author's *Política y Hacienda de Felipe IV* (Madrid, 1960), is an important contribution to the study of the Crown's financial policy in the reign of Philip IV, based as it is on previously unused documents from Simancas.

[49] Chaunu, op. cit., viii (2), pt. 2, pp. 1793–1851.

[50] For the Union of Arms, see my chapter in the forthcoming *New Cambridge Modern History*, vol. iv, and my *The Revolt of the Catalans. A Study in the Decline of Spain (1598–1640)* (Cambridge, 1963).

than that of the other regions of Spain. How far this assumption was correct, it is not yet possible to say. The various regions of the peninsula lived their own lives and went their own ways. A decline of Castile does not necessarily imply the simultaneous decline of the Crown of Aragon and Portugal, both of them living in different economic systems, and shielded by separate monetary systems from the violent oscillations of the Castilian coinage.

Yet, if we look at these peripheral kingdoms, we may well think that the prospects were a good deal less hopeful than Olivares believed them to be. Aragon: a dry, impoverished land. Valencia: its economy dislocated by the expulsion of the Moriscos. Catalonia: its population growth halted about 1625,[51] its traditional trade with the Mediterranean world contracting after the plague of 1630. Portugal: its Far Eastern Empire lost to the Dutch under Philip III, its Brazilian Empire in process of being lost to the Dutch under Philip IV.

Even if Olivares overestimated the capacity of the other territories of the peninsula to bring him the help he needed, he none the less knew as well as anyone else that he was engaged in a desperate race against time. If France could be beaten swiftly, the future would still be his. Then at last he could undertake the great reforms which only awaited the return of peace, and which would enable Castile to devote itself as effectively to the task of economic reform as it had already devoted itself to the successful prosecution of the war. In 1636, at Corbie, he very nearly achieved his aim. A little more money, a few more men, and French resistance might have crumbled. But the gamble—and Olivares knew it *was* a gamble—failed, and, with its failure, Olivares was lost. The Franco-Spanish war inevitably turned after Corbie into the kind of war which Spain was least able to stand: a war of attrition, tedious and prolonged. Such a war was bound to place heavy strains on the constitutional structure of the Spanish Monarchy, just as it placed heavy strains on the constitutional structure of the French Monarchy, since Olivares and Richelieu were compelled to demand assistance from, and billet troops in, provinces which had never been assimilated and which still possessed their own semi-autonomous institutions and their own representative bodies. The Spanish Monarchy was particularly vulnerable in this respect, since

[51] Catalan population problems are admirably treated in J. Nadal and E. Giralt, *La Population Catalane de 1553 à 1717* (Paris, 1960).

both Catalonia in the east, and Portugal in the west, were uneasily and unsatisfactorily yoked to the central Government in Madrid. When the pressure became too great, as it did in 1640, they rose up in arms against that Government, and Castile—for so long the predominant partner in the Monarchy that it took its superiority for granted—suddenly discovered that it no longer possessed the strength to impose its will by force.

The great crisis in the structure of the Monarchy in 1640, which led directly to the dissolution of Spanish power, must therefore be regarded as the final development of that specifically Castilian crisis of 1590–1620 which this essay has attempted to describe; as the logical dénouement of the economic crisis which destroyed the foundations of Castile's power, and of the psychological crisis which impelled it into its final bid for world supremacy.

It seems improbable that any account of the *decline of Spain* can substantially alter the commonly accepted version of seventeenth-century Spanish history, for there are always the same cards, however we shuffle them: mortmain and vagabondage, governmental ineptitude, and an all-pervading contempt for the harsh facts of economic life. Instead of continuing to be indiscriminately scattered they can, however, be given some pattern and coherence. Yet even when the reshuffling is finally done and all the cards are fairly distributed, it remains doubtful whether dissent will be possible from the verdict on Spain of Robert Watson's *History of the Reign of Philip III*, published in 1783: 'her power corresponded not with her inclination';[52] nor from the even sterner verdict of a contemporary, González de Cellorigo: 'it seems as if one had wished to reduce these kingdoms to a republic of bewitched beings, living outside the natural order of things'[53]—a republic whose most famous citizen was Don Quijote de la Mancha.

[52] p. 309.

[53] *Memorial de la Política*, p. 25 v.

VIII

QUEEN CHRISTINA AND THE GENERAL CRISIS OF THE SEVENTEENTH CENTURY[1]

Michael Roberts

IT is usual nowadays to consider the cluster of revolutions which occurred in the 1640s and 1650s as an acute phase of a chronic disorder, more or less common to all parts of Europe, which we have become accustomed to call the General Crisis of the Seventeenth Century. There does not seem, however, to be any great measure of agreement as to what the nature of that crisis was. And indeed, generalizations which are to fit movements as apparently dissimilar as the revolt of Portugal and the English Civil War are not, perhaps, very easy to devise; and Masaniello and Andries Bicker are certainly strange bedfellows. This paper does not purport to offer any solution to the problem: it attempts only to give some account of a crisis which seems so far to have been left out of consideration in discussions of it, and to examine how far events in Sweden square with the theories which have been put forward to explain the revolutionary movements elsewhere.

It is, of course, quite true that the Swedish crisis of 1650 did not issue in any violent upheaval. But, as Professor Trevor-Roper has remarked,[2] the revolutionary situation did not necessarily lead to revolution: revolution, to become explicit, must 'depend on events

[1] This paper is an expansion of the A. L. Smith Lecture for 1962, delivered in the Hall of Balliol College, Oxford, on 9 Mar. 1962. (From no. 22, 1962.)

[2] H. R. Trevor-Roper, 'The General Crisis of the Seventeenth Century', *Past and Present*, no. 16 (1959), p. 51 (repr. above, ch. 3; the quotation is at p. 83).

and errors'. But that it *was* a revolutionary situation seems undeniable; and Swedish observers saw it as part of the general European epidemic, which Oxenstierna, more philosophical than the rest, resignedly accepted as a seasonal fever which must run its course. The Swedish Council spent many perplexed hours debating the news from England and France; it had its eye on the troubles in Holland and Naples; it was interested in Portuguese independence; and Chmielnicki did not escape its observation. Per Brahe feared that Sweden was being infected by revolutionary doctrines imported from abroad; Jakob de la Gardie lamented that 'They want to do as they have been doing in England, and make us all as like as pig's trotters. . . . *Est res pessimi exempli.*' There was a '*spiritus vertiginis*' abroad: as Christina observed, 'neither king nor *parlement* have their proper power, but the common man, the *canaille*, rules according to his fancy'. In October 1650 Oxenstierna confessed that he was afraid to visit his country houses; and his son Erik predicted that the peasants would break their masters' necks when they got home from the diet. The burghers, too, were affected: Schering Rosenhane, in an imaginary conversation between representatives of the four Estates, published in this year, makes the nobleman accuse the burgher of aiming at a '*populare imperium*'. And Oxenstierna, in a moment of unwonted depression, told his colleagues in Council, '*Ferrum*, that is the only *consilium*.'[3]

The fear of a social war was thus very real in 1650. It was no new thing. Throughout the Regency (1632–44) Oxenstierna had always in mind the danger of a peasant revolt, and was very apt to urge it as an argument against heavier taxes, or wider privileges for the nobility: it was not for nothing that Grotius had sent him detailed reports about the Nu-Pieds.[4] And the nervousness per-

[3] [*Svenska*] R[*iks*] R[*ådets*] P[*rotokoll*] xiii, pp. 17, 103, 117, 163, 165, 182, 214, 282–3, 298; xiv, pp. 9, 16, 81, 175, 358; xv, p. 128: *S*[*veriges*] R[*idderskaps och*] *A*[*dels*] R[*iksdags*] P[*rotokoll*] iv, pp. 420, 433; *H*[*andlingar rörande*] *S*[*kandinaviens*] *H*[*istoria*] xxi, pp. 123, 137; *A*[*xel*] O[*xenstiernas*] *S*[*krifter och*] *B*[*refvexling*] 2nd ser., iii, pp. 544, 553; [Schering Rosenhane], *Samtal emellan Juncker Päär, Mäster Hans, Niels Andersson Borgare och Joen i Bergha Danneman,* in *Samling af Curieusa Samtal* . . . (Uppsala, 1768). Rosenhane, it is interesting to note, in 1650 also published a book on the Fronde, entitled *Observationes Politicae super Galliae Motibus*: 'Riks-Rådet och Öfverståthållaren Friherre Schering Rosenhanes Lefverne, af honom sielf beskrifvit', *Nya svenska biblioteket*, ii (Stockholm, 1763), p. 610.

[4] G. Wittrock, *Regering och allmoge under Kristinas förmyndare* (Uppsala, 1948), pp. 76–77, 156, 216, 239, 371; C. T. Odhner, *Sveriges inre historia under*

sisted after 1650 too: the outbreak was indeed aborted, but the threat remained. In December 1651 the elder Messenius[5] said at his trial: 'There is plenty of resolution all over the country; all they need is a leader.' In 1653 it was reported that there was a design to massacre all nobles. At the diet of 1655 the peasants openly threatened insurrection. And in 1660 both Per Brahe and Elaus Terserus thought the country near to civil war.[6]

The crisis of 1650 was compact of many elements.[7] It was a social crisis above all; but it was a constitutional crisis too, as the Fronde and the Civil War were. It was, quite obviously, a food

[5] Arnold Messenius was arrested for sending an anonymous letter of seditious tendency to the future Charles X. On interrogation he involved his father, Arnold Johan Messenius, who then vainly tried to shield his son by taking all the blame himself. Both were executed in December 1651. Arnold Messenius was undoubtedly playing on prevailing discontents to try to tempt the heir to the throne into something like treason; and he probably hoped to enlist the faction that was hostile to the Oxenstiernas. At his trial he reported compromising remarks by such prominent persons as the burgomaster of Stockholm, Nils Nilsson, and a member of the Council, Bengt Skytte (later emphatically denied by both of them). But there never seems to have been anything more than loose and dangerous talk in the affair: it was certainly not the 'widely-ramifying conspiracy' of the textbooks. See Verner Söderberg, *Historieskrifvaren Arnold Johan Messenius* (Uppsala, 1902), and the report of the interrogation in *RRP* xv, pp. 209 ff, 353–63.

[6] *RRP* xv. p. 243; S. Bonnesen, *Karl X Gustav* (Lund, 1958), p. 48; G. Wittrock, *Regering och allmoge under Kristinas egen styrelse* (Uppsala, 1953), p. 35: cf. Johan Ekeblad's disagreeable experience in 1652: *Johan Ekeblads bref* (Stockholm, 1911), i, p. 110; G. Wittrock, *Carl X Gustafs testamente* (Uppsala, 1908), pp. 128, 238.

[7] The crisis is well documented; besides *RRP*, *SRARP*, and *HSH* xxi (which has the parliamentary diary of a member of the Clergy, Jonas Petri) we have now *P*[*räste-*] *S*[*tåndets*] R[*iksdags*] *P*[*rotokoll*] i (Stockholm, 1949). Unfortunately *Borgarståndets riksdagsprotokoll före Frihetstiden* (Uppsala, 1933), begins only in 1654. The literature includes Wittrock, *Regering och allmogen under Kristinas egen styrelse*; B. Lövgren, *Ståndsstridens uppkomst* (Stockholm, 1915); N. Ahnlund, *Ståndsriksdagens utdaning* (Stockholm, 1933); S. I. Olofsson, *Drottning Christinas tronavsägelse och trosförändring* (Uppsala, 1953); R. Holm, *Joannes Elai Terserus* (Lund, 1906). Hj. Holmquist's *D. Johannes Matthiae Gothus* (Uppsala, 1903) unfortunately stops at 1648.

Drottning Kristinas förmyndare (Stockholm, 1865), p. 71; S. Lundgren, *Johan Adler Salvius* (Lund, 1945), p. 62; for Grotius' letters on the Nu-Pieds, *AOSB*, 2nd ser., ii, pp. 637, 639–40, 642, 648, 656, 670, 672, 674.

crisis, for the harvest was the worst Sweden had known for fifty years, or was to know for near fifty more: already in March the Stockholm bakers were fighting each other at the town gates for supplies of flour.[8] It gathered up into itself the struggles of parties and factions; but it concerned itself also with what contemporaries were pleased to call fundamental law. In one very important aspect the crisis was dynastic. And it was fought out, and the issue debated, in parliament.

The Diet which met in Stockholm in July 1650 sat for the unprecedented time of nearly four months; and it produced a concerted onslaught upon the nobility by the three lower Estates. That was unprecedented too. The lead was taken, unexpectedly, by the burghers; and all the lower clergy, with half the bishops, united with them to champion the peasants and attack the aristocracy. Preachers denounced from the pulpit nobles who allowed their horses to eat up all the corn, while the poor died of hunger. Political verses castigated the cruelties and oppressions of the landlords.[9] Respectable parsons declared passionately that there were too many nobles and too many foreigners in the country. The peasants complained that they were plagued by excessive labour services, deprived of their freeholds and their liberties, and degraded to 'a Livonian slavery'. The three lower Estates clamoured for a *reduktion*—i.e. for the resumption by the Crown of lands alienated to the nobility. And on 9 October they drew up a joint Protestation,[10] in which they demanded that henceforth there should be no alienation of Crown lands in perpetuity; that all Estates should enjoy equality before the law; that offices should be open to all upon a basis of merit, should not be discharged by deputy, and should be paid by fixed salaries; that private prisons and torture should be forbidden; that the formation of manors should be restricted to the scale laid down in 1562;[11] and that no title to alienated Crown lands should be considered good, once the

[8] *RRP* xiv, p. 78; cf. *SRARP* iv, pp. 307, 561.

[9] See, e.g. G. O. Hyltén-Cavallius and G. Stephens, *Sveriges historiska och politiska visor* (Örebro, 1853), i, pp. 343–55; Axel Strindberg, *Bondenöd och Stormaktsdröm* (Stockholm, 1937), pp. 95–100.

[10] Printed in *Handlingar til Konung Carl XI:tes Historia* (Stockholm, 1769), x, pp. 70–98.

[11] For the creation of manors, see M. Roberts, *Gustavus Adolphus, A History of Sweden, 1611–1632* (London, 1953–8), ii, pp. 54–55, and cf. ibid., p. 12 and n. 1.

Estates had called it in question. Hundreds of copies of the Protestation were disseminated throughout the country, after the diet was over; and for the next thirty years it became the great arsenal of argument of the unprivileged Estates. It is worth remarking that it challenged not only the existing social and political pattern, but also the whole imperial foreign policy of the preceding generation. 'What honour, what glory, has Your Majesty by the subjection of foreign lands, when some few only are allowed to possess them, and when on top of that they diminish the Crown's *Patrimonium* and property in the fatherland? Or what have we gained beyond the seas, if we lose our liberty at home?[12] It was a censure of Oxenstierna and all that he stood for;[13] and it echoed and amplified a sentiment which had been heard as long ago as 1634, when an anonymous pamphleteer had asked whether Gustav Adolf had not died for peasants, as well as for nobles?[14] And indeed the complaints of 1650 were for the most part not new. What lay behind them?

The root of the trouble undoubtedly was the massive alienations of Crown lands and revenues which had taken place since 1611, and especially since 1648.[15] The alienations were of various types. Some were sales either of Crown lands or of Crown revenues, for cash, or by way of offset against indebtedness, and such revenues might be either rents (if they came from Crown peasants) or taxes (if they came from freeholders). Others were donations: free gifts, without any obvious *quid pro quo*. It is tempting to see in the sales of land another instance of the revolutionary effects of the inflated military budgets which the Thirty Years War brought with it. But if by this it is meant that the wars drove Sweden to live on capital, the conclusion is untenable. Sweden's continental armies were for the most part meant to operate on self-balancing accounts. Up to

[12] *Handlingar til Konung Carl XI:tes historia*, x, pp. 84–85.

[13] On 9 July 1650 the clergy censured 'him who had brought the Crown to many needless expenses . . . (thereby understanding a particularly high personage among the lords)': *HSH* xxi, p. 70.

[14] Wittrock, *Regering och allmoge under Kristinas förmyndare*, i, pp. 57–58.

[15] For a discussion of the alienations and their implications, see Eli Heckscher, *Sveriges ekonomiska historia från Gustav Vasa*, i (Stockholm, 1936), pp. 301–55; S. Clason, *Til reduktionens förhistoria* (Uppsala, 1895); Sven A. Nilsson, 'Reduktion eller kontribution?', *Scandia*, xxiv (1958); Robert Swedlund, *Grev- och friherreskapen i Sverige och Finland* (Uppsala, 1936); E. Ingers, *Bonden i svensk historia*, i (Stockholm, 1943).

1654, moreover, more than twice as much went in donations as in sales; and no less than 62 per cent of the alienations occurred after 1648—that is, in years of peace. No: the sales of land and revenues were rather a deliberate change in fiscal policy, conceived originally not as a hand-to-mouth expedient, but as the replacement of a miscellaneous income in kind by a more convenient income in cash: you cannot well pay an army of mercenaries in ox-hides or salt herring. In exchange for a lump sum, the Crown divested itself of revenues which were troublesome to handle, and imposed instead indirect taxes, which Oxenstierna pronounced to be 'pleasing to God, hurtful to no man, and not provocative of rebellion'.[16] Hence the taunting question of the clergy in 1650, who inquired whether Christina was to be crowned Queen of the Swedish lands, or Queen of tolls and excises.[17] It was argued, moreover, that land alienated to the nobility was more productively used than before, and hence would ultimately enrich the State by way of indirect taxation.[18] Sale of lands and revenues, in fact, was defended as a step towards more modern methods of finance.[19] But such arguments were less easy to apply to donations. At best, donations were legitimate rewards for good service. The end of the war in 1648 saw a swarm of officers home from Germany clamouring for favours; and perhaps it was inevitable that some gratifications should be accorded. But Christina made no effort to keep them within bounds. She took pleasure in giving; she had neither interest in, nor grasp of, finance; and after 1652 seems to have been cynically indifferent to the distresses of a Crown she had

[16] Odhner, op. cit., p. 227. Hence Oxenstierna's insistence, as early as 1633, that the nobility must waive their exemption from customs dues: *HSH* xxvi, pp. 265–6: cf. *AOSB* 2nd ser., iii, p. 337. They did surrender it in 1644, but only in exchange for improved privileges in other respects. See F. Lagerroth, *Statsreglering och finansförvaltning i Sverige till och med frihetstidens ingång* (Lund, 1928), pp. 59–61.

[17] *HSH* xxi, pp. 75, 82. The archbishop reported that the Nobility received the question '*risu*'. Oxenstierna had no opinion of the clergy as economists: see *SRARP* v, p. 207.

[18] A good summary of these arguments in *Samtal*. . . , pp. 55–57.

[19] And on other grounds too: in 1660 Per Brahe remarked that 'a king's income ought not to consist in hens, eggs, butter, flax and such small gear as peasants give . . . but in tolls, *régales* on mining, and revenues of that sort': Wittrock, *Carl X Gustafs testamente*, p. 128. In 1654 M. G. de la Gardie attributed a very similar remark to Axel Oxenstierna: R. Fåhraeus, *Magnus Gabriel de la Gardie* (Stockholm, 1936), p. 63.

already decided to renounce. Donations were given faster than the land registers could record them, sometimes were given twice over; and the confusion was made worse by the activities of an exchequer official who sold forged titles to applicants.

The effects were startling. Twenty-two of the most favoured families obtained lands worth one-fifth of the ordinary revenues of the State. The area of noble land in Sweden more than doubled between 1611 and 1652; in Finland it sextupled. In the more eligible provinces of central Sweden scarcely any land was left in royal hands. Royal revenues dropped from 6.36 million silver dollars in 1644 to 3.79 million in 1653.[20] Civil servants went without wages, the peacetime maintenance of the army was disorganized, even the Court was in financial straits: it was said that the Queen had no money to buy firewood, and occasionally no food in her larders.[21] War taxes had to be continued in peacetime; extraordinary taxes which had been levied only after specific parliamentary grant came to be treated as ordinary revenue which needed no parliamentary sanction. The nobility was of course exempt from all ordinary taxation, for itself and its domestics; and its peasants paid taxes at half-rates, except for those attached to a manor, or living near it, who were totally exempt. The privileged position of the peasants of the nobility was a consequence of, and was balanced by, their obligation to pay dues and give services to their lords: the Crown imposed taxes at only half-rates, so that the other half might go to the noble. The less the Crown took, the more the lord got. It is obvious, then, that the total exemption of peasants on manors presented a strong inducement to establish as many manors as possible; and in the 'thirties and 'forties manors were indeed created by the score, to the great concern of the Regents.[22] Very many of them were fraudulent, mere tax-dodging devices; but they were defended on the ground that the absence of any custom of primogeniture imposed an obligation to provide a fitting establishment for every child in the family.[23]

Colaiste Oideachais Mhuire Gan Smal Luimneach

[20] Bonnesen, op. cit., p. 32.

[21] 'Nils Skunks självbiografi' (*Tidningar utg. i Uppsala* [1777]), p. 36.

[22] For the question of the limitation of manors, and the effects of their creation, see *RRP* x, pp. 319, 366; *PSRP* i, p. 151; *SRARP* iii, pp. 125–7; iv, p. 353; v, pp. 14, 102; Wittrock, *Regering och allmoge under Kristinas förmyndare*, pp. 258, 437, 441.

[23] See Christina's approving comments on the social effects of primogeniture in England, in *RRP* xiv, p. 48; and cf. Oxenstierna in *SRARP* iii, p. 47.

The social consequences of this situation began to be alarming when the alienations to the nobility took the form, not of Crown lands, but of tax-revenues from freehold peasants. The nobility might then be considered to have a direct interest in increasing the burden of taxation; since it was into their pockets, not into the exchequer, that the taxes of such freeholders were now paid.[24] They fell very easily into the habit of regarding these freeholders as their tenants—to use Per Brahe's significant phrase, as mediate, and not immediate, subjects of the Crown.[25] They came to think of themselves as having a right, not merely to the peasant's taxes, but ultimately to his land—a *dominium eminens*, as against the peasant's *dominium utile*. If a freeholder was three years in arrears with his taxes, the Crown was entitled to declare his land forfeit; and nobles to whom taxes had been made over tried to apply the same principle. Freehold peasants found themselves threatened with degradation to the relatively rightless position of peasants of the nobility, liable to eviction without compensation, burdened with intolerable labour services, made to ride the wooden horse, imprisoned in private dungeons, harried by the lord's agents, restricted in their freedom of movement, blackmailed into obedience by the lord's power to designate them for conscription.[26] The immemorial freedom of the Swedish yeoman was menaced by German customs, imposed very often by new lords who were indeed Germans, and imitated by Swedes who had picked up German social attitudes during the wars: it was revealing that Per Brahe should have remarked that the demands of the peasants would never be tolerated in Germany. At no other

[24] Their interest seems obvious, as the Clergy pointed out in 1650 (*PSRP* i, p. 203; and see *Handlingar til Carl IX:tes historia*, x, p. 91); but they do not seem in fact to have pursued it very vigorously. The question is complex and controversial: see, e.g. H. Swenne, *Svenska adelns ekonomiska privilegier 1612–1651* (Göteborg, 1933), especially p. 311; E. Brännman, *Frälseköpen under Gustav II Adolfs regering* (Lund, 1950) and Sven A. Nilsson's review of Brännman in *Historisk Tidskrift*, 2nd ser., xv (1952), pp. 404–15.

[25] 'We are all *subditi regni*, the peasants *mediate subditi*, but we *immediate*': *RRP* xiv, p. 343.

[26] For a defence of the nobility (which, however, largely ignores the crucial question of the freehold peasants) see Swenne, op. cit. His argument on conscription (pp. 229, 232) is controverted by Christer Bonde's remark in 1655: 'It is certain that the only means to keep the peasant under discipline is conscription': *SRARP* v, p. 54 (cf. ibid., iii, p. 95); and by Christina herself (*HSH* xxi, p. 87).

moment in Swedish history would a Marshal of the nobility have dared to say, 'It is extraordinary that persons who were formed for servitude should be deemed free.'[27] The implications were the more serious, because it was freehold revenues, rather than Crown lands, that constituted a majority of all the alienations; and also because these developments threatened the *political* destruction of the peasantry as an Estate. Nowhere in Europe was an Estate of peasants so firmly entrenched in the constitution as it was in Sweden; nowhere else had it such acknowledged constitutional rights. But the Estate represented freehold and Crown peasants only, and drew its members only from them. Thus the depressing of more and more of them to the status of peasants of the nobility threatened the whole Estate with eventual (and perhaps speedy) extinction. And as more and more of the revenue from taxation was diverted into the nobles' pockets, fiscal burdens necessarily fell with increased weight on the taxpayers that remained.[28]

The burghers and the clergy felt the force of this, and had besides grievances of their own. The burghers were coming to resent the favoured position of the nobility in the competition for offices.[29] The clergy, drawn very often from the peasantry, or at least living very close to them, sympathized with their sufferings. They themselves complained of alienation of Church lands to the nobility, arbitrary evictions from the glebe, illegal withholding of tithe (especially on manors), abusive extension of the right of presentation to livings: even the bishops grumbled that they were treated like the nobility's stable boys.[30] But apart from these particular grievances, Clergy and Burghers united with Peasants in

[27] *RRP* xiv, 333, for Per Brahe's remark; *SRARP* v, p. 86, for Christer Bonde's. He was sharply rebuked by Oxenstierna, who had earlier observed, 'though they be *glebae addicti*, yet they are not slaves': ibid., iv, p. 345.

[28] And, equally, as the number of crown peasants diminished the burden of labour services fell more heavily on them. Swenne found instances of peasants who had to travel 150 km. to get to the place where their services were to be performed: op. cit., p. 146.

[29] See pp. 216–17. They had other grievances against the nobility too: *RRP* xiii, p. 11; xv, p. 198.

[30] *RRP* xiv, p. 331. For the Clergy's grievances, see *PSRP* i, pp. 64, 89, 127, 164, 189, 269 ff; *SRARP* iii, pp. 46, 75; v, p. 75; *HSH* xxi, pp. 76, 272. For a vivid explanation of the effects of manor-creation on the economic position of the clergy, see *AOSB* 2nd ser., xii, p. 590 (Baazius to Oxenstierna, 19 Aug. 1637).

1650 because they feared that the whole social and political balance of the state was in danger of being upset. As Archbishop Lenaeus remarked: 'When the nobility have all the peasants subject to themselves, then the Estate of Peasants will no longer have a voice at the diet; and when the Estate of Peasants goes under, Burghers and Clergy may easily go under too . . . ; and since the Estate of Nobles has all the land in the kingdom under its control, where is then the crown's power? For he who owns the land is the ruler of the land; and thereby a *servitus* introduced into the country.'[31]

The tactics which the lower Estates now adopted, and the financial problem itself, had important constitutional implications.[32] Since 1632 the Diet had made significant constitutional advances. Its monopoly of legislation had been tacitly admitted. Its consent to new taxes, and to further conscriptions—though not to the raising of loans or alienation of lands and revenues—was now recognized to be necessary;[33] and its limitation of the duration of such grants had already had the effect of ensuring regularity of summons.[34] By the 1640s it had finally surmounted the danger—so fatal to the parliaments of Germany—of being supplanted for all ordinary purposes by a committee of its own members. Its forms of business were steadily developing. On more than one occasion individual Estates had taken a firm stand on the principle of 'redress before supply'. The debates on the Form of Government in 1634 had produced the suggestion that during a minority sovereignty reverted to the Estates; and the principle of ministerial responsibility to parliament had at least been adumbrated. In 1647 an opposition pamphlet had made startling claims for the Estates to participate directly in the choice of the great officers of government.[35] The *Riksdag* was indeed still far behind the English

[31] *HSH* xxi, p. 145; cf. the bishop of Växjö's remarks, *PSRP* i, p. 172.

[32] For a discussion of the constitutional problem, see Ahnlund, op. cit.; F. Lagerroth, *Frihetstidens författning* (Stockholm, 1915): Erland Hjärne, *Från Vasatiden till frihetstiden* (Uppsala, 1929).

[33] As Oxenstierna remarked in 1643: 'If it were here as in other countries, that one could call the Estates together and say: so much is required. . . . But here it is not so': *RRP* x, p. 301.

[34] Sam Clason, 'Om uppkomsten af bestämde perioder för den svenska riksdagens sammanträde', *Historisk Tidskrift*, 1st ser., xii (1892).

[35] *Mestadeles ständernas och goda patrioters betänkande om regementsformen* (printed in *SRARP* iii, pp. 409–14). See L. Stavenow, *Om riksrådsvalen under Frihetstiden* (Uppsala, 1890), pp. 1–11, for the constitutional background to this claim.

Parliament—it wholly lacked the initiative, and the idea of parliamentary privilege had not even been conceived—but one would have said that it was moving, and consciously moving, in the same general direction.

In 1650 it appeared to make a sudden leap forward. The right of free speech was firmly asserted. The three lower Estates held joint committee meetings, formulated joint resolutions, and claimed (in contradiction of the *Riksdag*-Ordinance of 1617) that a majority of Estates was decisive. They carried the principle of 'redress before supply' to the point of threatening to break up the Diet. With typical constitutional antiquarianism, they clamoured for the obsolete remedy of a General Eyre (*räfste- och rättareting*). Their debates resounded with novel appeals to 'fundamental law'. Above all, they asserted their right to the initiative. Against all precedent they deferred consideration of the Government's Proposition, and proceeded instead to formulate their own resolutions. To conservative statesmen, nothing in 1650 seemed more shocking, more subversive of good order, more truly revolutionary, than this.[36] Everything suggests, in fact, that the Diet of 1650 could have been a turning-point in parliamentary history, comparable, perhaps, with 1641 in England: now, one would suppose, the foundations were laid for the developments which after 1718 were to make the Swedish Diet the most advanced and most powerful representative assembly in the world. But in fact, the constitutional struggles of 1650 were curiously unfruitful. Solid progress began only in 1660, when the nobility took over some of the constitutional principles enunciated ten years before; it was not till 1675 or so that the lower Estates resumed their constitutional advance; and after 1680 they were content to practise parliamentarism by the grace of an austerely paternal sovereign. From the point of view of the Diet's

[36] *RRP* xiv, p. 370, *SRARP* iv, p. 328; *Samtal*, pp. 14, 18, where Juncker Päär says: 'to begin on *gravamina*, and prefer them before the government's Proposition, I hold to be *praeposterum*, untimely, and not to be practised in our constitution. For though the German Estates have begun to usurp the Emperor's place at the Diet, that is a different kind of state, and by doing so they have brought the Emperor to that condition, that his power consists only in grand titles, and more in a seeming than in realities; and how it has gone in England since the Estates began upon the same fashion, is sufficiently manifest to us'; cf. Oxenstierna's remarks to Whitelocke in 1654: Bulstrode Whitelocke, *A Journal of the Swedish Embassy* (1855), ii, pp. 278–81.

development, 1650 was a flash in the pan, almost a missed opportunity.

The explanation lies, of course, in part in the fact that the lower Estates were not primarily concerned with constitutional issues. They propounded innovating doctrines only as a means of waging the social struggle. They made no attempt to revive the controversies of 1634: the question of the divisibility of sovereignty, and the claim of the Estates to a share in it—which was so important to the Frondeurs—was not raised in 1650. The last thing they wanted was to curtail the power of the Crown for the benefit of parliament: it was one of their essential contentions that the Crown was too weak already. Their attitude to the prerogative was naïvely pragmatic and oddly ambivalent: for instance, they asserted the absolute right of the Queen to resume lands alienated by her predecessors, but maintained that she was restrained by the fundamental laws of the kingdom from making alienations in future.[37] Their indifference to constitutional issues appears most conspicuously in regard to the power of the purse. The alienations had put the monarchy quite at the mercy of parliament: the Government was now dependent on parliamentary grants if it were to carry on at all.[38] But the lower Estates had no notion of exploiting this situation: on the contrary. Their object was to make the Crown *independent* of parliamentary supply—as Gustav Vasa had been,[39] and as Charles XI was almost to be. The Queen was to live of her own.

If the Estates were thus indifferent to the constitutional possibilities, the Queen was not. And for her, in a much broader sense, 1650 was indeed a constitutional crux. From the beginning of the fifteenth to the end of the eighteenth century, Swedish history derives its inner dynamic from the tension resulting from the pull of two conflicting constitutional forces: on the one hand an aristo-

[37] The Nobility took the opposite line—that Christina was entitled to alienate freely because Sweden was now a hereditary and not an elective monarchy; a curious inversion of their historic role: *HSH* xxi, p. 155.

[38] Lövgren, op. cit., p. 32. It is of course true that the lower Estates resented having to pay the heavier indirect taxation which the Crown's loss of direct revenues made necessary; and they also objected to the uncertainty and variability of the yield of customs and excises: Lagerroth, *Statsreglering och finansförvaltning*, p. 63.

[39] As Christina herself remarked: *RRP* xiv, p. 345; cf. Oxenstierna's comment ibid., 353.

cracy which combined the assertion of its interests with the defence of constitutional liberties; on the other a monarchy which could count on popular support by seeming to protect the little man against exploitation. Between these two extremes the pendulum had swung back and forth, and would continue to swing, until Anckarström's bullet gave a crude and bloody retort to the bloodless revolution of a 'Patriot King'. In this perennial oscillation the Form of Government of 1634 occupied a dubious place. By those who sponsored it, it was regarded as establishing a *monarchia mixta*, a constitutional balance in which 'the King's sovereignty, the Council's authority, and the reasonable rights and liberties of the Estates, are properly preserved to them'.[40] But there were many who feared that it was intended to subject the monarchy to oligarchical control, to reduce the sovereign, as Schering Rosenhane somewhat tritely remarked, to the position of a Venetian Doge, perhaps to prepare the way for a return to electoral monarchy and a crowned republic on Polish models.[41] If the Form of Government was to be considered as a permanent arrangement, and not merely as providing for a minority, it certainly seemed to make government independent of the participation of the monarch. The Council, moreover, which claimed to be (as the Parlement of Paris also did) a mediator between the Crown and the nation, was an ominously close corporation of representatives of a few great families. It included no less than three Oxenstiernas; and when in 1648 a cause between the Oxenstierna and Bielke families came to the Council on appeal, it was found that almost all the members were related either to one family, or to the other, or to both.[42] Christina's paternal uncle, John Casimir, and her half-uncle, Karl Karlsson Gyllenhielm, were profoundly uneasy at this situation; and Karl Karlsson certainly feared that the Vasas might be edged off the throne. They instilled their fears into Christina. Men like Johan Skytte, and, later, Johan Adler Salvius, were jealous of the Oxenstiernas, and disapproved of their policies both at home and abroad, much as Marillac disapproved of Richelieu's, and for some

40 Printed in E. Hildebrand, *Sveriges regeringsformer 1634–1809* (Stockholm, 1891), p. 2.

41 See Christina's comments, *RRP* xiv, p. 309; and cf. xiii, pp. 344, 362. It was not without significance that Per Brahe in 1660 should have said that nowhere was '*senatoris officium* so noble' as in Sweden, Poland, Denmark and Russia: Wittrock, *Carl X Gustafs testamente*, p. 206.

42 *RRP* xii, p. 312.

of the same reasons. They found support in secretaries of state such as Lars Grubbe and Lars Nilsson Tungel: a 'rule of secretaries', after all, was traditionally the monarchy's alternative to reliance on the services of the high aristocracy. From this group came the radical pamphlets of the 'forties, pamphlets which combined an advanced constitutional programme with scarcely-veiled attacks upon the Chancellor—pale Nordic analogues of the *Mazarinades*.[43]

The situation—dynastic and constitutional—was made acute by Christina's decision not to marry, which became final in 1649. From that moment, the future, not only of the dynasty but of the monarchy itself, seemed to her to be bound up with her ability to obtain the acceptance by the Estates of her cousin Charles as her successor. The Council debates of 1649 were remarkable for exchanges of extraordinary acerbity between the Queen and her servants;[44] but by shock tactics and skilful diplomacy she carried her first objective: in 1649 Charles was recognized as heir to the throne. It remained to secure his recognition as hereditary Prince, and so ensure the succession to his descendants; and it was with this objective that Christina confronted the Diet of 1650.[45]

The conflict between the Estates gave her the lever that she needed. The three lower Estates were as anxious as she was to avert the possibility of an aristocratic republic: resistance to her programme was to be expected only from the nobility. She proceeded therefore to incite the commonalty to attack the first Estate. She received their deputations with words of compassion and encouragement; she urged them to object to the nobility's privileges; she posed as the protector of the poor; and when the

[43] Lövgren, op. cit., pp. 18–27, 31–37; Ahnlund, op. cit., pp. 229–30; Lundgren, *Salvius*, pp. 194–6, 242–4. Oxenstierna notoriously sided with parliament against Charles I, and often expressed the view that Charles (and Laud) had only themselves to thank for their troubles. In December 1651 the younger Messenius, at his trial, recalled that his father had told him how Oxenstierna had one day remarked, 'I think, Messenius, that you are in too much of a hurry to be Chancellor here in Sweden', and had been answered, 'And I think that you are in too much of a hurry to be King here in Sweden': *RRP* xv, p. 211; but cf. p. 239.

[44] See esp. *RRP* xiii, pp. 343–6.

[45] For the succession-question, see Olofsson, op. cit.; N. Ahnlund, *Drottning Kristinas tronavsägelse*, in *Från Medeltid och Vasatid* (Stockholm, 1933); C. Weibull, *Drottning Christina* (Stockholm, 1934), H. Rosengren, *Karl X Gustaf före tronbestigningen* (Uppsala, 1913).

onslaught showed signs of flagging, she took measures to reanimate it. She had the Vasa knack of popularity; and she may even have had some vague sympathy for the victims of aristocratic oppression. She was well aware that she was playing with fire; but she judged the hazards to a nicety. By the end of August she had the nobility running to her for the protection of the Crown:[46] it was a curious anticipation of the situation which made possible the revolution of 1772. Her price, of course, was the acceptance of Charles as hereditary Prince; and the frightened magnates were glad enough to close the bargain. She then coolly threw over her parliamentary allies. She had never intended agreeing to a *reduktion*, which she regarded as an intolerable infringement of her prerogative; and she now forced the lower Estates to drop it from their programme. The popular front thereupon collapsed. The clergy were given a sop in the shape of a long-sought grant of privileges; the peasants were offered an ordinance limiting labour services; the leaders of the burghers were given official promotion to posts at a reassuring distance from Stockholm. The trial and execution of Messenius and his son, in December 1651, emphasized the Queen's dissociation of herself from the tribunes of 1650, and gave a severe fright to the court-faction which had been intriguing with them; and in the euphoric atmosphere of total victory she could in 1652 even reconcile herself with Oxenstierna.

Such was the crisis of 1650. How does it accord with the explanations that have been propounded for the general European crisis?

It is not easy, certainly, to regard it as a 'crisis of production', induced by the failure of a still feudal society to provide an elastically-expanding market for mass-produced goods.[47] Sweden at this period was only beginning to be an industrial country. Production of copper reached a peak just in 1650 and the ensuing decade, and the later decline was not due to the limited capacity of the market; while iron production shows a fairly steady expansion throughout the century. Swedish trade was increasing, not decreasing; and in the 1650s and 1660s Swedish shipping began to get an appreciable share of Baltic commerce. And it is not until

[46] *HSH* xxi, p. 140; cf. *SRARP* iv, pp. 420, 422.

[47] E. J. Hobsbawm, 'The General Crisis of the European Economy in the Seventeenth Century', *Past and Present*, no. 5 (1954), esp. pp. 39–42 (repr. above, ch. 2; see pp. 14–18).

the 1670s, perhaps, that any signs are visible that Sweden was becoming a less attractive field for foreign investment. In short, there seem to be few signs of that 'slackening of spontaneous economic development and of the development of capitalism' which M. Mousnier sees as typical of the period.[48]

On the other hand, there are obvious parallels between the predicament of the Swedish freeholders and the fate of the peasantry of eastern Europe; and it is plain that the crisis of 1650 in one aspect represents resistance to what in Germany was termed *Bauernlegen*. But the resemblance does not go very deep. The 1640s and 1650s no doubt saw the beginnings of the large compact domain based on consolidation of strips, evictions, and perhaps enclosure; and the creation of a manor was often the first stage in this process. But it was still only beginnings, affecting only a small percentage of noble land; and most landowners still preferred to secure themselves against harvest failures by having isolated farms well scattered over the country. In any case, the Swedish landlords were innocent of the economic motives which lay behind *Bauernlegen*. They had little idea of large-scale agriculture for a market, or for export; they lived on the rents and taxes and services their peasants rendered them: a *Grundherrschaft*, in fact, not a *Gutsherrschaft*.[49] Many of them spent a good deal more than their fathers had spent; and to meet the drain they tried, of course, to extract more from their peasants, who naturally complained. But in fact the margin for exploitation was small. Ordinary taxes, or rents, were already deliberately fixed at a level which, for the peasant who paid them, left enough (but not much more than enough) to maintain himself and his family; and war taxes probably took most of what remained. Yet at least the tax-collector and the lord's bailiff were not competitors for the peasant's resources, as they were in France. The share of the Crown and the share of the lord were fixed; and the nobility were under no temptation to incite the peasantry to refuse taxes in order that they might pay the rent.[50] And although dreadful cases of noble cruelty did occur, most land-

[48] R. Mousnier, *Les XVIe et XVIIe siècles* (Paris, 1954), pp. 150–1.

[49] See Arthur Montgomery, 'Tjänstehjonsstadgan och äldre svensk arbetarpolitiken', *Historisk Tidskrift*, 1st ser., liii (1933), pp. 246–7; Heckscher, op. cit., i, pp. 323–8.

[50] Contrast B. Porshnev, *Die Volksaufstände in Frankreich vor der Fronde* (Leipzig, 1954), pp. 90, 440; cf. *RRP* x, p. 414.

lords realized that to ruin their peasantry was shortsighted policy: as Gustav Bonde remarked, 'it is better to milk the cow than to hit it over the head'.[51] Oppressed peasants could and would go elsewhere, when their short leases were up; and the ordinary courts could and did protect the poor man and punish the oppressor.[52] In 1650 the peasants at the Diet told horrific stories of landlords who exacted 500 or 600 days' labour service in the year from each farm; but in 1652 the Estate of Nobility was ready enough to accept an ordinance fixing the maximum for extraordinary labour services at eighteen.[53] What spurred on the peasants in 1650 was not so much actual oppression (which was probably not usual), as the fear of oppression, and above all the fear that they might lose security of tenure, personal liberty, and political rights.

Nevertheless, the alienations of Crown lands and revenues did result in both the absolute and relative enrichment of a small class. It was not that the Crown conferred a gratification by selling below the market price, as in some other countries:[54] a price of thirty-three and a third years' purchase was attractive only because prospective, unspecified and non-material advantages entered into the reckoning.[55] It is true, of course, that the nobility's increased wealth was relatively quickly dissipated by massive prestige-spending,[56] and also by the rapid dispersal of estates which followed from the absence of primogeniture or entail. But still the great landlords undoubtedly did very well. They had not been weakened by the

[51] G. Wittrock, 'Riksskattmästaren Gustaf Bondes politiska program 1661', *Historisk Tidskrift*, 1st ser., xxxiii (1913), p. 53.

[52] See H. Munktell, 'Till frågan om böndernas ställning vid 1600-talets mitt', *Historisk Tidskrift*, 2nd ser., vi (1943); and cf. Christer Bonde's complaint, *SRARP* v, p. 43.

[53] Swenne, op. cit., p. 151; Wittrock, *Regering och allmoge under Kristinas egen styrelse*, p. 188.

[54] Contrast Trevor-Roper, op. cit., p. 45 (repr. above, at p. 76).

[55] This seems to have been a price based on the yield to the crown of the so-called 'determinate revenues', and it was high probably because there was a tacit agreement that the buyer should also be entitled to the 'indeterminate revenues': in instances where the price was based on a figure which included the 'indeterminate revenues' it tended to be about twenty-two years' purchase: Heckscher, op. cit., i, pp. 309–13. For 'determinate' and 'indeterminate revenues', see M. Roberts, *Gustavus Adolphus*, i, p. 311.

[56] For standards of aristocratic luxury, see W. Karlsson, *Ebba Brahes hem* (Lund, 1943); Claes Annerstedt, *Om samhällsklasser och levnadssätt under förra hälften af 1600-talet* (Stockholm, 1896); and Ellen Fries, *Ur svenska adelns familjeliv i gamla tider* (Stockholm, 1910).

price-revolution, since their incomes were mostly in services and in kind; nor were they affected by the recession in prices after about 1640—a recession which was in any case somewhat masked in Sweden.[57] The alienations were the most comprehensive change in the ownership of land since the Reformation, and indeed were of even greater social significance; for they created, as the Reformation had not, a *new* landed nobility. Thus Sweden *is* an example of 'a shift in social forces arising from changes in the ownership of land'—which Vicens Vives held to be one of the constituent elements in the general crisis.[58] And the concentration of wealth in the hands of one class coincided with an absolute decline in the standard of living of the peasantry.[59] The aristocracy grew richer at the expense of the rest of society. Not least, at the expense of the Crown.

It is one of the peculiarities of the Swedish crisis, that it was not an attack upon the Crown. In Sweden the burdens imposed by the State were never so intolerable as to provoke serious insurrection, though unjust bailiffs now and then might come to violent ends; and after 1613 the peasant had no need (as he had in France) to seek the protection of a lord against the depredations of a royal army. Since the later 1630s taxes had ceased to be farmed; Sweden had neither *gabeleurs* nor *fermiers*; and a comparatively high percentage of the taxes actually paid seems in fact to have reached the treasury.[60] The reduction of taxation was in 1650 only a subordinate objective; and that objective, it was believed, could be attained, in alliance with the Crown, by measures of social reform rather than by the assertion of constitutional rights. The attack was rather upon the class which had appropriated the apparatus of government, and seemed likely as a consequence to push the Crown into the background. The reign of Gustav Adolf had seen the reconciliation of the high nobility with the monarchy: for twenty years the secular struggle of the two great forces in Swedish constitutional history was pretermitted; the pendulum, it seemed, had ceased to swing. It was not Oxenstierna's fault that the struggle

[57] Heckscher, op. cit., i, pp. 646–51.

[58] J. Vicens Vives, 'Estructura administrative estatal en los siglos XVI y XVII', *XIe Congrès International de Sciences Historiques*, 1960: Rapports, iv, p. 8.

[59] Heckscher, op. cit., i, pp. 420–2.

[60] The situation in this regard seems to have changed for the worse after 1660.

was now resumed. From 1632 to the day of his death, Oxenstierna pressed upon his colleagues a policy of moderation which would permit the reconciliation to be maintained. Gustav Adolf, he came to think, had had the better of the bargain between them, and after 1632 the balance was tipped a little the other way; but the oligarchical implications of 1634 were never fully exploited. Oxenstierna insisted that the nobility must be ready to make voluntary contributions, and be willing to waive its exemption from taxation on occasion; it must be careful to give no opening to its enemies by abusing its privileges, or making unwarrantable demands for their extension; it must give visible evidence of responsibility and patriotism; and above all must avoid committing itself to the defence of indefensible positions.[61] Erik Oxenstierna inherited this policy from his father, and made it the basis of the partial *reduktion* of 1655; and Klas Rålamb and Gustav Bonde would try to maintain it in the 1660s. The aristocracy had, on the whole, a high sense of public duty. Clientelage never developed into a political danger. Sweden could show no analogue to Korfitz Ulfeld, Condé, or Radziejowski—except for Patkul, and he was a Balt—and anything like a Fronde of the princes was unthinkable. It was a slander to accuse Oxenstierna of seeking to weaken the Crown by alienations, and so force it to depend on a *Riksdag* in which the first Estate would have the preponderant voice.

Nevertheless, Christina's suspicions were natural enough; and it was she who broke the alliance that had bound her father and Oxenstierna together. But the movement of 1650 might just as well have been directed against the Crown as against the nobility; for the crisis was produced quite as much by Christina's folly and extravagance as by the greed of a rapacious aristocracy. From this point of view, indeed, the crisis is classifiable in Professor Trevor-Roper's terms, as a protest against the waste and profusion of an extravagant Renaissance Court.[62] But the Court, and the appendages to the Court, were far too small for this to be a complete or satisfactory explanation, and only by juggling with words can we

[61] *SRARP* iii, p. 44; v. pp. 22–23; *RRP* x, pp. 315, 319, 366; and cf. ibid., x, p. 562; xiii, p. 258.

[62] cf. Trevor-Roper, op. cit. (above, ch. 3). In 1644 court expenses came to 3.1 per cent of the total budget; in 1653 to 12.3 per cent, or, if Maria Eleonora's and Prince Charles's be included, 20 per cent: Olofsson, op. cit., p. 75. Court etiquette became more elaborate under Christina: Odhner, op. cit., pp. 355–6; Rosengren, op. cit., p. 189.

view the problem in terms of 'Court' against 'Country'.[63] The element of parasitism in Swedish society was inconsiderable; monopolists were rare birds; the Church was free of pluralism and absenteeism, and no churchman had held ministerial office for a century. What was amiss was the high aristocracy's near-monopoly of power; and one could, no doubt, describe this situation as a 'refeudalization' of society.[64] But the term sounds strange and jarring in a Swedish context. For historically the rule of Oxenstierna is to be seen as the realization of those plans of administrative reform which had been propounded by the aristocracy half a century before; as the defeat of the casual and *ad hoc* methods associated with the 'rule of secretaries'; as the placing of the task of government in the hands of the class best fitted by education and legal training to discharge it. By 1650, however, experience was showing that this involved social evils which made the price too high. Nor, perhaps, was it the most modern solution any longer. A new secretary-class, bigger, better and more respectable than the old, and reinforced by a newly-aspiring and newly-importunate lesser nobility, stood ready as an alternative government. And from this angle it *is* possible to describe 1650 as the clash of rival oligarchies,[65] the first skirmish in a battle which would not be fought out for another thirty years. In Gustav Adolf's reign the central administration 'went out of court'; in 1634, Oxenstierna endowed the State with modern bureaucratic machinery; and in 1680 the new bureaucrats wrested the State from the control of his successors—not so much because they were more efficient than the old aristocracy (Oxenstierna, after all, was the prince of administrators) as by sheer weight of numbers, and above all by union with the arch-bureaucrat who now occupied the throne. The alliance of Charles XI and Erik Lindschöld, considered in this light, meant much the same as the alliance of Gustav Adolf and Oxenstierna—it meant that the monarchy harnessed the forces of

[63] cf. the suggestive remarks of E. H. Kossmann in 'Trevor-Roper's "General Crisis": a Symposium', *Past and Present*, no. 18 (1960), p. 11. Nor was there any question (before the annexation of Skåne) of a clash between regionalism and centralism, or of any serious collision between the traditional power and prestige of provincial magnates and the administrative encroachments of bureaucracy.

[64] Vicens Vives, op. cit., p. 16.

[65] cf. D. H. Pennington and L. Stone, in 'Seventeenth Century Revolutions', *Past and Present*, no. 13 (1958).

progress. In 1611 those forces lay in the high aristocracy, in 1680 in the petty nobility. And 1650 is the date when the monarchy begins to swap horses. Christina quite missed the significance of what was happening. But Charles XI was perhaps the only really successful example of what Professor Trevor-Roper has called the 'Puritanism of the Right';[66] and it was that cause (among others) that triumphed in 1680. He stood for austerity, order, devotion to duty, balanced accounts, and, as a necessary consequence, peace: in 1680 the opposition of the 1640s and 1650s has become the Government.[67] The Crown really does turn back the clock; finance in Oxenstierna's style is abandoned; the King really does try to live of his own: an odd programme, we may think, for the forces of progress; but at least it realized some of the objectives of 1650. It was a solution born of necessity and defeat; but it was based on popular support. And indeed, without that support the establishment of absolutism would have been impossible in Sweden, for there was no state in Europe where a standing army was so little fitted to be an instrument for suppressing popular liberties. The break which some have discerned in the history of the seventeenth century[68] comes in Sweden in 1680, not in 1650; and only then is the ideal of mixed monarchy finally overthrown. And the differing outcome of the two crises depends not only on the differing personalities of Christina and Charles XI, but equally on the fact that in 1650 the political alliance of the lesser nobility with the unprivileged Estates had not yet had time to mature.

The common objective which drew them together was the attainment of office. And in this matter the position in Sweden was very different from that in most European countries. For there never was a time, in all Sweden's history, when offices were sold by the Crown—though there came to be a time when they were sold by their possessors.[69] A few offices—that of county court judge, for instance—were in practice hereditary in great noble families,

[66] Trevor-Roper, op. cit., p. 49 (above, at p. 80).

[67] Contemporaries did not fail to remark that Johan Gyllenstierna was Johan Skytte's grandson.

[68] Trevor-Roper, op. cit., pp. 33–34 (above, at pp. 62–63).

[69] The so-called *ackord* system, by which an office-holder provided himself with a lump sum on retirement by the sale of his office to his successor, seems to have arisen in the generation after 1680, when Charles XI, by prohibiting any further donations, made some such expedient necessary.

and were often executed by deputy;[70] and in Christina's reign we hear of the gift (but not the sale) of offices in reversion (a practice condemned by the Clergy in 1655 as conducing to a breach of the Tenth Commandment);[71] but venality of offices in the French sense simply did not exist, and the absence of it does not seem to have entailed a greater degree of corruption than elsewhere—at least, in Oxenstierna's time—although some historians will no doubt feel that it ought to have done so.[72] It might therefore appear superfluous to touch on the controversy as to whether the revolutionary movements of the mid-century were directed against office-holders, or engineered by them.[73] But in fact this matter of office-holding was important in Sweden too; and it certainly helped to range Burghers and Clergy on the Peasants' side in 1650.

For both Estates wanted offices, and both saw the nobility blocking their way. The representatives of the burghers at the Diet were no longer mainly merchants or traders; they were professional municipal officials, 'royal burgomasters' paid by the Crown, civil servants, men learned in the law, very often with a degree from Uppsala. As Schering Rosenhane's parson put it: 'in former times we had good old merchants for burgomasters, who

[70] Around the mid-century the absenteeism of these *häradshövdingar* was heavily attacked: *SRARP* iv, pp. 216, 417; *HSH* xxi, p. 237; *RRP* xii, p. 342; xv, p. 509.

[71] *PSRP* i, p. 342.

[72] Vicens Vives, op. cit., pp. 20–21; Jacob van Klaveren: 'Die historische Erscheinung der Korruption, in ihrem Zusammenhang mit der Staats- und Gesellschaftsstruktur betrachtet', *Vierteljahrschrift für Sozial- und Wirtschaftsgeschichte*, xliv (1957), pp. 289–324. Klaveren would no doubt attempt to explain the comparative purity of Swedish official life either as a consequence of the absolutism of Charles XI (since it is his thesis that absolutism inhibits corruption), or perhaps as evidence of the weakness of the 'Zwischengruppen' in Swedish society: 'Die Mittelschichten waren die Brutstätten der Korruption. Dies gilt allgemein sowohl für die traditionellen Zwischengruppen wie für die vom Fürsten geschaffene Beamtenschaft'; op. cit., p. 312. But the change from oligarchy to absolutism made, if anything, for greater rather than less corruption: see E. Ingers, *Erik Lindschöld* (Lund, 1908), i, pp. 212–15; Alf Åberg, *Karl XI* (Stockholm, 1958), pp. 67, 112–13, 121; and the sale of offices by their owners was systematized only after the victory of parliamentarism in 1720: contrast K. W. Swart, *Sale of Offices in the Seventeenth Century* (The Hague, 1949), p. 116.

[73] cf. R. Mousnier, in 'Trevor-Roper's "General Crisis": a symposium', *Past and Present*, no. 18, pp. 18–25 (repr. above, pp. 97–104).

understood trade and commerce, and thought not beyond their own concerns, but drove their trade as best they could; but now, since burgomasters have begun to speak French and Italian, and have a book or two under their arm when they come to the office, it is become vulgar to speak of salt and cloth, for they must be telling us what Tacitus says, and how things stand at Court'.[74] Such men wanted a career open at the top; and at the Diet of 1650 they threw up leaders in the persons of Nils Nilsson and Nils Skunk—the first professional political lawyers in Swedish history. So too with the clergy, who desired official appointments for their sons. It happened that in the 1650s Sweden was suffering from a glut of priests; and in the absence of vacant livings the sons of the manse were looking to a career in the civil service, with the result that the university was turning out far too many graduates in the contemporary equivalent of Modern Greats: as Magnus Gabriel de la Gardie said in 1655, 'there are more *literati* and learned fellows, especially *in politicis*, than means or jobs available to provide for them, and they grow desperate and impatient'.[75] Sweden was acquiring a learned proletariat of unemployed academics; and de la Gardie, as Chancellor of Uppsala, was driven to the heroic remedy of making the examinations harder, and cutting down the number of bursaries. In 1650 the prospects for such persons were poor. For the nobility claimed a preference for all the better jobs; and though the bureaucracy was increasing slowly, the nobility was increasing so fast that there was no keeping track of it.

During the reign of Christina the process which Mr. Stone has called the inflation of honours[76] reached heights that would have staggered James I. In ten years she doubled the number of noble families, and sextupled the number of counts and barons. She ennobled army contractors, chancery secretaries, importunate creditors, land agents of the aristocracy, customs inspectors, her

[74] *Samtal*, p. 29. From the short autobiographical notes made by Nils Skunk in 1668 it is pretty clear that it was to him that Rosenhane was referring: 'Nils Skunks självbiografi', in *Tidningar utg. i Uppsala* (1777), pp. 33–39. And cf. *SRARP* iv, p. 427; and Tom Söderberg, *Den namnlösa medelklassen* (Stockholm, 1956), pp. 118, 121–2.

[75] Sven Edlund, *M. G. de la Gardies inrikespolitiska program 1655* (Lund, 1954), pp. 40–41, 51–52, 64; cf. *SRARP* iv, p. 625. This well bears out Trevor-Roper, op. cit., pp. 52–53 (above, at pp. 84–85).

[76] Lawrence Stone, 'The Inflation of Honours, 1558–1641', *Past and Present*, no. 14 (1958).

court tailor, a round dozen of court physicians, droves of army officers, Germans, Dutchmen, Scots—there was no end to them.[77] The flood of new peers was so great that there was not enough land in the market for all of them to acquire estates; and we hear of counts for whom the Crown found it impossible to provide counties.[78] And this meant that they were shut out from the essential financial advantage of noble status. The war was over; the prospects in the army were poor; and the new nobility was therefore driven back on the civil service, only to be confronted with equally hungry competitors, of better blood than they. These were the old petty nobility, whose lineage was longer than its purse; men who had backed the abortive sumptuary ordinances of the 1640s because they could not afford to keep up with French fashions, men who demanded to be allowed to club together in twos or threes to provide one collaborative cavalryman by way of knight-service, men with only two or four horses, who complained loudly of the expense of Christina's coronation.[79]

It was against the pre-emptive claims of such persons that the lower Estates in 1650 advanced the demand for appointments to be made on merit alone. They failed; for on this occasion the nobility was united against them, and the Queen in the end let them down. But their cry for a *reduktion* was destined five years later to split the apparently solid front of the first Estate. By 1655 the latent tensions and antagonisms within the peerage had risen to the surface.[80] The

[77] *Samtal*, p. 5, where *Juncker Päär* says: 'You see yourself by daily experience, that he who anyways addresses himself to ensure honour and virtue, and does any good service, can without difficulty come into the Estate of Nobility, whether his origins be in the Estate of Clergy, Burghers, or Peasants . . . and when he is come thereto, he has a like right and access to high office with any other . . .But that any should leap into the highest posts straight from his pepper-bags or his dung-cart is a thing whose consequence you may well imagine'. Johan Ekeblad commented: 'We have now arms and escutcheons by the hundred. Herr Carl Krusse (*sc.* Kruus) has now joined the mob they call counts': *Johan Ekeblads bref*, i, p. 195. For the bad quality of some of the new nobility, see *SRARP* iii, p. 238; iv, p. 433; v, p. 301; *Riksrådets memorial till K.M:tt, 1665* (printed in *Den svenska Fatburen*, 1769), p. 113; R. Swedlund, 'Krister Bonde och reduktionsbeslutet 1655', *Karolinska Förbundets Årsbok* (1937). And for the whole question, Tom Söderberg, op. cit., pp. 94–99, 105, 112.

[78] Swedlund, *Grev- och friherreskapen i Sverige och Finland*, pp. 134–5.

[79] *SRARP* v, pp. 55, 260; iv, p. 431; iii, pp. 24, 41; *RRP* xiv, pp. 339, 383.

[80] For the tensions within the Nobility, see *SRARP* iii, pp. 215, 219; iv,

refusal of members of the historic families to enter the civil service at the bottom of the ladder; the pretensions of counts and barons to a superiority over the untitled nobility; the divergent interests of those who had, and those who had not, great estates; the contempt of the old aristocracy for *parvenus;* the lack of any common interest between the Brahes and Bondes and Bielkes on the one hand, and the poor rustic squires on the other—all these things destroyed the ability of the aristocracy to resist a *reduktion*, for they made many nobles its most fervent advocates.[81] For from the point of view of the office-holding noble, the clinching argument for a *reduktion* was, that it would enable the Crown to be regular in the payment of wages. It was this argument which led them to ally with the lower Estates, and which turned them into supporters of the revolution of 1680 and the new bureaucratic absolutism of Charles XI. Thus the struggle of the peasants against deteriorating conditions becomes potentially revolutionary (in 1650) only when it receives the support of the other non-noble Estates; and is successful (in 1680) only when that support is reinforced by a section of the nobility, and by the alliance of the Crown. And even then success comes only incidentally, as a by-product of quite other conflicts. For the events of 1680, in fact, registered first the emancipation of the monarchy from oligarchical control, and secondly the victory of the petty nobility over the high aristocracy. And the bureaucracy of which that nobility was the backbone can plausibly be equated with the high *bourgeoisie* in other countries.[82] They were hard-working, respectable, and of solid but (as a rule) not immoderate means, and to most of them their salaries were important. Some of them were nobles, some not; but all might hope to be, when they reached the appropriate grade in the service.[83] It is not easy to contend, as Porshnev argued in regard to

[81] *Riksrådets memorial . . . 1665*, pp. 110–11, 115; Wittrock, op. cit., pp. 44–47; *SRARP* iv, p. 267; Sven A. Nilsson, 'Reduktion eller Kontribution?', *passim*, and p. 106.

[82] See, in general, Tom Söderberg, *Den namnlösa medelklassen* (which, however, dissents from the view taken above); and Sten Carlsson, *Svensk ståndscirkulation, 1680–1960* (Stockholm, 1950).

[83] Sten Carlsson, op. cit., pp. 21–22.

pp. 181, 192, 217, 362, 454, 584; v, pp. 237, 241; Swedlund, 'Krister Bonde och reduktionsbeslutet' *passim*; Edlund, op. cit., pp. 45, 239; Wittrock, 'Riksskattmästaren Gustaf Bondes politiska program', pp. 48–49.

the office-holding class in France, that their very success feudalized them, converted them into defenders of the aristocratic exploiting classes, and deprived them of their *bourgeois* characteristics.[84] The charter of their liberties, the tangible evidence of their victory, was the Table of Ranks of 1680, which laid it down that in civil life, as well as military, status in the social hierarchy should henceforth depend not on birth, but on rank, and rank itself upon service and merit.[85] After 1718 the high aristocracy made a brief attempt to recover political power, as they did in France in 1715. They were unsuccessful, in the one instance as in the other; and in 1739 the triumph of 'democracy' within the first Estate once more revealed the alienation of the bureaucracy from the old families. The Age of Liberty, despite constitutional appearances, is the true successor to the absolutism of Charles XI; for it is the age of bureaucratic rule in alliance with the quasi-sovereign Estates, who have stepped into the vacuum of power left by the overthrow of unlimited monarchy. And the deliverance—or the catastrophe—of 1772 was possible only because, as so often happens, the bureaucratic class in course of time developed an exclusiveness which made it vulnerable. It may seem a far cry from 1650 to 1769; but the two situations are in many ways not dissimilar;[86] and it is not altogether fanciful to trace the political ancestry of Kepplerus to Nils Skunk.[87]

The example of Sweden, then, does little to make easier the

[84] Porshnev, op. cit., p. 479; and Vicens Vives, op. cit., pp. 15–16. As M. Mousnier remarks: 'tous les officers aspirent à devenir juridiquement nobles. Ils ne deviennent pas de ce fait des féodaux ni des gentilshommes'. And again, 'Une noblesse de service, une noblesse dans laquelle on est classé par le service envers le Prince, incarnant l'Etat, est-ce la même chose qu'une féodalité?': R. Mousnier, in ' "Serviteurs du Roi". Quelques aspects de la fonction publique dans la société française du XVIIe siècle', *XVIIe Siècle*, nos. 41–43 (1959), pp. 5, 6.

[85] S. Bergh, 'Rangstriderna inom adeln under 1600-talet', *Historisk Tidskrift*, 1st ser., xvi (1896), *passim*, and p. 149.

[86] It was scarcely by accident that some of the more important documents on the crisis were printed for the first time in 1768–9. And it is no less significant that Anders Schönberg, in his *Historiska bref om det svenska regeringssättet* (1773) should have taken the line that the social struggles of 1650 were now (after Gustav III's *coup*) better forgotten: op. cit. (new edn. 1850), ii, pp. 149–50.

[87] For Kepplerus, see *The European Nobility in the Eighteenth Century*, ed. A. Goodwin (London, 1953), p. 148.

provision of a plain answer to the enigma of the general crisis; for it is pretty clear that Sweden does not exactly fit any of the generalizations which have been put forward to explain it. No doubt we are not entitled to demand of a historical explanation that it should explain everything, or be true for all cases. Yet the case of Sweden may reasonably be held to present features of more than local interest: the country resembled a western European state a good deal more closely than did (for example) the Ukraine; and in 1650 Stockholm looks much nearer to the centre of the revolutionary movement than (for instance) Naples or Amsterdam. If we are really determined to bring the Cossacks and the Ironsides within the scope of a single explanation, it does not seem legitimate to leave Sweden out of the reckoning. Is it too much to hope for an explanation which will accommodate Nils Nilsson as well as John Pym, embrace Oxenstierna no less than Zuidpolsbroek,[88] and find room for Archbishop Lenaeus side by side with Cardinal de Retz?

[88] For Zuidpolsbroek, see J. E. Elias, *Geschiedenis van het Amsterdamsche Regentenpatriciaat* ('s Gravenhage, 1923), pp. 145–9.

IX

THE CHARACTER OF ELIZABETHAN CATHOLICISM*

John Bossy

I

AN account of Elizabethan Catholicism must begin as a commentary on the term most frequently used to describe it, the 'Old Religion'. What answers to this description is a Catholicism less concerned with doctrinal affirmation or dramas of conscience than with a set of ingrained observances which defined and gave meaning to the cycle of the week and the seasons of the year, to birth, marriage and death. This has been aptly termed 'survivalism'.[1] It should probably not be thought of either as particularly localized, or as from the beginning associated with one section of the population rather than with another. But being a predominantly social sentiment it could persist only where there was a social institution to support it; and the support of those institutions controlled by the Government had been withdrawn. This left those rapidly diminishing areas in which public authority was still virtually in private hands, and the relatively independent seigneurial institutions of the countryside. Nobles or gentlemen who felt the insufficiencies of the new-found religion more strongly than the inducements of the Court could retire to their 'estates': to the seigneurial household, its buildings, lands, and the village or villages which it dominated. Within this unity the rites and

[1] A. G. Dickens, 'The First Stages of Romanist Recusancy in Yorkshire', *Yorks. Arch. Jl.*, xxxv (1941), p. 181.

* From no. 21 (1962).

observances which had disappeared from public view could be preserved, adapting themselves to, and mutually supporting one another.

The geography of Catholicism was broadly established by the relative strength of this institution, by the negative factors of difficulty of access for the machinery of government, distance from an economically dominant town, the presence of widespread rural industry or an active maritime coast. One can distinguish three types of unit: the bastard-feudal connections of the borders; the numerous small but independent seigneurial households in areas which, though settled, were not easily in reach of Government influence, and backed on ground inaccessible or unsubdued;[2] and the larger but increasingly scattered households of the rest of the country, the centre of substantial complexes of land, with a tradition of wider dominance and large-scale hospitality, occupied by families which by marriage and scale of life merged into the lesser peerage.[3] Contrary pressures did not so much prevent the existence of the Catholic household as compel it to be larger if it was to survive.

Of bastard-feudal Catholicism there is not much to be said. It carried on the tradition of private allegiance and of war with neighbours and with the Government,[4] of which the Northern Rising in 1569 was little more than a large incident; it was doomed to incoherence and failure. After this débâcle, though islands of it survived into the seventeenth century, there were no large clienteles left, and without them the will to aristocratic revolt, even with foreign encouragement, was powerless. The flight of the surviving leaders cleared them out of England, and they did nothing abroad except produce the last manifesto of the old order, the *Treatise of Treasons against Queen Elizabeth*.[5]

The resources and resilience of properly seigneurial Catholicism

[2] Examples in J. S. Leatherbarrow, *The Lancashire Elizabethan Recusants* (Chetham Society, 1947), p. 86; A. G. Dickens, 'Extent and Character of Recusancy in Yorkshire in 1604', *Yorks. Arch. Jl.*, xxxvii (1948), pp. 40 f.

[3] e.g. the Arundells, in A. L. Rowse, *Tudor Cornwall* (London, 1941), pp. 342 f; the Treshams, in M. E. Finch, *The Wealth of Five Northamptonshire Families* (Northants Record Society, xix, 1956), pp. 80 f.

[4] The case of the Cholmleys in J. J. Cartwright, *Chapters in the History of Yorkshire* (Wakefield, 1872), pp. 162 f; Dickens, 'First Stages', p. 176.

[5] T. H. Clancy, 'Political Thought of the Counter-Reformation in England' (London University Ph.D. thesis, 1960), p. 26, etc.

were greater. In so far as the old religion was a cycle of fasts and feasts, withdrawal to the seigneurial household limited it by paring off such public elements as festivals and processions, but left it substantially intact. Fasting, for example, was admirably adapted to the household régime. If the household contained a priest, who could at the same time act, or be disguised, as tutor, steward, or something similar, and especially if there was a chapel, the traditional regularity could be preserved without much loss. In the bigger houses the liturgical cycle merged indistinguishably with the cycle of hospitality. At Easter or Christmas there would be a large company and sung Masses; the musicians who served for the Mass would also serve for the entertainment, and it was presumably on these occasions that Byrd's Masses were first performed.[6] The integration of religion into the household accounts for a fact which has been universally observed as characteristic of Elizabethan Catholicism, the importance of the position occupied in it by women. The same process can be observed in those aspects of religion concerned with the bonds of continuity. These also tended to be withdrawn from the public order of the parish into the private order of the household: marriages and christenings would take place there, and as for burial, if the parish priest could not be influenced or circumvented, the occasion would be ringed around with the traditional rites observed in private and later with Masses for the Dead and the general commemoration of All Souls.[7] Here was a religion of communal observance and mutual obligation, binding the living to one another and to the dead.

Lord Vaux, presented in May 1581, along with 'his household and familiars and divers servants', for not coming to his parish church of Harrowden, 'did claim his house to be a parish by itself'.[8] This was putting the case in a nutshell. Whatever the legal ground for Vaux's claim, his attitude was clearly that of the Catholic gentry as a whole. For them, the integration or reintegration of religion into the household was not simply a second best; it brought the positive advantages of control over the priest, freedom

[6] G. Anstruther, *Vaux of Harrowden* (Newport, Mon., 1953), pp. 247 f, 168 f; Rowse, *Tudor Cornwall*, pp. 352, 373.

[7] Dickens, 'First Stages', p. 170; Leatherbarrow, *Lancashire Elizabethan Recusants*, pp. 121 f; *Victoria County History of Oxfordshire*, ii, pp. 44 f; Anstruther, op. cit., p. 233.

[8] Anstruther, op. cit., p. 113.

from inappropriate sermons, and from civil and ecclesiastical supervision. More generally it served to bind together gentlemen, servants and tenants in the unity of the seigneurial household, to establish loyalty to it as practically superior to all other loyalties, to confirm the position of the gentleman as mediator between his dependants and public authority.[9] The result may be regarded as a revival of the proprietary church, a sort of 'natural economy' in religion. For the advantages it brought, a recusancy fine, if it came to that, might not be too much to pay.

But this sort of Catholicism by no means necessarily involved recusancy.[10] As a complex of social practices rather than a religion of internal conviction, it offered no barrier to the degree of attendance at the parish church required to preserve the integrity of the household; a sufficient dissociation could be expressed by not communicating, by keeping one's hat on or talking during the sermon. For the first twenty years of the reign the minimum of conformity was almost universally observed by men who within their own households continued to live as Catholics; and this with no sense of strain or moral discomfort. All that was implied was a distinction in the order of society between what was the Queen's and what was one's own; freedom of conscience meant the free decision of the mode of existence of one's household. The Government, at least provisionally, accepted the distinction, and conflict either interior or exterior was minimal.

When conflict came, it came as a struggle between two notions of social obligation, and was fought in the debatable land between the order of the household and the order of government. The household was most obviously vulnerable from below; from the recalcitrant servant appealing to public authority over the head of his master, by the act of informing. Personal trouble, desire for reward, sense of public duty or religious conviction could all play their part; and one informer, who knew when there would be a priest, a well-attended Mass, or a large company assembled for a feast, could destroy a household.[11] Once the information had been given, or the arrest made, the point of conflict shifted to the

[9] Note the case in Rowse, op. cit., p. 349.

[10] Dickens, 'First Stages', p. 157 and *passim*; Anstruther, op. cit., pp. 77 f.

[11] Leatherbarrow, op. cit., pp. 86, 90; Anstruther, op. cit., p. 238; Rowse, op. cit., pp. 352, 363; Evelyn Waugh, *Edmund Campion* (London, 1935), pp. 155 f.

allegiance of the tenants and neighbours who would have to indict, convict, or value lands for composition. Here again the strength of the seigneurial bond might make it difficult to assemble a jury, to get a conviction or a realistic valuation of property.[12] Where it proved insufficient, the gentleman was left with a sense of outrage and betrayal; Sir Thomas Tresham complained of being 'beaten with juries' and brought face to face with 'perjured caitiffs' produced 'most falsely to swear to my prejudice'.[13] After the event, loyalty might be rewarded; and the informer who was foolish enough to stay or reappear in the locality was likely to get beaten up by the friends and servants of the man he had informed against.[14] The gentleman could of course himself contribute to a weakening of the bond of loyalty, and notably if, as Tresham did, he went in for ruthless enclosure, depopulation and rack-renting.[15] Bad feeling or open warfare between himself and his tenants was disastrous; and if, as has been suggested, the Elizabethan Catholic gentry were as a whole unenterprising landowners,[16] this would help to account for it. Nothing could replace loyalty. This was perhaps a wasting asset, and Henry Garnet had reason to preach on the text: 'Gentem auferte perfidam/Credentium de finibus.'[17] But the extent to which the Catholic household survived into the seventeenth century shows that it still had a good deal of wear in it.

The order of the household, the integration into it of the practice of religion, and the preservation of its integrity, were the subjects with which the Elizabethan Catholic gentry were largely occupied. It is difficult to discover what they thought of public matters, or to define a general political attitude which they would share. They were not as a class specially articulate, and the one general statement with which one might associate them, the *Treatise of Treasons*, does not really represent them. To argue from

12 G. H. Ryan and L. J. Redstone, *Timperley of Hintlesham* (London, 1931), pp. 53 f; Rowse, op. cit., pp. 347 f; H. Bowler, 'Some Notes on the Recusant Rolls', *Recusant History*, iv (1958), pp. 188, 194.

13 Anstruther, op. cit., p. 129.

14 Rowse, op. cit., p. 378; Anstruther, op. cit., pp. 87 f, 216.

15 Finch, *Wealth of Five Northamptonshire Families*, pp. 87 f; cf. R. H. Tawney, 'Rise of the Gentry', *Econ. Hist. Rev.*, 1st ser., xi (1941), p. 16.

16 J. E. Mousley, 'The Fortunes of some Gentry Families of Elizabethan Sussex', *Econ. Hist. Rev.*, 2nd ser., xi (1959), pp. 478–9.

17 At Coughton, Warwicks., All Saints 1601: Anstruther, op. cit., p. 281.

revolts and conspiracies to a general sense of antagonism towards the Crown,[18] is a temptation which should probably be resisted. It was certainly possible for a habit of violence bred in the local conflict to extend to violence against the Government; but this was in either case a counsel of despair rather than a typical reaction. The independent gentry had nothing to do with the Northern Rising, and all that can be deduced from the fate of conspiracies like the Babington or Gunpowder Plots is that, as a whole, they disapproved of them as making even more difficult their task of maintaining the integrity of their households. Allowing for nuances of outlook between the bigger gentry and the small men from remoter parts, we are likely to represent them most fairly as having a conception of their relation to the Queen which did not wholly coincide with her own, and generally refusing to admit that this was so.

Men who saw their relation to their inferiors in terms of fidelity could hardly envisage otherwise their relation to the Queen. They thought of this as a direct personal relationship, as is clear from the declaration of loyalty and allegiance made by the most important of them at the time of the Armada' a declaration which they evidently considered as involving those from whom they claimed fidelity themselves.[19] They did not think of the State as a generality comprising individuals: there was the 'estate' of the Queen, and there were their own 'estates'.[20] There were therefore two circuits of loyalty: that which bound their dependants to themselves, and that which bound themselves to the Queen. These should be kept distinct. They objected to royal interference with their own 'estates' not only because it undermined the loyalty to them of their dependants, but because it implied on the part of the Queen a mistrust in the loyalty to her which they never ceased to proclaim. Whatever disturbed this hierarchy, they resented. Heresy disturbed it by upsetting the spiritual order which sanctioned it; fidelity and heresy were incompatible because heresy was infidelity to God. Protestantism particularly disturbed it because it was a religion of

[18] H. R. Trevor-Roper, *The Gentry, 1540–1640* (Economic History Review, Supplement no. 1), pp. 38 f.

[19] *Historical Manuscripts Commission, Fifth Report*, Appendix, p. 406.

[20] cf. J. E. Neale, 'The Commons' Privilege of Free Speech in Parliament', *Tudor Studies presented to A. F. Pollard* (London, 1924), pp. 280 f; P. Laslett, Introduction to Filmer's *Patriarcha* (Oxford, 1949), p. 18, etc.

'basket-makers and beer-brewers'.[21] But the Pope had no more right to interfere with it than anyone else, and they took no notice when he relieved them of their duty of fidelity to the Queen.

The ideas that the Queen's 'estate' was entirely her own business, as their own was theirs, and that she could not act against the order of which she was the central point, could only be reconciled with each other and with the facts by the time-honoured fiction of evil counsellors. Responsibility for the situation must lie with the new men, raised 'one from book, the other from buttery', who had insinuated themselves into her confidence, and whose ultimate aim was to reduce England to a popular state.[22] When the attempt to by-pass evil counsellors and bureaucratic machinery by appealing directly to the Queen produced no result,[23] they were left nursing the hope that in God's good time she would wake up to the situation, or a new reign restore the true order of things. But this assumption was a matter of social necessity rather than of internal conviction. Attachment to an order which had disappeared, dependence on a hierarchy of relationships repudiated from above and undermined from below, a sense that their history was being made for them by powers which they did not understand and could not control—these bred insecurity, disorientation, and a feeling of general decline. Whether they continued to conform outwardly or took the plunge into recusancy, they could provide themselves with no practical object but the preservation within their households of a conscience conceived as passive.

II

Elizabethan Catholicism, however, is to be understood neither purely as the Old Religion nor in purely seigneurial terms. It is to a large extent dominated by elements foreign and in many ways antagonistic to those already described, and which are to be accounted for as part not of the history of the gentry, but of that of the clerk. For their origins we must go to the humanism of the universities, to men in whom the sense of criticism and intellectual

21 Clancy, 'Political Thought of the Counter-Reformation in England', pp. 37 f, 65.

22 ibid., pp. 39, 47.

23 Anstruther, *Vaux of Harrowden*, p. 154.

renovation was not distinguished from the idea that the unity of Christendom was the only preservative of truth. In 1558 this state of mind remained especially strong at Oxford; when it became obvious that it was not acceptable to the new Government, those who shared it took themselves abroad, to continue their work in the more congenial climate of Louvain.[24] The Louvainists were not unduly worried about the present, or concerned for the future; the traditional structure of Church order, of belief and practice, seemed to them part of the order of the Universe; there had always been heresies and schisms, but as a violation of this order they could not finally prosper. In the meantime they must get on with their work as clerks, examining and purifying traditional doctrine with the best techniques available, and defending it against the attacks of heretics. At the worst, they would have to see that this work was safeguarded and carried on by successors who, when the time came, would be ready for the task of restoring true religion in England.[25] Some of them saw the need for a more energetic approach; but there was no radical change of outlook until they were joined by a new generation of clerks, drawn to Catholicism from motives perceptibly different from their own, and totally different from those of the Catholic gentry; men for whom it appeared not as a withdrawal from the Elizabethan order in favour of something older, but as a reaction against it in favour of something better.

The decline of the clergy in sixteenth-century England is a familiar topic. We are used to seeing the reorganization of the Church as a victory over it of lay society, diminishing its resources and lowering the status of the clerk; imposing a makeshift order which disguised problems so that laymen could get on with their business without hindrance; reorientating the universities to the function of seminaries for gentlemen, and implying in the long run the evolution of the clerk into the clergyman.[26] The relevance of this scheme of affairs to the growth of Puritanism is generally recognized; it is also a prime element in the formation of Eliza-

[24] A. C. Southern, *Elizabethan Recusant Prose* (London, 1950), pp. 18–26, 43–50.

[25] Note Allen's remarks in M. Haile, *An Elizabethan Cardinal: William Allen* (London, 1914), p. 76.

[26] Christopher Hill, *Economic Problems of the Church from Archbishop Whitgift to the Long Parliament* (Oxford, 1956); M. H. Curtis, *Oxford and Cambridge in Transition* (Oxford, 1959); F. Caspari, *Humanism and the Social Order in Tudor England* (Chicago, 1954).

bethan Catholicism.[27] Between 1568 and 1575 a number of Oxford clerks left their fellowships and went abroad, among them Gregory Martin and Edmund Campion of St. John's, William Reynolds of New College, and Robert Parsons of Balliol.[28] They were younger and more diverse in origin than those who had gone to Louvain. Few of them were gentlemen, or came from parts of the country where seigneurial Catholicism was strong; they were clerks first and last. Most of them had at some time been attracted to Protestantism, and all had conformed in some degree to the new establishment. Catholicism meant for them not conformity to traditional forms of belief and behaviour, but a conversion, a religion individual and interior. What they were against was lay supremacy and intellectual compromise; they saw themselves as sounding an 'alarm spiritual against foul vice and proud ignorance';[29] they had as much as Milton the idea of a people purified by truth. The story that William Reynolds and his brother John reciprocally converted one another to Calvinism and Catholicism[30] may well be apocryphal, but conveniently makes the point. The content of their belief was poles apart; but the conditions from which it sprang were the same, and the forms in which it expressed itself were remarkably similar.[31]

The difference between these men and the Louvainists was that they saw the Elizabethan settlement not as unnatural, but as intolerable, and not doomed to collapse of itself but likely to continue indefinitely if nobody did anything about it. The conscience whose rights they affirmed was a public conscience, coterminous neither with the gentleman's liberty of withdrawal nor with the right to argue from a safe distance; it demanded Reformation. They bitterly criticized the Marian régime because it had not reformed, but had contented itself with external observance;[32] they could not be satisfied simply with attempting to restore it. Some-

[27] William Haller, *The Rise of Puritanism* (New York, 1957 edn.), pp. 39 f; Parsons, in *C(atholic) R(ecord) S(ociety)* ii, pp. 50 f; Clancy, op. cit., p. 67.

[28] Southern, op. cit., pp. 51–54.

[29] Campion's *Challenge*, printed in Southern, op. cit., p. 154.

[30] Wood, *Athenae Oxonienses* (London, 1813 edn.), i, col. 613.

[31] cf. C. S. Lewis, *English Literature in the Sixteenth Century, excluding Drama* (Oxford, 1954), p. 439.

[32] Parsons, *Memorial for the Reformation of England* (ed. Edward Gee, as *The Jesuit's Memorial, 1690*), pp. 20 f; *CRS*, ii, pp. 54–57.

thing different had to be invented; and it was already, gradually and tentatively, being invented by one of the Louvainists, William Allen. Allen had been forced by illness to return to England and had been able to see that a policy of reliance on Providence would end in the extinction of Catholicism in England. When he returned to the Netherlands he founded the college at Douai. In his motives there was a mixture of old and new: the college was to continue the work of Louvain as the older men died out, and it was to capture men who were unhappy in the English universities. It was only in the course of establishing it, and almost by accident, that he hit on the idea that it should train a new generation of priests to be sent back to England immediately. What had been first conceived as a sort of dissident university created by the clerks for themselves became the spring of a missionary venture which demanded a renovation of the very idea of the clerk.[33] Allen described what had happened when he said that they must not wait for better times, but make them. Certainly, in Campion's phrase, the enterprise was God's, and being God's could not be withstood; but it was quite clear to them that the enterprise of men was the only instrument of the enterprises of God.[34]

By this mental revolution the clerks revivified Catholicism in England. Their Catholicism offered a pole of attraction for men unsatisfied with the conditions of the Elizabethan settlement, such as until then only Protestantism could provide. It could be presented, as Parsons presented it in his *Book of Resolution*, in terms which had a universal appeal; the book's effect on people as diverse as the future Benet of Canfield and the playwright Robert Greene, and the fact that it could be widely distributed by Protestants with only minor changes, prove that he had touched a general need.[35] Allen, Parsons, Campion and their collaborators were doing far more than providing spiritual cement for the households of the Catholic gentry. They had acted as clerks; they wanted to affirm the independence of the clerical order and to rediscover for it an

[33] Philip Hughes, *The Reformation in England*, iii (London, 1954), pp. 282–96; Allen, in Southern, op. cit., pp. 18–20, and *Letters and Memorials of William Cardinal Allen*, ed. T. F. Knox (London, 1882), pp. 31–37.

[34] *Allen Letters*, p. 367; Southern, op. cit., p. 155.

[35] H. Thurston, 'Catholic Writers and Elizabethan Readers', *The Month*, lxxxii (1894), pp. 463 f; *The Repentance of Robert Greene* (reprinted with *A Groatsworth of Wit*, London, 1923), pp. 12 f; *Autobiography of Benet of Canfield*, in J. Brousse, *Life of Angel of Joyeuse, etc.* (Douai, 1623), pp. 20 ff.

echo in the minds of people at large. They had not refused one form of lay supremacy in order to confirm another. In this lay the grounds of later conflict.

The pursuit of the clerical enterprise demanded a great variety of connected activities. Allen directed the seminary, at Douai and then at Rheims, until 1585, and assembled from clerks who had left England a remarkable group of professors. He and they trained the newcomers in both the humanities and the scholastic disciplines, in cases of conscience, in preaching and controversy, preparing them for the tasks of a renovated priesthood which they would have to assume when they returned to England. The seminary was an institution without written statutes, functioning on enthusiasm and the practical inspiration of Allen; its power of attraction proved such that new foundations had to be created, first in Rome, then in Spain. The priest, once back in England, was left on his own: without priestly dress, without a church, without a hierarchy above or below, with no refuge in the continuity of material institutions and objects. In what might be a state of continuous alarm, he had to survive, to say Mass, administer the sacraments, preach and reconcile; to denounce the menace of external compromise; to try to infuse into a baffled squirearchy his own impetus and sense of the future; to offer himself as evidence of a spiritual adventure not to be found in the established Church. This metamorphosis of the clerk into a man of action could not be allowed to suppress his character as a man of thought and scholarship. The mission itself demanded books: simple explanations of doctrine, books of spiritual encouragement and direction, statements on doubtful points of practice, manifestoes, martyrologies. But at the same time the work of the Louvainists had to be continued: controversy and apologetic, technical works of theology, above all the new version of the Bible, done largely by Gregory Martin.[36]

This activity was the root of the matter, but it could not operate in a vacuum. Not only had the modes of spiritual action to be invented, but also the temporal structure which would support them. The seminary provided one pole of action; the other could not be firmly established without modifying the Catholic household in England so that it became an instrument of the enterprise—constructing priests' holes, dismissing doubtful servants, evolving

[36] Southern, op. cit., *passim.*

new lines and methods of communication.[37] To link the two, a network of routes was needed, converging on the sea and demanding the intervention of the merchant and the sailor. All along the north-west coast of Europe, from Antwerp to San Lucar de Barrameda, merchants and agents oiled the wheels of the enterprise: English or half-English, men who had been trading there for years or new men put there for the purpose, but in either case men who knew the world of commerce and long-range communication.[38] They operated at the junction between the continental network and the routes in and out of England; they arranged passages, gave directions, lent money, saw to its conveyance, received under their own name goods to be sold for the benefit of an *émigré*, cashed bills of exchange; they received and forwarded letters, gathered news and passed it along the line to Douai, Rheims or Rome. This last in particular developed into a highly organized machinery the importance of which, in the conditions of the sixteenth century, can hardly be overestimated.[39] Themselves, or in conjunction with printers local or *émigré*, they saw to the printing of books, or received them from presses inland, packed them up in bales of merchandise and sent them into England.[40] Without them, and without the network of communications on which they operated, the mission is inconceivable. In the absence of the income from property and tithes on which the Church had lived for centuries, the creation of a new priesthood meant calling on most of the resources of Europe in communications and financial techniques; it meant exposure to the great movements of economic change, and vulnerability to every political disturbance; it demanded flexibility and imagination. This was a far cry from the

[37] Anstruther, *Vaux of Harrowden*, p. 241; Dickens, 'Extent and Character of Recusancy in Yorkshire in 1604', pp. 38–39; D. Mathew, *Catholicism in England* (London, 1948), p. 51.

[38] e.g. Richard Verstegan at Antwerp: *Letters and Despatches of Richard Verstegan*, ed. A. G. Petti (*CRS*, lii, 1959), pp. xl f; Humphrey Shelton and Ralph Letherborough at Rouen: J. A. Bossy, 'Elizabethan Catholicism: The Link with France' (Cambridge University Ph.D. thesis, 1961), p. 80; for San Lucar, A. J. Loomie, 'Spain and the English Catholic Exiles, 1580–1604' (London University Ph.D. thesis, 1957), pp. 170–87.

[39] Petti, op. cit., pp. xv–xxxvi; cf. P. Sardella, *Nouvelles et spéculations à Venise au début du XVIe siècle* (Cahiers des Annales, i, 1948), pp. 9, 16, 83.

[40] *Letters and Memorials of Robert Persons*, ed. L. Hicks (*CRS*, xxxix, 1942), pp. lxvi f; Petti, op. cit., p. xxiii.

routine of the Catholic household in the north or the midlands. It is impossible, without a great deal more investigation, to tell how far the mission was financed by the profits of landownership, and how far from other sources like trade, book publication and foreign pensions.[41] But it is clear enough that the independence of the clerks depended on the existence of means of supply alternative to those provided by the Catholic gentry, and the impetus and unity of their action on the mastery of techniques of which the latter had the dimmest comprehension. By its very existence, the clerical enterprise redrew the map of English Catholicism and tended to redress the dominance within it of a seigneurial social structure and seigneurial ways of thought. The fact that 'merchant' came to be used by Catholics as the conventional periphrasis for a priest[42] is not entirely accidental or insignificant.

If the mission could not function apart from the communications and commerce of Europe, neither could it function in isolation from its politics. Its routes ran through, its bases were established in, foreign countries; it depended on governments whose goodwill was far from automatic. If this goodwill lapsed it had to be sought elsewhere. It was necessary to gain the support of groups within the country which could ensure, either that the government remained favourable, or that the *émigrés* would be protected if, for reasons of internal or external policy, it turned against them. On these grounds at least, some degree of political activity was called for; and since no government or faction would be anxious to support them if it had an interest in preserving the *status quo* in England, the protection of the mission implied at least a passive co-operation in attempts to overthrow it. The initiative was not primarily in the hands of the *émigré* priests; but once the question had been raised their attitude was clear. What had driven them to do what they were doing was a demand for reformation. The mission could supply some of the deficiencies in the existing situation and prepare the way for something better, but it could not act on the causes of the trouble; it could not change the laws

[41] For the cloth trade, Loomie, op. cit., p. 190; Petti, op. cit., pp. xli, xliii; Allen on the rate of exchange, *Allen Letters*, pp. 127, 132 f.

[42] An early instance in Anstruther, *Vaux of Harrowden*, p. 187. On the general point, see H. R. Trevor-Roper, 'Religion, the Reformation and Social Change', *Historical Studies*, iv: *Papers read before the Fifth Irish Conference of Historians* (London, 1963), pp. 35–36 and esp. n. 35.

by which the state of religion in England was enforced and protected. These would not change unless somebody made an effort to change them. They had no access to Parliament; rebellion, in view of the condition and outlook of the Catholic gentry, could never be more than a weak auxiliary; they were therefore forced back on foreign intervention, which might range from verbal good offices to a declaration of war, but must involve in the last resort the threat of force. They concluded that the nature and success of what they were doing demanded intervention of this kind, and the negotiation which would procure it; and deduced from the Marian disaster and the failure of earlier attempts that they could not afford to leave this to the *émigré* gentlemen, but must do it themselves. Neither Allen nor Parsons believed that political action could solve the problems with which they were faced; it did not dispense from the fundamental need to renovate English Catholicism, immediately, from within.[43] But the alternative to politics was quietism and a passive trust in providence, and if they had thought in these terms they would never have begun the mission at all.

The outcome of their involvement in English and continental politics was a number of statements of political principle which register the progress of their experience. They had of course learnt in the schools a political theory derived from Aristotle; but the pressure of the sixteenth century on the clergy tended to supplant this tradition in favour of theories of monarchical divine right. The situation of the Elizabethan clerks gave them a motive for holding on to the tradition and reformulating it in terms appropriate to the time. But they had first to survive their feudal inheritance. Had the Catholicism of the gentry remained dominant, nothing could have been done but to bolster the position of the *Treatise of Treasons* with the theory of papal supremacy. Allen, in the *Defence of Sir William Stanley* and the *Admonition to the Nobility and People of England and Ireland*, did little more than attempt to revive the ideal of the Christian knight and the tradition of the crusade.[44] Except that the fiction of evil counsellors was dropped and the Queen attacked directly, no progress was made. But the circumstances of the enterprise, in particular the situation of the *émigrés* in the France of

[43] cf. Parsons, in Hughes, op. cit., p. 329.

[44] *Defence of Stanley*, ed. T. Heywood (Chetham Society, 1851), pp. 20, 25 f, 32; *Admonition*, ed. J. Mendham (London, 1842), p. 7.

the Catholic League, forced them to think again.[45] The machinery of the mission, its bases, communications and finances, put them in contact with the urban elements of the League, clerical and lay, and gave them experience of the kind of political opposition which Catholicism in England was totally unable to furnish. The result was the *De justa Reipublicae Christianae in Reges impios et haereticos Authoritate* of William Reynolds.[46] Much of the book recapitulates, for the benefit of the Guises, the politics of the crusade; but forced at the same time to appeal to the Leaguer bourgeoisie, Reynolds utilizes in his attack on absolute monarchy and its courtiers the themes of property, moral rectitude, civic pride, and the examples of republican Rome. If most of the argument is feudal, the principles are Aristotelian. Political society results from the natural association of men necessary to supply fully their physical, intellectual and spiritual needs; the magistrate is necessary to secure the objects of association; the form of magistracy is dependent on the choice of the people concerned, and therefore alterable. Hereditary monarchy is the best alternative, but neither monarchy nor the principle of succession is inviolable. The king who violates the conditions of his office becomes a tyrant; the people may depose or, if he persists in his tyranny, kill him; it may alter the normal course of succession when this endangers the satisfactory performance of the office. The commonwealth is not created for the king, but the king for the commonwealth.[47] What Reynolds had begun was completed in the *Conference about the next Succession* (1595), the work of several *émigré* hands, but probably to a large extent of Parsons and Richard Verstegan. In it the principles drawn by Reynolds from the case of France are applied to the situation of England pending the death of Elizabeth; but the crusading elements have been eliminated, and only the Aristotelian theory of the commonwealth is left.[48] Reflection on the problems posed for them by the doubtful succession to Elizabeth led at least one of the

[45] For the relation between the *émigrés* and the League, Bossy, op. cit., pp. 30–143; J. H. M. Salmon, *The French Religious Wars in English Political Thought* (Oxford, 1959), pp. 34–36.

[46] For this authorship, C. H. McIlwain, *Constitutionalism and the Changing World* (Cambridge, 1939), pp. 178–82.

[47] cf. J. N. Figgis, *Political Thought from Gerson to Grotius* (New York, 1960 edn.), pp. 182–7.

[48] Clancy, 'Political Thought of the Counter-Reformation in England', pp. 111–27.

émigré clerks into republicanism;[49] and it was logical that Verstegan, who had a vital function in the machinery of the enterprise, should have been one of the earliest promoters of the anti-Norman view of English history.[50]

Their involvement in the League encouraged the Elizabethan priests to formulate a political theory which corresponded to the character of their enterprise. They used their inheritance as clerks to put forward these ideas on a general theoretical ground which ensured for them not only survival but a steadily increasing resonance throughout the seventeenth century. It was not, of course, among the Catholics that they flourished.

III

Between the outlook of the gentry and that of the clerks, coexistence was in the long run impossible. During the twenty years or so after the foundation at Douai, the dynamism of the clerks succeeded, on the whole, in carrying the gentry with it; but from the beginning there were what Parsons described as 'domestical difficulties'. There was trouble over occasional conformity: Parsons's *Brief Discourse why Catholics refuse to go to Church* (1580) drew a rejoinder from Lord Montague's chaplain to the effect that they did not.[51] The attempt of some of the new priests to follow the easier rules for fasting introduced by the Council of Trent caused so much ill-feeling that the Jesuit Jasper Heywood had to be recalled from England on account of it.[52] That these were more than minor misunderstandings is apparent from the fact that Allen's manifesto in support of the Spanish invasion, the *Admonition*, is almost exactly contemporary with the declaration of allegiance to Elizabeth made by the leading Catholic gentlemen.[53] This conflict, which during the 1580s the heroic atmosphere of the mission tended to suppress in England itself, broke out openly among the *émigrés*. One of the *émigré* gentlemen, Charles Paget, had a violent argument with Parsons, complaining 'against priests

[49] Roger Smith, in PRO SP 12/269/27.

[50] Christopher Hill, *Puritanism and Revolution* (London, 1958), pp. 60, 73, n. 2; cf. above, notes 38–40.

[51] Hicks, *Persons Letters*, pp. xxxi f.

[52] Parsons, in *CRS*, ii, pp. 176 f.

[53] cf. Burghley, in Hughes, op. cit., iii, p. xxvi.

in general and against Mr. Dr. Allen in particular . . . why he and other priests and religious men should meddle in public matters of our country and not . . . gentlemen, . . . repeating often . . . why priests did not meddle with their breviaries only and the like';[54] and the quarrel grew into a feud which gained in bitterness and ramifications as time went on. This was not simply an argument as to whether clerks should interfere in politics; what was at issue was the entire clerical enterprise, and the will to Reformation from which it sprang, as the scandal caused by Parsons's *Memorial for the Reformation of England*[55] makes clear. It is unlikely that Paget's opinions were fully shared by more than a minority of the *émigré* gentry; but a gentleman could only take the opposite view if he was willing to be absorbed into the machinery of the enterprise, to leave his destiny in the hands of the clerks. This certainly happened; but an initial enthusiasm could equally well turn sour.

The problem had a more intimate side. The priest arrived in England without either exterior signs of his priesthood or the structure of a clerical order behind him; he did not appear as a priest, but as a gentleman, a soldier, or a servant. This was evidently necessary for the purposes of the mission, but the ambiguity had its dangers. Settled in a Catholic household, supported by its head, outwardly or really acting, perhaps, as his steward, the priest would tend to be assimilated to the role he had adopted. The only alternative role to that of a superior servant was that of a gentleman who received hospitality as an equal. If then he was to defend his independence he had to assert not his status as clerk but his status as gentleman.[56] From this point it was a short step to affirming that Catholic priests were gentlemen, while the clergy of the established Church were not.[57] The case of John Gerard is enough to show that a priest could live as a gentleman without losing his original impulse; but to walk the tightrope in this way demanded gifts which not all the priests had, and the danger was that the disguise would absorb the personality. A priest who had got into the habit of wearing secular clothes in

[54] ibid., p. 331.

[55] Paget, in PRO SP 12/267/67, denounces it as being 'to the prejudice of the Nobility and ancient custom and laws and privileges of England'.

[56] William Watson, *Decacordon of Ten Quodlibetical Questions* (London, 1602), pp. 49–53.

[57] Southwell, *Humble Supplication*, ed. R. C. Bald (Cambridge, 1953), p. 7; Allen and Campion, in Clancy, op. cit., p. 228.

England and kept it up when, for one reason or another, he returned abroad, justified the suspicion of continentals; the more so when, as in the case of Gilbert Gifford, he considered that one of the marks of the gentleman was the use of the brothel.[58]

The absorption of the priests into the gentry could hardly be avoided without the reconstruction of a clerical order. But the idea of the missionary priest as conceived by Allen was not easily reconcilable with the forms of an established order. To provide the necessary foundation of independence, it must be visible, and visibility implied recognition by the Government, mutual acceptance of the *status quo*, and abandonment of the original purpose of the mission. The Jesuits were relatively immune from this difficulty, since they had behind them the support of a religious order whose organization could without great change be adapted to the conditions of work in England. The seminary priests were more vulnerable: there were far more of them; as a body, they were amorphous; and their training could not be as thorough as that of the Jesuits. For them, a demand for order could scarcely mean anything but a return to things as they had been before the Reformation: benefices, a hierarchy of promotion, bishops, government and jurisdiction according to canon law. After rejecting several attempts on the problem, the Papacy tried to solve it in 1598 by the appointment of an Archpriest and twelve assistants; but by this time the situation had got too far out of control, and too involved with other causes of dispute, for this solution to be universally accepted.[59] Along with the hankering after orthodox procedures, there grew among the priests a mistrust of the methods of Allen and Parsons and a tendency to equate them, and the outlook from which they sprang, with the innovations of Puritans.[60] Some of the priests were tempted to neglect the mission while they tried to secure the sanction of the Government for some minimal form of order which would provide status and recognition. The consequence was division and dispute, conducted with a degree of violence and irrationality which suggests that the problem of status

[58] *Autobiography of John Gerard*, ed. P. Caraman (London, 1951), pp. 164–171; T. G. Law, *Jesuits and Seculars in the Reign of Queen Elizabeth* (London, 1889), p. lxxii; *Cal. State Papers, Foreign 1586–88*, p. 483.

[59] J. H. Pollen, *Institution of the Archpriest Blackwell* (London, 1916), *passim*.

[60] Clancy, op. cit., pp. 142 f; Christopher Bagshaw, in *The Wisbech Stirs*, ed. P. Renold (*CRS*, li, 1958), pp. 14, 41.

concealed difficulties of a psychological order. The conditions of the mission, the threat of torture and execution, could place a priest under intolerable strain. It was a relief to be able to blame, not the Government, but the Jesuits; the bitterness and persistency with which it was pursued gave to the attack on the Jesuits the character of a pseudo-enterprise.

The outcome of these conflicts was the enunciation, by a number of secular priests who came to be called Appellants, of an argument and a programme. Catholic priests, they said, were loyal to the 'state', that is to the Queen and the order of society. The ideas and practice of the Jesuits were subversive of all order, political and ecclesiastical. They were responsible for turning the mission into a political machine in the service of the Spaniards, and a religious enterprise on the 'Calvinist' model. The position of the Government, that it persecuted not for religion, but for treason and sedition, was amply justified. If both the Pope and the Queen could be convinced that the Jesuits had perverted the mission from its original object, the Pope would deprive the Jesuits of any connection with it, and the Queen cease to persecute. A clear distinction was made between Allen, now safely dead, and Parsons; to Parsons were attributed such divergences as had occurred during Allen's lifetime, and the total perversion of the mission since his death. In this way some of the priests came round to the position which had been held from the beginning by many Catholic gentlemen, with whom they joined forces in the attack on the Jesuits. The priests reproduced arguments first put forward by the gentlemen, adopted the language and outlook of lay supremacy, and modelled their programme on that of the gentry by taking up for themselves the idea of an oath of allegiance.[61] The clerk was to be not only a gentleman, but a gentleman bound by a personal obligation to the Queen which would take precedence over all others. There was a clear contradiction between this idea and that of reconstructing the clerical estate,[62] but for the moment this could be ignored.

This reorientation was furthered by a new development, the revival of courtly Catholicism in England. The dominant religion of the Elizabethan Court was the gentleman's Puritanism of Sir Philip Sidney, which was much closer to the religion of the Court of Catherine des Médicis than the latter was to English Catholicisms

[61] Hughes, op. cit., iii, pp. 392 f.

[62] Bossy, 'Elizabethan Catholicism: The Link with France', pp. 291 f.

either clerical or lay.[63] But there remained throughout the reign a strain of indigenous courtly Catholicism, of which the most permanent representative was Lord Henry Howard. This had raised its head at the time of the proposed marriage between Elizabeth and the Duke of Anjou, and though the failure of this project led to the emigration of several of those who had supported it, the strain did not die out. Howard continued to navigate the rocks and shoals of Elizabethan politics until he arrived triumphantly at the reign of James; the rump of the party produced, in exile, the legitimist and *politique* pamphlet generally known as *Leicester's Commonwealth*.[64] The thesis that Catholicism, rightly understood, was the natural religion for a courtly society began towards the end of the reign to make an impression at the English Court, and a trickle of conversions resulted, which was to turn into a steady flow in the seventeenth century. This kind of Catholicism was evidently not compatible with that of the Elizabethan clerks; Catholicism could only become respectable if their ideas were extruded from it. The Court converts came into the disputes to reinforce those who were trying to reorganize English Catholicism from within,[65] and to supply the piece missing from the programme of the gentry by restoring contact with the Court.

What finally ensured the success of the opposition to the clerical enterprise was the pressure of the European political situation within which it operated. Here the change in Spanish policy after the death of Philip II was probably less important than the failure of the League in France. The success of Henry IV cleared out of France those *émigré* establishments which had not already been forced to go by the disruption of the Civil War. The King of Spain was not prepared to allow things to be said and done in his own dominions which he had been willing to pay to have said and done in France;[66] and no resettlement of English *émigrés* in France was permissible except on the understanding that they renounced their

[63] F. A. Yates, *French Academies of the Sixteenth Century* (Studies of the Warburg Institute, xv [1947]), pp. 224 f.

[64] J. A. Bossy, 'English Catholics and the French Marriage', *Recusant History*, v (1959), p. 2; Clancy, op. cit., pp. 100 f; J. Lecler, *Toleration and the Reformation* (New York–London, 1960), ii, pp. 374 f.

[65] Notably Henry Constable: G. Wickes, 'Henry Constable, Poet and Courtier', *Biographical Studies* (*Recusant History*), ii (1954), p. 272; and see below.

[66] The chapter on tyrannicide was left out of the second (Antwerp) edition of *De justa Reipublicae Christianae* . . . : Clancy, op. cit., p. 111.

Leaguer past and accepted the new régime. As in England, conversion could only be proved by some such demonstration as joining enthusiastically in the hue and cry after the Jesuits. Certainly, the revival of France provided new possibilities of political leverage; but despite the efforts of the Papacy it proved impossible to bring simultaneous pressure from France and Spain to bear on the favourable situation offered by the death of Elizabeth. The political readjustment in Europe split the *émigrés*, and to some extent the Catholics in England as well, into two groups, one depending on the Spaniards and the other on the French. From this point a common enterprise was impossible; the internal disputes were taken up and institutionalized by the political machinery of Spain and France; and both halves of the clergy were driven to accept the principles of monarchical orthodoxy from which the League had temporarily liberated them.[67]

By the beginning of the seventeenth century the conflict between the gentry and the clerks was turning decisively in favour of the gentry. Those who attacked the clerical enterprise were developing their own outlook; those who had participated in it were conducting a withdrawal which left their opponents in possession of the field. The result was a Catholicism which Allen, Campion and Parsons would have had some difficulty in recognizing.

The point of view of the gentleman opposition emerges most clearly from the *Examen pacifique de la Doctrine des Huguenots* of the convert courtier and poet Henry Constable.[68] Driven into print by the assassination of Henry III, Constable defends the order of Church and State as part of the providential order of the Universe; self-help, as practised by the League, is a usurpation of the prerogatives of God which can only lead to chaos. Clerks are not to be trusted, since they have a vested interest in disagreement and their disputes are the spark of civil war. He denies the importance of differences between Catholics and Protestants, and urges the enlightened laity to a 'union effectuelle' which will where necessary cover a gentleman's agreement to differ. The majority of Catholics and Protestants, who do not in any case understand what the arguments are about, will fall in behind, and the clerk be put in his

[67] Bossy, 'Elizabethan Catholicism: The Link with France', *passim*.

[68] See D. Rogers, 'The Catholic Moderator', *Recusant History*, v (1960), p. 224.

place.[69] The book was written before Constable became a Catholic, and his conversion no doubt entailed the abandonment of some of the opinions expressed in it; but it certainly did not involve a change in its original assumptions. These are closely parallel to those already implied in *Leicester's Commonwealth*; but a Catholicism founded on them could find little room for the *Book of Resolution*, and none at all for the *Memorial for the Reformation of England*. Nor, *a fortiori*, could it find room for the political theory of Reynolds and the *Conference about the next Succession*. In 1600 the gentleman *émigrés* in Paris produced their counterblast, the *Discovery of a counterfeit Conference*. This was an assertion of James's right to succeed Elizabeth on the grounds of the absolute inviolability of hereditary succession, studded with phrases like 'the sacred state of regal dignity', and dismissing as blasphemous the argument for the primacy of the commonwealth over the king.[70] In this scheme of political and social order, the functions of the clergy became largely ceremonial. It meant abandoning the ultramontanism which the clerks of the enterprise had seen as the only salvation of their order, and adapting Gallican principles to the circumstances of England. The priests who accepted it tried to salvage the clerical order by a form of episcopal Gallicanism;[71] but, ground between the Government and established Church on the one hand, and the Papacy on the other, this could never make much headway. The only form of Gallicanism possible in England was the royalist Gallicanism of the defenders of the oath of allegiance, inspired from time to time with the idea of reunion with the sounder elements of the Church of England.[72] Among both the gentry and the priests the seventeenth-century programme of Catholic royalism for royal Catholicism was in an advanced stage of preparation at the beginning of the reign of James I.

In face of this programme the survivors of the clerical enterprise were driven to a progressive modification of their positions which brought them, not to agreement with their opponents, but to an

[69] *Examen pacifique*, esp. *Epistre au lecteur* and c. 6; cf. the sonnet to St. Michael in *Diana*: *The Sonnets and other Poems of Henry Constable*, ed. W. C. Hazlitt (London, 1859), p. 53.

[70] *Discovery*, pp. 70, 90 f; Clancy, op. cit., p. 128.

[71] Notably Richard Smith: Philip Hughes, *Rome and the Counter-Reformation in England* (London, 1942), pp. 329 ff.

[72] e.g. M. Nédoncelle, *Trois aspects du problème anglo-catholique au XVIIe siècle* (Paris, 1951), pp. 7–41.

outlook which in practice came to much the same thing. In his last years Parsons whittled down his opposition to the oath of allegiance to a point where the theoretical objection was severed from most of its practical consequences.[73] In the *Treatise concerning Policy and Religion* of his friend Thomas Fitzherbert, the signs of weariness are evident. Fitzherbert had become a priest, then a Jesuit, late in life; he speaks with the authentic voice of the Catholic gentleman. Convinced of the 'natural imbecility of man's wit', faced with a providence inscrutable both because it works by miracle and because it permits virtue to suffer affliction and vice reward, he counsels the abandonment of human activity in favour of pure contemplation.[74] Though the book was intended as an attack on the *politique* view of religion which underlay Constable's *Examen pacifique*, the general effect is remarkably similar. The two traditions could exist happily enough together.

That Fitzherbert's reflection on the problems of politics and religion could end up as a treatise of mystical contemplation, is significant of the new direction which English Catholicism was taking. What gave vitality to Elizabethan Catholicism was a refusal to accept the accomplished fact, an 'alarm spiritual', a demand for reformation. Its dominant expression was action. To this the religion of social convenience offered a direct negation, but no adequate alternative. An inner experience could only be met by another inner experience, a religion of action by a religion of contemplation. It is in this light that we shall best understand one of the most striking developments in the history of English Catholicism at the beginning of the seventeenth century—the revival of the Benedictine order.[75] So far as the Elizabethan priests, seminary or Jesuit, had been working in a tradition, it had been that of the friars;[76] the reappearance of the monks was the rediscovery of a form of the religious life more in harmony with the social foundations of Catholicism in England. Where the Capuchin Benet of Canfield, writing in the atmosphere of the Leaguer emigration, had attempted a synthesis of the active and the contemplative life, the

[73] Clancy, op. cit., pp. 159 f.

[74] *Treatise,* Preface para. 6, pp. 18 f, 48, 83 f, etc.; Clancy, op. cit., pp. 316 f; L. I. Bredvold, *The Intellectual Milieu of John Dryden* (Ann Arbor, 1934), pp. 25 f.

[75] J. McCann *et al., Ampleforth and its Origins* (London, 1952), pp. 81 f.

[76] Clancy, op. cit., pp. 146 f.

Benedictine Augustine Baker, treating action as distraction, took as the culmination of religious experience the state of passive contemplation in which nothing, not even the humanity of Christ, was to come between the soul and God.[77]

From the gentleman's theology of Henry Constable to the spirituality of Augustine Baker there is a world of distance; but Constable had a hand in the refounding of the Benedictines,[78] and the thread which runs between them is visible enough. Taken together, the conservatism of the opponents of the clerical enterprise, the pessimism of those who survived it, and the religion of contemplation, constitute a whole whose tendency is unmistakable; an ideology formed out of reaction or withdrawal from that of Allen, Campion and Parsons, and destined to supersede it as the dominant outlook of English Catholicism until the French Revolution, if not beyond. Loyalty supplanted enterprise. The history of Elizabethan Catholicism is a progress from inertia to inertia in three generations.

[77] Aldous Huxley, *Grey Eminence* (London, 1956 edn.), pp. 77–90; David Knowles, *The English Mystical Tradition* (London, 1961), pp. 151–87. I need hardly say that I am grossly simplifying.

[78] J. McCann, op. cit., pp. 86 f.

X

THE NOBLES, THE PEOPLE, AND THE CONSTITUTION*

Brian Manning

I

IN subordinating the Church to the State the Henrician Reformation inaugurated the phase in English history which it is illuminating to call absolute monarchy.[1] This term has clear significance and obvious application to English conditions even if we do not go beyond the sense in which it was employed in England during the sixteenth and early seventeenth centuries, that is to describe a king whose power was not restricted by pope or emperor.[2] It marks, therefore, a sharp break with the medieval State and the assumption of absolute authority by the secular nation-State embodied in the person of the monarch. It means, further, a concentration of power in the Crown in contrast to the dispersion of power in the medieval State. Development in this direction was not new; but the culmination of earlier tendencies towards absolute monarchy received sufficiently dramatic expression in the Reformation to warrant the dating of a new period in the history of the State.

[1] For introduction to discussion of the state in the sixteenth and seventeenth centuries see A. D. Lindsay, *The Modern Democratic State* (Oxford, 1943); and H. J. Laski, *The Rise of European Liberalism* (London, 1936).

[2] C. H. McIlwain, *The High Court of Parliament* (New Haven, 1910), pp. 128–30, 144–5; and the same author's *Constitutionalism Ancient and Modern* (Ithaca, New York, 1947), pp. 166–7.

* From no. 9 (1956).

The unwillingness of historians to recognize that there was ever in England a form of State corresponding to the absolute monarchies of the continent[3] at first took the form of focussing attention on Parliament and interpreting its position as if it were already a part of a system of constitutional government that was not then even conceived. What happened at the Reformation was that the Crown 'resumed' the ecclesiastical authority 'usurped' by the Papacy: this was more than a legal fiction designed to conceal a revolutionary extension of royal power; it was a statement that the role of Parliament did not consist of granting anything to the King but of declaring what authority had always resided in the Crown.[4] Parliament was, as it remained for Coke, the King's highest court,[5] the place where the greatest controversies concerning the realm were decided. A medieval institution, Parliament survived into the sixteenth and seventeenth centuries not so much as a representative assembly but because it was a court; an integral part of the legal system through which the King governed.[6]

The King governed through councils as well as through courts, not always differentiated; Parliament was the King's great council as well as his highest court. The Reformation resulted in more clear-cut arrangements for the government of the Church than existed in the State. As Supreme Head of the Church the King became as absolute a ruler in the ecclesiastical sphere as in fact he was already in the temporal—he was the source of all authority. From his great council of Parliament he learnt what was necessary for the maintenance of good government in the State; likewise the representatives of the clergy in Convocation had the function of informing him what was needed for the well-

[3] F. Hartung and R. Mousnier, 'Quelques Problèmes concernant la Monarchie Absolue', *Relazioni dei X Congresso Internat. di Scienze Storiche* (Firenze, 1955), vol. iv, where England is equated with the absolute monarchies of the continent.

[4] K. Pickthorn, *Early Tudor Government: Henry VIII* (Cambridge, 1934), chaps. ix–xiii.

[5] McIlwain, *The High Court of Parliament*: whatever the limitations of this work on the medieval side it retains great value for the period under discussion.

[6] For the relation of Parliament to the legal system and for an excellent examination of the whole structure of government in the sixteenth century see W. S. Holdsworth, *A History of English Law*, 3rd edn. (London, 1945), vol. iv.

governing of the Church and the preservation of true religion. But, unlike Parliament, Convocation was not a court; the jurisdiction of the royal supremacy over the Church was exercised through the Court of High Commission developed under Elizabeth;[7] Convocation lacked the place in the legal system of the Church possessed by Parliament in the legal system of the State, and so lost significance. At the same time the hierarchical system which supported monarchical absolutism belonged to the very nature of the Church under such a government; it consigned the lower clergy and their representatives in Convocation to an inferior position; the reality of government of the Church through bishops appointed by the Crown was not concealed. Resistance of the lower clergy took the form of clerical Puritanism, which, in seeking to reduce the power of the bishops, also threatened the absolutism of the monarchy.

It is, of course, true that the Reformation extended the competence of Parliament; the State, whose highest court and council it was, now encompassed the Church. But the effective increase of power lay with the Crown. Parliament was cut off from the Church by the royal supremacy, and the constitutional opposition in the early part of the seventeenth century admitted the limitation of the power of Parliament in ecclesiastical matters.[8] The separation of the Church and Parliament and the linking of Church and State by monarchical government in both spheres, safeguarded the authority of the Crown: by his power in the State the King had the means to ensure that the Church was no check on his authority; by his power in the Church the King had a strong base for his authority in the State.

The peculiar pre-eminence of Parliament arose from the presence there of the nobles and bishops, sitting in person, the heads of both the secular and the ecclesiastical hierarchies, with a personal and immediate relationship to the sovereign; and there also was the King, the life of parliaments. Parliament, then, formed the Estates of the Realm, the highest institution of that hierarchical system which lay at the heart of medieval society. Thomas Wilson indicates that hierarchy was considered no less the basis of the

[7] For a study of the relations of Church and State in the period of absolutism see R. G. Usher, *The Rise and Fall of the High Commission* (Oxford, 1913).

[8] M. A. Judson, *The Crisis of the Constitution* (New Brunswick, 1949), p. 89.

State than of the Church when in *The State of England* (1600) he described the nobles and bishops as 'nobilitas major' and the gentry, lawyers and lower clergy as 'nobilitas minor'.[9] The lesser landowners like the lower clergy belonged to the hierarchy of the ruling class and sat, through their representatives, in the lower house of Parliament, as the clergy through their representatives sat in the lower house of Convocation. The lesser nobility of gentry could not be assigned to the subordinate position of the lower clergy, because the gulf that separated them from the greater nobility was not so wide as that which divided the ordinary clergy from the bishops. Further, the gentry were more important since society rested on the ownership of land; they were no mere agents but active participators in shaping the system of government, something from which the lower clergy were barred.

From this it appears that the underlying nature of the absolute monarchical State was government through and in the interests of a ruling class of landowners.[10] The power of that class in the sixteenth and early seventeenth centuries does not make the term absolutism inapplicable to the English State in that period. In the later Middle Ages the nobility steadily pushed the English State towards the assumption of authority over the Church which culminated in the Reformation.[11] This marked a break with the medieval State. But although the form of the State changed, its social basis did not; and this explains the continuity between the medieval period and the sixteenth century noted by many historians. Foremost in that continuity was the survival of Parliament and it is still commonly supposed that because of this England never had a period of absolutism. But the way in which the rule of the big landowners is institutionalized depends on local conditions. In England Parliament remained an institution which preserved the position of the landlords as the ruling class. In a pamphlet published in 1641 Sir Thomas Aston wrote, '. . . It hath been the method of former times, that the Parliament, the Primates, the Nobiles, with the minores nobiles, the Gentry,

[9] T. Wilson, *The State of England* (1600), ed. F. J. Fisher (Camden Miscellany, vol. xvi), p. 23.

[10] J. E. Neale, *The Elizabethan House of Commons* (London, 1949) gives a good picture of the English ruling class of the sixteenth century and its relation to the institutions of government.

[11] F. M. Powicke, *The Reformation in England* (Oxford, 1941).

consult and dispense the rules of government, the plebians submit to and obey them.'[12] The effectiveness of Parliament in fulfilling this function was facilitated by the bridling of the independent power of the towns; the towns were less of a threat to the authority of the State because they were dominated by the landowners. This overcame the dispersion of power that marked the medieval State and made possible the concentration of power which characterized the absolute State: power was not only concentrated in the State but also reconcentrated in the landlords. In the sixteenth century the boroughs had come to be represented in the commons by the gentry,[13] so that Parliament corresponded to a unified ruling class; the gentry also controlled local government. The gentry and Parliament were not set up over against the State, they were an integral part of it. Nor was the ruling class a collection of disparate local governing oligarchies; it was a class with a sense of common interest and national solidarity. This community of interest and nationalism overrode local and economic variation and played an essential part in the establishment of the absolute State under Henry VIII and Elizabeth.

Parliament was not a check on the Crown so long as the monarchy reflected the interests of a more or less united ruling class. Of course that unity was never complete; there were degrees of wealth and power and conflicts of economic interest among the landlords, and these stresses found expression in resistance to the centralization of State power, which favoured the richer and more powerful and fostered some economic interests rather than others. But, in general, during the sixteenth century, the dominant need of the ruling class was for a strong central government. They needed it because of the long-term decline in their control over the peasantry. Increasingly the landlords had come to see the advantage of a stronger State as an instrument to bolster up their economic power and to reinforce their hold over the peasants. The landlords' attitude towards the State comes out clearly in the pamphlet by Sir Thomas Aston quoted earlier. Arguing against the thesis that Presbyterianism could provide a means of strengthening the power of the nobility over the people, he makes an illuminating comparison with Scotland. There, he says, the peasants are more dependent on their lords than in England, so

[12] T. Aston, *A Remonstrance against Presbytery* (1641).

[13] Neale, op. cit., chap. vii.

the lords are able to dominate the Presbyterian system, and through it keep control of the Church and the monarchy. But in England the people are more powerful and can be kept in obedience to the nobility and gentry only by a strong monarchy, and by the centralization of authority in Church and State which would be undermined by Presbyterianism.

The period of absolutism was inaugurated by the dissolution of the monasteries, which economically refloated the ruling class and recruited into it from below by endowing new families. For some time before this landlords had been seeking to reconstruct their economic power by means of enclosures and rent-raising, but such measures provoked peasant discontent[14] and made necessary a strong central government to reinforce politically the economic and social power of the landlords. However, this led the absolute monarchy into the dilemma which it never solved and which caused its downfall. If it gave the landlords a free hand it was faced with peasant revolts which might overthrow the ruling class; if it restrained the landlords and protected the peasants it was confronted by a revolt in the ruling class which might endanger the monarchy. This is precisely what happened in the reign of Edward VI; a free hand for the landlords produced peasant uprisings and attempts to restrain the landlords caused the downfall of the government of Protector Somerset. From the reign of Elizabeth the absolute monarchy inclined to the policy of restraint because the dominant influences among the landlords came to see that the best guarantee of their political power lay in keeping agrarian relationships reasonably stable.

The big landlord no longer played the decisive role in shaping the economy; its base rested on the small producers in agriculture and industry and its development lay in the direction of capitalism.[15] Stability depended on restricting the growth of capitalism, and that was the economic policy of the absolute monarchy.[16] At

[14] R. H. Tawney, *The Agrarian Problem in the Sixteenth Century* (London, 1912).

[15] M. Dobb, *Studies in the Development of Capitalism* (London, 1946); the discussion between Sweezy, Dobb and Takahashi, *The Transition from Feudalism to Capitalism* (London, 1954: reprinted from *Science and Society*); E. Kosminsky, 'The Evolution of Feudal Rent in England', *Past and Present*, no. 7 (April, 1955).

[16] E. Lipson, *The Economic History of England*, 5th edn. (London, 1948), vol. ii, pp. cv–cxv, cxvi–cxvii; vol. iii, *passim*. L. Stone, 'State Control in Sixteenth Century England', *Econ. Hist. Rev.*, xvii (1947). For a brilliant

the same time capitalism developed under the shadow of absolutism because it benefited from the system of internal order established by that form of government. The State, like the landlords, needed the financial services of the capitalists, primarily the merchants, but that was not new; the novelty was that the military and strategic requirements of the absolute monarchy led it to foster in some degree the emergence of industrial capitalism.[17] That did not at first run counter to the interests of the ruling class because they sought the backing of the State to exploit the new economic developments; this resulted in the system of monopolies by which the State aimed to keep control of industry and through which fortunate members of the ruling class shared in the profits. Certain commercial and urban elements, particularly the bigger merchants, found their interests satisfied by the system of monopolies and controls; their close relationship with the nobility and gentry marked socially the harmony which existed between them in politics.[18] The merchant cliques ruled the towns and exploited trade and industry in alliance with the local landowners. But industry escaped from the restrictions of the towns into the countryside where it permeated agrarian relationships. Under Elizabeth the State tried to keep control of industry by applying on a national scale the policy of regulation maintained by the towns; thus illustrating that the necessity for a strong central government lay in the need to enforce nationally what local power had once sufficed to maintain.

The economic problems of the landlords, however, produced divisions in the ruling class. The struggle for a share in the economic resources of the State led to the contest for offices, which underlay many of the political quarrels in the ruling class during the period of absolutism. But, more fundamental, a section of the landlords, particularly those most exposed to the influence of the development of the economy towards capitalism, kicked against policies which denied them a free hand to pursue agrarian

[17] J. U. Nef, 'The Progress of Technology and the Growth of Large-Scale Industry 1540–1640', *Econ. Hist. Rev.*, v (1934).

[18] P. Laslett, 'The Gentry of Kent in 1640', *Cambridge Historical Journal*, ix (1948).

---

survey of economic policy during the period of absolutism see R. H. Tawney, *Religion and the Rise of Capitalism* (London, 1926).

change.[19] These discontented landlords tended to find supporters among the small industrial producers of town and country, whose interests were sacrificed by the whole economic policy of the absolute monarchy, and among whom Puritanism gained its main strength. This alliance in the end accomplished the downfall of absolutism.

II

The lack of a standing army and the absence of a bureaucratic system of local government, the existence of Parliament and the common law, did not weaken the monarchy. It was the reverse, for these circumstances preserved the supremacy of the aristocratic society in which the monarchy was embedded and from which it drew its strength. Its weakness sprang from any weakening of that society and from any divergence between the monarchy and any important section of the ruling class. In that sense the absolutist State was a balance between the monarchy and the nobility and gentry. The significance of this is brought out in the speech of the Lord Keeper at the opening of the Long Parliament: 'From the throne turn your eyes upon the two supporters of it, on the one side, the stem of honour, the nobility and clergy, on the other side, the gentry and Commons. Where was there, or is there in any part of the world, a nobility so numerous, so magnanimous, and yet with such a temper that they neither eclipse the throne, nor overtop the people, but keep in a distance fit for the greatness of the throne. Where was there a Commonwealth so free, and the balance so equally held, as here? And certainly, so long as the beam is so held, it cannot be otherwise. . . .'[20]

This was the balance of the constitution, which M. A. Judson in her study *The Crisis of the Constitution* demonstrates to be the dominating idea in constitutional and political thought in the early part of the seventeenth century; but she explores only the idea without reference to its social significance, which comes out in the Lord Keeper's speech. She represents the constitutional crisis as revolving round the balance between the prerogatives of the the Crown and the rights of the subject, both of which were considered absolute: the question was one of harmonizing the two

[19] C. Hill, *The English Revolution 1640* (London, 1940).

[20] *Speeches and Passages of this Great and Happy Parliament* (London, 1641).

independent spheres. The question was not, as G. L. Mosse tries to argue in his book *The Struggle for Sovereignty in England*, a contest for absolute power between the King and Parliament, nor, as Holdsworth and others have held, a conflict between rival interpretations of the constitution. There was no Hobbesian conception of sovereignty on either side in the dispute, nor were the two sides in disagreement about the fundamentals of the constitution. Opponents and supporters of the first two Stuarts both agreed that there were absolute powers of the Crown which could not be questioned and absolute rights of the subject which could not be invaded by the prerogative. The trouble arose when the financial and administrative problems of the government led to legally-upheld interpretations of the prerogative which in the opinion of many people undermined the rights of the subject and upset the balance of the constitution. The object of the parliamentary opposition was to restore that balance by reaffirming the rights of the subject and making them inviolate against invasion by the prerogative. The failure of the Petition of Right to re-establish the harmony at which it aimed led to the revolutionary measures of the Long Parliament to secure the rights of the subject. Then many, who considered that Charles I had unbalanced the constitution in the direction of the prerogative, came round to the opinion that the leaders of the commons were undermining the monarchy and unbalancing the constitution in the direction of the rights of the subject. This, Miss Judson thinks, produced the Civil War.

Does this thesis really explain the Civil War? According to it both sides were fighting for more or less the same balanced constitution, both fearful of too great a concentration of power; the parliamentarians afraid that the King was still too powerful to be trusted to work the constitution with due regard to the rights of the subject, the royalists convinced that the threat to the rights of the subject now came from a parliament which had become too powerful. In Miss Judson's opinion the Civil War was a tragic misunderstanding which could have been avoided. Her analysis of the constitutional crisis applies well enough to the period up to 1628, thereafter it becomes less illuminating. She ignores highly significant factors which had entered into the situation by 1641 and totally changed the nature of the crisis. Before considering what these were it is necessary to put the original crisis into a somewhat different perspective.

The rights of the subject were the rights of property, and the stock argument for the difference between the English monarchy and continental absolutisms is that the King could not take the property of his subjects without their consent in Parliament.[21] Miss Judson says that this inviolability of property was the barrier to absolutism, but is it supposed that continental absolutisms were not based on the rights of property?[22] The maintenance of these rights was the guarantee that the State remained firmly based on the existing ruling class. The financial problem was common to all absolute monarchies. The question was how to ensure that the main burden of supporting the State fell on the lower rather than the upper classes; the fact that this was achieved through Parliament instead of through the formal exemption of the ruling class from taxation does not make the English monarchy different in kind from the continental absolutisms. The adjustment between the financial needs of the State and the interests of the nobility and gentry had to be institutionalized in some form, and this could be done either in Parliament or by formal privilege. Parliamentary taxation was the privilege of the English ruling class. Parliament harmonized the interests of the central government and that class. So long as that harmony existed the monarchy was absolute, little enough was heard about rights, and Parliament was in no way a check on the Crown. The characteristic theory was that the King could do everything necessary for good strong government provided he did not lose the affection of his people, that is so long as he retained the confidence of the ruling class. Harmony within the ruling class began to disappear in the reign of James I and as a result there was bound to be discord between the monarchy and part of that class. In the speech quoted above the Lord Keeper had to appeal to the identity of interests between the Crown and the nobility because by 1640 an important section of the nobility was no longer convinced of that identity: on the one hand they did not sufficiently 'overtop the people' and on the other hand the 'distance fit for the greatness of the throne' had become too great. Absolutism consisted in the dependence of the Crown on the nobility and gentry. As they were losing power, and as the monarchy tended to surmount that dependence, absolutism col-

[21] This was by no means absolutely so: see McIlwain, *The High Court of Parliament*, p. 316.

[22] Hartung and Mousnier, op. cit.

lapsed: historically that was the fate of all absolute monarchies. It was in these circumstances that Parliament emerged in a new role, no longer an instrument of government but a check on government.

III

Gardiner argued that at the beginning of the seventeenth century the choice before England was between the ideas of Bacon and Coke.[23] Bacon's political philosophy amounted to something like 'enlightened absolutism',[24] a strong State seeking to reconcile the old order with the new. He had no wish to change the social basis of the State[25] but he recognized that Puritanism had developed an appeal and characteristics menacing the existing social order and form of State. This he thought was due to it being forced underground by persecution, and the remedy he propounded was to permit religious freedom up to the point 'where zeal tends to degenerate into sedition.'[26] The danger he saw was disunity in the ruling class due to the alliance of discontented elements with the Puritans; but their Puritanism was not deep or extreme, and probably approximated to Bacon's own anti-clericalism. He condemned clerical intolerance and the bigotry of the bishops, and advocated strong State control of the Church and limitation of the power of the episcopate. He saw the needs of the new order in intellectual freedom and reform of the law; both could be achieved only by a strong State. He wanted to rationalize the whole legal system and reduce it to order, simplicity and certainty. His proposal—something like a codification of the law—was a restatement of the law by means of two digests, one of case law, and the other of statute law.[27] He discovered in the changes going on around him the philosophy of the new society, more universal than Puritanism and more directly related to the coming transformation, the

[23] S. R. Gardiner, *History of England 1603–1642* (London, 1895), vol. i, pp. 146–7, 164, 194, 297–9, 435–6; vol. ii, pp. 35–42, 122–4, 191–209, 272–83; vol. iii, pp. 1–36.

[24] G. P. Gooch, *Political Thought in England from Bacon to Halifax* (Oxford, 1915), p. 13.

[25] J. W. Allen, *English Political Thought 1603–1660* (London, 1938), p. 57.

[26] W. K. Jordan, *The Development of Religious Toleration in England 1603–40* (London, 1936), pp. 457–72.

[27] Holdsworth, op. cit., vol. v, pp. 249, 485–9.

philosophy of science. These two movements—science and law reform—were at the centre of the seventeenth-century revolution. Since the middle class on the whole still accepted the absolute monarchy and hoped to gain through it the conditions which favoured their development, Bacon's conceptions might have acted as the bridge between the old order and the new.

Coke, also, formed a link with the new world in stretching the law to uphold the right to freedom of trade.[28] He reflected the movement in the ruling class at the accession of James I in favour of relaxation of some of the rigidities of the Elizabethan system.[29] But this movement did not look to the power of the State to achieve its ends, as did Bacon; on the contrary it sought to reduce control by the central government. It was felt that there had been a tendency for the monarchy to become more powerful than was required to maintain the existing social order. The more the State tried to do the greater was the pressure on the ruling class who had to operate the system: the gentry were overworked[30] and the nobility found the services demanded of them costly.[31] Coke, in seeking to recover business being lost by the common law courts to Chancery, the Admiralty, and Court of High Commission, stumbled on the theory which fitted the situation. He attempted to resurrect the medieval constitution and developed the ideas of the supremacy of the common law and the absoluteness of rights. This would permit a relaxation of central control while preserving intact the predominance of the existing ruling class. Despite his quarrel with the central authority in the Church, the High Commission, Coke was no enemy to bishops. 'If no bishops, then no laws,' he is reported to have said, 'if no laws, no kings.'[32] And he underlined the common interest of nobles, bishops, and judges in his conception of Magna Carta, which was central to his constitu-

[28] D. O. Wagner, 'Coke and the Rise of Economic Liberalism', *Econ. Hist. Rev.*, vi (1935).

[29] E. P. Cheney, *A History of England from the Defeat of the Armada to the Death of Elizabeth* (London, 1914), p. 64.

[30] E. M. Leonard, *The Early History of English Poor Relief* (Cambridge, 1900), p. 178.

[31] L. Stone, 'The Anatomy of the Elizabethan Aristocracy', *Econ. Hist. Rev.*, xviii (1948): although marred by error and exaggeration this article still contains an important hypothesis and valuable material.

[32] Quoted by G. L. Mosse, *The Struggle for Sovereignty in England* (Michigan, 1950), p. 150; and see chap. viii for a good analysis of Coke's ideas.

tional ideas: 'My lords, your noble ancestors, whose places you hold, were parties to Magna Carta. . . . And you, my lords the bishops . . . are commanded *fulminare*, to thunder out your anathemas against all infringers of Magna Carta. . . . And all worthy judges that deserved their places have ever had Magna Carta in great estimation.'[33] Coke believed that the monarchy would find all its necessary powers upheld at the common law. James I, who made some attempt to move in the direction of Bacon's ideas, experimented in this other way also. He allowed the prerogative to be tested in the courts, which Elizabeth would never have done. Inevitably the judges upheld the absolute power of the Crown, since without precedents to guide them they had to fall back on the basic principles of the common law. The result was to strengthen the power of the Crown. Coke had seen the common law as a means of keeping the central government within bounds and harmonizing the interests of the State and the ruling class. This concept now collapsed. The independent authority which he mapped out for the common law proved non-existent. His denial of the generally accepted doctrine that the judges were the King's advisers led to his dismissal.[34]

Coke's leadership of the common lawyers derived from his efforts to extend the business of their courts.[35] The chief common lawyers, it seems, were an almost hereditary caste[36] into which Coke had not been born but whom he outdistanced in fanatical devotion to their interests. He led something like a revolt of the robe, and with his dismissal this passed over into the parliamentary opposition. The opposition of the lawyers reflected discontent in the ruling class, for, as Notestein says, the common lawyers 'interlocked with the gentry, or were its retainers, in much the same relation that the lawyer class in America holds to our gentry, the manufacturers'.[37] This was the period in which Miss Judson shows that opposition was dominated by the upholding of rights. But the nationalism of the gentry tended to turn against the monarchy and join with the

[33] Quoted by J. W. Gough, *Fundamental Law in English Constitutional History* (Oxford, 1955), p. 40.

[34] J. R. Tanner, *English Constitutional Conflicts of the Seventeenth Century 1603–1689* (Cambridge, 1928), p. 36.

[35] Usher, op. cit., pp. 149–55.

[36] Holdsworth, op. cit., vol. v, pp. 341–4.

[37] W. Notestein, *The Winning of the Initiative by the House of Commons* (British Academy, Raleigh Lecture, 1924), p. 50.

middle-class criticism of Stuart foreign policy. Out of this appeared a new theory asserting that as the representative of the people Parliament had a special concern in the welfare of the nation. Coke resisted this development and denied the competence of Parliament in foreign affairs. He led the Opposition into the Petition of Rights,[38] which like Magna Carta declared the law; it took nothing from the Crown. His object was to uphold the rights of the ruling class and reconcile the discontented elements with the monarchy. Coke's constitutionalism was essentially conservative; when it came to the Civil War its adherents were royalists,[39] or the extreme right wing of Parliament, pushed increasingly into the King's camp or into neutrality.

Coke's ideas did not act as a bridge between the old order and the new. He put new strength into the common law but preserved obsolete doctrines and all its enormous technicality and complexity. Codification of the law never came about but the division of the common lawyers in the Civil War seems to have been between conservatives and reformers. The cause of law reform was identified with the cause of parliament: to take one example, Rolle, whose *Abridgement* came near to being a digest of the whole law, became a judge of the King's Bench in 1645, Chief Justice in 1648, and worked with the Protectorate until 1655.[40] The common law was being torn in contradictory directions by the social stresses of the seventeenth century; an instrument of the absolute State, on the one hand it was being called upon to uphold the rights of the ruling class, and on the other to come to terms with the new society that was coming into existence. The Long Parliament and the Interregnum provided the great formative time in the development of the common law, rather than the period of Coke. The common law after 1660 was scarcely the common law of Coke; it was established on a new base and to meet the needs of a new world.[41]

The problem of preserving the existing social order against the challenge of a totally different conception of society produced disunity within the ruling class and provided the framework of the constitutional crisis. But, under James I and in the early years of

[38] E. R. Adair, 'The Petition of Right', *History*, v (1920–1).

[39] F. D. Wormuth, *The Royal Prerogative 1603–1649* (Ithaca, New York, 1939), p. 119.

[40] Holdsworth, op. cit., vol. v, pp. 375–6.

[41] Laski, op. cit., p. 151.

the reign of Charles I, the social question itself was not at the centre of the constitutional crisis, which was primarily a crisis within the ruling class. The constitutional conflict developed from disagreements about policy in the council and amongst the nobility. This conflict cannot be separated from the struggle for place and profit. The nobility looked to the Crown to provide the honours, employments, and economic resources, on which depended their social pre-eminence; but there were not enough to go round. As one aristocratic faction moved into favour its disappointed rivals tended to drift into opposition. The gentry looked to the nobility for leadership and patronage. Opposition to the King in the House of Commons reflected the opposition of certain nobles. In 1621 the Earl of Southampton was the real leader of the opposition in the Lower House; in 1626 the Earl of Pembroke was behind the parliamentary attack on the Duke of Buckingham. Opposition came from disappointed office-seekers and was a means of gaining royal favour, but opposition would not have gone to the lengths it did if there had not been real and serious disagreements about the management of affairs.[42]

Colaiste Oideachais Mhuire Gan Smal Luimneach

IV

Both James and Charles felt that the monarchy needed the reinforcement of that disinherited section of the ruling class, the Catholics, to counterbalance the alliance of the discontented nobles and gentry with the Puritans.[43] Their experiments in that direction strengthened the fear of popery in the ruling class. Their other policy was to bolster up the authority of the Church and restore its economic power, which had been continuously undermined in favour of the Crown and the lay landlords during the sixteenth century. James I's attempt to use the prerogative to effect this ran into opposition from Coke and from the nobility and gentry, to whose interests it ran counter. At the same time there was a reaction in the Church against its subordination to the State. Some Jacobean divines demanded a greater degree of inde-

[42] C. H. Firth, *The House of Lords During the Civil War* (London, 1910), pp. 4–43; A. Thomson, 'John Holles', *The Journal of Modern History*, viii (1936); D. H. Willson, *The Privy Councillors in the House of Commons 1604–1629* (Minneapolis, 1940), pp. 116–90.

[43] Jordan, op. cit., p. 102.

pendence for the Church and exalted the function of the clergy.[44] This developed into the Laudian High Church movement which, in response to the decline in the economic and social status of the clergy and to the menace of Puritanism, elevated the office of the priesthood and asserted the necessity of hierarchy. There was truth in the Long Parliament criticism that the Laudians sought to make the Church superior to the State. Charles I faced with growing discontent in the ruling class found himself forced increasingly to depend on the Laudian clergy.[45] In return they upheld the monarchy. In identifying Puritanism with sedition and attack on social order, the Laudian bishops, although themselves economically and socially divorced from the nobility,[46] were in reality the front line of defence of that class. But the King's reliance on them increased the opposition in the ruling class. The enhanced power of the Church and its relieving the Crown of some of its dependence on the nobility and gentry, widened the cleavage between the King and the ruling class, who sought to keep the monarchy and the Church in dependence on themselves.

The gentry were antagonized by interference with their control over their own parish clergy, and their hostility fused with the resistance of many of the lower clergy to the increased autocracy of the hierarchy. The Root and Branch Petition accused the bishops of subjecting all the clergy to their sole authority 'and so by degrees exempting them from the temporal power', and encouraging them to 'despise the temporal magistracy, the nobles and gentry of the land'.[47] Charles I's employment of clerics and the Laudians' interference with the ecclesiastical patronage of the nobility and gentry, were bitterly resented. Falkland complained that the bishops aimed at obtaining power 'to dispose as well of every office as of every benefice'.[48] Finally, the aristocratic attitude towards the Laudian clique is well summed up in Lord Say's speech to the Long Parliament: 'My Lord of Canterbury, a man of mean birth, bred up in a College (and that too frequently falls out to be in a faction), whose narrow comprehension extended itself

[44] Allen, op. cit., pp. 129–35.
[45] Jordan, op. cit., p. 121.
[46] D. Mathew, *The Social Structure of Caroline England* (Oxford, 1948), pp. 69–70.
[47] *The Constitutional Documents of the Puritan Revolution*, ed. S. R. Gardiner (Oxford, 1906), p. 138.
[48] Quoted by Allen, op. cit., p. 348.

no farther than to carry on a side in the college, or canvass for a Procter's place in the University, being suddenly advanced to the highest places of government in Church and State, had not his heart enlarged by the enlargement of his fortunes, but still the maintaining of his party was that which filled his thoughts. . . .'[49]

The Laudian clergy and the part of the ruling class which supported Charles I developed a theory of the King's absolute power for the welfare of the people, and there were tentative steps towards seeking to reconstruct the social basis of the monarchy on popular support. In so far as this involved invasion of the rights of the nobility and gentry it further worsened the position of the Crown, and popular support was not gained. In reality this 'welfare' policy was actuated by fear and distrust of the people: popular discontent was mounting during the period of the Personal Government and the privy councillors were acutely aware that in the face of widespread disorder the government would rapidly collapse.[50] They employed the methods by which Elizabeth had protected the nobility and gentry from the people, but this time the government had as much to fear from the opposition in the ruling class. More important, the intensification of the Elizabethan system of economic controls and the attempts of the Crown to exploit commerce and industry, brought in the urban middle class against the monarchy and transformed aristocratic discontent into a revolutionary movement. Admirers of the *ancien régime* have displaced the Liberal picture of an enlightened opposition by the Conservative picture of an enlightened government. The government was 'national' and 'progressive' where the opposition was 'local' and 'traditional', the government seeking the welfare of all and the opposition defending selfish vested interests. It is true that the opposition was local and traditional in so far as it was the opposition of the ruling class in defence of the old order. But, as I have tried to show, there was no single way of defending the old order to the satisfaction of the whole ruling class; Charles I's policy was equally the defence of the old order, but the way chosen alienated a powerful section of the ruling class. The dissidents allied with the middle class whose opposition *was* national and

[49] *Two Speeches by . . . Viscount Say*, BM E. 198 (16).

[50] This is an impression gained from the *Calendar of State Papers Domestic* and other printed collections of letters: see D. G. C. Allan, 'The Rising in the West 1628–31', *Econ. Hist. Rev.*, v (1952–3).

progressive, and the contradiction between the two classes had not yet become apparent.

The beginning of the alliance between noble and bourgeois opposition led Charles to dispense with Parliament, and those members of the ruling class who discerned in the changing situation a threat to the social order came round to the opinion of the need for strong government. One of these was Strafford: 'The authority of the King is the keystone which closeth up the arch of order and government, which keeps each part in due relation to the whole. . . .'[51] In other words keeps each class in its place, the counterpart of Laud's conception of hierarchy. But partly divorced from its social base, the financial difficulties of the monarchy led it to invade the property rights of the nobility and gentry, and that provoked the explosion. Property, however, was not the monopoly of a class, and its broad dispersion through society was the source from which a revolutionary capitalism was emerging. The cry of property in danger united a wide movement behind the nobility and gentry, not only the urban middle class, but the small producers in town and country, the mass of the people. The idea of property in the seventeenth century was not just the creed of a few rich men but a potentially revolutionary gospel which could overthrow the established order. No longer was the idea of property merely a defence of the old order but a challenge to that order—a demand to free the small producers from the exploitation of the existing system. This merged with the middle class hostility to government interference with economic activities and their demand for the removal of restrictions on production. It further embraced the section of the ruling class which saw the solution to their economic problems in a régime of economic freedom which would give a free hand to landlords. There were contradictions here with the interests of the mass of the people, contradictions between landlords and peasants, capitalists and small producers; but the cause of economic freedom opened up opportunities to the small producers, even if ultimately it degraded the majority of them into a wage-earning proletariat. Puritanism found its strength amongst the industrial small producers and was the ideology of a powerful popular movement,[52] but it was also the ideology in which capitalism found expression and the means to

[51] Quoted by Judson, op. cit., p. 147.

[52] See the profound study by W. Haller, *The Rise of Puritanism* (Columbia, 1938).

mould society to its own image,[53] thus marking the link between petty-production and the emergence of a revolutionary capitalism. Puritanism and property united the revolutionary movement, although both were destined to be the sources of division when the landowners and the middle class repudiated the popular movement. The middle class provided the leadership for the popular movement: it was said that Prynne, Burton, and Bastwick, whose persecution during the Personal Government aroused great popular sympathy, belonged to the three professions with most influence over the people, those of lawyer, divine, and physician. The professions were seeking a higher social status than accorded them by an aristocratic society. The 'enlightened administration' of Charles I could not solve the social problem; it could only maintain the *status quo*, and that is true of all philosophies that promise progress through enlightened administration only.

Revolt in Scotland precipitated the collapse of the monarchy, but its downfall had already been made certain by the refusal of the majority of the ruling class to collaborate with it any longer. After the failure of the Short Parliament the nobility forced on the King the Long Parliament. It looked upon itself as a Constituent Assembly, and great hopes were aroused. The popular movement hung upon the actions of the Long Parliament, convinced that a new age had dawned and that the poor and unlearned were about to come into their own; its pressure forced forward the revolution and obliged the ruling class to resort to force to defend the existing social order. The popular movement was not merely the reflex of economic distress, it was carried forward by the cries of Liberty and Reformation, and it had its own aims distinct from and conflicting with those of the landlords or middle class. A petition got up in Cheshire 'amongst the Common People' and 'concealed from the Gentry' criticized tithes and the excessive fines imposed by landlords on their tenants; it demanded the abolition of episcopacy and the vesting of ecclesiastical jurisdiction in the congregations, which, it argued, 'would learn landlords more compassion'.[54] It was in reaction to this petition that the royalist party first began to form itself in Cheshire. Captain Venn, Member of Parliament for the City, one of the most important revolutionary leaders, later accused by royalists of engineering the tumults in London, which

[53] Tawney, *Religion and the Rise of Capitalism*.
[54] Aston, op. cit.; and the *Cheshire Petition*, BM 669f4(8).

played the decisive part in the events of 1641, is in fact to be found trying to keep the popular insurrection under control.[55]

J. W. Allen, in his *English Political Thought 1603–60*, rejecting the idea that religion was the basic cause of the Civil War, had to fall back on distrust of the King; and Miss Judson takes the same view. Allen thought that the division over the abolition of episcopacy did not mark the beginning of the cleavage in the ruling class which led to civil war. The dispute was not about religion but merely about the best method of bringing the Church under the control of the nobility and gentry. Falkland, arguing in favour of the retention of episcopacy, said that it should be possible so to tie up the bishops by law that they would not dare to act 'otherwise than we would have them'.[56] The object of those who advocated the abolition of episcopacy was by this means to bring the Church under the control of the State. However, what Allen ignored was that the basic question in this dispute turned upon the nature of the State that the Long Parliament was to establish. It was no longer fundamentally a question of the relation of the nobility and gentry to the Church but of whether the State was still to be based on the nobility and gentry. The division over episcopacy was acutely significant because those who wished to retain the bishops argued that if they went down the ruling class went down as well.

Allen was mystified because agreement on the constitution seemed perfectly possible in 1641, yet the country drifted into civil war in 1642; the view that agreement was perfectly possible and merely postponed until 1660 is also expressed by Miss Judson. The reason for this approach is that both look upon the conflict as essentially within the ruling class. If that were the case religion would provide the only coherent explanation of the breakdown. But in fact the breakdown was caused by the intervention of the popular movement, which pushed a section of the ruling class reluctantly into revolution, and persuaded the middle class to make their bid for power. This factor received inadequate attention in Christopher Hill's important pioneer interpretation *The English Revolution*.

The Root and Branch Petition caused the fundamental division.

[55] *A True Relation of the Most Wise and Worthy Speech Made by Captain Ven* (1641), BM E. 181(21).

[56] Quoted by Allen, op. cit., p. 349.

The supporters of episcopacy were frightened by 'the long tail of this blazing star', the popular demonstrations in favour of the petition. Digby argued that the time had come to resist the popular movement,[57] but Fiennes replied that it might be more dangerous to deny the people what they asked in their present mood than to grant it. 'If we shall throw their petition behind the door . . . it may seem an act of will in us. And whether an act of will in us may not produce an act of will in the people, I leave to your consideration.'[58] But Edmund Waller, one of those who remained with Parliament after the outbreak of the Civil War in the hope of sabotaging the revolution, gave a clear picture of the acute danger which now faced the ruling class. If the 'outwork' of episcopacy were taken 'by this assault of the people, and withall this mystery was once revealed, that we must deny them nothing when they seek it thus in troops, we may in the next place have a hard task to defend our property, as we have lately had to recover it from the prerogative. If . . . they prevail for an equality in things ecclesiastical, this next demand may be Lex Agraria, the like equality in things temporal.' If it be alleged that episcopacy is against Scripture '[I] am confident that whenever an equal division of lands and goods shall be desired, there will be as many places in Scripture found out, which seem to favour that. . . . And as for the abuses where you are now in the Remonstrance told, what this and that poor man hath suffered by the Bishops, you may be presented with a thousand instances of poor men, that have received hard measure from their landlords.'[59]

At the beginning of the Long Parliament Charles I appeared powerless in the face of the opposition his rule had aroused; it was the popular movement which caused the first division amongst his opponents. As it developed, that movement drove the bulk of the ruling class to the side of the King, with whose power their own was fundamentally identified. The middle class were confident of their ability to keep control of the popular movement and to use it as the means to achieve power. Their theorist was Henry Parker. He argued that insurrection of the people was the only check on tyranny, but 'till some way was invented to regulate the motions

[57] *The Third Speech of Lord Digby to the House of Commons* (1641), BM E. 196(30).

[58] *Speeches and Passages of this Great and Happy Parliament* (London, 1641).

[59] *A Speech Made by Master Waller Esquire in the Honourable House of Commons* (1641), BM E. 198(30).

of the people's voluminous body, I think arbitrary rule was most safe for the world. . . .' 'Long it was ere the world could . . . find out an orderly means whereby to avoid the danger of unbounded prerogative on this hand, and too excessive liberty on the other. . . .'[60] The new theory was the sovereignty of Parliament; power derived from the people but was embodied in the representative assembly. Thus Parliament could call upon the people to resist the King but the people could not disobey the orders of their representatives, to whom they had made over absolutely their right of resistance. A small section of the ruling class, in the face of the popular movement, saw the best chance for the survival of their power in an alliance with the wealthy middle class. Their attitude was expressed in the old prophecy of Bishop Williams, ex-Lord Keeper: 'The Puritans would carry all things at last. . . . No one was wise who permanently opposed himself to the people of England.'[61]

The Army Plots marked the beginning of the counter-revolution in the ruling class; they were provoked by the realization that 'some turbulent spirits, backed by rude and tumultuous mechanick persons . . . would have the total subversion of the government of the state'[62]: their aim was as much to force the King to stop appeasing the revolution, as to use force against the popular uprising. The intervention of the popular movement totally changed the nature of the constitutional crisis. The contest for office played its part in the early stages of the Long Parliament in the manoeuvres of the aristocratic factions.[63] But this factor was super-

[60] H. Parker, *Observations upon some of his Majesties late Answers*, p. 14 (*Tracts on Liberty in the Puritan Revolution*, ed. W. Haller, Columbia, 1933, vol. ii, p. 180). See W. K. Jordan, *Men of Substance* (Chicago, 1942), chap. v.

[61] Quoted by D. Masson, *The Life of Milton* (London, 1859–94), vol. i, p. 636.

[62] *Examination of Sir John Coniers by a Committee of the House of Lords* (1641), BM E. 148(17).

[63] For an account of the part played by disappointed office-seekers in the downfall of Strafford see R. R. Reid, *The King's Council in the North* (London, 1921), pt. iv. For an examination of the significance attached by Clarendon to the struggle for office in the early stages of the Long Parliament see B. H. G. Wormald, *Clarendon: Politics, History and Religion 1640–1660* (Cambridge, 1951). H. R. Trevor-Roper, *The Gentry 1540–1640* (Economic History Review, Supplement no. 1) seems to me to misunderstand the part played by the struggle for office in the constitutional conflict and to interpret the civil war in the light of factors which, although important until 1641, thereafter ceased to be decisive.

seded in 1641: the anonymous author of the *Letter Found in the Privy Lodgings at Whitehall* pointed out that the people were so resolved that if their present leaders were bought off with places they would set up new leaders.[64] The Civil War cannot be regarded as a vast struggle for office or a great revolt against centralization. The struggle was not against central power but for control of central power. The great majority of the ruling class rallied to the defence of their state. The revolutionary middle class assumed the leadership of the popular movement, which henceforth determined the direction of events. The royalists said that they were fighting for the cause of the nobility and gentry, the parliamentarians said that they were fighting for the cause of the people: it seems quite likely that both were right.

[64] *A Copy of a Letter Found in the Privy Lodgings at Whitehall* (1641), BM E. 163(4).

XI

STRAFFORD IN IRELAND: A REVALUATION*

Terence Ranger

UNTIL recently the orthodox interpretation of the career of Thomas Wentworth, Earl of Strafford, seemed very firmly established. After centuries of melancholy vicissitudes, Strafford's reputation was rescued in the 1920s and 1930s. Dr. O'Grady provided the Irish groundwork of the new interpretation with his *Strafford and Ireland* in 1923; Lady Burghclere re-examined the whole career of Strafford in her two-volume biography in 1931; in 1935 Miss C. V. Wedgwood perfected and popularized the new interpretation in her immensely successful *Strafford, 1593–1641*; Lord Birkenhead, though without reference to these predecessors, bestowed the seal of his approval upon their interpretation with another biography in 1938.[1]

Out of this flurry of biographical activity there emerged a consistent and attractive picture. Strafford's Irish deputyship, which had provided the majority of the indictments against him at his trial, now became the central achievement around which the new interpretation was built. To Lady Burghclere, indeed, Strafford's part in the 'unprofitable experiment' of personal government was small. 'It is by his Irish record', she wrote, 'that he must stand or fall.' To Miss Wedgwood, who saw Strafford's significance as wider than this, the conclusions drawn by O'Grady and

[1] W. H. A. O'Grady, *Strafford and Ireland*, 2 vols. (Dublin, 1923); Burghclere, *Strafford*, 2 vols. (London, 1931); C. V. Wedgwood, *Strafford, 1593–1641* (London, 1935); Birkenhead, *Strafford* (London, 1938).

* From no. 19 (1961).

Lady Burghclere on his Irish administration seemed applicable to his career in England also.

All these writers saw Strafford's deputyship as 'the classical example of English administration in Ireland'. 'At last', writes Dr. Kearney, summarizing the orthodox view in his excellent recent book on Strafford, 'a lord deputy was appointed who was both efficient and incorruptible and who was determined to maintain the highest possible ideal of government. . . . On the one hand he was seen as the lord deputy who acted in the interests of the smaller proprietors against the greater, and on the other as a statesman who, though he crushed the Irish woollen trade, was yet sufficiently far-sighted to establish linen as a substitute. Alternatively he has been seen as leading a crusade against the vested interests of a corrupt society in the name of a higher, traditional social code.'[2] To Miss Wedgwood these ideals of efficient and incorrupt government and the protection of the poor against the rich were typical of Strafford's thought whether in Ireland or in Yorkshire. At Court he supported the alleged Laudian policy of paternal social protection for the poor and avowed himself an enemy of the self-seeking and shallow courtiers. And everywhere and at all times he assumed that efficient government, honest administration, benevolent social policy, could only be based upon a strong monarchy supported by a strong Church.

Strafford's aims, then, as they were described by his biographers of the 1930s, were ones with which it is easy to feel sympathy. Yet despite his great ability and his honesty of purpose he was doomed to failure and destruction. This was partly due, thought his biographers, to the strength, cunning and versatility of the adversary; partly due to flaws in his own nature—or perhaps more correctly to virtues which weakened him as a statesman but became him as a man. Too good for the seventeenth-century world, Strafford, a 'simple and generous man . . . fearless in the pursuit of what he believed to be right', was broken by it.[3]

So the interpretation of the 1930s assumed the character not only of scientific re-appraisal but of high tragedy. Strafford was depicted in language of dramatic exaltation. His enemies were described as 'sharks' or 'jackals' or as 'sinister executioners of a pre-determined sentence'. The final effect in all these biographies

[2] H. F. Kearney, *Strafford in Ireland, 1633–41* (Manchester, 1959).

[3] Wedgwood, op. cit., pp. 346–7.

was to depict the last great contest between Strafford and his enemies in terms of 'the pack in full cry after the stately quarry penned against the wall, fighting undauntedly for life and dear honour'.[4]

Despite, or perhaps because of, this emotive and melodramatic language the interpretation produced by these biographers survived, and in surviving became an orthodoxy. Yet it was always based upon a coincidence of accidental or ephemeral factors. One was that it was peculiarly the interpretation of its period. The prevailing attitude of the inter-war years allowed for Strafford's rehabilitation on his own terms—for these biographers were largely inspired by Strafford's own vision of the contest. The politicians of both right and left were re-establishing the respectability of authoritarianism and undermining the 'whig' concepts of the primacy of individual liberty and the rights of property. Strafford as the strong man who tried to protect the poor against the unbridled appetites of plutocrats and Puritans was an attractive image to elements both on the right and left of intellectual developments.

Two other factors, however, enabled the unopposed creation of this sort of interpretation. One was that professional historians were denied access to the great mass of Strafford's papers at Wentworth Wodehouse. This meant that all the biographers relied largely upon Knowler's eighteenth-century edition of a selection of Strafford's papers—for Lady Burghclere and Lord Birkenhead, who were allowed to consult the other documents, were not equipped to make much use of them—and Knowler's selection had been made with the intention of presenting Strafford's own view of events in its clearest and most convincing form.[5] Finally the interpretation rested upon the curious accident that for Strafford's Irish career his biographers depended almost entirely upon Dr. O'Grady. Dr. O'Grady's book had all the appearance of a piece of pioneer research work. But not only did it run counter to the typical Irish view of Strafford, because O'Grady's hatred of the 'new English' settlers, with whom Strafford most spectacularly strove, overcame any reservations that an Irish historian might otherwise be expected to feel towards Strafford's Irish

[4] Burghclere, op. cit., ii, p. 261.

[5] *The Earle of Straffordes Letters and Dispatches*, ed. Wm. Knowler, 2 vols. (London, 1739).

policies in general; it was also, in Dr. Kearney's unsparing but just words, 'a strange mixture of confused information, weird prejudice and chronological anarchy'.[6] The Irish foundation upon which so much was built was, in fact, thoroughly unsound.

None of these factors still obtain. The spirit of the post-war period has been one of disillusionment with authoritarianism, whether of the right or the left, and as far as historians are concerned attention has been directed more to problems of 'structure' than to problems of personal and political morality. The Strafford papers are now deposited in the Sheffield Public Library and open to the inspection of any qualified scholar; already the new evidence which they contain has enabled Mr. J. P. Cooper to produce a valuable article on Strafford's personal fortune which sets him firmly in the patronage context of his time. Finally, the current revival of Irish historiography has produced as one of its major achievements Dr. Kearney's account of Strafford's Irish administration which entirely supersedes O'Grady's unreliable work. Despite Miss Wedgwood's gallant reiteration of the traditional view in the first volume of her narrative history of the Civil War, the time is evidently ripe for a reassessment of the significance of Strafford's career.[7]

Mr. Cooper's article and Dr. Kearney's book go some way towards establishing a new view and a much longer way towards destroying the old one. Mr. Cooper's examination of Strafford's private financial affairs, together with Dr. Kearney's chapter on 'Personal Profit', cast much light on Strafford as a crusader 'against the vested interests of a corrupt society in the name of a higher, traditional code'. The two accounts show Strafford accepting the Irish deputyship at least partly for reasons of profit and making from Irish sources an income of some £13,000 a year; selling offices in his gift as deputy, including those of judicial officers and judges; resisting royal invasions of his patronage not only because

[6] op. cit., p. x.

[7] J. P. Cooper, 'The Fortune of Thomas Wentworth, Earl of Strafford', *Econ. Hist. Rev.*, 2nd ser., xi (1958); C. V. Wedgwood, *The King's Peace* (London, (1955). Since this paper was first published, Miss Wedgwood has in fact made her reassessment of the significance of Strafford's career in *Thomas Wentworth, First Earl of Strafford, 1593–1641, A Revaluation* (London, 1961).

they hindered efficient government but also because they reduced his chances of profit and influence; using that influence to gratify friends and promising to obtain 'hansomly and secretly' £2,000 for a client of Laud's; confusing, in a way astonishing to modern notions, the finances of the State with his own adventures in the farming of tobacco and customs. Mr. Cooper tells us that 'if Strafford's gains were considerable so were those which he secured for the crown' and that 'of those who looked for favour at the court of Charles I many sought and found less honourable ways to thrive than Strafford'. Dr. Kearney is less kind. Pointing out that an annual income of £13,000 made Strafford one of the richest men in Britain, he comments that Strafford's despised Irish official enemies could hardly have done better in so short a time. 'Strafford', he writes, 'was typical of the general run of seventeenth-century Irish politician.'[8]

Dr. Kearney's book continues this process of bringing Strafford down to earth out of the clouds of glory trailed by his own correspondence and by the biographies of the 1930s. Dr. Kearney has little time for Strafford as a crusader and sees little, if any, difference between him and the 'sharks' and 'vultures' of Irish life. He has not much more time for him as the inventor of a sound land policy designed to safeguard the interests of the smaller landowner or as the creator of an enlightened economic policy. In fact, Dr. Kearney, who has the advantage of knowing a great deal about Irish administrative and economic developments in the decades before the arrival of Strafford, does not see him as an initiator at all.[9] The instruments of 'Thorough' were not Strafford's creation; 'like so many other things' the plan for the plantation of Connacht 'did not originate' with Strafford; during Strafford's deputyship economic policy was dictated as before by 'the economic situation in England', and so far from originating a coherent economic policy Strafford merely 'carried on in the way that his predecessors, Chichester, Grandison and Falkland had done, creating nothing but destroying nothing'; finally, 'the supposed violent contrast between the land policies of Strafford and those of his predecessors did not exist'. Dr. Kearney shows, in short, that 'the novelty' of

[8] Strafford's total annual income was some £19,000 a year in the 1630s. The annual income of his greatest Irish adversary, the Earl of Cork, was £20,000 a year.

[9] Kearney, op. cit., chaps. 1, 2, 4, 10, 11.

Strafford's Irish career 'has either been overstated or misunderstood'. He shows, moreover, that as far as the oppressed Irish were concerned, there was no reason for gratitude to Strafford, whose administration in no way improved their condition; and that, for the Anglo-Irish themselves, Strafford's deputyship saw the beginning of a catastrophic decline in influence and power.

Dr. Kearney does distinguish certain novel features in Strafford's deputyship—but here again he departs from the established view. So far from Strafford being unable to depend upon his 'faithless master', as the orthodox version has it, Dr. Kearney shows that 'for the most part Strafford could rely upon the support of Charles I' and that this gave the deputyship a strength it had never before enjoyed. So far from Strafford evolving a policy to suit Irish conditions and unappreciated either by King or Parliament, as the orthodox version holds, Dr. Kearney shows that the King's support enabled Strafford to ignore Irish pressures and to become 'the first lord deputy to succeed at any rate for a time in carrying out a policy which had been conceived in England without regard for existing interests in Ireland'. So far from the Irish rebellion springing from the removal of Strafford and the abandonment of his policies, Dr. Kearney shows that it was Strafford's implementation of his policies which provoked discontent from all sections of Irish society and was thus responsible for the rising. In two respects Dr. Kearney agrees with the conventional analysis. He agrees that Strafford's success in solving the Irish financial problem was unprecedented and remarkable; and he agrees that Strafford initiated a new religious policy. To Dr. Kearney, however, 'the seeds of eventual disaster lay within Strafford's financial achievements' and Strafford's religious policy was 'completely misconceived' and 'destined to arouse grave discontent'. His final judgement on Strafford's deputyship is that it was 'an overwhelming failure' and that it 'proved to be a passing interlude between the two great revolutions of seventeenth-century Ireland—the Ulster plantations and the Cromwellian Settlement'.

Not much is left of the old version. All Dr. Kearney gives us is an energetic and opinionated administrator, with a capacity for self-delusion, enforcing bad old policies with a new efficiency and with disastrous results. That Mr. Cooper and Dr. Kearney are in general right to put Strafford firmly in the contemporary patronage context can hardly be doubted. That Dr. Kearney is in general right in his account of Strafford's Irish administration can hardly be doubted either, in view of the evidence he gives and the other evidence now available. But a doubt still lingers. Is this all one can say about Strafford? And if it is, why did Strafford become a key figure in English politics so that he had to be called in to save the King and had to be destroyed by Parliament? It is the purpose of this essay to suggest that Mr. Cooper and Dr. Kearney have not said the last word on Strafford, even on Strafford's career in Ireland, though what they have said is true.

The reason why there remains more to say about the significance of Strafford's Irish deputyship even after Dr. Kearney's careful account, and why what remains to be said is actually the most important aspect of all as far as English history is concerned, is that Dr. Kearney quite explicitly regards Strafford's Irish administration as primarily an episode in *colonial* history. This is, of course, a very proper and illuminating way to regard it and chimes with the increasing tendency to regard Anglo-Irish relations as colonial in the same sense as Anglo-Indian relations; to emphasize the *difference* between England and Ireland and to emphasize that Irish history cannot be treated as though it were an extension of English; to emphasize the clash of two or more cultures as the essence of the Irish situation. From the point of view of Irish history—and Dr. Kearney's book is a proclamation of the fact that there is such a thing as Irish history—this is a perfectly satisfying approach. But when it comes to asking what was the significance of Strafford's deputyship in *English* history, or even to asking what was the prime purpose of Strafford's government in Ireland, this emphasis upon the colonial character of Ireland's relationship with England is not helpful.

Strafford's Irish deputyship did, after all, become a key issue in English politics and we certainly cannot explain that in terms of English interest in colonial administration. If Strafford's Irish administration caused concern in England it was not because of the differences between Irish and English life but because of the similarities. It was because the English opposition felt that Strafford's policies in Ireland were relevant to the central issues of English politics.

For if Irish society was very different from English society in most ways, there was at least one important respect in which it was similar. Both countries possessed influential groups of Protestant landowners whose land had in many cases previously belonged to the Church and who depended for security of title on the operation of a modernized common law system. In England the relationship between this group and the Crown was the most important issue of contemporary politics. Now, the Irish group was in many ways unlike its English counterpart. It was nothing like so large, of course; nor so diversified, for even in Munster, where the attempt to recreate English society had been longest on foot, there was no equivalent of the great body of middling landowners who played so important a part in English county life. Moreover, the Irish group lacked the self-confidence of the English aristocracy and squirearchy. Few of the 'new English' landowners came of great families; the atmosphere of Irish landed society was provincial and painfully derivative. For these and other reasons English aristocrats or gentlemen often found themselves out of sympathy with the 'new English' landowner or official when travelling in Ireland. Moreover, the interest of the English landowners as a group often conflicted with the interest of Irish landowners as a group, particularly over such matters as the economic regulation of Irish life and the prohibition upon the export of Irish agricultural produce.

Nevertheless, in other ways the 'new English' ruling group in Ireland shared important common characteristics and interests with the English 'country' opposition. Indeed, they not only shared the essential characteristics of Protestantism, dependence upon land for wealth, and dependence upon the common law for security, but possessed them in a purer or more marked degree. To them, Protestantism was not only a safeguard against the restoration of Church lands and a religion which claimed allegiance for national and historical reasons, but also a mark of race and class, and they regarded a lapse into Catholicism as the equivalent of 'going native'. The established Irish Church, influenced by this attitude and faced by the constant competition of the Catholic 'underground', was austerely Protestant, not to say Puritan. In Ireland there was no room for the Laudian solution, which there seemed to undermine the whole basis of 'new English' supremacy. For their wealth, the 'new English' depended almost entirely upon land and office. There was little industrial development and those who did invest in industry, like the Earl of Cork, made little profit out of it. Commerce, too, was relatively undeveloped and was dominated by the Anglo-Irish of the towns with whom the 'new English' had nothing like the alliance which existed between the English landed and commercial classes. Revenue came largely from land and then not from the direct capitalist exploitation which Professor Tawney postulates as so important in England, but from rents.

In the management of an Irish estate, then, the skills of the lawyer were more important than those of the agriculturalist or businessman. Moreover, because so many Irish estates had been so recently and so dubiously acquired and because of the confusion created by differing land policies and differing titles in the past, the 'new English' landowner came to rely for his security peculiarly upon the operation of the common law system. He needed the enunciation of principles of law which would safeguard the man in possession against any claimant, whether it was the Crown or the Church or the dispossessed Irishman; which would protect the purchaser of land from the consequences of fraud or carelessness committed before his purchase; which would prevent the Crown or the Church from using the same methods of unscrupulous stretching of the letter of the law and downright 'force and fraud' which had built up so many estates in the first place. He needed a legal system which would allow him to break inconveniently long leases or to weary through constant delay and expense a smaller rival. Because the establishment of the common law system in the greater part of Ireland was entrusted to the 'new English' officials and planters; because the Anglo-Irish had been replaced in judicial positions by 'new English' judges who had to look for their chances of profit to the patronage of great landowners or to successful land speculation on their own account; because the scope of prerogative justice in Ireland was limited by the restrictions which the King imposed upon Strafford's predecessors in the deputyship; the 'new English' were able to build up the sort of common law system they desired. It was a system in which a royal judge, on discovering a dangerous weakness in a landlord's title, could write to warn him rather than inform the Crown; in which the salaries of provincial judges could actually be paid by a local landowner, as was the case in Munster; in which juries were peculiarly dependent on their landlords; in which, as Strafford wrote, 'all the judges . . . bend themselves to pronounce that for law which makes for the securing of the subjects' estate wherein they have so full an interest'.[10]

If on the one hand the 'new English' magnates represented the essential qualities of the English opposition in heightened form, on the other hand the lord deputy could exercise in Ireland an executive authority considerably more extensive than that exercised by the King himself in England. In practice this power had not in the past been exercised because of the distrust which had attached itself to the various lord deputies. Prior to Strafford's arrival Ireland presented the paradoxical spectacle of a country in which royal interests were systematically disregarded, royal possessions systematically filched away, and royal revenues steadily diminished, but in which royal power was potentially immense. Strafford was authorized to exercise this power in full and did so. Thus a clash between these two forces—one representing in an extreme form the characteristics of the English opposition and the other representing in an extreme form the power of the English Crown—on the issues of religion, land-rights and the common law was bound to appear to English spectators as a gesturing and melodramatic dumb-show prefacing a tragedy to be played later in England.

Nor were English observers mistaken in viewing the matter in this way. Strafford himself saw his relations with the 'new English' as an extension of the Crown's relations with the English opposition and his statements to his allies in England show quite clearly that he regarded the Irish and the English dilemmas as essentially one. His correspondence with Laud in 1633 shows him urging upon the Archbishop the execution of a common policy in both countries—a policy aimed at defeating the common lawyers and Puritans. 'Tis true, my lord,' he wrote to the Archbishop on 22 October 1633, 'the common lawyers have a great sway in the administration of justice yet not of that papal plenipotency but that they may be contained and brought within the bounds of sobriety and moderation of ancient times. . . . For myself I vow to your Grace that there shall be no such narrow considerations fall into my counsels as my own preservation till I see my master's

[10] Strafford to Coke, 7 Dec. 1633 (Strafford MSS., letter book 5, pp. 27–29); Harris to Sir Richard Boyle, April 1609 (A. B. Grosart, *The Lismore Papers*, 2nd ser. [London, 1887], i, pp. 130–1).

power set out of wardship and above the expositions of Sir Edward Coke and his year books.'[11]

Dr. Kearney is inclined to leave aside such declarations of purpose as these and to regard the concept of 'Thorough' as another of Strafford's self-delusions, primarily because it involved no real change of policy in Irish affairs as such. But Strafford was not really interested in Irish affairs as such and was content to follow established policies in dealing with them. He was, however, the first to realize that Ireland could be made of central importance to English politics and that through the great power of the Crown in Ireland the desirable solution could be tried out there before it was applied in England. Twice again, at least, in the seventeenth century Ireland was used in the same way: once when Henry Cromwell and Lord Broghill put into effect in Ireland their policy of basing the Cromwellian régime upon men of substance and property before they attempted to extend it to England with the offer of the kingship in the second Protectorate Parliament; again when in the last years of Charles II and the first years of James II the catholicizing policy of the Crown was adopted first in Ireland. And through his alliance with Laud, Strafford's policy was linked with a similar attempt in Scotland—just as Henry Cromwell's Irish experiment was linked with the similar Scottish experiment of Broghill and Monck. Strafford was, indeed, attempting to effect 'a policy which had been conceived in England without regard for existing interests in Ireland',[12] but in its most important aspects it was not a colonial policy at all.

With such an intention, Strafford's Irish policy was bound to become a crucial issue in England. But what made it an issue of such urgency was Strafford's own vision of the nature of the struggle between the King and his political opponents. To him it was from the first not a political contest susceptible of manoeuvre and compromise but a fight to the death in which he must either triumph or perish. As early as 1632, he saw himself as a sailor at sea in a storm, but 'let the tempest be never so great, I will much rather put forth to sea, work forth the storm, or at least be found dead with the rudder in my hands'; in 1633 he and Laud were like men walking on ice which might at any moment break; later he was like Caesar 'who besett by . . . conspirators on all parts, and

[11] Strafford to Laud, 22 Oct. 1633 (Strafford MSS., letter book 8, pp. 34–35).
[12] Kearney, op. cit., p. 220.

at last struck by Brutus, threw his vestment over his head'.[13]

Strafford's sense of crisis was not the result of profound foresight. It was, rather, a matter of temperament. 'I shall do the king's business and the business of the church', he told Laud in October 1633, 'in spite of the devil. Naturally I work against the stream and being of a cold constitution . . . exercise keeps me in warmth and heat.'[14] There was not a desperate crisis in 1632 or 1633; the Civil War was not then inevitable; the divisions need not have sharpened into irreconcilability. But Strafford, naturally working against the stream, with his sense of urgency and his overpowering personality, did much to import into the contest the desperateness and finality which he had always seen there. In 1632 Strafford believed that it was his head or the heads of the opposition: in 1640 it really was his head or theirs: Strafford's vision had been realized at least partly because he had all along been acting as though it was true.

The chief result of Strafford's sense of urgency and the chief cause of the intensification of the contest in Ireland and hence in England was the adoption of methods which were objectionable not only to landlords with something to hide, but to those who had respect for law and convention. The rights of the Crown and Church, Strafford told Laud, could not 'be recovered unless a little violence and extraordinary means be used for the raising again as there has been for the pulling down'.[15] Strafford was as good as his word, and violence and extraordinary means were extensively used.

Thus Strafford's deputyship was marked by a conscious, urgent and unscrupulous assault upon the 'new English'. To understand this assault in detail we must look at it again outside the colonial context. Indeed, to Dr. Kearney, looking at it from within the colonial context, no contest is visible at all. Strafford, he says, prosecuted personal quarrels with some of the 'new English' but he kept many of them in office and made use of their services. He did not abandon the planatation policy as such but rather applied it

[13] Strafford to Carlisle, 1632 (quoted in Wedgwood, op. cit. [1935], p. 225); Strafford to Laud, 25 May 1639 (quoted in Burghclere, op. cit., ii, p. 165); Strafford to Laud, 22 Oct. 1633 (Strafford MSS., letter book 8, pp. 34–35).

[14] Strafford to Laud, 31 Oct. 1633.

[15] Strafford to Laud, 10 Mar. 1635 (Strafford MSS., letter book 6, pp. 144–152).

with more vigour. And despite his animadversions on the conduct of the 'new English' on his arrival in Ireland, by the end of his deputyship 'he was playing a similar kind of game in Irish land to that of the men whom he criticized so severely'.[16] Dr. Kearney's attitude is understandable. Looked at from an Irish point of view there was little difference between Strafford's land policy and that of his predecessors or between his solicitude for the interests of the Irish and that of the 'new English' group. Whoever benefited from Strafford's manoeuvres, as Dr. Kearney points out in his examination of Strafford's plantation of the Birnes' Country which is discussed below, 'those who were worst off' were the native Irish. To them it did not matter whether the owner of what had once been their land or the landlord who collected their rents was the Crown or Strafford himself, or Sir William Parsons. Nor did it matter to them whether the Crown got its proper rents or the established Church its proper maintenance. But to Strafford it mattered a great deal. He did not, of course, think that ownership of land in Ireland by Englishmen was in itself wrong—it was to him still the best way of 'civilizing' Ireland. Nor did he think it wrong for a landowner to make a profit greater than could be obtained in England, since some compensation had to be given for the risks of settlement in Ireland. What he did think wrong was the making of this profit at the expense of the Crown and the Church. What Strafford attacked was the whole structure of concealment, of royal patents acquired on misinformation, of suppression of knight service tenure, of false impropriations, of very long leases of Church or Crown land at very low rents, and so on.[17] Where his attack was successful it did not help the Irish tenant at all nor did it alter the fact that land was increasingly in 'new English' hands. It was not meant to. But it did help to restore the revenues and the influence of the Crown and of the established Church.

To get a sense of the combination of cunning, idealism and self-interest which characterized Strafford's methods we must look at a specific example. The story of the plantation of Birnes' Country, to which reference has already been made, may be taken as one such example. To Dr. Kearney, who has not unravelled the

[16] Kearney, op. cit., p. 178.

[17] See Terence Ranger, 'Richard Boyle and the making of an Irish fortune, 1588–1614', *Irish Historical Studies*, x (no. 39, Mar. 1957).

full story, it is an illustration of his thesis that Strafford was a typical seventeenth-century politician. The truth is more complex and more interesting. Birnes' Country was a stretch of fertile coastal land in Wicklow, amounting to some 80,000 acres in extent. It was occupied by the senior branch of the O'Byrnes. It was coveted by a group of Irish officials on the one hand—including Sir William Parsons, Master of the Irish Court of Wards, and Lord Ranelagh, the Lord President of Connacht—and on the other hand by one of Charles I's minor favourites, James Hay, Earl of Carlisle. The perfected technique for displacing Irish occupiers was the discovery of a royal title to the land concerned. Here both sides had an advantage—Carlisle had a grant of the land from the King if he could prove a royal title; Parsons and Ranelagh had the 'proofs' necessary to do so. Before Strafford's arrival Parsons and Ranelagh, with the connivance of their ally, Lord Justice Cork, had been playing a traditional 'new English' game, seeking so to weary and obstruct Carlisle and his agents that they would finally agree to sell the royal grant. In fact on the eve of Strafford's arrival Carlisle's agent did agree to sell the grant to Parsons and Ranelagh for £5,000.

Strafford's appointment as deputy changed the situation because he was a great friend of the Carlisle family. He was asked by Carlisle to investigate the matter and as soon as he arrived in Ireland he issued a commission of inquiry. Parsons and Ranelagh were naturally alarmed at this and at other signs that Strafford intended to attack them and their allies. Sir William therefore approached Strafford with a superbly dishonest scheme. He frankly confessed that he could prove a royal title and had been obstructing Carlisle in the hope of getting the land himself. But he now offered the opportunity to Strafford. Strafford should inform Carlisle that his best hope of profit was to accept a composition of £10,000 from the O'Byrnes. He should then pay Carlisle the money himself; acquire the grant; and entitle himself to land worth £3,000 a year. Parsons offered to see that the royal title was found in return for Strafford's favour and a promise to consult him on all matters of importance.[18]

It was, in a sense, a test case. Parsons was approaching Strafford

[18] Kearney, op. cit., pp. 174–8; letters to Carlisle in letter book of Richard Boyle, Earl of Cork, 1629–31 (Boyle MSS., Chatsworth); Strafford to Charles I, 17 Sept. 1634 (Strafford MSS., letter book 3, pp. 128–9).

with the sort of proposition which had made him indispensable to former deputies. If Strafford had been the crusader for public morality depicted by his biographers he would presumably have rounded on Parsons and driven him from office. If he had been a typical seventeenth-century politician he would either have followed the course of personal profit and accepted Parsons's offer or the course of personal obligation and informed Carlisle. In fact he did none of these things. He told the King of Parsons's offer but, while admitting that such behaviour deserved punishment, he favoured instead a project to use £15,000 from the Irish exchequer with which to buy out Carlisle so that the land when found for the King would actually come into the direct possession of the Crown. Carlisle was to be persuaded that the £15,000 came from a composition raised by the O'Byrnes. Parsons himself should be persuaded that Strafford was entering into the bargain on his own account. The King approved this astonishing suggestion; a warrant authorizing the expenditure of £15,000 from the Irish exchequer on purposes unspecified was issued; the trusting Carlisle accepted Strafford's assurances and was paid his £15,000; the duped Parsons proved the King's title to the land and the O'Byrnes were dispossessed. As a result the Crown obtained land worth £2,000 a year in rents and Strafford was granted as his reward two manors in the area worth more than £1,000 a year.

This most unorthodox transaction demonstrates admirably the truth of Sir Thomas Roe's observations that Strafford was 'a servant violently zealous in his master's ends and not negligent in his own'. The Crown profited most; Strafford profited considerably. As Dr. Kearney says, the real losers were the Irish tenants of the area. But neither the Carlisle family nor Sir William Parsons can have been very happy when they realized what had happened. Carlisle had trusted a friend and as a result had been fobbed off with the lesser bargain while Strafford himself profited. Parsons had surrendered his own hopes of profit but he had not obtained the power over Strafford that he naturally hoped would result from complicity in such a bargain and instead his duplicity had been revealed to the King. It is not unreasonable to suggest that this incident of Birnes' Country may have had something to do with the famous transfer of Lucy Carlisle's platonic affections from Strafford to Pym and almost certainly had everything to do with the hatred which Parsons and Ranelagh henceforth nursed against Strafford.

Illuminating though the story of the Birnes' Country is, it omits two features of Strafford's attack on the 'new English' which are of the utmost importance—his manipulation or overriding of the law and his recovery of Church property. These features may be illustrated by a brief examination of Strafford's attack on the Earl of Cork. The Earl of Cork had no services to offer Strafford of the sort offered by Parsons. He was, on the other hand, the greatest landowner in Ireland and Strafford knew that his wealth had largely been acquired by the sort of swindling of the Crown and the Church that he so abhorred. Strafford therefore determined to make Cork pay for his past frauds. There was little he could do about the frauds against the Crown because Cork had bought off royal inquiries in 1629 and had then achieved, through the favour of Lord Keeper Coventry, a comprehensive regrant of all his lands from the Crown giving him the completest security against further questioning. Here Strafford had to be content with bringing a criminal prosecution against Cork in the court of Castle Chamber, based on the most dubious of his past transactions, and with fining him £15,000. (It was typical of Strafford that he used this money to accomplish the Birnes' Country business, thereby adding another twist to his fooling of Parsons.) There remained the lands of the Church. Cork held long leases or fee farms of most of the Bishop's lands in the See of Lismore; he also held episcopal land in other sees and lands of deaneries, treasurerships, archdeaconries, lazar houses, hospitals and colleges, all at nominal rent. In addition he enjoyed the tithes of several livings supposedly impropriate. Most of the property had been leased by former bishops to the men from whom Cork had purchased the land but in some cases the transactions had been his own. One such case was the basis of the charge in Castle Chamber which resulted in the recovery of numerous impropriations for the Church as well as a £15,000 fine for the King. The rest of the Church property had to be assaulted piecemeal. Strafford went about it with astonishing care. Full lists of Cork's Church property were drawn up, even down to scraps of a few acres. The most exhaustive inquiries were made into his titles. Then through a series of legally dubious challenges the attack was launched.[19]

[19] The whole question of Strafford's relations with Cork is discussed in

To appreciate what Strafford was undertaking, we must remember that many of Cork's leases dated from the reign of Elizabeth and that the land concerned had been out of the hands of the Church for thirty or forty years. We must appreciate also that Cork was protected by the accepted principles of Irish law which held that long leases made by churchmen prior to the Act of State prohibiting them were valid and that in any case bona fide purchasers were to be protected from challenges arising from any irregularity in the lease. It was established practice, also, that the final appeal in such matters as disputed impropriations should be to the common law courts, 'where your lordship may judge', wrote Strafford to Laud of one case concerning the Earl of Cork's impropriations, 'what good measure the poor man may expect from a jury against the earl'.[20] Obstacles such as these Strafford swept aside. He obtained royal letters giving the court of Castle Chamber the right to make final decisions in Church causes without appeal to the common law. And he evolved a whole series of ingenious legal challenges to Cork's titles, or rather employed Sir George Radcliffe to evolve them.

Radcliffe, whose importance in this role has been insufficiently appreciated, soon produced an objection to all Cork's leases from the Bishop and other Church officials in the diocese of Lismore. Radcliffe maintained that the See of Lismore was 'really united' with the See of Waterford and that all leases of land in Lismore should have been approved not only by the Dean and Chapter of that diocese but also by the Dean and Chapter of Waterford. Strafford sent this opinion over to the English judges in 1635. 'I expect the return of opinions on Sir George Radcliffe's case', he wrote to Laud in July 1635, 'and then have at the great house of Lismore. My fingers itch to fetch it back to the church.'[21] But the judges were shy of the case, as they often were when faced with Radcliffe's legal ingenuities, and would not commit themselves. Strafford had to wait until the death of Bishop Boyle of Lismore

[20] Strafford to Laud, 10 Mar. 1635 (Knowler, i, p. 380).
[21] Strafford to Laud, 14 July 1635 (Strafford MSS., letter book 6, pp. 199–209).

Terence Ranger, 'The Career of Richard Boyle, first earl of Cork, in Ireland, 1588–1643' (thesis presented for the degree of D.Phil. Oxon., which is to be published as a book by the Clarendon Press).

and Waterford in January 1636 gave him a chance to appoint a bishop who would prosecute Cork in the Castle Chamber, from which there was now no appeal in ecclesiastical causes. Bishop Atherton, once appointed, proved as Strafford had predicted a fit 'terrier for the unkenneling an old fox'.[22] He began suits against Cork for all the lands and rights leased by his predecessors on the grounds that the leases had not been approved by the Chapter of Waterford and was so strongly supported by Strafford and Bramhall that he was able to force Cork to a composition which greatly increased the revenues of his See. This success was followed up by new appointments to the archdeaconry, the treasurership and the deanship of Lismore and suits were begun by the new incumbents for the land leased by their predecessors, again on the same grounds of the inadequacy of the leases. These attacks were also successful. By means of a legal quibble as trifling as any which Cork had himself exploited in the past and by virtue of a pressure as partisan as any he had exercised, Strafford had succeeded in breaking down a structure which it had taken Cork thirty years to build.

Cork was similary pursued in the other bishoprics where he held lands from the Church. Chappel, the new Bishop of Cork, recovered the revenues of his See through the use of a novel and alarming weapon—a commission issued by Strafford which allowed him to apply for the sequestration of any lands that he *supposed* 'to be detained from his see'. It was certainly arbitrary to grant sequestration before any demonstration of title and merely on supposition, but Chappel was able to obtain the sequestration of all Cork's rents from Church property in his diocese, and to collect them himself until Strafford's downfall. Cork and his agents always wrote of 'this illegal commission' but there was nothing they could do to oppose it. In Cloyne the new Bishop, Synge, also demanded the return of land which had originally belonged to his See. Here Cork defended himself particularly stubbornly since he had acquired this land by an exchange of property with another great Munster landowner and he felt an outraged innocence when confronted with Synge's demands. But Synge was able to threaten him by producing an ancient document purporting to show that half Cork's barony of Inchiquin was really the property of the Bishop of Cloyne and although the claim was very far-fetched, it

[22] Strafford to Laud, 9 Mar. 1636 (ibid., pp. 292–9).

was enough 'as things now go on in favour of the church' to force Cork to negotiate with him.[23]

Strafford's method of recovering impropriations was equally irregular. His practice was to appoint a minister to a living on grounds of lapse; then the minster was encouraged to complain to Castle Chamber that the owner of the impropriation was withholding his tithes; the Attorney-General was instructed to present the minister's case; Strafford then handed down his judgement, which almost invariably favoured the Church, and was invariably followed by the rest of the board. In such cases Strafford was initiator, prosecutor and judge. It was little wonder that legal opinion in England was shocked at such procedures and that Lord Keeper Coventry expressed himself of the opinion that lapse should first be proved before presentation and that there should be appeals in Church causes from the Irish Castle Chamber to the English Chancery. Strafford was savagely scornful of such doctrine and made no concessions other than to give the initiative in bringing cases into the hands of his bishops.[24]

Just as there were other transactions like the Birnes' Country affair, so these assaults upon Cork were the model for wider assaults on the holders of Church property. Cork lost most and the attack on him was most thorough but the methods pioneered in his case were very generally used. Thus the reclamation of Church land did not only make Strafford more personal enemies nor did it only delight the small man by the spectacle of the humiliation of the great. It struck at the small landowner also, whether Catholic or Protestant, and caused bitter resentment. 'Here has been an infamous libel cast out against me', reported Strafford in March 1635, 'the author sure was popish and vents part of the discontent they carry secretly in their bosoms. The language is very venomous but the effect is that in private causes I am indifferent just but that if the king or the church be concerned there is no right to be expected from me; that I bring in new laws and proceed in the plantations with an intent to overthrow the old law and in time the old religion.' The anxiety of the Catholics over Strafford's plantation policy was not likely to strike many chords in Protestant

[23] The sources for these paragraphs can be found in Terence Ranger, op. cit., chaps. 9 and 10.

[24] See esp.: Strafford to Laud, 22 Oct. 1633 (Strafford MSS., letter book 8, pp. 34–35); Strafford to Laud, Dec. 1633 (ibid., letter book 6, pp. 3–9).

breasts whether in Ireland or England. But their anxiety over Strafford's partiality towards Church and Crown was a different matter. On this issue the 'popular' opposition in England heard not only the cries of the Catholics but of fellow Protestants. 'Like wolves', wrote the Earl of Cork's agent, Walley, 'the churchmen now look and con about where to snatch and catch a prey, not regarding either right or wrong, but where they set on they must be served and no people so ravenous as they, for they grow insatiable . . . as they are now backed there will be no more questioning of titles or interests but present possession.' 'We are like to suffer very much misery', wrote a small 'new English' landowner in Munster, 'between the church and the subsidies. The one, I think, will take from us all our lands and the other all our monies.' These were outcries which the English opposition heard with much alarm and fellow feeling.[25]

Of the propriety of Strafford's actions in cases like these there may be some dispute. Strafford himself believed that because the Crown and the Church had been defrauded in the past and because the common law could make no reparation for their losses, it was right to sweep away legal quibbles or to exploit legal quibbles against the landowner. Strafford's biographers of the 1930s all agreed that he was justified in this opinion. Yet objections to his actions came not only from self-interested landowners but also from lawyers who believed that it was completely wrong for the government itself to strain and manipulate the law and thus to introduce the element of the arbitrary and the uncertain. To put it at its lowest there is more substance in this view than Strafford's biographers were prepared to admit. At any rate, whatever one may feel about their propriety, there can be no doubt about their unwisdom. In transactions like the Birnes' Country affair Strafford was making enemies, losing friends and leaving himself open to damaging allegations against which only the King could defend him. In his attack on the owners of Church property Strafford was attempting to undo the work of thirty or forty years and even if he did not have time to complete the task of demolition it was clear that no property-owner in Ireland could count himself secure under Strafford's rule. Just as historians have always blamed Mary

[25] Strafford to Coke, 2 Mar. 1635 (Strafford MSS., letter book 5, pp. 175–190); Walley to Cork, 7 Aug. 1639 (Boyle MSS., Chatsworth, vol. 19, no. 69); John Boyle to Cork, 29 May 1640 (ibid., vol. 21, no. 19).

I for her folly in supposing that it would be possible to restore the monastic lands, or blamed Laud for his folly in supporting a policy of enforced uniformity and ecclesiastical resumption in Scotland, so they should blame Strafford for the supreme lack of political judgement shown in his attack on the Irish common law as a bulwark of property rights. Together with Laud's Scottish policy, Strafford's Irish administration was fatal to the Personal Government of Charles I. The English opposition could be in no doubt of the implication of Charles's policy when they heard of the arrogance of Strafford's demanding bishops; of Sir George Radcliffe's latest cleverness; of the latest rebuke delivered by the the Lord Deputy to a judge clinging to the old concepts of property law.[26] In this sense there was a profound truth in the charge brought against Strafford at his trial that he had attempted to subvert the fundamental laws of the kingdom.

One last point must be made. Strafford did not only sharpen the conflict because of the melodrama in his personal view of it; nor did he only confirm the worst suspicions of the English opposition. He also attracted to himself personally a hatred even greater than might have been expected. The 'new English' landowner and the Parliamentary opposition regarded Strafford not only as an enemy but as a treacherous and immoral enemy. For this they had from their own point of view much justification. Strafford was one of those idealists who are so sure of their own rectitude and so certain of the justice of their own ends that they cut through or exploit conventional social morality. Strafford despised the conventions of patronage and the concepts of personal obligation which alone gave a sort of moral discipline to Irish society. He despised them—and he exploited them with supreme short-term success. Strafford was always able to outwit the very experienced and able men around him in Ireland because he was unpredictable—both in the sense that he would do things which were not, in seventeenth-century Ireland, done; and also in the sense that he would do things which did not seem to be politically possible. He was always doing either the unexpected or the unthinkable. We have already seen examples of this—in his disregard of his obligations towards Carlisle; in the simple duplicity of his handling of complaints against Cork in the Castle Chamber, where he would privately command a curate to complain and publicly bully him

[26] Strafford to Coke, 7 Dec. 1633 (Strafford MSS., letter book 5, pp. 27–29).

for doing so. There are innumerable other examples. One such is his handling of Cork while the attack on him was being prepared. Strafford deliberately deceived Cork into a feeling of false security by helping to arrange a match between Cork's eldest son and his own niece, Elizabeth Clifford, and by giving Cork and his friends the sort of assurances which in the normal operation of the patronage system would have meant the close alliance of the two men. Then, when the attack was prepared, Strafford did what he could to have the marriage broken off. This disregard for the normal conventions continued throughout his assault on Cork. Strafford thought nothing of assuring Clifford that he was with great difficulty restraining the King from ordering that charges be brought against Cork, at the very moment that he was, in fact, urging the King to allow him to bring such charges. He thought nothing of promising Cork that he would not write to England on a particular aspect of the case and then immediately writing several pages to Laud about it.[27]

Even when Cork and the other 'new English' discovered that they could not take the new Lord Deputy at face value, they were still baffled by him. To Cork, for instance, it was obvious that when Strafford fell out with his last great 'new English' ally, Lord Chancellor Loftus, he would need to look about for new friends. It did not occur to Cork that Strafford could be intending to carry on without any allies of significance in Ireland and consequently Cork refused to join in Loftus's attack on Strafford and offered his alliance to the Lord Deputy. But Strafford did intend to carry on without allies and rejected Cork's overtures out of hand. Such a decision was incomprehensible to the shrewd Irish politicians but Strafford relished the fact that they saw him as 'one of the oddest deputies that ever came here'. To them he was, in Sir William Parsons's words after Strafford's fall, 'that strange man'—unpredictable, faithless, hateful with his sermons about public morality and his great possessions, with his code of honesty of purpose and his frequent betrayals of their social code. It is this rather than the vileness of Strafford's enemies which accounts for the bitterness of the attack on him in 1640.[28]

Strafford, then, was not a man above all consideration of self, with a splendid and feasible policy, betrayed by his master. But he

[27] Ranger, op. cit., chap. 10.
[28] Strafford to Laud, 22 Oct. 1633 (Strafford MSS., letter book 8, pp. 34–35).

was more than an exceptionally energetic and self-deluded seventeenth-century politician. He was a man who not only saw his role in heroic terms but who actually tried to effect the impossible. He was a man so far from typical that his 'oddity' aroused the resentment and hatred, half selfish, half honest, of other men. As we have seen, Dr. Kearney believes that the fateful Irish rebellion was precipitated by Strafford's deputyship. In addition, his policy and his personality powerfully contributed to the disaster in England itself and to the implacable character of the opposition to the Crown. Strafford was, above all, a man who brought disaster.

Colaiste Oideachais Mhuire Gan Smal Luimneach

XII

THE ALIENATED INTELLECTUALS OF EARLY STUART ENGLAND*

Mark H. Curtis

THREE hundred years ago Thomas Hobbes, the inveterate critic of Oxford his Alma Mater and her sister Cambridge, laid a heavy charge against the two ancient English universities. He found them guilty of breeding sedition. 'The core of rebellion . . . ,' he wrote in passion, 'are the universities'.[1] As he developed his specifications against them, he likened them to the wooden horse of Troy. Out of them had poured in the years preceding the English Civil War, just as earlier in the centuries of popish superstition, the chief corrupters of the King's loyal subjects. They produced and let loose upon Stuart England both Puritan ministers and disobedient ambitious gentlemen. He put his point in these words:

> As the Presbyterians brought with them into their churches their divinity from the universities, so did many of the gentlemen bring their politics from thence into the parliament. . . . And though it be not likely that all of them did it out of malice, but many of them out of error, yet certainly the chief leaders were ambitious ministers and ambitious gentlemen; the ministers envying the authority of bishops, whom they thought less learned; and the gentlemen envying the privy council, whom they thought less wise than themselves. For it is a hard matter

[1] *Behemoth* in *The English Works of Thomas Hobbes of Malmesbury*, ed. Sir William Molesworth (London, 1840), vi, p. 236.

* From no. 23 (1962).

for men, who do all think highly of their own wits, when they have also acquired the learning of the university, to be persuaded that they want any ability requisite for the government of a commonwealth. . . .[2]

As this passage suggests, Hobbes traced back the streams of rebellion to a source in the courses of study at Oxford and Cambridge. The divinity imbibed at the two universities enabled the Presbyterian clergy to appear to the people as men more righteous than others—the only true ministers of Christ and ambassadors of God. It gave to their preaching the power to bring men into great dependence upon them and provided the doctrines that taught Englishmen to look upon the King and the bishops as their oppressors. The politics that the universities instilled came from the study of Greek and Roman history and philosophy. In reading about the deeds and thoughts of the famous men of antiquity, young gentlemen learned to extol popular government 'by the glorious name of liberty' and disgrace monarchy 'by the name of tyranny'.[3] Thus, by the education that they provided, Oxford and Cambridge bred the seducers of the people and brought the kingdom to disobedience and rebellion.

For those who enjoy comparative studies of historical movements, Hobbes's indictment of the universities will provide much titillation. It will excite comparison with charges made in other post-revolutionary periods and perhaps provoke the formulation of some general law of human behaviour. My purpose in outlining it here is, however, less exalted. I find it interesting because it points to an important but slighted aspect of early Stuart England.[4] Up to a point I agree with Hobbes. The universities were dangerous to English society in the early seventeenth century. I also agree that their success in educating divines and young gentlemen

[2] ibid., pp. 192–3.

[3] ibid., pp. 168, 193–6.

[4] Christopher Hill has briefly treated the subject of this paper in examining the effect of pluralism on the Church. See his *Economic Problems of the Church* (Oxford, 1956), pp. 238–9. Although we have arrived at our conclusions independently and although each of us has used slightly different terms to explain the phenomenon, our findings with respect to the clergy are fundamentally the same. My purposes in elaborating on the matter are to present as fully as possible the evidence upon which these conclusions are based and to show how this type of analysis can also be extended to include laymen.

was the source of this danger. I part company with the crusty philosopher and opinionated observer of his own times at two points: in making the universities the principal cause of rebellion and in specifying that the courses of study pursued at Oxford and Cambridge necessarily and almost inexorably inspired disloyalty and disobedience.

To make such qualifications of Hobbes's argument is not to deny that the English universities provided opportunities for Puritans to instil their ideas and attitudes in the minds of young men nor to discount entirely the possibility that learning in the *literae humaniores* might arouse sympathy for popular forms of government. Elsewhere and at considerable length I have shown that the university Puritans—though harassed—were never suppressed in the early seventeenth century and remained a significant faction at both Oxford and Cambridge until the 1630s.[5] Occasionally a rash man among them made pronouncements that would seem to justify Hobbes's judgement. On Palm Sunday, 1622, William Knight, an Oxford don, preached a sermon at St. Peter's in the East which expounded the offensive doctrine that in disputes over religion it was lawful for subjects to oppose by force of arms the ungodly decrees of their sovereign. He had found some of his arguments in a Heidelberg professor's recently published book—a Calvinist commentary on St. Paul's teachings on obedience to civil authorities in the thirteenth chapter of Romans.[6] Likewise reading in classical literature, especially in classical history, sometimes suggested dangerous reflections on contemporary affairs. In commenting on Tacitus's account of the transformation of Rome from a monarchy to a republic Isaac Dorislaus, Lord Brooke's professor of history at Cambridge, described the power of the Roman people under their kings, related the details of Tarquin's attack on their liberties, and finally fell to justifying his countrymen, the Dutch, for defending their liberties against the oppressions of Spain. In short, according to one report, 'he was conceived of by some to speak too much for the defence of the liberties of the people, though he spake with great moderation and with an exception of such monarchies as ours. . . .' In the end, even though he squared

[5] Mark H. Curtis, *Oxford and Cambridge in Transition, 1558–1642* (Oxford, 1959), pp. 207–11, 225–6.

[6] Anthony Wood, *The History and Antiquities of the University of Oxford*, ed. John Gutch, 2 vols. (Oxford, 1796), ii, pp. 341–5.

himself with the Cambridge authorities, Dorislaus discontinued his lectures.[7]

Some of the teaching and influences at Oxford and Cambridge, as these examples indicate, undoubtedly strengthened Puritan consciences and quickened love of liberty, yet the content of university education, despite Hobbes, was not the direct cause of resistance to authority and ultimately of civil war. One would have to be as authoritarian as Hobbes himself both to ignore the short-sightedness and foolishness of one side and to lay all the blame on the other: in other words, to overlook official acts that first generated discontent and then exacerbated it. And what is perhaps more to the point, neither Puritanism nor love of liberty gave rise to serious radical or revolutionary proposals before 1641. Puritanism, to be sure, sought changes in ecclesiastical ceremonies and discipline, but until 1630 the early Stuart Puritans were on the whole more moderate than their Elizabethan forerunners and would have probably settled for changes that could have been accommodated to episcopacy. Furthermore, despite the fears of James I, Puritanism led few if any men before 1646 to adopt republican views in political affairs. Neither did ambitious gentlemen advance such seditious ideas before the Civil War. A learned Member of Parliament might compare Buckingham to Sejanus, but he hastened to protest his loyalty to Charles and expressed no desire to pull down monarchy with the favourite.[8]

The effect of university education on Stuart politics operated in more subtle but nonetheless significant ways than those that Hobbes condemned. The universities were dangerous—though not the 'core of rebellion'—because they were, paradoxical as it may seem, too successful in carrying out their primary task of training men for service to Church and State. As vigorous, effective institutions of higher education they unwittingly worked against the

[7] C. H. Cooper, *Annals of the University of Cambridge*, 4 vols. (Cambridge, 1842–52), iii, p. 201.

[8] In his speech delivered on 10 May 1626 at the impeachment of Buckingham, Eliot explicitly stated that the commons did not in any sense 'lay an odium or aspersion on his majesty's name; they hold him spotless. . . .': John Rushworth, *Historical Collections* (London, 1721), i, p. 354. In explaining his words after his imprisonment Eliot said that 'he, in none of these examples, [intended] to parallel times, or any other person, but the Duke': *Commons Journals*, i, p. 861. Cf. Harold Hulme, *The Life of Sir John Eliot* (London, 1957), p. 143.

peace and tranquillity of the realm not because they instilled subversive doctrines but because they prepared too many men for too few places. Having been geared to the extraordinary demands for trained men which the Elizabethan Church and State made upon them, they poured out more educated talent than early Stuart society in its unreformed condition could put to work in ways that would contribute either to its own health or to the satisfaction of the individuals concerned. As Lord Chancellor Ellesmere so succintly put the matter in a conference between the bishops and the judges as early as 1611:

> It is somewhat hard . . . that £8 per annum should be thought a sufficient maintenance for him who hath *curam animarum* when many in this company doth make better allowance to their grooms who have but *curam equorum* and I think that we have more need of better livings for learned men than of more learned men for these livings, for learning without living doth but breed traitors as common experience too well sheweth.[9]

The success of the universities thus became a double-acting acid within early Stuart society: in the first place it exposed the depths of abuse in the old corruption and hence made it less tolerable than ever, and at the same time it precipitated an insoluble group of alienated intellectuals who individually and collectively became troublemakers in a period of growing discontent with the Stuart régime.

The men to whom the term 'alienated intellectuals' is herein applied are not to be understood as being primarily an economically oppressed and exploited class. As I shall show below, some undoubtedly had reason to think of themselves in such ways, yet most of them probably received adequate livings in one form or another. Nor were they wholly unattached or isolated within English society. Frustration rather than exploitation or absolute isolation was the common experience of these men. They suffered frustration in the pursuit of their professions or careers, for opportunities to use their training and talents to the full were not available to them. As a consequence they frequently had to accept

[9] Conference between the bishops and the judges before the privy council on the jurisdiction of the Court of High Commission, 23 May 1611, Folger Lib. MS. V.a. 121, f. 124.

posts or roles which, no matter how remunerative, could not entirely satisfy them. These positions gave them employment and livelihood but left them restless and critical because they neither offered sufficient challenge to their sense of duty nor appeased their self-esteem and desire for recognition and honour. If in time some satisfactions did accrue to them, they frequently came in ways that were perverse. In other words these men, both clergymen and laymen, while they were within Stuart society, did not share all the opportunities, privileges, and responsibilities that were the perquisites of full unequivocal membership in that community. Being thus to some degree alienated from it, especially from its inner circles, they simultaneously viewed certain aspects of it with greater realism and objectivity than many of their contemporaries and yet on critical occasions acted and spoke irresponsibly. They were, to use a modern phrase, 'angry young men', but 'angry young men' whose bitterness grew to be far more intense than that of their twentieth-century counterparts.

To appreciate the growth of an alienated class among the clergy, one must recall the conditions of the Elizabethan Church that provided extraordinary stimulus to university development in the late sixteenth century. It is well known, for instance, that immediately after Elizabeth's accession, the Church had need for large numbers of educated clergymen. By 1558 England had in the short space of twenty-five years passed through a succession of religious changes, going from medieval Catholicism to Henrician Catholicism, to moderate Protestantism, to radical Protestantism, and finally back to communion with Rome. Aside from leaving the ordinary Englishman uncertain about what he should believe and how he should worship, these changes had decimated the clergy: many suffered deprivation; some resigned. At the accession of Elizabeth not only were ten bishoprics vacant but at least 10 to 15 per cent of the parish churches were without incumbents. In the dioceses of London and Canterbury some populous archdeaconries had vacancies in one-third of their parishes. Pluralists and unordained readers could not and did not make up for these deficiencies. Furthermore, only a small fraction of the clergy holding livings were qualified and licensed to preach. In many places such a condition had existed for at least five years; in some for a decade or more. At any time and place in the life of the Church such a condition would have been serious. In a Protestant country still in the throes of the Reformation it was perilous.[10] The only remedy lay in training sufficient clergymen to preach and to minister to the spiritual needs of the nation.

In the face of such conditions ecclesiastics exhorted the magnates and gentlemen of England to support the universities and urged Oxford and Cambridge to double and redouble their efforts to educate a learned clergy. Bishop John Jewel, the great apologist for the Church of England, pleaded on one occasion:

> View your universities: view your schools, which ever have been nurseries to this purpose [of training ministers]. Alas! how many shall you find in both the universities, and in all the schools through England, not only that are already ripe, but also that are minded to the ministry? If they be not found there, alas! where think you to have them? . . . Think you that they will spring out of the ground, or drop down from the heavens? No, no, they be of you, and must be bred and reared amongst you. If there be none to be found, nor hope of any to be hereafter, be you well assured that acts of parliament and proclamations are not enough to content the conscience of the people, and to build up the temple.[11]

During the years of Elizabeth's reign the state of the Church underwent considerable improvement. In 1603 it was still far from perfect, but the worst of the abuses had been overcome and in some respects further changes could not have been made without fundamental reorganization of the economic foundations and territorial divisions of the parishes. No government of the time, even though it had some awareness of the nature of these problems, could conceivably undertake these radical reforms. Indeed they only came with the general transformation of English institutions and society that took place in the nineteenth century. Within such limits, however, there had been significant changes. In 1603, according to a survey of the clergy made at the command of the King, there were in the 9,244 parishes in England and Wales, 4,830 licensed preachers and 3,804 men with university degrees.

10 W. H. Frere, *The English Church in the Reigns of Elizabeth and James I* (London, 1924), pp. 104–9.

11 'Sermon on Haggai, i. 2–4', in *The Works of John Jewel*, ed. John Ayre (Parker Society, Cambridge, 1847), ii, p. 999. For similar sentiments, see *The Works of James Pilkington, B.D.*, ed. James Scholefield (Parker Society, Cambridge, 1842), p. 593.

Many of the rest of the clergy had undoubtedly spent some time in the universities.[12]

The most perplexing abuses still left in the Church were largely the consequences of the difficult and extremely complex economic problems of the Church, the nature of which Christopher Hill has skilfully delineated in his recent book. Pluralism and non-residency quite naturally arose from them. Although in the largest diocese of the realm, pluralists had decreased in number between the years 1585 and 1603 from 140 to ninety, a low estimate for the state of the Church as a whole in 1603 shows that 1,000 clergymen still held 2,500 livings.[13] Furthermore, in the seventeenth century pluralism was probably rising. Between 1600 and 1640 the number of pluralists in the dioceses of Oxford and Worcester increased from eighteen to thirty-three. By the latter date, even defenders of the Establishment were calling the cathedral chapters—the haunts of the worst pluralists—'receptacles for drones and non-residents'. Such evidence would appear to indicate that in the early seventeenth century the number of good livings in the Church available to university men was if anything in decline.[14]

Under the circumstances it is difficult, to say the least, to estimate how many new ministers the Church needed each year. At best such an estimate can only be an approximation. The available statistics are neither complete nor entirely reliable. Yet even a rough idea, so long as it is conservatively formulated, will help in giving concreteness to an understanding of the nature and size of the class of alienated intellectuals.

Two factors must be used in making such an estimate: (1) the

[12] R. G. Usher, *The Reconstruction of the English Church*, 2 vols. (London and New York, 1910), i, p. 241. Usher made his tabulations from BM MS. Harl. 280, f. 157. Another version of the results of this survey is to be found in Add. MS. 38139, ff. 254v–55. This is apparently a copy of the report shown by Archbishop Whitgift to Sir Peter Manwood. It gives a total of 9,044 instead of 9,244 parishes in England and Wales and 4,792 preachers instead of 4,830. I have used Usher's figures because whatever error they may contain is of the kind that will make my estimate of the oversupply of clerical candidates on the conservative side, i.e. too small rather than too large.

[13] R. G. Usher, *Reconstruction*, i, p. 211. Usher thought that this estimate was too high, but for reasons that seem more cogent to me than Usher's opinion, Hill believes that it is, if anything, too low. See Hill, *Economic Problems of the Church*, pp. 225–6.

[14] Hill, op. cit., pp. 226–7, 230.

total number of church livings or places and (2) the longevity of clergymen in early Stuart times. Of these the first can be calculated more exactly than the second. As noted earlier, the best contemporary ecclesiastical surveys put the number of parishes in England and Wales at the figure of 9,244. There were as well approximately 1,200 non-parochial church livings in cathedrals, universities, and colleges. Of these latter places 674 were in cathedrals or collegiate churches like Westminster Abbey. The total number of places can therefore with some certainty be set at 10,500. Since pluralism had come to stay, a realistic calculation must also take it into account. Using the conservative estimate cited above, namely that 1,000 clergymen held 2,500 livings or, to put it more usefully, 1,000 clergymen held 1,500 livings in addition to their principal ones, the total of 10,500 livings in England and Wales must be reduced for the purposes of this analysis to 9,000.

To determine the number of clergy needed in the Church annually, this total must now be divided by a factor that is an estimate of the longevity of the clergy after ordination. Although this is a much more uncertain matter than calculating the number of actual places in the Church, one point to remember in this connection is that the life expectancy of a man who had in the seventeenth century survived the hazards of infancy, childhood, and adolescence was much longer than that of the population at large. Guideposts for making such an estimate can therefore be found in a couple of samples of the population made up largely of adults or near adults whose living conditions would not be far different from those of the clergy themselves. I have, for instance, taken as one sample all the persons born between the years 1558 and 1640 whose names begin with the letter F and for whom the *Dictionary of National Biography* gives data about births and deaths. The average life span of this group, despite the fact that it includes men like Thomas Felton and Guy Fawkes whose lives were cut short by the executioner, was 61 years and their median age at death was 63 years.[15] Another sample can be found in the matriculants in Gonville and Caius College, Cambridge, for whom much vital information is published in the admirable catalogue compiled by John Venn. In this case it appears that the average life span of

[15] This group is made up of 148 persons, of whom three died between the ages of 21 and 30, twelve lived to be over 80 and one over 90. Most of them, 104 or more than two-thirds, died between the ages of 51 and 80.

an Elizabethan or Jacobean student was 60 years. This result, of course, is based on a group of persons several of whom died from plague or other causes in college before they had reached their majority.[16] In either case these figures suggest that a man who was ordained at the canonical age of 23, or within a few years thereafter, could in the seventeenth century usually expect to serve the Church for thirty years or a little more. In actuality, those matriculants of Caius College who later became ordained and for whom vital information is known served on the average for a period of twenty-nine years and eight months.[17] Therefore a factor of twenty-seven years and six months for the average term of service for a clergyman in the seventeenth century would seem to be a conservative estimate. Applying it to the total number of places in the Church results in an estimate that normally 327 vacancies would occur each year.

The usual source of supply for vacancies in the Church was the pool of men educated in the universities. In the course of the Elizabethan period Oxford and Cambridge had geared themselves to meet an unusual demand for trained talents in both Church and State. By the close of Elizabeth's reign, they were drawing abreast of the needs of the Church and in the first decade of the Stuart period they had, I believe, surpassed them. Both enrolments and the number of graduates increased rapidly in the last half of the sixteenth century. In 1564 Cambridge had a membership of only 1,267 privileged persons. By 1622 it was reported to have more than 3,000 students. The number of degrees granted rose proportionately. In the first five years of Elizabeth's reign only fifty-four men a year proceeded B.A. at Cambridge. Thirty years later this number had grown to 177 a year. This development reached its peak in the seventeenth century. For the years 1617 to 1637 Cam-

[16] In making this sample, I did not use all the matriculants, but only those for selected years: namely, for the years 1565/6 to 1569/70 inclusive, 1585/6 to 1589/90 inclusive, and 1605/6 to 1609/10 inclusive. John Venn, *et al.*, eds., *Biographical History of Gonville and Caius College*, 5 vols. (Cambridge, 1897–1948), i, pp. 57–66, 126–41, 189–209. This sample totals 105 persons. A higher proportion of this group than of the first died young. Three died under the age of 20 and seven between 21 and 30. Only five became octogenarians. Again over two-thirds of them—seventy-three to be exact—died between the ages of 51 and 80.

[17] ibid., length of service varied in these cases from four years to fifty years after ordination.

bridge turned out an annual average of 266 B.A.s. Oxford experienced similar changes. In the decade from 1571 to 1580 matriculations at Oxford averaged 191 a year. After jumping to 340 a year in the succeeding decade, they declined slightly and levelled off at approximately 300 a year in the early seventeenth century. Again the record of degrees granted followed the same pattern. In the five years from 1571 to 1575, 103 men a year proceeded B.A. at Oxford. In the five years ending in 1621, the graduates at Oxford numbered 222 annually. By the 1630s, though a slight decline had occurred, the total was still well above the Elizabethan average.[18]

To sum up the situation, the two universities were in the early seventeenth century graduating more than 450 men each year and were matriculating another 200 to 250 who did not take degrees. Of course, not all these men sought careers in the Church. One of the striking features of Elizabethan England was that young gentlemen began to flock to the universities. By 1600 the sons of the gentry and nobility may have outnumbered the students of lesser status in Oxford and Cambridge. Under these circumstances probably only 75 per cent or 337 of the annual number of graduates and only 40 per cent or ninety of the annual number of non-graduates can be considered candidates for the ministry. In other words, of the total number of students going down each year from the universities, about 427—or 100 more than were needed—were available to supply vacancies in the Church.[19]

Evidence that the universities were meeting, and indeed surpassing, the needs of the Church is not wanting. In the years 1606 and 1607, 97 per cent of the men ordained in the diocese of Lincoln were university trained and nearly 90 per cent of these university men were graduates.[20] Even more revealing is a story that can be

18 Cooper, *Annals of Cambridge*, ii, pp. 207, 269; iii, p. 148; Venn, op. cit., i, p. xxi, n.1; Andrew Clark, ed., *Register of the University of Oxford*, vol. ii, in 4 parts (Oxford, 1887–9), pt. ii, p. 410; pt. iii, p. 448; Curtis, *Oxford and Cambridge in Transition*, pp. 3–4, 150; Bodl. Lib. MS. Wood F. 14. I am indebted to Mr. Lawrence Stone for the information about Oxford B.A.s in the 1630s.

19 Venn concluded from two samples of Caius graduates that in the early seventeenth century 78 per cent of them took orders. *Biographical History of Caius*, i, p. xxi, n. 1.

20 C. W. Foster, *The State of the Church . . . in the Diocese of Lincoln* (Linc. Rec. Soc., 1926), i, p. lviii.

discovered by comparing visitation records from the first decade of the seventeenth century with those dating from the 1630s. A good series of these exist for the diocese of London and there one can see that by the 1630s many parishes that earlier had only a vicar or a curate now have both vicar and curate and sometimes a schoolmaster as well, all with degrees.[21] Miss Barratt, in her study of the clergy in the dioceses of Oxford, Worcester, and Gloucester, found the same kind of evidence, and with respect to the curates learned that they were not only more highly educated in the 1630s than before but also more permanently situated, perhaps because they had less opportunity to improve their state by moving. She remarks:

> It was rare throughout the sixteenth century for a curate to have a degree. . . . They were a wandering class rarely settling for long in one parish. . . . In Oxford diocese the curates of the sixteen thirties were a very different group of men. Of 46 who subscribed on being licensed to curacies between May 1631 and October 1635 each except one described himself as either a master or a bachelor of arts, and call books from 1630 to 1641 show that these men were serving cures for longer periods.[22]

The conditions in which the supply of clergymen was greater than the need for them gave the authorities in the Church a great advantage in dealing with Puritans who refused to conform to ecclesiastical laws and regulations. But of even greater importance was the part it played in creating a class of dissatisfied and alienated intellectuals within the clergy. As the shortage of ministers was transformed into an oversupply, this change brought the abuses within the Church into even more prominence than ever before. Now they began to affect in direct, immediate, and painful ways the prospects and fortunes of a small but growing number of articulate people. Abuses such as pluralities and non-residence, which even James I and Bancroft acknowledged as undesirable, became in the eyes of these men and their sympathizers intolerable evils. Impatience with them could be heard in the way that critics

[21] London Guildhall Lib., MS. 9537, vol. x (Episcopal visitation book, 1607), vol. xiii (Episcopal visitation book, 1628), vol. xiv (Episcopal visitation book, 1636), and vol. xv (Episcopal visitation book, 1637).

[22] (Miss) D. M. Barratt, 'The Condition of the Parochial Clergy from the Reformation to 1660, with Special Reference to the Dioceses of Oxford, Worcester, and Gloucester' (D.Phil. thesis, Oxford, 1949), pp. 49–51.

refuted arguments used to justify them. To the claim that pluralities were necessary in order to provide large enough clerical incomes to encourage learning, the House of Commons, invoking experience as their authority, answered that 'pluralists heaping up many livings into one hand do by that means keep divers learned men from maintenance, to the discouragement of students and the hindrance of learning'.[23]

Discouraged some students of divinity may have been, but few of them suffered the despair that would have made them give up their studies. Hence the universities continued to provide them the usual rewards for their academic achievements and they departed to find such posts as they could. The large majority of them did, of course, eventually get regular livings, even though many were of small value. Of the surplus, some became chaplains in private households. More than a few magnates in Stuart England patronized discontented clerics, both those who had recently come from the universities and others whose places after suspension or deprivation had been filled by university men. One or two little-known examples will show the extent of the practice: Lord William and Lady Elizabeth Russell gave aid and maintenance to several silenced ministers in the first decade of the seventeenth century, including Thomas Taylor and Humphrey Fenn; Lord de la Warr in those years gave refuge to the notorious Anthony Erbury.[24] Other graduates for whom there were no places found a vocation in teaching school or in practising medicine. Most, however, either eked out a living as underpaid curates or entered a calling which though it was in the Church was not of it—that of a lecturer.

The position of curates in the early seventeenth century cannot be fully defined until more investigations like Dr. Barratt's have revealed for representative dioceses of the realm their number, status, and degree of conformity to ecclesiastical laws. At this stage it is nonetheless worthwhile to note the factors that probably contributed to a sense of alienation among them. In the first place they were the lowest paid among the financially hard-pressed clergy.

[23] 'Petition concerning Religion, 1610', J. R. Tanner, ed., *Constitutional Documents of the Reign of James I* (Cambridge, 1930), p. 79.

[24] PRO Star Cham. Proc. 8/252/1, a case in which Lord Russell tried to break his wife's will because he thought she had been over-generous to these men at the expense of her son's inheritance; PRO SP 15/8, no. 23.

Rarely did their stipends amount to more than £10 per annum.[25] Secondly they did not have any security of tenure. Their livings were not benefices or freeholds in the sense that they had an interest in them guaranteed either by ecclesiastical or common law. In other words they could be dismissed without the legal proceedings required in cases of deprivation of vicars and rectors. These two characteristics of their status could and did give rise to restlessness and discontent. In 1621, for instance, a Master of Arts who was curate of Newton chapel in the parish of Winwick, Lancashire, grew envious of his more fortunate neighbour, the rector. He became a convert to Rome, and conspired with some Catholic gentry of the parish to spread libels about his superior and to trump up charges in hopes of getting him deprived. Although suits before High Commission and Star Chamber and a near escape from death led him to recant and to make a public apology for his uncharitable dealings, his case aptly illustrates the kind of disruptive behaviour to which frustration might tempt ambitious men.[26] Outside Lancashire and the north such reactions more often than not contributed to the mounting tide of Puritanism. The fact that these decades saw most curacies filled by degree men only aggravated the situation.

Speaking qualitatively, lectureships were an even more disruptive outlet for the energies and talents of surplus clergymen than underpaid curacies. A lecturer was a stipendiary preacher who may or may not have held a regular church living but whose activities as a lecturer were not under the same kind of control as those at the parish clergy. He customarily preached or lectured at times other than the ordinary church services, most frequently on weekday mornings or afternoons. In the Elizabethan period the practice of establishing lectureships had in some measure compensated for the lack of preachers in the Church. In the early Stuart period it had become a means of circumventing the control of preaching by the ecclesiastical authorities. In these years it enjoyed tremendous growth in popularity, especially in the towns and under the patronage of the guilds and liveried companies by which it may be said to have perpetuated the medieval religious functions of those

[25] C. Hill, *Economic Problems*, pp. 113, 205–6.

[26] PRO Exch. K.R., Eccl. Docs., E. 135, 13/4, f. 105; Star Cham. Proc. 8/175/19, Josiah Horne, parson of Winwick *versus* John Gee, clerk, *et al.*; John Gee, *The Foot out of the Snare*, 4th edn. (London, 1624), pp. 95–96.

bodies. In some cases the lecturers received their salaries directly from patrons; in others they were hired by the aldermen of incorporated boroughs or cities who paid them from the revenues of the corporations; increasingly, however, they were supported by the proceeds of endowments bestowed on parishes and corporations. Professor W. K. Jordan has pointed out in his study of English philanthropy that in the eighty years from 1580 to 1660 a total of £70,267 18*s*., or 2.27 per cent of all charitable gifts for the much longer period from 1480 to 1660 was left for the establishment of lectureships. The greater part of this sum was given in the years from 1601 to 1640. In those four decades just preceding the Civil War the amount bestowed upon lectureships—£46,253—far exceeded the sum of £37,540 donated to increase the stipends of the parish clergy.[27]

The feature of lectureships that made them attractive objects of Puritan philanthropy caused embarrassment to the Stuart monarchs and their ecclesiastical officials. The lecturer did not have to be instituted by the bishop or his officers and was not subject, once he had received his licence to preach, to the same kind of episcopal control as the parish clergy. As James I was acute enough to sense, he belonged to 'a new body severed from the ancient clergy of England as being neither parsons, vicars, nor curates'.[28] In 1622 James tried rather anxiously to curb lecturers. He decreed that henceforth they had to be specially licensed by the Court of Faculties. In applying to that body for a licence they had to exhibit both the recommendation of a bishop and the 'fiat' or formal grant of permission from an archbishop confirmed by the Great Seal.[29] The very complexity of these regulations shows the anomaly of their position. Still they were not subjected to rigorous control until after 1633 when Laud's fear and dislike of them finally energized a policy of suppression. Thereafter visitation articles for dioceses governed by Laud's lieutenants contained special queries to uncover irregularities in the conduct of lectureships. The spirit with which these were administered burns even yet in the words used

[27] W. K. Jordan, *Philanthropy in England, 1480–1660* (London, 1959), pp. 300, 312–13, 375.

[28] 'Directions concerning Preachers (1622), sec. 6', PRO SP 14/132, no. 851; printed in Henry Gee and W. J. Hardy, *Documents illustrative of English Church History* (London, 1896), p. 518.

[29] ibid.

by Bishop Wren's Vicar-General to denounce lecturing in the diocese of Norwich in the year 1636. He wrote: 'The laic contributions and support hath made the ecclesiastic persons and ceremonies wag and dance after their pipe from whom they receive their livelihood.' He added: 'if his majesty shall in his princely care abolish that ratsbane of lecturing out of his churches . . . we shall have such a uniform and orthodox Church, as the Christian world cannot shew like; your lordship will excuse my silly zeal'.[30]

One aspect of the lecturers' reputation might make one suspect that they were not persons who would come within the compass of this study. More often than not since the seventeenth century they have been characterized as lacking in gravity and learning. Why this opinion took root and persisted so long can only be explained in terms of a prejudice so strong that it blinds men to the facts before them. For instance, an officer of the Bishop of Lincoln who during a visitation of that diocese in 1614 made a careful investigation of the lecturers was a victim of such a prejudice. His blindness appears in the recommendations that he made to reform the conduct of lectures. He urged among other things that the Bishop should 'exhort the doctors, bachelors of divinity, and masters of arts to undertake this great business and that non-graduates and bachelors of arts be totally left out'. In the light of the information that he compiled about the Lincoln lecturers this recommendation was fatuous. Of the seventy lecturers whom he listed by name, the degrees of two were unknown to him, only two were described by him as non-graduates, and only ten were Bachelors of Arts. Of the remaining 80 per cent, forty-nine were Masters of Arts, six were Bachelors of Divinity, and one was a Doctor of Divinity.[31] Although no comprehensive statistics of this sort are readily available for other dioceses, many cases like that of the learned and widely admired John Preston, Master of Queens'

[30] Bodl. Lib. MS. Tann. 68, ff. 2, 68v–69. The visitation articles concerning lecturing in the diocese of Norwich are to be found therein.

[31] 'A Visitation in the Diocese of Lyncolne, Anno Domini 1614', BM Add. MS. 5853, ff. 166v–168. This is William Cole's transcript of a copy of a manuscript furnished to Strype by Ralph Thoresby. I have collated my transcript with the original now in the Muniment Room of the Dean and Chapter of Lincoln Cathedral, MS. A4/3/43, and have found it accurate. This report has also been printed in *Associated Architectural Societies Reports and Papers*, vol. xvi, pt. i (Lincoln, 1881), pp. 31–54, a publication now hard to come by.

College, Cambridge, who preferred a lectureship to a bishopric, can be easily cited. There were of course exceptions to this as to other generalizations. One fraud in the diocese of Peterborough, who outraged both Puritans and reliable churchmen, claimed falsely that he had a degree from Trinity College, Dublin, a place sufficiently remote so that perhaps he thought his lie might escape detection.

As well-trained and respectably educated as the lecturers may have been, they were known in the seventeenth century as unreliable persons—unquiet spirits who were both arrogant and factious. The Lincoln visitor of 1614 criticized the men he investigated for behaving as if they believed in the parity of ministers. 'Oft time', he wrote, 'the man of lower degree, yea sometimes the non-graduate, is preferred in his course of preaching and in their sitting at table . . . even before the bachelor of divinity.' Neither did they show sufficient regard for the Canons of 1604. In their preaching they affected a method of preaching peculiar to themselves and censured any other 'as carnal, or at the best . . . academical'. They drew the multitudes who heard them to the conceit 'that the preaching of the Word is [not only] a principal, but even the sole and only means of man's salvation, and that all religious worship consists only of speaking and hearing'. By these signs they all appeared to him to be the 'factious spirits' that lectureships characteristically attracted.[32] All these comments reflect an uneasiness with the lecturers, partly because they did not fit neatly into the normal pattern of ecclesiastical life and partly because they exhibited an *esprit de corps* that both originated in their peculiar specialized function and marked their self-conscious alienation from the rest of the clergy. As most of them did not have regular church livings, they escaped the arduous cares of parish administration and the pastoral ministry. But they were denied in return the personal satisfaction of doing the full job for which they were called and trained. Their preoccupation with their own special duties would therefore tend to give them as compensation an exaggerated opinion of how important these were in the service of God and their fellow men. All of these features of their outlook and position distinguished them as men belonging to, and comprising the largest contingent of, the body of alienated intellectuals among the clergy.

[32] BM Add. MS. 5853, ff. 167v–168.

A vivid phrase from a speech in the Parliament of 1621 provides a link between the clerical and lay side of this story. In attacking the evil of the sale of offices, a member of the House of Commons said: 'That in the cheapness of all things offices grow dearer and are indeed of a greater price than benefices.'[33] Although this particular person opposed the sale of offices because buyers needed to resort to acceptance of bribes and extortion of excessive fees to recover their costs, and not because it prevented well-qualified men from serving the monarch, his words give an indication that in the State as well as in the Church offices were hard to come by. G. E. Aylmer has recently shown that such sentiments rose from actual conditions and not merely from the bitterness of disappointed office seekers.[34] In his analysis of the system of office-holding in the early seventeenth century, he shows that rigidity had set in. Opportunities to win honour and profit for oneself and to advance the good of one's prince and commonwealth were not growing in the financially hard-pressed Court of James I and were probably declining in Charles I's reign after 1629. Furthermore, under James I galloping venality and creeping monopoly had combined to poison the sources of patronage. They were not only distasteful but frequently revolting to some well-intentioned, prospective servants of the State. Complaints about the Court and the indignities of waiting on patrons and winning influence—complaints that are levelled against every system of patronage—took on in these years overtones of disillusionment and even disgust that had formerly been less obvious. Although merit, as Aylmer notes, might still recommend a candidate for office to a patron, patrimony operating through a system of purchases and reversions usually determined who held places under the Stuarts. The disregard of merit became especially flagrant in the days of Buckingham's ascendancy, when he virtually monopolized the distribution of patronage.

All of these points are relevant to this discussion of the role of the universities in the growing discontent with the Stuart régime.

[33] William Noy's speech, 3 May 1621, as reported by John Pym, *Commons Debates*, 1621, ed. Wallace Notestein, F. H. Relf, and H. Simpson, 7 vols. (New Haven, 1935), iv, p. 295; for other versions, see ibid., ii, p. 341; iii, p. 151; v, p. 137; vi, p. 131; and cf. i, p. 606.

[34] G. E. Aylmer, 'Office Holding as a Factor in English History, 1625–42', *History*, xliv (1959), pp. 229–232; see also Aylmer, *The King's Servants* (London, 1961), chap. iii; chap. iv, sec. iv.

Through most of the sixteenth century when the Tudors were increasing the power and responsibilities of the central Government, and therefore the chances for men to serve their prince, matters had been different. To be sure patronage and influence greased the wheels of the State then as later, but it seems to have been a less sticky and less contaminating kind of lubricant than that used in the seventeenth century. Moreover the changes that were both limiting and causing distaste for places in the service of the Prince were occurring just at the time that the universities were reaching the peak of their Renaissance development. As a result of what has been called a 'cultural revolution', young gentlemen and noblemen had since Elizabeth's accession been coming to Oxford and Cambridge in rising numbers. In the period between 1603 and 1640 this movement reached flood tide.[35]

The growing enrolment of young gentlemen in the universities is, however, only part of the problem. Another is related to what the sons of the gentry and nobility learned there. This is not to say that Hobbes was correct in denouncing the study of classical history. He was not, but one aspect of university education did generate discontent. The humanists of the sixteenth century, whose criticism of the university curriculum had wrought significant changes in the arts course, had taught Englishmen a lesson that they retained for at least a couple of generations. Not only did they effect a change in social ideals so that learning was accepted as one of the attributes of a gentleman but they instilled the idea that learning in the *literae humaniores* imparted that peculiar wisdom and judgement needed in the conduct of public affairs. Hence university men among the gentry had reason to pride themselves on being especially qualified to serve the State. The new scholars who appeared in Oxford and Cambridge may not indeed have all come to read for degrees but most of them were there to equip themselves for the life that hopefully lay before them. Gabriel Harvey sensed this fact as early as the 1580s. Forty years later Henry Peacham showed that this attitude toward university education had become a commonplace. In his book *The Compleat Gentleman* he warned his younger readers that in going to the university they were leaving childish things and entering on adult life and that the

[35] J. H. Hexter, 'The Education of the Aristocracy in the Renaissance', *Journal of Modern History*, xxii (1950), pp. 1–20; Curtis, *Oxford and Cambridge in Transition*, chap. iii.

industry and conduct shown there would be telling factors in determining their success or failure in later careers.[36] The practical consequences of such attitudes can be found in the letters of application written to patrons of the period. Wherever the applicant could honestly do so, he set forth the educational qualifications he had gained at the universities. One typical suitor, who was not blind to his own faults, asked the Earl of Salisbury to consider him for the post of clerk of the council in a letter that reads in part: 'I was brought up 18 years past in the University of Cambridge, having been master of arts and fellow of Jesus College, where though I played the truant yet I think I did not altogether lose my time.'[37]

Thus again the success of the universities—and in this connection perhaps someone ought also to give attention to the Inns of Court—was breeding trouble for the Stuarts. Oxford and Cambridge were striving to give young gentlemen the knowledge that would make them skilled and wise in the service of the monarch and to indoctrinate them with a sense of the high calling for which they were supposedly destined. Instead they seem to have prepared a goodly number of them for frustration. When one contrasts, for instance, the mediocrity that Professor David H. Willson found generally characteristic of the Privy Council under the first two Stuarts with the abilities of men like Sir Edwin Sandys, Sir John Eliot, John Pym, and John Selden, to name but a few university men who were actively interested in politics but failed to find satisfying positions in the King's service, the consequences of this conjunction of circumstances can begin to be fully appreciated.[38] Here again the outpouring of university men into a world unable to put their trained talents to constructive use generated impatience with the old corruption and helped create the body of men who would be among its most formidable opponents. Even as early as 1625 the feelings expressed by some of these men were becoming ominous in tone. One Member of Parliament, in sharply criticizing

[36] Henry Peacham, *The Compleat Gentleman*, ed. G. S. Gordon (Oxford, 1906), p. 38.

[37] Robert Kayle to Sir Michael Hicks, 13 May 1605, BM MS. Lansd. 89, f. 105. Kayle wanted Salisbury's help in securing the place and asked Hicks to intercede with Salisbury for him. There are many other examples of letters like this one among Hicks's papers.

[38] David H. Willson, *The Privy Councillors in the House of Commons, 1604–1629* (Minneapolis, 1940), pp. 82–98.

the sale of honours and offices, spoke in these terms:

If worthy persons have been advanced freely to places of greatest trust, I shall be glad. [But] Spencer was condemned in . . . 15 Edward II for displacing good servants about the king and putting in his friends and followers. . . . The like in part was laid by parliament on de la Pole.[39]

To understand that Oxford and Cambridge as effective institutions of higher education had been instrumental in creating a group of alienated intellectuals does not, of course, account for the principles and policies that suggested alternatives to the unreformed society of Stuart England. It merely explains how maladjustments within English society produced discontented individuals who provided some of the leadership to the opposition. On the other hand it was not merely historical accident that these men more often than not voiced Puritan religious doctrines and liberal constitutional ideals in expressing their criticism of what was, and in delineating their vision of what could be. The changes in Oxford and Cambridge that had made them successful institutions took place under the aegis of social, intellectual, and religious movements to which these opposition doctrines and ideals also owed some of their origins and nurture. It was therefore natural for the alienated intellectuals to find the means of remedying the abuses from which they suffered in idealisms so closely woven into the fabric of their existence. Hobbes, it can thus be seen, overstates his case against the universities by making the courses of study the source of rebellion. Although experiences at Oxford and Cambridge may have heightened awareness of opposition principles and may have increased capacities to understand and apply them, no such drastic indictment of the universities is needed to explain the espousal of Puritan and republican ideas by university men. In this matter Ellesmere was both more observant and more profound than Hobbes when he said that 'learning without living doth but breed traitors as common experience too well sheweth'.

Perhaps the proper conclusion to this paper is a word of caution, not to weaken what has been set forth but to keep it in perspective. At no time in the early Stuart period was this group of clergymen and laymen whom I have designated alienated intellectuals large in

[39] Speech in the parliament held in Oxford, 25 Aug. 1625, BM MS. Harl. 6846, f. 166v.

numbers. In the whole period from 1603 to 1640 the universities had probably enrolled less than 25,000 students. The proportion of those who became frustrated and alienated because their society had no satisfying callings for them would probably be no more than 15 to 20 per cent of that total. Furthermore, as far as the clergy was concerned, the graduates who could not find regular livings in the Church were only a part of the group of discontented critics. As Christopher Hill has shown, the economic privation suffered by many parsons also engendered restlessness and protest. Nor must it be forgotten that some men who held good livings were critics because of their principles. The importance of the group described did not, however, arise from its numerical strength, but rather from the character and training of its members. They were a significant segment of the educated, talented, sensitive, conscientious men in Stuart society—men who would be capable of giving leadership and direction to the causes that they shared in common with others. For that reason understanding of the social conditions that produced them—especially the unwitting role of the universities and other institutions of education—helps to explain the rising storm that shattered the Stuart system of government and swept England into the agonies of Civil War.

Colaiste Oideachais Mhuire Gan Smal Luimneach

XIII

WOMEN AND THE CIVIL WAR SECTS*

Keith Thomas

IN the seventeenth century, as at most other times, the family was the lowest unit of English society, but then especially it formed an intimate framework for the activity of everyone. 'Who anywhere', asked a preacher in 1608, 'but is of some man's family, and within some man's gates?'[1] Great efforts were made by the State and by local authorities to see that everybody was attached to a household, and the government displayed a strong prejudice against bachelors and masterless men. Upon the good management of families, it was universally agreed, the well-being of the commonwealth depended, an opinion which the inadequacy of contemporary methods of police and local government did much to justify. Those who thought about such things, moreover, knew from Aristotle and the Old Testament that the family was the oldest political society and that out of it emerged all subsequent government, either, as the Royalists were to hold, through the King's inheritance of original patriarchal power, or, according to more liberal thinkers, through the heads of families covenanting together to form a commonwealth. But one did not have to be a philosopher to realize that the father still retained much of his power. He was entitled to exact complete obedience from all his household and particularly from his children in such matters as choice of a career or marriage, for which his permission was essential. Indeed it was doubtful how far the State could interfere with the exercise of his

[1] W. Crashawe, *The Sermon preached at the Crosse, Feb. xiiij 1607* [London, 1608], p. 173.

* From no. 13 (1958).

powers within the family. As for matters outside the household, the master's voice spoke for all. In the seventeenth century references to 'popular consent' usually meant the consent of householders, and this class was smaller than one might think. The size of a household would, of course, vary according to the importance of the householder, but, to take an admittedly extreme example, Sheffield in 1615 was said to have a total population of 2,207: of these, only 260 counted as householders, women, children, servants and the poor making up the remainder.[2]

Since the Reformation the family had also become the lowest and most essential unit of government in the Church. The head of the household was required to see that his subordinates attended services and that children and servants were sent to be catechized. He was expected, moreover, particularly by the Puritans, to conduct daily worship at home and to see to the general spiritual welfare of all in his household. In return, the Church used its jurisdiction to preserve domestic order. The master was both king and priest to his household and upon his functioning adequately as such, it was felt, depended both the prosperity and the obedience of his family.

The place of women was determined in theory, and to a great extent in practice, by a universal belief in their inferior capacity and by reference to the specific commands for their subjection to be found in Genesis and the Epistles of St. Paul. Woman's destiny was marriage, preferably at an early age, and then the hazards of continual childbearing. She was allowed a voice in neither Church nor State, and it was expected that she should stay at home and busy herself with the (admittedly considerable) affairs of the household. As a married woman she could own no property, at least not by common law; her chief ornament was silence, and her sole duty obedience to her husband under God. The Puritans, by their exalted conception of family life, their protests against wife-beating and the double standard of sexual morality, and their denunciation of the churching of women, with its origin in the primitive view of woman as shameful and unclean, had done something to raise women's status, but not really very much. If the wife was a partner, she was still an inferior one. As for the much-vaunted Puritan love,

[2] J. Hunter, *Hallamshire . . .* , ed. A. Gatty (London, 1869), p. 148 (quoted in H. M. and M. Dexter, *The England and Holland of the Pilgrims* [London, 1906], p. 7).

it should be remembered that it came after marriage, not before; and that, as a popular manual remarked, 'we would that the man when he loveth should remember his superiority'.[3]

This patriarchal view of the family was given added meaning by the widely prevailing system of domestic production and by the practical self-sufficiency of most country households. It was seen as natural and reasonable, for, in the absence of a science of anthropology, and with the experiences of foreign travel still ill-digested, no one seriously imagined that any other form of family unit could exist; and finally it was invested with divine sanction by all the religious teaching of the day. If Christ's own remarks on the subject of the family had been ambiguous, none the less, later Christian teaching had taken it as fundamental and He himself had drawn upon it to symbolize the ideal relationship of God with man and of men with each other. And by contrast perhaps with the Middle Ages, the 'insistent theme' in Puritanism is that of God's Fatherhood. 'The word *Father*', wrote Sibbes, 'is an epitome of the whole gospel'.[4] The family was an integral part of what Dr. Tillyard has called the Elizabethan World Picture. This picture, if we leave out the astronomical trappings and take its main theme, which was that the structure of society in all its details was divinely ordained and must never be tampered with, was as much Caroline as Elizabethan. It stood for those twin concepts which had so powerful an emotive force for contemporaries—order and unity. To question the family, the place of women, or any other part of the social order, was to flaunt nature, reason and, above all, the will of God. It could only result in chaos and anarchy.

In this paper I wish to discuss the impact upon this patriarchal family in general and on women in particular of the Civil War sects. By these I mean the successors of the separatists who first appeared in Elizabethan England, who emigrated to Holland or to America to set up their independent congregations, or who continued to meet at furtive conventicles in this country, until they reappeared in great numbers in the early days of the Long Parliament, after which they enjoyed a large measure of practical toleration throughout the Interregnum. They were known by a

[3] J. Dod and R. Cleaver, *A Godly Forme of Housholde Government* . . . (London 1614), sigs. L5r–v.

[4] *Works*, ed. A. B. Grosart (Edinburgh, 1862–4), v, p. 25. See G. F. Nuttall, *The Holy Spirit* . . . (Oxford, 1946), p. 63.

variety of names—Brownists, Independents, Baptists, Millenarians, Familists, Quakers, Seekers, Ranters—and they represented a wide diversity of theological opinion. What they had in common was that they all were *sects*, that is, they believed in a pure Church, they made spiritual regeneration a condition of membership and insisted upon separation from a national Church which contained ungodly elements. More often than not they believed in the complete self-government of individual congregations; they usually thought in terms of direct inspiration by the Holy Spirit; and they tended to depreciate the role of a ministry, of 'outward ordinances' and of human learning. Their assertion of the spiritual equality of all believers led to an exalted faith in private judgement, lay preaching, a cult of prophecies and revelations, and culminated in the Quaker doctrine of the spirit dwelling in all men.

It is well known how in political matters this consciousness of direct relationship with God proved a great source of strength and these beliefs with their frequently democratic implications became a powerful solvent of the established order. I wish to argue here that their impact was felt not only by the State but also by the family.

From the very beginning the separatists laid great emphasis upon the spiritual equality of the two sexes. Would-be members of a congregation had to give proof of their individual regeneration, women as well as men. There was no reason to believe that women were any less likely to pass this test, nor were there any grounds for denying that a woman might be regenerate when her husband was not. And once admitted to the sect women had an equal share in church government. 'It followeth necessarily', wrote John Robinson, 'that one faithful man, yea, or woman either, may as truly and effectually loose and bind, both in heaven and earth, as all the ministers in the world'.[5]

Furthermore, women were numerically extremely prominent among the separatists. It is impossible to obtain a very accurate view of the size of the various sects in the seventeenth century, and even harder to ascertain the relative proportion of females in the overall total. Nevertheless, what evidence we do have is extremely suggestive. In the episcopal returns and indulgence documents of the reign of Charles II conventiclers are frequently described as being 'chiefly women', 'more women than men', 'most silly

[5] *Works*, ed. R. Ashton (London, 1851), ii, p. 158.

women' and so on. During the Civil War period it was a favourite gibe against the sectaries that their audience consisted chiefly of the weaker sex. Information extant about individual congregations suggests that it was quite usual for women to preponderate. At Norwich in 1645, for example, the congregation contained thirty-one men and eighty-three women. Of the twelve founder members of the Baptist church at Bedford in 1650, eight were women.[6] From the beginning of the eighteenth century individual church covenants and church books are more plentiful and afford numerous examples of the women being in a majority. This, of course, was by no means the rule and it is quite easy to produce instances of congregations where the opposite was the case. We should remember too the importance of women in religious bodies which were not sects—among the Scottish Presbyterians,[7] and the Roman Catholics in England, where, for a time, the law made it easier for a woman than a man to be a recusant. It is possible indeed to hold for the seventeenth century a theory of the greater natural religiosity of women. Many of them had more time for piety; they were less used to saving themselves by their own exertions, and their experiences in child-birth made them far more conscious of the imminence of death. Yet, when all the obvious objections have been made, it still remains true that in the sects women played a disproportionate role; and they received from them correspondingly greater opportunities.

There were said to be more women than men in the first large body of English separatists, in London in 1568;[8] and we know that later many left their husbands to go overseas to the Netherlands with Browne and Harrison.[9] These were not women of exceptional education or opportunity. Many, no doubt, had never left home

[6] G. L. Turner, *Original Records of early Nonconformity under Persecution and Indulgence* (London, 1911–14); J. Browne, *History of Congregationalism and Memorials of the Churches in Norfolk and Suffolk* (London, 1877), p. 254 n.; *The Church Book of Bunyan Meeting, 1650–1821*, ed. G. B. Harrison (London, 1928), p. v.

[7] The Scottish Privy Council reported of the field conventicles in 1684 that 'women were the chief fomenters of these disorders', *Register of the Privy Council of Scotland, 1683–4*, ed. P. Hume Brown (Glasgow, 1915), pp. 247–9, 367. See also (B. Whitelocke), *Memorials* (London, 1682), p. 512, and J. Anderson, *The Ladies of the Covenant* (Glasgow, 1851), *passim*.

[8] A. Peel, *The first Congregational Churches* (Cambridge, 1920), pp. 22, 32.

[9] *Tracts ascribed to Richard Bancroft*, ed. A. Peel (Cambridge, 1953), p. 88.

before and there is evidence to suggest that well over three-quarters of them were illiterate.[10] The sectaries attracted persons who in all probability had previously never been active members of any church. Coming from a lower order of society,[11] they were perhaps more used to mixing with women on a basis of rough and ready equality—or perhaps they were influenced by the greater freedom enjoyed by women among the Dutch—at all events the upshot was that the separatist churches made considerable concessions to women in the sphere of church government.

For this there was a good deal of precedent. In the Middle Ages anti-clerical movements frequently ended by exalting the claims not only of laymen but of lay women. The Lollards, for example, encouraged women to read the Bible and to recite the Scriptures at their meetings; several deposed on examination that perfect women were capable of the priesthood, and there is some evidence of actual preaching by Lollard women.[12] Even Occam admitted the possibility of some future occasion when the whole male sex might err and the true faith maintain itself only among pious women.[13] After the Reformation it was not unusual for Protestant leaders to admit that under exceptional circumstances, in a heathen country, for example, women might be allowed to preach as a temporary expedient.[14] But this conclusion was reluctant and largely theoretical and it was left to the radical sects to work out the logical consequences of the extreme Protestant position.

Among the English congregations in Holland opinion had varied. Francis Johnson thought that women should concern

[10] T. G. Crippen, 'The Brownists in Amsterdam', *Trans. Congregl. Hist. Soc.*, ii, 3 (1905), p. 171. Of the women married between 1598 and 1617 eighteen out of one hundred and fifteen could sign their names.

[11] The low social status of the leaders of the Family of Love is noted by W. Wilkinson, *A Confutation of certaine articles* (London, 1579), f. 30v.

[12] *Fasciculi Zizaniorum*, ed. W. W. Shirley (Rolls Series, London, 1858), pp. 422–3; *Registrum Johannis Trefnant*, ed. W. W. Capes (Canterbury and York Soc., London, 1916), pp. 341, 345–7, 364.

[13] G. V. Lechler, *John Wycliffe and his English precursors* (London, 1884), p. 47; *Dialogus*, I.v, xxxii, in *Monarchiae S. Romani Imperii* (Francofordiae, 1621), iii, p. 503.

[14] *Most fruitfull & learned Commentaries of Doctor Peter Martir* (London, 1564), f. 93r–v. A similar opinion was held by Voetius, D. Nobbs, *Theocracy and Toleration* (Cambridge, 1938), p. 135. In 1538 John Lambert was burned after admitting to this view, *The Acts and Monuments of John Foxe*, ed. S. R. Cattley (London, 1837–41), v, pp. 207–8.

themselves with household affairs, and in any case maintained that effective power should remain with the elders rather than be given to the congregation as a whole.[15] Henry Ainsworth felt that women should be present at all deliberations, but not be allowed to speak.[16] John Robinson went further and argued that, although in the normal course of events they might not prophesy, they could at least confess before the congregation, witness transactions, speak on them, 'yea, in a case extraordinary, namely where no man will, I see not but a woman may reprove the church, rather than suffer it to go on in apparent wickedness'.[17] John Smyth, the Se-Baptist, although against women speaking in times of prophecy, tended to the view that 'women, servants, and children admitted into full communion, yet under age', might 'give voice in elections, excommunications, and other public affairs of the church'.[18]

Practice on the Continent varied also. Women sometimes held minor church offices;[19] they voted occasionally on important Church matters, as in 1633 when the church at Rotterdam was remodelled and Hugh Peters installed as minister,[20] and it is very likely that they took some part in the practice of lay preaching which began in Holland at this time.[21]

But all this was nothing to what took place when the sects returned to England in the early 1640s. In the formation of small independent congregations women often played a leading part and in the outbreak of lay preaching they joined with enthusiasm. Many of the London Independent congregations far outstripped the practice of the sectaries on the Continent by allowing all their members, women included, to debate, vote and, if not preach, then usually at least to prophesy, which often came to much the same thing.

[15] F. Johnson, *A Christian Plea conteyining three treatises* (n. pl., 1617), p. 307; H. M. and M. Dexter, op. cit., p. 465.

[16] H. Ainsworth, *An Animadversion to Mr. Richard Clyfton's Advertisement* (Amsterdam, 1613), p. 34.

[17] J. Robinson, *A Justification of Separation* (1610), in B. Hanbury, *Historical Memorials relating to the Independents, or Congregationalists* (London, 1839–44), i, p. 214; *Works of John Robinson*, ed. Ashton, ii, pp. 215–16.

[18] *The Works of John Smyth*, ed. W. T. Whitley (Cambridge, 1915), i, p. 256.

[19] C. Burrage, *The early English Dissenters* (Cambridge, 1912), i, p. 253.

[20] Burrage, op. cit., ii, p. 272; R. P. Stearns, *The strenuous Puritan, Hugh Peters, 1598–1660* (Urbana, 1954), p. 77.

[21] On which see W. T. Whitley, 'The rise of lay preaching in Holland', *Trans. Congregl. Hist. Soc.*, v, 5 (1912).

Preaching by women had thus probably begun among certain Baptist churches in Holland and was to be found in Massachusetts by 1636.[22] When it became common in England in the 1640s[23] its main centre, like that of most sectarian activity, was London. A woman preached weekly at the General Baptist church in Bell Alley in Coleman Street,[24] but we also know that there were women preachers outside London, in Kent, Lincolnshire, Ely, Salisbury, and Hertfordshire,[25] and as far afield as Yorkshire[26] and Somerset.[27] Indeed one of the most advanced Baptist churches in this respect was probably that of John Rogers in Dublin, where women held all the privileges (though not the offices) of male members. Rogers was forthright in his condemnation of any attempt to exclude women from Church government. 'Most men do arrogate a sovereignty to themselves which I see no warrant for', he wrote.[28] But, even among the Baptists, men showed a marked reluctance to relinquish this sovereignty and, even in Dublin, Rogers's views on the place of women seem to have alienated half his congregation.[29]

It was of course among the Quakers that the spiritual rights of women attained their apogee. All the Friends were allowed to speak and prophesy on a basis of complete equality, for the Inner Light knew no barriers of sex. Fox and his followers declared that women's subjection, decreed at the Fall, had been eradicated by the sacrifice of the Redeemer. 'Man and Woman were helps meet . . . before they fell; but after the Fall, in the Transgression, the Man was to rule over his Wife; but in the restoration by Christ . . . they are helps meet, Man and Woman, as they were before . . . the

[22] R. Barclay, *The inner life of the Religious Societies of the Commonwealth*, 3rd edn. (London, 1879), pp. 155–6.

[23] There are isolated references to women preaching in England before 1640. See A. Lake, *Sermons* (London, 1629), iii, pp. 67–78, discussed by T. G. Crippen in *Trans. Congregl. Hist. Soc.*, i, 3 (1902), pp. 192–4.

[24] T. Edwards, *Gangraena*, 2nd edn. (London, 1646), i, p. 116.

[25] ibid.; *A Discoverie of six women preachers* (London, 1641); *The Brownists conventicle* (n.pl., 1641), p. 6.

[26] Whitelocke, *Memorials*, p. 403.

[27] Edwards, *Gangraena*, i, p. 218 (misprinted as 118).

[28] J. Rogers, *Ohel or Beth-shemesh* (London, 1653), p. 463 (misprinted as 563). See also J. H. Taylor, 'Some seventeenth century Testimonies', *Trans. Congregl. Hist. Soc.*, xvi, 2 (1949).

[29] E. Rogers, *Some account of the Life and Opinions of a Fifth-Monarchy-Man* (London, 1867), p. 33.

Fall.'[30] As for the ministry of women, it is held, as a modern Quaker puts it, that 'those Scriptures which enjoin silence upon women . . . refer to local or temporary conditions which have now passed away'.[31] The women who walked under the Spirit were not under the Law.[32] Women were priests as much as men.[33] Christ was one in male and female alike.[34]

As a result the female sex played so large a part among the Quakers that it was rumoured at first that the sect was confined to them alone.[35] Women were the first Quaker preachers in London, in the Universities, in Dublin and in the American colonies;[36] and from 1671 regular Women's Meetings, organized on a country-wide basis, gave women their share in church government.[37] It should not be thought that all this was accomplished without serious opposition from within the Society of Friends itself.[38] The Women's Meetings developed only slowly and even at the beginning of the eighteenth century women did not really enjoy completely equal status, at least not in matters of discipline anyway.[39] Nonetheless, the significance of the

[30] G. Fox, *A Collection of many Select and Christian Epistles* (London, 1698), ii, p. 323.

[31] J. S. Rowntree, *The Society of Friends: its faith and practice* (London, 1901), p. 21. Contrast the ecstatic passage in M. Fell, *Womens speaking justified* (London, 1667), p. 11, with the protest by Z. Crofton, *Catechizing Gods Ordinance* (London, 1657), p. 102: 'Oh consider, Brethren, is paternal power any less now under the Gospel than before and under the Law'.

[32] 'If you be led of the spirit, then you are not under the Law.' G. Fox, *The woman learning in silence* (London, 1656), p. 1. Cf. (W. Fiennes, Viscount Saye and Sele), *The Quakers reply manifested to be railing* (appended to *Folly and Madnesse made manifest* [n.pl., 1659]), p. 132.

[33] Fox, *Epistles*, ii, p. 244.

[34] ibid., pp. 6, 31, 372, and *passim*; Fox, *The woman learning in silence, passim*; W.C., *The moderate enquirer resolved* (n.p ., 1671), p. 33; R. Barclay, *An Apology for the true Christian Divinity*, 8th edn. (Birmingham, 1765), pp. 281–2. Counter arguments based on scripture could be of no avail: 'And if there was no Scripture for our Men and Womens Meetings, Christ is sufficient, who restores man and woman up into the image of God . . . as they were in before they fell: so He is our rock and foundation to build upon'. Fox, *Epistles*, ii, p. 388.

[35] *State Papers collected by Edward, Earl of Clarendon* . . . (Oxford, 1767–86), ii, p. 383.

[36] Nuttall, *The Holy Spirit*, p. 87.

[37] A. Lloyd, *Quaker Social History, 1669–1738* (London, 1950), p. 112.

[38] See E. Fogelklou, *James Nayler* (London, 1931), pp. 141–2.

[39] Lloyd, op. cit., p. 118.

Quaker contribution to women's emancipation is enormous.

The main scriptural obstacle in the way of women preachers was, of course, the prohibition of St. Paul, but this could be countered by reference to the prophet Joel;[40] and so we read of a lace woman prefacing her sermon by remarking, 'That now those days were come, and that was fulfilled which was spoken of in the Scriptures, that God would pour out of his Spirit upon the handmaidens, and they should prophesy.'[41]

Not unnaturally the principle that the Spirit bloweth where it listeth proved itself an extremely powerful solvent of the established order. Under the outpourings of even its most extravagant female adherents we can detect, if in exaggerated form, the claims of women to be heard in their own right. In sixteenth-century Switzerland an Anabaptist had given 'herself out for the Queen of the World and Messias for all women'.[42] In seventeenth-century England Richard Hubberthorne encountered 'an impudent lass that said she was above the apostles'.[43] Jane Holmes, a Quaker, had a fever which transformed her into 'a wild eyrie spirit, which . . . kicked against reproof, and would not come to judgement'.[44] Women claimed to be able to perform miracles, like Susannah Pearson, who acted the part of Elisha and tried to raise a young man from the dead.[45] Great feats of endurance were performed, such as that of Sarah Wight in 1647, who was believed to have fasted for fifty-three days.[46] Many claimed the power of prophecy as did the irrepressible Lady Eleanor Douglas.[47] Others like Anna Trapnel[48] were gifted with an almost endless capacity for the com-

[40] Joel ii. 28–29.

[41] Edwards, *Gangraena*, i, p. 117.

[42] R. Baillie, *Anabaptism* (London, 1647), p. 11.

[43] E. Brockbank, *Richard Hubberthorne of Yealand* (London, 1929), p. 91.

[44] M. R. Brailsford, *Quaker women, 1650–1690* (London, 1915), p. 22.

[45] G. F. Nuttall, *James Nayler. A fresh approach* (Supplement no. 26 to *Journ. Friends Hist. Soc.* [1954]), p. 15; cf. the story of the woman at Newbury in *A looking-glas for sectaryes* (London, 1647), pp. 3–7.

[46] Nuttall, *James Nayler*, pp. 9–10.

[47] S. G. W(right), 'Dougle Fooleries', *Bodl. Qtly. Rec.*, vii (1932); C. J. Hindle, *A Bibliography of the printed pamphlets and broadsides of Lady Eleanor Douglas*, rev. edn. (Edinburgh Bibliog. Soc., 1936). For other examples of female prophecy see *The wonderfull Works of God* (London, 1641), and E. Channel, *A message from God* (n.pl., 1653).

[48] See anonymous folio vol. in the Bodleian Library (S. 1.42.Th.), and the account by B. Dobell in *Notes and Queries* (21 Mar. 1914), pp. 221–2. Her

position of ecstatic religious verse. It is difficult for us to recapture the apocalyptic atmosphere in which all this took place,[49] but the challenge offered by these events to traditional ideas on the passive and subordinate role of women in the Church and in society is obvious. As Anna Trapnel remarked, 'Whom the Son makes free, they are free indeed.'[50] And it is clear that the horrified chorus of opposition to these women preachers and mystics derived its fury from something more than their defiance of St. Paul. The greatest offence of Mrs. Anne Hutchinson, the leader of Antinomianism in Massachusetts, was not a purely theological one. As Hugh Peters said to her, 'You have stepped out of your place; you have rather been a husband than a wife, and a preacher than a hearer; and a magistrate than a subject, and so you have thought to carry all things in Church and Commonwealth as you would, and have not been humbled for this.'[51] Anne Wentworth, who wrote delirious verse, was regarded as 'an impudent hussy, a disobedient wife . . . , one that run away from her husband, and the like'.[52] And it is interesting to remember that a hundred years earlier the same had been said of Anne Askew, the Protestant martyr. Forced into a loveless marriage against her will, she had left her husband and reverted to her maiden name.

It should not be thought that all women visionaries of this period were ardent feminists. Elizabeth Warren, for example, who was one of the most prominent writers of the 1640s, published reluctantly, 'conscious to my mentall and sex-deficiency',[53] dilated

[49] cf. Lord Brooke, *A discourse opening the nature of that Episcopacie* (1642), p. 107, in *Tracts on Liberty in the Puritan Revolution, 1638–1647*, ed. W. Haller (New York, 1933–4), ii, p. 151.
[50] A. Trapnel, *The cry of a stone* (London, 1654), p. 47.
[51] *Antinomianism in the Colony of Massachusetts Bay, 1636–38*, ed. C. F. Adams (Prince Soc., Boston, 1894), p. 329.
[52] *The Revelation of Jesus Christ unto Anne Wentworth*, p. 20.
[53] E. Warren, *The old and good way vindicated* (London, 1646), sig. A3r.

---

fasting and trances are described in *The Clarke Papers*, ed. C. H. Firth (Camden Soc., London, 1891–1901), ii, pp. xxxiv–xxxv. See also *The Publick Intelligencer*, 13 (1655); pp. 193–4, and C. Burrage, 'Anna Trapnel's Prophecies', *Eng. Hist. Rev.*, xxvi (1911). Hobbes seems to refer to her in *The English Works*, ed. Sir W. Molesworth (London, 1839–45), vi, p. 398. For another sectarian poetess see *The Revelation of Jesus Christ . . . unto . . . Anne Wentworth* (n.pl., 1679).

upon women's greater susceptibility to error,[54] and urged obedience to all whom God had placed in lawful authority.[55] But she was exceptional and most of these women declared without hesitation that the Spirit of God was to be revealed 'as soon to his handmaids as his men servants'.[56]

With the sectarian women also were popularly associated advanced views on marriage and divorce.[57]

'We will not be wives
And tie up our lives
To villainous slavery'

was the chorus of a ribald skit on the 'holy sisters',[58] a form of literature which had great vogue at this time.[59] After the Reformation matrimony was no longer regarded as a sacrament, and this had left the way open for the Brownist view of marriage as a purely civil contract,[60] and hence one which could be terminated on the non-performance of either of the two parties. Moreover, the rigid application of the sectarian view that it was necessary to separate from the ungodly and to join the regenerate gave an added sanction to divorce and re-marriage, as the Brownists had also demonstrated.[61] The Anabaptists had held 'that wives of a contrary religion may be put away, and that it is lawful for them to take others'.[62] This, however, could work in reverse, and Milton's

[54] idem, *Spiritual thrift or, Meditations* (London, 1647), p. 81.

[55] idem, *A Warning-peece* (London, 1649), p. 40.

[56] Lady E. Douglas, *The star to the wise* (London, 1643), p. 12.

[57] e.g. *Antinomianism in the Colony of Massachusetts Bay*, p. 314; *The routing of the Ranters* (n.pl., n.d.), p. 5.

[58] *Rump, or an exact collection of the choycest Poems and Songs* (London, n.d.), ii, p. 196.

[59] For some examples see *Rump*, i, pp. 2, 18, 43, 47, 55, 82, 88, 152, 162, 194–5, 359; ii, pp. 158–9, 164, 193–8, 199–200; *The Brownists Synagogue* (n.pl., 1641), p. 4; R. Carter, *The Schismatick stigmatized* (London, 1641), p. 15; *A wife, not ready made, but bespoken*, 2nd edn. (London, 1653), p. 16.

[60] e.g. Burrage, *The early English Dissenters*, i, p. 144; ii, p. 54, 56.

[61] *Tracts ascribed to Richard Bancroft*, p. 7; S. B(redwell), *The rasing of the foundations of Brownisme* (London, 1588), pp. 39–40, 115–16.

[62] E. Pagitt, *Heresiography*, 4th edn. (London, 1648), p. 12. See also Edwards, *Gangraena*, i, p. 34; ii, pp. 141, 179; D. Featley, *The Dippers dipt* (London, 1645), p. 29. Cf. the view ascribed to the German Anabaptists that marriage was polluted and no better than fornication where both parties were not enlightened by the true faith: *Mock-Majesty or the siege of Munster* (London, 1644), p. 11, quoting *A warning for England* (n.pl., 1642), p. 15. More extreme was the view of the Free Brothers, that 'women did sin in

writings on divorce had left loopholes of which women could avail themselves. In New England the followers of the Ranter, Gorton, asserted 'that it is lawful for a woman who sees into the mystery of Christ, in case her husband will not go with her, to leave her husband and follow the Lord's House; for the Church of God is a Christian's home, where she must dwell . . . and in so doing, she leaves not her husband, but her husband forsakes her'.[63] Such behaviour was not confined to New England and from the early 1640s we find evidence of sectary women casting off their old husbands and taking new, allegedly for reasons of conscience. The most celebrated instance was that of Mrs. Attoway. This formidable lady after one of her sermons, we are told, approached two gentlemen and 'spake to them of Master Milton's doctrine of divorce, and asked them what they thought of it, saying it was a point to be considered of; and that she for her part would look more into it, for she had an unsanctified husband, that did not walk in the way of Sion, nor speak the language of Canaan'.[64] Shortly afterwards, she attached herself to one, William Jenney, who, it appears, had also been troubled by an unsanctified consort, but who resolved his dilemma by deducing 'from that Scripture in Genesis where God saith *I will make him an help meet for him*, that when a man's wife was not a meet help, he might put her away and take another; and when the woman was an unbeliever (that is, not a sectary of their church) she was not a meet help, and therefore Jenney left his wife, and went away with Mistress Attoway'.[65] Nor was this an isolated case.[66]

[63] R. Baillie, *A dissuasive from the errours of the time* (London, 1645), p. 145. 'The odiousness of this point was further manifested unto me (remarked Roger Williams) by the speech of Ezekiel Hollimer's wife saying that she counted herself but a widow' (ibid.).

[64] Edwards, *Gangraena*, ii, pp. 10–11.

[65] ibid., iii, p. 27. See the account in D. Masson, *The Life of John Milton* (London, 1859–94), iii, p. 189, et seq.

[66] Other examples are to be found in Carter, *The Schismatick stigmatized*, and H. Ellis, *Pseudochristus* (London, 1650).

---

having intercourse with their husbands who were still heathens, but they did not sin when having intercourse with brethren': E. B. Bax, *Rise and fall of the Anabaptists* (London, 1903), p. 38. Even Presbyterians would apply the principle of separation where Roman Catholic husbands or wives were concerned: *A religious scrutiny concerning unequal marriage* (London, 1649).

Luimneach
Mhuire Gan Smál

There was, of course, nothing new about this association of women and small religious sects. 'From the Montanist movement onwards,' wrote R. A. Knox, 'the history of enthusiasm is largely a history of female emancipation'.[67] Women seem to have played a disproportionate role in the history of mysticism and spiritual religion. Almost all the medieval sects from the Manichaeans to the Waldenses, the Donatists to the Cathars, received to a marked degree the support of women and welcomed them, sometimes as influential patronesses, but more often, and more to our purpose here, as active members on a basis of practical equality.[68] To contemporaries this represented nothing more than Satan working through his usual channels, but to us it is hardly surprising that women were attracted to those groups or that form of religion which offered spiritual equality, the depreciation of educational advantages, and that opportunity to preach or even to hold priestly office which they were otherwise denied. Membership of the sects outside the Church or mysticism within it allowed women self-expression, wider spheres of influence and an asceticism which could emancipate them from the ties of family life.

The same factors must have operated among the women of the Civil War sects.[69] They could play no active part in the Church of England nor in the Catholic Church, several of whose leaders had publicly lamented that the Reformation had placed Bibles in hands which would have been better occupied with a distaff.[70] The

[67] R. A. Knox, *Enthusiasm, a chapter in the History of Religion* (Oxford, 1950), p. 20.

[68] S. Runciman, *The Medieval Manichee* (Cambridge, 1947), pp. 15, 18–19, 23, 74, 131, 156–7; D. Obolensky, *The Bogomils* (Cambridge, 1948), pp. 50, 135, 199; R. M. Jones, *Studies in mystical religion* (London, 1909), pp. 46–47, 141, 145, 191; Bax, *Rise and fall of the Anabaptists*, pp. 59–61, 146, 155–6, 196, 247, 309. There is a list of medieval women mystical writers compiled by H. E. Allen in *The Book of Margery Kempe*, ed. S. B. Meech (EETS, London, 1940), i, pp. lix–lx. For the Lollards see ibid., pp. lvii, 259, 315, and for the role of women in a modern sect E. D. Andrews, *The people called Shakers* (New York, 1953).

[69] The parallel was noticed by J. Cranford, *Haereseo-Machia* (London, 1649), p. 29.

[70] 'Nunc translationibus istis in linguam vernaculam factum esse cernimus, ut quas lanam texere sub id tempus magis expediebat, eae sibi docendi quoque potestatem iam arrogaverint:' S. Hosius, *De expresso dei verbo* (Antverpiae, 1561), sigs. 161v–162r. This text was frequently cited by English Protestant writers, e.g. J. White, *The way to the true Church*, 2nd

Presbyterians campaigned for the minor office of church widow, and all Puritans agreed that women could and should instruct their families in religious matters. But that was all and it is not to be wondered at that for some women the sects proved more attractive.

Contemporaries had other explanations to offer. Women were weaker in capacity and more easily led astray. False teachers were like 'those Amalekites, who (in the absence of the men) very stoutly smote Ziglag, and took captives the women'.[71] Thomas Edwards reproached the sectaries for their activity 'among common people (and especially the female sex) apt to be seduced, strong in their affections, and loving too much Independency, but weak and easy in their understandings, not able to examine grounds and reasons, nor to answer you'.[72]

Nor was the error of these women regarded as entirely innocent. Some perhaps might have been seduced merely by dint of their native imbecility, but in others ambition and a desire to upset the established order were quickly detected. Women, John Brinsley shrewdly observed, were not allowed to concern themselves with the discipline and government of the Church 'and hereupon they grow discontented, and fall into dislike with the present state of the Church; and that discontent layeth them open to Satan's delusions, who readily worketh upon such an advantage'.[73] Dissatisfied with her present state, woman was ready to better her condition by any means propounded to her.[74] Mrs. Hutchinson

[71] R. Hooke, *The Laver of Regeneration and the Cup of Salvation* (London, 1653), p. 58 (I Sam. xxx. 1–2).

[72] T. Edwards, *Antapologia: Or, a full answer to the Apologeticall Narration* (London, 1644), p. 250.

[73] J. Brinsley, *A looking-glasse for good women* (London, 1645), p. 8.

[74] ibid., p. 11.

impressn. (London, 1610), pp. 21–22; *An humble Supplication to the Kings majesty* (1620), in *Tracts on Liberty of Conscience and Persecution, 1614–1661*, ed. E. B. Underhill (Hanserd Knollys Soc., London, 1846), p. 204; Philolaoclerus, *The private Christian's Non Ultra* (Oxford, 1656), p. 19. Cf. J. Dod, *Bathshebaes Instructions to her sonne Lemuel* (London, 1614), pp. 61–62: 'The Jesuits . . . which do so straightly tie the women to the wheel and spindle, as they do cut them off and bar them from all conference touching the word of God, as absurd and far unbeseeming their sex'. Religious women in the Middle Ages were usually urged to return to the distaff; cf. Runciman, *The Medieval Manichee*, p. 159, n. 4; *The Book of Margery Kempe*, p. 129.

and her followers, said Johnson, had 'their call to this office from an ardent desire of being famous'. The six women preachers, reported in a pamphlet of 1641, 'seemed to be ambitious, and . . . they would have superiority'.[75] Such women were 'puffed up with pride' and 'vainglorious arrogance, to preach in mixed congregations of men and women, in an insolent way, so usurping authority over men'.[76] It was intolerable, wrote Vicars, 'to see bold impudent housewives, without all womanly modesty, to take upon them . . . to prate . . . after a narrative or discoursing manner, an hour or more, and that most directly contrary to the Apostle's inhibition', all under a pretence of New-Light, from the prophecy of Joel.[77]

Prynne went further and said what others doubtless thought, namely that the Independents allowed women to vote, speak or preach in their congregations simply as a means of securing their membership. These concessions were not only contrary to the doctrine and practice of the Apostles; they were nothing more than 'a mere politic invention to engage that sex to their party'.[78]

But whatever its causes, the Anglicans and Presbyterians were agreed as to the enormity of the conduct of both the sectaries and their female adherents. They condemned the 'unwarrantable rashness and presumption of some women in embracing, and engaging themselves in new ways without the privity of their husbands . . . to whom they are so far in duty bound, as to take their advice . . . to acquaint them with their intentions, and the reasons of them, desiring their consents'.[79] For a woman to forsake the church of which her husband was a member and to join another without his consent was monstrous and unnatural. That those 'who lie in the same bed, and in the eye both of God's Law and Man's are both one, should yet be of two churches, it is such a solecism, such an absurdity in Christianity, as . . . the world never saw practised, much less heard pleaded for until this last age'.[80] 'Next to the debauching a woman into forbidden embraces' came 'this alienat-

[75] *Johnson's Wonder-working Providence 1628–1651*, ed. J. F. Jameson (New York, 1910), p. 186; *A Discoverie of six women preachers*, p. 5. [76] *A Spirit moving in the women preachers* (London, 1646), p. 3. [77] J. Vicars, *The Schismatick sifted* (London, 1646), p. 34. [78] W. Prynne, *A fresh discovery of some prodigious new wandring-blasing-stars, & firebrands* (London, 1645), p. 47. Cf. sig. A2r. [79] Brinsley, *A looking-glasse*, p. 16. [80] ibid., p. 41. He held that for a woman to engage herself to a church without her husband's consent was a direct infringement of her divinely ordained duty of submission.

ing of those two, whom God hath made one, and no person has power to put asunder either in body or mind.'[81]

The growth of sectarianism certainly seemed likely to provoke direct conflicts of loyalty within the family. 'I pray you tell me', demanded Katherine Chidley, 'what authority [the] unbelieving husband hath over the conscience of his believing wife; it is true he hath authority over her in bodily and civil respects, but not to be a lord over her conscience.'[82] The enemies of the sects argued that the growth of schism was undermining the unity of the family. They pointed to sectarians who held that any form of religious compulsion in the family, including family prayers, was unlawful,[83] and to others who attacked the authority hitherto exercised by heads of households in matters of Church government.[84] In short, the growth of the sects, it was asserted, was reducing the practice of household piety, alienating the affections of members of the family towards each other, and worst of all, rending the bonds of obedience which held them together.

As to this there was no doubt that when the direct issue presented itself—obedience to one's husband or obedience to one's church—then the church had to come first. In 1658 Jane Adams excused her absence from the Baptist meeting at Fenstanton by explaining that her husband would not let her come. She was sharply reminded that there were limits to the authority a husband could exercise and that she must come unless restrained by force.[85] The records of a London Baptist church reveal an earlier and more complicated affair in 1654, concerning Eleazar bar Ishay, a Jew, who had been persuaded to become a Baptist so as to be able to marry a widow, named Rebecca Hounsell, who was a member of the congregation. The trouble began when Eleazar (who seems to have been somewhat promiscuous in his religious affections) carried off their first-born to be baptized, or, as the church put it, 'sprinkled', by the Presbyterians. The indignant Baptists promptly

[81] J. Nalson, *The Countermine*, 3rd edn. (London, 1678), p. 138.

[82] K. Chidley, *The justification of the Independent Churches of Christ* (London, 1641), p. 26.

[83] *These Trades-men* (1647) (broadside), reproduced in *Tracts on Liberty in the Puritan* Revolution, i, facing p. 56.

[84] *Severall votes of tender conscience* (n.pl., 1646) (broadside).

[85] *Records of the Churches of Christ, gathered at Fenstanton, Warboys, and Hexham, 1644–1702*, ed. E. B. Underhill (Hanserd Knollys Soc., London, 1854), p. 242.

delivered him over to Satan, but his wife, anxious to avoid a similar fate, tried to excuse her share in the sprinkling by appealing to the obedience which wives owed to husbands. This plea only exacerbated matters, and Peter Chamberlen replied on behalf of the church that it was a great sin for her to put her duty to her husband before her duty to her church. Was it not made clear by the Scriptures, he asked, 'that whosoever forsaketh not husband and wife, etc., for Christ's sake is not worthy of him'? As a result she too was expelled from the Church.[86]

Such incidents notwithstanding, the separatists seldom maintained that they wanted more from the family than liberty of conscience and worship. Apart from this the web of obedience was to be maintained intact. 'No difference, or alienation, in religion, how great soever', John Robinson had said, 'either dissolves any natural or civil bond of society; or abolisheth any the least duty thereof.'[87] This commonplace of contemporary political theory was urgently reiterated in the writings of the leading separatists[88] and in the official confessions of the Congregational and Baptist churches.[89] Just as the ungodly magistrate must be obeyed unless his commands were directly contrary to the word of God, so was obedience due on the same terms from wives, children and servants to their superiors. As William Gouge had remarked much earlier, 'Though an husband in regard of evil qualities may carry the image of the devil, yet in regard of his place and office, he beareth the Image of God.'[90] It was completely in accordance with their stated principles that as soon as they took on institutional form even the most radical sects became conservative as regards the organization and discipline of the family. The Quakers were notoriously

[86] Bodl. Lib. MS. Rawlinson, D 828, *passim*.

[87] Hanbury, *Historical Memorials*, i, p. 435.

[88] Ainsworth, in Hanbury, op. cit., i, p. 279; F. J. Powicke, *Henry Barrow, Separatist* (London, 1900), p. 127; Smyth, in Barclay, *The inner life*, App. to chap. vi, p. xii; R. Williams, *The Bloudy Tenent of Persecution*, ed. E. B. Underhill (Hanserd Knollys Soc., London, 1848), p. 341; *Works of T. Goodwin* (Edinburgh, 1861–5), iv, p. 122; Rogers, *Ohel or Beth-shemesh*, p. 75; *Ancient bounds* (1645), in *Puritanism and Liberty*, ed. A. S. P. Woodhouse (London, 1938), p. 255.

[89] *A Declaration by Congregational Societies in and about the City of London* (1647), in Hanbury, op. cit., iii, pp. 261–2; B. Cox, *An Appendix to a Confession of Faith* (London, 1646), p. 12.

[90] W. Gouge, *Of Domesticall Duties, eight treatises*, 3rd edn. (London, 1634), p. 275.

patriarchal and the Baptist churches continued to punish rebellious wives and servants.[91] For the sects, as for the Presbyterians, spiritual equality was to remain strictly spiritual only.

Yet it would be misleading to pretend that all was as it had been. Religious divisions within the family had reproduced in miniature the dilemma created by the same divisions with the State. After the Reformation the dissenting minorities had been confronted by the problem of obedience to the ungodly magistrate. The solution to this conflict of loyalties was to be the separation of Church and State, leaving the latter a purely secular organization existing only for the convenience of its members. The way was then open for the emergence of ideas of contract and popular government, political liberty thus becoming, as Figgis said, 'the residuary legatee of ecclesiastical animosities'.[92]

We do not find an exact parallel in the history of the family, for, then as now, no religious body would recognize it as no more than a secular social unit. But we must not underestimate the importance of sectarian claims to limit the father's authority in the sphere of conscience, for it was precisely the supposedly divine origin of his position and his role as household priest which had mattered; in the family, as in the commonwealth, it was religion which had kept the subject in obedience. It was, wrote Nalson, 'the only bond of union, the only maintainer and preserver of those respective dutie which are owing from one to another, in those little primitiv societies of mankind'. If that bond was lacking, then 'neither t' obligations of nature, education, or reason, are powerful enou to keep men within the limits of their duty'.[93] For servants, h Gouge, 'God's fear is the ground of all good obedience and fa fulness'[94] and as for wives, 'if the fear of God possess not

[91] e.g. *Records of the Churches of Christ gathered at Fenstanton*, pp. 73, Brown, *John Bunyan*, tercentenary edn. (London, 1928), p. 231; Robinson, 'Baptist Church discipline, Part II', *The Baptist Qtly.*, n i, 4 (1922), p. 184.

[92] J. N. Figgis, *Studies of political thought from Gerson to Grotius, 1414–* edn. (Cambridge, 1923), p. 118. For some general remarks on see T. M. Parker, *Christianity and the State in the light of histor* 1955), chap. viii.

[93] J. Nalson, *The true liberty and dominion of Conscience vindicate* (London, 1678), p. 13.

[94] Gouge, *Of Domesticall Duties*, p. 658; cf. *The Works of . . . Dr* (London, 1653), p. 191.

hearts, though they be the weaker vessels [they] do oft make their husbands plain vassals to them'.[95]

These remarks are not intended to suggest that seventeenth-century religion was a disreputable device on the part of heads of families to keep down their inferiors, to say with Mr. Schlatter, for example, that it was 'well calculated to serve the interests of employers',[96] but rather that religious teaching, even in the later seventeenth century, inherited the traditional static, hierarchical view of society, invested as it was with divine sanctions, and used as a framework inside which all the Christian virtues of love and charity were to operate. Virtue was relative to function and, if obedience was required from below, then kindness and consideration were demanded from above.

But once the religious sanction was taken away or weakened, then the whole of society was subject to challenge and rescrutiny from a new point of view—that of reason, natural right, popular consent and common interest. The Leveller principle that men and women were born free and equal and could only be governed by their own consent had implications for the family as well as for society in general. As Filmer said, it meant that 'every infant at the hour it is born in, hath a like interest with the greatest and wisest man in the world . . . not to speak of women, especially virgins, who by birth have as much natural freedom as any other, and therefore ought not to lose their liberty without their own consent'. Or, as another pamphleteer realized, 'if this principle were true, that all subjection and obedience to persons and their laws stood by virtue of electing them, then . . . all women at once were exempt from being under government'.[97] Some of the petitions to Parliament in this period show that women were well capable of

[95] Gouge, op. cit., p. 193; cf. F. Cheynell, *A plot for the good of Posterity* (London, 1646), p. 28: 'Do not forget your beloved wife . . . she will never be at your command unless you teach her to be at Christ's command'.

[96] R. B. Schlatter, *The social ideas of religious leaders, 1660–1688* (London, 1940), p. 86.

[97] *The anarchy of a limited or mixed monarchy* (1648), in *Patriarcha and other political works*, ed. P. Laslett (Oxford, 1949), p. 287; Edwards, *Gangraena*, iii, p. 154. The place of women in the Leveller movement is a subject well worth investigation: see for some remarks M. A. Gibb, *John Lilburne, the Leveller* (London, 1947), p. 174, and J. Frank, *The Levellers* (Cambridge, Mass., 1955), pp. 105, 199.

grasping the implications for themselves.[98] As for the Fifth Commandment, 'the great dispute', said Rainsborough at Putney, 'is, who is a right father and a right mother . . . for my part I look upon the people of England so, that wherein they have not voices in the choosing of their (civil) fathers and mothers—they are not bound to that commandment'.[99]

During the Civil War and Interregnum the very foundations of the old patriarchal family were challenged in a number of ways which have not been mentioned in this paper. Among them may be numbered the Civil Marriage Act, the lively discussion of polygamy[100] and of marriage within the forbidden degrees,[101] and the unusual part played by women in war, litigation,[102] pamphleteering, and politics;[103] the appearance in English of continental feminist writings,[104] and the attacks, sometimes by women themselves, on their limited educational opportunities,[105] their confinement to domestic activity,[106] their subjection to their husbands,[107]

98 E. A. McArthur, 'Women petitioners and the Long Parliament', *Eng. Hist. Rev.*, xxiv (1909).

99 *Puritanism and Liberty*, p. 61.

100 *A dialogue of Polygamy* (London, 1657) (from the Italian of Ochino); *A remedy for uncleanness* (London, 1658); *The Ladies Champion* (n. pl., 1660). Cf. C. Hill, 'Clarissa Harlowe and her times', *Essays in Criticism*, v, 4 (1955), p. 336.

101 *Little Non-Such: or, certaine new questions moved out of ancient truths* (London, 1646), which may, however, be intended to be satirical. See the remarks of E. Sirluck in *Complete Works of John Milton*, ii (New Haven and London, 1959), App. C.

102 Particularly in petitioning for the release of their husbands and in compounding for delinquent estates. Their importance in the latter respect led Dr. Denton to remark, 'women were never so useful as now'. F. P. Verney, *Memoirs of the Verney family during the Civil War* (London, 1892), ii, p. 240. Cf. *The Knyvett letters (1620–1644)*, ed. B. Schofield (London, 1949), p. 147.

103 McArthur, op. cit. For the frequent satire provoked by women's political activity see *Catalogue of the pamphlets . . . collected by George Thomason, 1640–1661*, ed. G. K. Fortescue (London, 1908), ii, index s.v. 'Women'.

104 Anna Maria à Schurman, *The learned maid*, trans. C. Barkdale (London, 1659).

105 *The womens sharpe revenge* (London, 1640), pp. 40–42; Marchioness of Newcastle, *Poems and fancies* (London, 1653), sig. A3v.

106 *The womens sharpe revenge*, p. 42; S. Torshell, *The womans glorie*, 2nd edn. (London, 1650), p. 2; Marchioness of Newcastle, *The Philosophical and Physical opinions* (London, 1655), sig. B2v.

107 *The womens sharpe revenge*, p. 77; *Now or never: or, a new Parliament of Women* London, 1656), pp. 3–4.

and the injustices of a commercial marriage market.[108] We should remember also the campaign against entails and primogeniture,[109] the emergence of a political theory which took as its primary unit not the family but the individual and, in the background all the time, a slow decline in the self-sufficiency of the country estate and in the household as a unit of production.

In this paper only one of the influences which led to rescrutiny of the nature and purpose of the family has been discussed—the impact of the religious sects. Their numbers were never great, they affected only certain classes and certain areas to any extent, and their social radicalism was undoubtedly much exaggerated by their opponents. Even Thomas Edwards, their most voluble opponent, admitted that he was concerned less with actual happenings than with what he thought would be long-term consequences, scarcely perceived by the separatists themselves.[110] In company with much other contemporary thought, the more radical views on the family went underground at the Restoration. The old apocalyptic vision was dimmed and in the stolid and respectable dissenters of the eighteenth century it is hard to recognize the fervent separatists of our period.

As regards the place of women, the long-term effects of separatism were probably small. Appeal to divine inspiration was of very questionable value as a means of female emancipation. The whole emphasis was placed upon the omnipotence of God and the helplessness of his chosen handmaid should she be thrown upon her own resources. 'I am a very weak, and unworthy instrument', wrote Mary Cary in the preface to one of her Fifth-Monarchy

108 *Now or never*, p. 5 (misprinted as 4); Z. S. Fink, *The Classical Republicans* (Evanston, 1945), pp. 72–73.

109 H. Peters, *A word for the Armie* (London, 1647), pp. 12–13; Stearns, *The strenuous Puritan*, pp. 310–11, 373 (Peters held that 'if daughters were ingenious and would work, they ought to have equal portions with sons', *Good work for a good magistrate* [London, 1651], p. 31); Champianus Northtonus, *The younger brothers advocate* (London, 1655); *The Works of Gerrard Winstanley*, ed. G. H. Sabine (Ithaca, New York, 1941), p. 413; *Puritanism and Liberty*, p. 64. Cf. J. Dod and R. Cleaver, *A plaine and familiar Exposition of the Ten Commandments*, 16th edn. (London, 1625), pp. 185–6. In New England the English law of inheritance had been radically altered: see J. M. Shirley, 'The early jurisprudence of New Hampshire', *Proc. New Hants. Hist. Soc.*, i (1872–88), p. 241.

110 T. Edwards, *Reasons against the Independent Government of particular congregations* (London, 1641), sig. *3r and p. 54.

pamphlets, 'and [I] have not done this work by any strength of my own, but have been often made sensible, that I could do no more herein . . . of myself, than a pencil, or pen can do, when no hand guides it: being daily made sensible of my own insufficiency to do anything as of my self.'[111] We should not overemphasize this objection: after all, Cromwell said the same sort of thing about his victories in battle without it noticeably diminishing their impact; but it does seem in this case that the language in which such writing was couched must have served to perpetuate the legend of women's inferiority. In addition, it is probable that the more exotic and extravagant of these female prophets and preachers only served to do harm to their own cause, since for most people they illuminated by contrast the virtues of the Marthas who stayed at home.

Nor does the sectarian insistence upon women's spiritual equality seem to have been of very great importance in the later history of female emancipation in general. It is true that the energy and resourcefulness of Nonconformist women was to be very evident in subsequent generations, but, for the most part, future feminist movements were to base their arguments less upon any renewed assertion of women's spiritual equality than upon natural right and a denial of any intellectual differences between the sexes. No plea for female suffrage was put forward during this period, so far as I can discover. The sectaries protested strongly against the view that 'the vote of the husband, or his joining to this or that true church, [doth] include the vote and joining of his wife and children under his government'.[112] Yet they failed to challenge the exclusion of women from political suffrage, even though that exclusion was based upon exactly the same grounds. Either they failed to see the analogy, or the strength of deeply rooted traditional ideas was too great to allow them to perceive its implications.

As for the family in general, it is not hard to see why patriarchal theory and practice subsequently appeared unaffected by the events I have tried to describe. For nearly thirty years after the Restoration all attempts at religious toleration were effectively resisted. The Clarendon Code and the later Stuart Poor Law were a deli-

[111] *The Little Horns Doom and Downfall* (London, 1651), sig. A8r.

[112] R. Hollinworth, *Certain Queres modestly (though plainly) propounded to such as affect the Congregational-way* (London, 1646), p. 28.

berate attempt to check the growth of that mobile and fluid society which many people in the 1640s thought toleration likely to produce. When a degree of tolerance was conceded in 1689 it came too late to have those effects upon the family which contemporaries had predicted. During the intervening period a corpus of Nonconformist casuistry had been evolved which in essentials was every bit as patriarchal as that of more orthodox religious teachers before the Civil War, and which refused to allow separatism anything more than purely spiritual implications. In addition, rigid insistence upon intermarriage within the sects had produced a number of little societies made up of families whose members were of the same religious complexion and which were therefore so composed as to make impossible the large scale recurrence of the sort of domestic situation which gave rise to conflicts of loyalty.

Did the family then emerge unscathed by the events of the Civil War period? It is hard to believe that it did. In a famous passage Clarendon declared that the relations between parents and children, masters and servants, were irreparably damaged by the divisions of the Civil War and the influence of the sects. 'Children asked not blessing of their parents. . . . The young women conversed without any circumspection or modesty. . . . Parents had no manner of authority over their children.'[113] It is difficult to assess the value of his account and even were it found reliable the situation it describes must have come about largely through factors other than those discussed here.

But this at least can be said. The Civil War sects contributed to the later development of the family by their contribution to the general process of substituting secular for divine sanctions for the arrangements of society. The orthodox arguments and texts for woman's exclusion from church office had been identical with those for her subordination in general. It was impossible now to attack the one without weakening the other. And in the family the demand for religious toleration led to the redefinition of the limits of paternal power. New standards of utility and reason were being sought to justify the subordination of men and women to each other. It was a search from which in the long run both women and the family were to benefit.

[113] *The Life of Edward, Earl of Clarendon* (Oxford, 1827), i, pp. 358–9.

XIV

THE QUAKERS AND THE ENGLISH REVOLUTION[1]

Alan Cole

I

FOR nearly thirty years after the defeat of the Levellers at Burford, no political party emerged which could claim the effective support of the English Radicals. Throughout this period the main centres of resistance were the Puritan sects and the history of the Radical movement of the time, therefore, is closely bound up with the history of religious dissent. It is this fact which lends peculiar interest to the history of the early Quakers. For the rise of the Quakers spans the period from the breach between Cromwell and the Radical movement to the emergence of the new Country party at the end of the 1670s; and conversely, the decline of Quakerism in England may be traced back to the final defeat of the popular movement and the political compromise of 1688. Moreover, the first Quakers had had close connexions with the earlier Radical movement. Like the Levellers, most of them came from the class of petty traders and handicraftsmen, although it is worth noting that the movement made more headway among the peasantry than the Levellers had done. Over half the early Quaker leaders were directly connected with the land, and throughout the century the movement remained strong in the rural districts of the north and

[1] This article is based in part on the writer's doctoral dissertation, 'The Quakers and Politics, 1652–1660', copies of which have been deposited in the libraries of the University of Cambridge, Friends' House, London, and Swarthmore College, Pa., U.S.A. (From no. 10, 1956).

west.[2] At least ninety of these men—Quaker pamphleteers even claimed the 'most part of them'—had been in arms for Parliament,[3] and some of them had played an active part in the political events of 1647–53. A contemporary diarist noted that 'severall levellers setled into Quakers',[4] and we know that Lilburne himself was a distinguished convert before his death.[5] Again, five members of the Nominated Parliament of 1653 are known to have become Quakers,[6] while in Bristol it seems that the bulk of the Radical party were among the earliest converts to the new religion in the autumn of 1654.[7] During the Protectorate, indeed, the Quakers were widely regarded as socially disreputable men of a discontented and factious humour; and in Ireland Henry Cromwell even regarded them as the government's most formidable opponents.[8]

It has often been argued that the Quakers, unlike the Fifth Monarchists and some of the Baptists, stood entirely aloof from war and politics.[9] In the light of recent research, many Quaker historians have been more cautious, despite the pacifist assumptions of latter-day Friends. But some other students of the seventeenth century have not hesitated to assert that the movement was

[2] The Quaker registers of births, marriages and deaths contain much useful occupational information which I have discussed in an article on 'The Social Origins of the Early Friends', *Jl. of the Friends' Historical Society*, xlviii (1957), pp. 99–118. For the social origins of 'The First Publishers of Truth', see E. E. Taylor, *Jl. F.H.S.*, xix (1922), pp. 66–81.

[3] M. E. Hirst, *The Quakers in Peace and War* (London, 1923), pp. 527–9.

[4] Diary of the Rev. John Ward, ed. C. Severn (London, 1839), p. 141.

[5] Since this article was originally published, it has been suggested that the Digger leader, Gerrard Winstanley, and some of his followers may also have become Quakers. See Richard T. Vann, *Jl. F.H.S.*, xlix (1959), pp. 41–46; ibid., l (1962), pp. 65–68.

[6] W. C. Braithwaite, *The Beginnings of Quakerism*, 2nd edn. (Cambridge, 1955), p. 119, n. 3.

[7] Several Quaker names will be found in the list of radical voters in the Parliamentary election of 1654 in *The Deposition Books of Bristol*, vol. ii, 1650–1654, ed. H. E. Nott and E. Ralph (Bristol Rec. Soc., 1948), pp. 180–1. One of the Independent candidates in this election, George Bishop, became a Quaker, and the other, Col. John Haggett, a sympathizer. Contemporaries also noted the connection between Friends and the Radical party: e.g. R. Farmer, *Satan Inthron'd in his Chair of Pestilence* (1657), pp. 43 ff; T. Ewen, *The Church of Christ in Bristol* (1657), pp. 10–11.

[8] J. Thurloe, *State Papers* (1742), iv, p. 508.

[9] cf. R. Barclay, *The Inner Life of the Religious Societies of the Commonwealth* (London, 1876), p. 193.

distinguished by its 'essentially quietist character'. Thus, one writer has claimed that the Quaker leader, George Fox, 'accepted the world in all its squalor and evil',[10] while Professor Trevor-Roper dismisses Quaker 'quietism' as the plebeian counterpart of the later Tory doctrine of non-resistance.[11] In this essay I hope to show that such judgements spring from a misunderstanding of both the nature and origin of the supposed pacifism of the early Friends. If we are to understand their position, therefore, we must first recall the political circumstances in which it developed.

II

During the 1640s the popular movement had played an important part in shaping events, tending both to drive the revolutionary movement forward and at the same time to precipitate divisions within the ranks of the revolutionary party. But whereas before 1649 the conflict between Cromwell and the army grandees and the popular movement was subordinate to their common struggle with the upholders of the traditional political order, in the 1650s that relationship was reversed and led, in 1660, to the restoration of Charles II. In the critical years 1647–9 the Levellers emerged for a time as an independent political force to demand political power on behalf of the mass of the people. Yet within a few weeks of the execution of the King, the defeat at Burford and subsequent collapse of the movement revealed the weakness and instability of the social groups from which the Levellers sprang. Moreover, it soon became apparent that without political power the Radicals had little hope of overcoming Conservative opposition to their other demands for further reform in Church and State. In 1653, when Cromwell made his last attempt to govern with the support of the popular movement, the assembly of nominees from the Independent churches was soon divided over tithes and other issues in much the same way as the General Council of the army in the years before 1649. In pressing for the abolition of tithes, the minority in the assembly was voicing the demand on which all the Radical groups of the period were most firmly united. But just as the grandees had opposed the extension of the franchise as a threat to

[10] G. Huehns, *Antinomianism in English History* (London, 1951), pp. 140, 144.

[11] H. R. Trevor-Roper, *The Gentry, 1540–1640* (Econ. Hist. Rev., Supplement no. 1), p. 43.

property rights, so the majority of Barebones's Parliament now resisted a proposal which challenged the very basis of the State Church and implied a major change in property relationships. Hence the dissolution of the Assembly and the establishment of the Protectorate clearly confronted the Radicals with the conflict between their demands for reform and the immediate possibilities of the historical situation. And in face of this dilemma, while some of the left-wing sectaries became absorbed in Fifth Monarchist plots and dreams of a military domination of the elect, many others abandoned the struggle and became increasingly ready to compromise with the 'powers of the earth'.

If their attitude towards Fifth Monarchist plots were the sole criterion, it would be easy to associate the Quakers with this latter trend. For despite the violence with which they denounced their opponents in word and print, and the tenacity with which they maintained their well-known testimonies against tithes and 'hat-honour', the Quakers themselves consistently repudiated accusations of their subversive designs. And although two Friends were reported to have been present at the meeting organized by the plotter, Wildman, in the autumn of 1654,[12] no Quaker was ever convicted of bearing arms against the government of the Commonwealth. Nor, in general, were they ever collectively identified with any of the political movements of the time. On the other hand, it is clear that the Friends were by no means consistent pacifists. It has been pointed out that early Quaker statements of their pacific intentions were primarily statements about the *cause* of war.[13] Following the epistle of St. James, the Quakers held that warfare arose from the lusts of men, and looked forward to a time when war and the need for coercion would cease to exist. It followed, therefore, that the Quaker 'seed' was redeemed from the occasion of the strife which prevailed among men. But, at the same time, they recognized the necessity in a 'fallen' world for a just State founded upon equal respect for men's persons and estates, and, as an official letter of 1656 indicates, accepted the responsibility of the saints to take office under it.[14] Moreover, in the

[12] S. R. Gardiner, *Commonwealth and Protectorate* (London, 1903), iii, p. 228, n. 3.

[13] Hugh Barbour, *The Quakers in Puritan England* (New Haven, 1964), p. 196. The point is made more explicitly in his original thesis, 'The Early Quaker Outlook upon "The World" and Society' (Yale Univ., 1952), sect. viiG.

[14] Braithwaite, op. cit., p. 313.

Commonwealth period, the Quakers consistently upheld the justice of the Parliamentary cause in the Civil War and indeed William Dewsbury, perhaps the most pacific of all the early Friends, was not alone in warning the rulers of the Protectorate that if they sought to set up the Beast of Nebuchadnezzar, 'which was the Kings power in these three Nations', they would be overturned like others before them.[15]

It is quite true that some Quakers had become disillusioned with political action by the experience of ten years of civil strife, and as early as 1650 Isaac Penington, for example, had written: 'if thou labourest for Freedom with all thy might, and a greater power oppose, what wilt thou gain by the contest?'[16] But it is important to note that Penington did not become a Friend until 1658, and a study of his Quaker writings suggests that he doubted, not the efficacy of political measures, but the willingness of any of the dominant parties in the Commonwealth to promote the principles for which the Radicals stood.

> There hath been often [he wrote], a naked, honest, simple pure thing stirring in the Army, which the great ones (seeing some present use of) fell in with, and improved for their own ends but destroyed the thing itself; so that it attained not to the bringing forth of that righteous liberty, and common good which it seemed to aim at (and did indeed aim at in those in whom the striving did arise) but was made use of as an advantage to advance them in their particular interest against their Enemies, and so set them up.[17]

Similarly, it was the recognition of social divisions, and not their pacifism, which explains why so many Quakers found it difficult to remain in the army; for when they saw that the army 'did not intend the thing which they did pretend, [they] durst not, for Conscience sake, continue any longer amongst them'.[18] Yet other Quakers retained their positions as long as they could, and when they were eventually cashiered for insubordination, they received the warm support of the Quaker leaders. It is unnecessary, therefore, as some writers have done, to look for the presence in

[15] W. Dewsbury, *A True Prophecie of the Mighty Day of the Lord* (1655), pp. 3–4.

[16] I. Penington, *A Voyce out of the thick Darkness* (1650), Preface.

[17] I. Penington, *To the Parliament, the Army, and all the Wel-affected in the Nation* (May 1659), pp. 2–3.

[18] G. Fox the Younger, *A Noble Salutation* (1660), p. 7.

the Quaker movement of conflicting wings. For if there is little evidence of the plots in which the militant party are supposed to have engaged, it is equally true that most other Quakers were far from adopting a doctrinaire pacifist position. Even Fox himself, who later claimed that he had 'never learned the postures of War', apparently made no attempt to correct the mistaken suggestion of one of his followers that he had once borne arms on behalf of Parliament.[19] Pacifism was not a characteristic of the early Quakers: it was forced upon them by the hostility of the outside world.[20]

The same is true in a more general sense of the Quakers' political position. The Quaker emphasis on the primary authority of the inner light and their rejection of the doctrine and ceremonial of a 'hireling ministry' challenged the foundations of the established ecclesiastical order. But their belief in human equality found expression, not only in their own democratic organization and in their attitude towards women, the Jews, and American Indians, but also in the demand for cheap justice and the reform and simplification of the law.[21] Again, the earliest Quaker declaration of faith included a pronouncement in favour of annual Parliaments,[22] while one Quaker writer criticized plural voting, the limitations of the franchise and the class-system of justice in the authentic tones of the Leveller pamphleteers of the previous decade.[23] If these echoes from the past were never embodied in a political programme, it was largely because the Quakers were too well aware of the power of propertied and clerical interests to influence elections to pin their faith in constitutional reform.[24] Hence the overriding importance which the Quakers, like other Radicals, attached to the abolition of tithes. For tithes were not only incompatible with religious liberty; they were also the main survival of the old economic order and more burdensome to the mass of the people than royal taxation had ever been. Moreover, as Richard Hubber-

[19] G. Fox, *Journal*, ed. J. L. Nickalls (Cambridge, 1952), pp. 379, 389; E. Pyott, *The West Answering to the North* (1657), pp. 3, 16.

[20] M. R. Brailsford, *A Quaker from Cromwell's Army* (London, 1927), p. 25.

[21] G. Fox, *The Law of God* (1658); *An Instruction to Judges and Lawyers* (1657), esp. pp. 17–31; *Fifty-nine Particulars* (1659), etc.

[22] E. Burrough, *A Declaration to all the World* (1657), pp. 5–6.

[23] G. Fox the Younger, *A Few Plain Words* (1659).

[24] ibid.; J. Fuce, *A Visitation by way of Declaration* (1659), p. 2.

thorne pointed out, they were the basis of the State Church, the main obstacle to political reform and the source of much of the strife of the past twenty years.[25]

Unlike Winstanley, the Quakers did not go beyond this attack on tithes to challenge the property system as such. On the contrary, some of them attacked tithes on the grounds that their exaction constituted an infringement of property rights; and while they apparently demanded that the clergy should suffer unconditional expropriation, lay impropriators were to be compensated for their loss.[26] Similarly, although some Quakers advocated the use of ecclesiastical and royalist lands for the relief of poverty,[27] and others even looked with favour on the community of goods which they believed had been practised by the early Christians, they consistently repudiated the charge that they sought the wholesale levelling of men's estates by political means.[28]

This was certainly not because the Quakers were unaware of the roots of moral and political problems in the social order. Fox himself commented on the social origins of crime,[29] and several Quaker writers enlarged on the beneficent moral effects of political and social reforms. But it was precisely because the Quakers recognized that the 'great ones of the earth' could not be relied on to carry out such reforms that they so often stood aloof from political movements. For in the second half of the seventeenth century, the conditions for the re-emergence of an independent popular movement did not exist: the yeomen and artisans of the old order had been decisively defeated, and the modern working class movement had not yet been born. When Isaac Penington surveyed the political scene in the spring of 1659, he remained confident that the Lord would eventually raise up a perfect instrument to complete his work on earth; but in the meantime he could only

[25] R. H(ubberthorne), *The Good Old Cause* (1659); *The Commonwealth's Remembrancer* (1659).

[26] J. Crook, *Tythes no property to nor lawful maintenance for a Gospel, powerful preaching Ministry* (1659), p. 1; A. Pearson, *The Great Case of Tythes* (1657), pp. 34 ff.

[27] R. Crane, *A few Plain Words* (1659), p. 4; F. Howgil, *One Warning more* (1660), p. 9; G. Fox, *Fifty-nine Particulars*, nos. 17, 29, 32.

[28] e.g. J. Nayler, *A True Discoverie of Faith* (1655), pp. 13–14; A. Parker, *A Discovery of Satans Wiles* (1657), pp. 39–40; J. Audland, *The Innocent Delivered* (1655), pp. 6–7.

[29] G. Fox, *To the Protector and Parliament* (1658), p. 12.

urge those who had been faithful to the good old cause to wait on the Lord.[30]

In this situation, the question of toleration, not political power, was the crucial issue for the Quakers, as for most other sections of Radical opinion. Hence they were mainly preoccupied with the struggle to propagate and preserve the purity of their faith, and were careful to avoid any political entanglements which might compromise this primary objective. This did not mean, however, that they were passive bystanders in the political struggle. On the contrary, in the first phase of its history, Quakerism was essentially a movement of protest against the suppression of the 'good old cause'. In the five years of the Protectorate alone, nearly two thousand Friends suffered imprisonment, and twenty-one of them died in gaol.[31] The Quakers' refusal to pay tithes or take oaths, their stubborn testimony against 'hat-honour' and insistence on simplicity of speech were not peculiar to them; but it was the characteristic mark of Friends that they invoked these symbolic actions as invariable rules of conduct demanded by their religion. Moreover, as we shall see, the Quakers lost no opportunity of pressing for the satisfaction of their demands in the political sphere. Indeed, so long as the Commonwealth and its once revolutionary army survived, they never quite abandoned the hope that there might be a return to the good old cause. And if they resisted the temptation to seek a short cut to victory through violence and political insurrection, the explanation is to be sought, not in the quietism of their doctrine, but in their insight into the common dilemma of seventeenth-century Radicals.

III

The political history of the Quakers during the Commonwealth period, therefore, is the record of their attempt to escape this dilemma, to reconcile their political hopes with their underlying mistrust of the social groups on which the Commonwealth rested. In the early years of the Protectorate, despite their disillusion with the course of events since the end of the Civil War, Friends' relations with Cromwell himself were often cordial. Fox himself

[30] I. Penington, *To the Parliament, the Army . . .*, p. 4.
[31] Braithwaite, *Beginnings of Quakerism*, p. 454.

was well received by the Protector in the spring of 1655,[32] and Quakers in general were inclined to look to him for protection against their enemies. Indeed, the Quakers recognized that Cromwell had once been an instrument of God and was still an obstacle to the worst excesses of persecution; and though they did not hesitate to reprove him for his failure to abolish tithes and reform the laws, they generally refrained from public denunciation of the Protector's Government.[33]

The course of events during the Protectorate, however, placed a growing strain on the relations between Cromwell and Friends. For although Cromwell sought to reconcile the interests of property with the Radical demand for liberty of conscience, he viewed with growing concern the Quakers' challenge to the conservative interests on which he relied. The mounting list of Quaker imprisonments, the introduction of anti-Quaker legislation, and the dismissal of Friends from positions in the army and local administration, all illustrate Cromwell's development, under the influence of conflicting pressures, back towards a conservative position.[34]

The deterioration in the situation was reflected both in the growing violence with which some Quaker pamphleteers attacked the government and in the heat of Fox's interview with Cromwell in October 1656.[35] Frequently, too, Quaker protests assumed eccentric and seemingly fanatical forms, such as the practice of walking naked through the streets in the manner of the Old Testament prophets, or, in Nayler's case, the notorious ride into Bristol on a donkey, as a sign of Christ's second appearance in his saints. But, at the same time, the private letters of the Quaker leaders reveal a more rational criticism of the implications of Cromwellian policy. Several Quakers seem to have sympathized with the objectives of the Protector's foreign policy, and Fox even advocated a Protestant war of liberation in Europe.[36] But when news was received of the disaster of English arms at Hispaniola early in the war with Catholic Spain, George Bishop wrote to

[32] Fox, *Journal*, pp. 197–200.

[33] Instead, the Quakers bombarded the Protector with letters, and many argued with him at private interviews. The Quakers, in fact, seem to have been among the pioneers of this type of political pressure.

[34] Fox, *Journal*, p. 280; Braithwaite, op. cit., pp. 218–19, 228–30, 443 ff.

[35] E. Burrough, *A Trumpet of the Lord* (1656); Fox, *Journal*, pp. 274–5.

[36] Letters to Cromwell printed in G. Fox and E. Burrough, *Good Counsel an Advice* (1659), pp. 26–27, 36–37.

Cromwell to point out the connection between his growing conservatism and the exhaustion of the revolutionary impetus of Puritanism at home and abroad. Reminding Cromwell that, in the Civil War, they had faced the opposition of propertied and clerical interests alike, Bishop declared that it was useless for Cromwell to shelter behind the argument of necessity to excuse his betrayal.[37] Indeed, both Fox and Edward Burrough (who rapidly became the chief political spokesman of the movement) warned Cromwell that by purging Quakers and rejecting their demands he was only weakening himself. For

If thou thus utterly deny the people of God in the day of thy prosperity, and thus wholy cast them out of thy service, they cannot stand by thee, nor own thee in the day of thy trouble, and such as thou cleavest unto may be a broken staffe in thy time of need.[38]

Similarly, in the spring of 1657, when Parliament was debating the proposal to make Cromwell king, the Quaker leaders vigorously opposed the plan and declared that Cromwell's acceptance would mean the destruction of him and his house.[39] By September of the same year, Burrough was writing to Cromwell warning him of the danger of a Restoration: surrounded by place-men and hypocrites, and facing the opposition of Royalists and Fifth Monarchy men, Cromwell was 'but the head of a disjoynted body', and his 'Dominions as a broken vessel that cannot easily be bound up, and as a bruised reed not to be confided in'.[40]

In face of this situation, the Quakers were driven deeper into political isolation; and in the last years of the Protectorate several Friends who were still in the navy sought their release.[41] But so long as Cromwell himself lived they displayed little inclination to side with any of the parties which were ranged against him. When, on the other hand, the army revolt in the spring of 1659 led to the

[37] Letter to Cromwell, July 1656, printed in Bishop's *The Warnings of the Lord* (1660), pp. 1–17.

[38] *Good Counsel and Advice*, pp. 15, 26–27.

[39] Fox, *Journal*, p. 289; *Good Counsel and Advice*, p. 9. Swarthmore MSS. vii, p. 38.

[40] *Good Counsel and Advice*, pp. 17–21.

[41] *Extracts from State Papers relating to Friends*, ed. N. Penney (Friends' Historical Soc., 1913), pp. 14, 27–28; T. Lurting, *The Fighting Sailor turned Peaceable Christian* (1710); J. Strutt, *A Declaration to the Whole World* (1659).

fall of the Protectorate and the restoration of the Rump of the Long Parliament, a flood of Quaker pamphlets welcomed the change and the revival of support for the 'good old cause' which it seemed to imply.

In the weeks which followed Friends seem to have acted for a time as a united political force.[42] Encouraged by the release of a number of Quaker prisoners, the Quakers in fourteen counties supplied the Council of State with lists of persecuting magistrates who ought to be removed, and suggested the names of 'moderate' men and Friends who might take their place.[43] Two petitions were presented to Parliament calling for the abolition of tithes, one of which, with 7,000 signatures, had been organized by Quaker women.[44] Meanwhile, the Quakers who had been expelled from the army were not backward in stating their case, and a semi-official declaration was issued indicating the willingness of Friends to serve the Commonwealth.[45]

But this activity was shortlived. In face of the threatening Royalist rising, the Rump was quite prepared to make use of sectarian military assistance, and a number of Quakers were appointed as commissioners for the militia in London, Bristol, and elsewhere.[46] But at the same time, the majority of members were unwilling to add to the strength of the Conservative opposition by acceding to left-wing demands on the question of tithes. Throughout the summer, the breach between the Rump and the Quakers grew rapidly wider, and though many Friends stood by the

[42] cf. J. F. Maclear, 'Quakerism and the End of the Interregnum', *Church History*, xix (1950), pp. 240–70.

[43] *Extracts from State Papers*, pp. 6–13, 105–15; Braithwaite, *Beginnings of Quakerism*, pp. 460–1.

[44] *The Copie of a Paper presented to the Parliament: and read the 27th of the fourth Moneth*, (July 1659); *These Several Papers was sent to the Parliament the twentieth day of the fifth Moneth* (July 1659).

[45] J. Crook *et al.*, *A Declaration of the People of God in scorn called Quakers* (1659).

[46] For the London Friends, see R. Rich, *Hidden Things brought to Light* (1678) pp. 28–29; *Acts and Ordinances of the Interregnum*, ed. C. H. Firth and R. S. Rait (London, 1911), ii, p. 1290. For the Bristol Friends, Parker to Fox, 7 Aug. 1659, Swarthmore MSS. iii, p. 143. In addition, Anthony Pearson was appointed in the north, Humphrey Lower in Cornwall, Thomas Curtis in Berkshire, Robert Duncon in Suffolk, and several other Friends in Wales. Cf. A. R. Barclay MSS. 169; *Acts and Ordinances*, ii, pp. 1320 ff; T. Lewis, *For the King, and both Houses of Parliament* (1661), p. 5.

government during Booth's rebellion in August,[47] there were others who hesitated. Fox himself did not condemn those of his followers who had taken office under the Commonwealth, but he warned them that they could not hope to achieve much by accepting such places, for 'there is little but filth & muck & dirt & drosse to be expected among them'.[48]

Hence when the army officers again expelled the Rump in the autumn of 1659, many Quakers regarded the *coup* as a judgement of God. According to Francis Howgil it was no crime in the eyes either of God or just men to remove parliaments when 'they will not hearken to the cry of their Masters [the People]'.[49] Indeed, in their defence of the military dictatorship against its opponents, several Quakers came closer to direct approval of armed resistance to unjust authority than at any other time in their history. Yet it is equally true that the Quakers' mistrust of the army grandees was unabated. In the previous spring, Parliament and army alike had rejected the logic of Cromwellian policy and restored the Republic. But neither faction would accept the Quaker argument that it was only by further reforms in Church and State that the Commonwealth might ultimately be established in peace. Hence the expulsion of the Rump served only to intensify the crisis of the Commonwealth. Alienated from the left-wing sects and their own rank and file, and faced with the combined opposition of Presbyterians, Royalists and Republicans alike, the rule of the officers was soon to collapse in chaos. For several weeks the Quakers oscillated between despair and the hope that the military dictatorship might yet pave the way for a further move to the left. In the last weeks of the Commonwealth, Quaker pamphleteers continued to pour forth appeals to a backsliding generation to return to the principles of the good old cause.[50] But they were now more than ever convinced that nothing further could be expected from the mighty and honourable of the earth, 'and while your eyes are upon them for help, your expectations shall be frustrated and your Hope shall be

[47] F. Howgil, *An Information, and also Advice* (1659), p. 7; T. Davenport, *This for the Parliament, Counsel, and the Officers of the Army* (Aug. 1659), pp. 7–8; G. Bishop, *The Warnings of the Lord* (1660), p. 35.

[48] Swarthmore MSS. vii, p. 157; Bristol MSS. v, p. 31.

[49] *An Information, and also Advice*, pp. 1–5.

[50] E. Burrough, *To the whole English Army* (Jan. 1659–60); F. Howgil, *One Warning more* (1660); J. Collens, *A Message from the Spirit of the Lord* (1660), pp. 4–5.

as the giving up of the Ghost'.[51] Only a new race of men, immune from the corrupting influence of power and property, might one day be able to revive the shattered hopes of the English Commonwealth.

IV

The fall of the Commonwealth, therefore, temporarily resolved the problem which had exercised the Quakers in the earlier years of their history. For there was no longer any question of Friends co-operating with the scattered remnants of the old revolutionary parties. On the contrary, in the light of their experience in 1659–60, some Quakers considered that even their earlier activity for the revolutionary cause had been a mistake,[52] and few of them experienced any difficulty in assuring the triumphant Royalists of their peaceful intentions.[53] But it is equally true that the Quakers declined to give their active support to the restored monarchy. As Burrough put it, 'this is the bondage of *Egypt*, but the children are free from it, and are not entangled concerning the things of this world'.[54] Thus the majority of Quakers had now come round to a pacifist position. It was in January 1661, when the abortive Fifth Monarchy rising had led to the arrest of 4,000 Friends, that they first issued the famous official declaration, 'that the Spirit of Christ which leads us into all Truth, will never move us to fight and war against any man with outward Weapons, neither for the Kingdom of Christ, nor for the Kingdoms of this World'.[55]

This development alone did not, of course, involve the Quakers' final exit from the political stage. Even in the period of bitterest disillusionment they indicated their willingness to co-operate with other groups in the pursuit of limited political objectives.[56] And if the hope of a Radical reformation of society and the State was fast

[51] Howgil, *One Warning more*, p. 13.

[52] T. Lewis *et al.*, *For the King, and both Houses of Parliament*, p. 5; E. Burrough, *A Visitation of Love* (1660), p. 10.

[53] An apparent exception among the better known Friends was Edward Byllynge. As late as November 1662, Byllynge refused to give an undertaking that he would never take up arms against the king. Cf. *Extracts from State Papers*, pp. 153–4.

[54] E. Burrough, *To the Beloved and Chosen of God* (1660), p. 6.

[55] G. Fox *et al.*, *A Declaration from the Harmless and Innocent People of God, called Quakers, Against all Plotters and Fighters in the World* (n.d.), p. 2.

[56] E. Burrough, *A Declaration from the People called Quakers* (Dec. 1659), p. 14.

receding from the horizon, they might still be expected to lend their support to any party which championed the cause of religious toleration. But for fifteen years after the Restoration, the Quakers, like most other dissenters, were almost exclusively preoccupied with the struggle for survival. Not until the growth of opposition to Charles II once more produced a party responsive to Radical demands were the Quakers again confronted with the problem of political action.

By the time that this party emerged, under the leadership of Shaftesbury and Monmouth, the Quaker movement was at the height of its strength. For the Quakers thrived on persecution, and in the intervening years, they had grown in numbers and perfected their organization. Braithwaite calculated that in 1660 there were between 30,000 and 40,000 Quakers—men, women and children. Twenty years later there may well have been twice that number; and at the end of the century it was estimated that they were as numerous as the Roman Catholics and all other Protestant dissenters combined.[57] It is worth noting that their organization had itself contributed in large measure to the Quakers' success. For unlike other Radical sects, the Quakers rejected the principle of the autonomous congregation, and though they lacked a permanent priesthood, the scattered Quaker Meetings were linked together under the guidance of itinerant preachers, supported by the voluntary contributions of individual Friends. Thus, by combining the democracy of the group with the centralized leadership of the principal Friends, the Quakers were able to develop an organization peculiarly well-adapted to the requirements of an unorthodox sect in a hostile world. In 1659, they had already demonstrated that this organization might be effectively used for political ends. And similarly, during the political struggle of 1675–80, first the 'morning meeting' of Quaker ministers and then the Meeting for Sufferings urged all Friends in the various localities to discuss collectively how they should use their votes at elections.[58]

We know that in practice Quaker support at this time was

[57] Braithwaite, *Beginnings of Quakerism*, p. 512; F. S. Turner, *The Quakers* (London, 1889), pp. 235–7. The Quaker registers of births, marriages and deaths which I have examined suggest that the movement probably reached its height *c.* 1680, though the decline in numbers did not become apparent until the second quarter of the eighteenth century.

[58] W. C. Braithwaite, *Second Period of Quakerism* (London, 1919), pp. 80, 98.

generally given to the Whig candidates. During the reaction in the 1680s it was said that if one of the Quaker leaders would give an undertaking that Friends would abstain from voting persecution would soon cease.[59] How close was the liaison between the Quakers and the new Country party is illustrated by the fact that a few years earlier Titus Oates himself had publicly defended the Quakers against a Tory charge that they were Jesuits in disguise.[60] Yet, in fact, the Quakers played an important part in the ensuing disintegration of the new Country party in face of the Tory reaction. During Monmouth's tour of the west of England in the summer of 1680, local Quakers watched his progress with sympathy but hesitated to approach him publicly for fear of making him too popular. And although a few of them may have gone to the aid of the rebel army at Sedgemoor five years later, the majority remained severely aloof.[61]

The Quakers, in short, were prepared to support the Whigs in a demand for religious toleration; but they were not willing to follow Shaftesbury and Monmouth into a new civil war. For the first Whig party rested on an unstable alliance between landowners and merchants and the dissenting sects against the French foreign policy of Charles II and the popish influence of the Duke of York. Events soon proved, however, that the great Whig families were not prepared to push their opposition to Charles to the extent of risking a revival of the former militancy of the left-wing sects.[62] And as the Whig notables transferred their allegiance to the Crown, so the new Country party likewise forfeited Quaker support.

In this connection, it is particularly important to observe the role of William Penn. A member, by birth, of the governing class, Penn was unlike both his fellow Quakers and the Radicals who followed Monmouth at Sedgemoor. But partly for that reason he was in a position to play a more conspicuous and illuminating part in politics than any other of his contemporaries. For unlike other Friends, Penn was actively concerned in the political struggle; and

[59] ibid., p. 112.

[60] *Letters to Wm. Dewsbury*, ed. H. J. Cadbury (Friends' Historical Soc., 1948), p. 62; *Jl. F.H.S.*, xlii (1950), pp. 67–69.

[61] Braithwaite, *Second Period*, pp. 92–93, 121–3; *Jl. F.H.S.*, xv (1918), pp. 141–2; ibid., xvi (1919), p. 134.

[62] cf. Iris Morley, *A Thousand Lives: an Account of the English Revolutionary Movement, 1660–1685* (London, 1954).

in 1678–9 he had been a leading Whig writer and agitator, acting as Algernon Sidney's election agent in two successive elections. Yet, like them, he was too keenly aware of the divergence of interest between the Whig notables and the dissenting sects to believe that a Whig victory would ensure the triumph of liberty of conscience. In June 1680, therefore, when the exclusion battle was at its height, Penn petitioned the Crown for a grant of land in America in payment of a debt to his father, the old Commonwealth admiral. For Charles, the situation presented a unique opportunity to rid himself of some of his most troublesome subjects at a moment of political crisis. For the Quakers, it meant the first real opportunity to realize their 'Holy Experiment' in the political sphere. By January 1681, with the help of the Duke of York, the boundaries of the new province of Pennsylvania had been agreed. Then, when the results of the elections for the Oxford Parliament were known, Charles granted the charter; and in the months following the dissolution of the third Whig Parliament, a steady stream of Quaker emigrants began to cross the Atlantic.[63]

The foundation of Pennsylvania, however, did not mean that the proprietor lost interest in developments in England. In 1685, after a first visit to his new province, Penn was back in England, and with his friend James on the throne, he presented himself at Court. Thus the Whig pamphleteer now became a Jacobite courtier. Penn himself later explained that his activity during this period was aimed at securing relief for individual Quakers and other Church and State dissenters. But more important was his role as the leader of the party of toleration, and the architect, with Robert Barclay, of the Quaker-Jacobite alliance. For Penn was a prominent supporter of James II's declaration of indulgence, although he opposed the use of the royal prerogative to force it on Parliament. Moreover, he supported the packing of Parliament with members sympathetic to the King's policy, and it was under his influence that a number of Quakers accepted political offices for the first time since the fall of the Commonwealth.[64]

[63] Fulmer Mood, 'William Penn and English Politics in 1680–81', *Jl. F.H.S.*, xxxii (1935), pp. 3–21.

[64] The salient facts of Penn's political career will be found in any of his numerous biographies, e.g. J. W. Graham (1916), C. E. Vulliamy (1933), W. I. Hull (1937), though his role in the history of the period has never been adequately explored.

Penn's pamphlets reveal that he regarded not the Catholics, but the Tories and the Church of England as the main enemies of the Radical sects. Thirty thousand Catholics, he argued, were numerically, economically and politically insignificant. Nor was James himself the real power, and if he attempted to abuse his position, he would soon discover his mistake.[65] Penn, therefore, anticipated the revolution of 1688, but at the same time he was playing for higher stakes than the half-hearted toleration of the Revolution Settlement. His aim was not only freedom of religious worship, but the removal of political disabilities from Protestant dissenters. In this objective, however, he was doomed to failure. After 1649 each successive attempt to form a political alliance capable of carrying the revolution of 1640 to a further stage had foundered on the conflict between the interests of property and the demands of the popular movement. If it was impossible to form such an alliance on the lines envisaged by Shaftesbury, it was equally impossible to do so on the basis of a hybrid association between the dissenting sects and a Catholic king. For the restored monarchy of 1660–88 depended for its survival on the class of merchants and landowners; and if the Quaker alliance with the monarchy depended on the weakness and isolation of a Catholic king, that very weakness ensured the defeat of the political hopes of Quakers and Jacobites alike.

Hence the revolution which brought to a victorious conclusion the struggle of the propertied classes for political power, also ensured the exclusion from political life of the dissenting sects. After 1688, Penn himself disappeared from the political scene, discredited by his past activities and his continuing contacts in Jacobite circles. At the same time a change came over the Quaker movement. In 1691, George Fox died. Fox had never been a political leader like Penn, but he was the very embodiment of the spirit of uncompromising passive resistance of the early Friends. For some years Fox had taken a less active part in the leadership of the movement, and in the years which followed his death a new generation of Quakers emerged, more willing to seek an accommodation with the outside world. In the eighteenth century, while some Friends became the successful pioneers of new financial and industrial techniques, the society as a whole settled down into the

[65] cf. 'Beati Pacifici' (Wm. Penn), *Good Advice to the Church of England, Roman Catholick and Protestant Dissenter* (1687), esp. pp. 48 ff.

group of respectable philanthropists we know today. But if it now became possible to speak of Quaker quietism, it is important to remember that this very quietism was at least partially due to the achievements of the first generation of Friends. On this side of the Atlantic their purely political activities had borne little fruit. But it was their stubborn resistance for more than a generation which ensured the limited toleration of 1688 and the survival, throughout the eighteenth century, of some of the radical ideas thrown up by the English Revolution of the century before.

INDEX

Colaiste Oideachais Mhuire Gan Smal
Luimneach